Lindsay Simpson is the author and ⟨...⟩ books, including the bestselling *Broth⟨...⟩* Milperra bikie massacre and *My Husband My Killer*, made into a telemovie of the same name. Both books were co-authored with Sandra Harvey. Her first novel, *The Curer of Souls*, was published in 2006. She is an award-winning journalist formerly of *The Sydney Morning Herald*, and is now the head of the journalism program and coordinator of the postgraduate writing program at James Cook University in Townsville.

Jennifer Cooke is an award-winning journalist for *The Sydney Morning Herald* and its former legal affairs reporter. She wrote *Cannibals, Cows and the CJD Catastrophe*, which won Australia's most prestigious popular science accolade for authors, the Eureka Science Book Prize, in 1999. She also co-authored *Done Like A Dinner*, a collection of true crime stories all linked to restaurants, with Sandra Harvey.

HONEYMOON DIVE

LINDSAY SIMPSON and **JENNIFER COOKE**

MACMILLAN
Pan Macmillan Australia

First published 2010 in Macmillan by Pan Macmillan Australia Pty Limited
1 Market Street, Sydney

National Library of Australia
Cataloguing-in-Publication data:

Simpson, Lindsay & Cooke, Jennifer.
Honeymoon Dive: the real story of the tragic honeymoon death of Tina Watson.

ISBN 9781405040129 (pbk.)

Watson, Tina.
Deep diving – Accidents – Queensland – Great Barrier Reef.

363.14

Typeset by Post Pre-press Group
Printed in Australia by McPherson's Printing Group

Papers used by Pan Macmillan Australia Pty Ltd are natural, recyclable products
made from wood grown in sustainable forests. The manufacturing processes
conform to the environmental regulations of the country of origin.

This book is dedicated to Sandra Harvey,
an amazing woman, co-author of both of us.
For Lindsay she was the best friend anyone
could hope to have.

Acknowledgements

Lindsay Simpson would like to thank her patient and loving husband, Grant Lewis, and their five children. Thanks also to fellow journalist, Leisa Scott, on whose Magnetic Island verandah, one balmy night, the idea for this book was born.

Jennifer Cooke would like to thank her husband, Brad Norington, and especially their two children for putting up with having a largely absent mother so soon after moving to the United States.

We appreciated the help of Steve Atchison, Joel Bernstein, Ryan Butler, Chris Carpenter, Craig and Corley Cleckler, Richard Coleman, John Cooke, Marie Damania, Kim Herman, Chris Lent, Xenia Lewis, Donna Singletary, Professor Thomas Walsh, Professor Victoria Jennings, Professor Nola Alloway, Dr John Wittig, Mark Williams, Anita W. Wolfe and our new friends in Birmingham, Alabama. They were among the many people, some of whom can't be named, who guided the authors on different sides of the globe while researching the intrigue and technicalities behind this fascinating story. Thanks also to Paul Crocombe from Adrenalin Dive for the visit to the *Yongala* site and to Rob Webster from Pleasure Divers. Lastly, thanks to our patient editor Brianne Collins, copy-editor Claire de Medici, publisher Tom Gilliatt and agent Lyn Tranter.

We are indebted to Truman Capote, pioneer of 'creative non-fiction'. We have drawn extensively upon primary sources such as transcripts, video footage, media accounts, interviews with eyewitnesses and discussions on internet sites to research this story. We have also visited key places of importance in the book.

May the truth come out so those people whose lives irrevocably changed after Christina Mae Watson's death can have some resolution.

When the SS *Yongala* sank in a cyclone almost a century earlier, the Marine Board of Queensland stated that its fate 'passes beyond human ken into the realms of conjecture, to add one more to the long roll of mysteries of the sea'.

Unlike the fate of the *Yongala*, however, there is one person who knows exactly what happened beneath the same ocean on 22 October 2003.

PROLOGUE

The Great Barrier Reef, at around 2300 kilometres in length, is so large that it is the only living formation to be seen from outer space. Divers from all over the world are drawn to this part of Australia. Apart from the spectacularly coloured coral gardens, there are more wreck dives on the north-eastern coast of Australia than anywhere else in the country. Nothing remains of the wooden sailing ships, battered in cyclones and wild weather, except for their ballasts and scattered coral-encrusted fittings. Ranked among the best wreck dive sites in the world, however, is a massive steel ship that has survived for almost a century on the ocean floor despite the shifting sands. On 23 March 1911, the SS *Yongala* steamed straight into the heart of a cyclone off Cape Bowling Green, south of Townsville in North Queensland, and sank with 121 souls on board who still lie entombed in their cabins.

Even on the sunniest day in the tropics, this lonely sweep of water is prone to fickle changes of wind and currents, making the seas treacherous for larger ships as the ocean suddenly bottoms out in shallower waters.

In the colourful wonderland above the ocean floor the

1

6000-odd divers who arrive each year to dive on the wreck can be carried away in a matter of minutes. That is, unless they cling to permanent mooring lines or anchor lines set up by visiting dive boats. But the unforgettable sight of the dark, ominous shape of the iron bow emerging 15 metres up from the seabed covered in coral and oysters, its manmade shape curiously clumsy compared to its swirling, colourful, native inhabitants, never fails to reward those who venture below.

Gabe Watson first heard about the SS *Yongala* at the dive shop where he had booked all his certification courses in his hometown of Birmingham, Alabama, in the United States. Gabe had wanted to dive the Great Barrier Reef since he was in high school. In five years, he had progressed through his open-water dive certificate to the status of certified rescue diver, one qualification below a dive instructor. His wedding date of 11 October 2003 was planned around the best diving conditions on the reef, a perfect destination for a scuba diving honeymoon. October was also when the green sea turtles began nesting, an important factor for his fiancée, Tina Thomas.

Gabe Watson is a big man, more than 1.9 metres tall, with a chubby, unremarkable face, close-set eyes, thin lips and, almost to offset the blandness of his face, a surprisingly aquiline nose in profile. The high school gridiron and basketball player is the eldest of three boys. He had spent much of his life sheltered by his parents from the harsher realities of life.

A few years earlier, Gabe would have been the sort of man fair-haired Tina Thomas, with a spontaneous, dimpled smile, would have spurned. Gabe lacked Tina's effervescent social skills, often traded sarcasm for conversation, and could be surly and withdrawn. But as her twenties crept on, Mr Right became more elusive. Tina had plenty of beaux, including a broken engagement. By her twenty-sixth birthday, however, she was still not betrothed. Tina had been her younger sister's maid of honour and a bridesmaid at girlfriends' weddings. Gabe, also twenty-six, didn't believe in long engagements. When his proposal finally came, the booking of the honeymoon, the purchase of a marital home and the wedding date all occured within six months, giving Tina little time to plan for the event she had spent most of her life dreaming about. As well as preparing for her marriage, her husband-to-be had insisted that she gain her open-water dive certificate so she could scuba dive on their honeymoon.

In October 2003, the newlyweds joined the two million annual international tourists to visit the Great Barrier Reef, the world's largest World Heritage area, to dive on the wreck that had been dubbed Townsville's *Titanic*. The Watsons left Townsville late on the evening of 21 October 2003 aboard the *Spoilsport*, the 30-metre catamaran that would transport them to the wreck.

On deck in the early morning light, the passengers were swallowed by the endless sea and sky. Cape Bowling Green shimmered on the far distant horizon to the west, a whisker of land cast up by another epoch. The ocean changed from shades of aqua to turquoise with the climbing sun, its depths hidden where the water became an impenetrable blue, hiding the ship's graveyard below.

By 11.27 a.m. on the day of her first ocean dive with her rescue diver husband, Tina was pronounced dead, after being pulled from the bottom of the ocean by master scuba instructor Wade Singleton.

Later, Gabe would tell police that he knew little about the conditions around the wreck until after Tina's death, in spite of the evidence from other passengers about the in-depth briefings that morning. It was to be the first of many inconsistencies in his recounting of what happened after he abandoned Tina to her freefall towards the ocean floor.

But it would be more than five years until Gabe Watson was charged with his new wife's murder, and another year before he was behind bars serving time for her manslaughter.

CHAPTER 1

The most prominent landmark visible on the top of Red Mountain in Birmingham, Alabama, is Vulcan, the Roman God of metalwork. In his right hand, he holds a spear. With his squat neck and muscled torso, his massive feet pushed into Roman thongs, he towers over the city and the panoramic view of its sprawling suburbs. The statue, the world's largest in cast iron, symbolises all that is Birmingham: big, brash and proud, the largest city in the state of Alabama. Red Mountain and Shades Mountain are the two ridges that flank the city. It was within Red Mountain that Birmingham's forebears discovered the equivalent of gold: limestone, iron ore and coal. Between 1860 and 1960 there were more than 100 active ore mines inside the mountain, and the local foundrymen used the iron ore to cast the statue. The Vulcan's birth was rushed through in seven months by an Italian sculptor, who was rewarded at the 1904 St Louis Fair when the sculpture won first prize. Once overshadowed by burgeoning southern cities like neighbouring Atlanta, from that moment on, Birmingham hastily rode on the back of the mineral boom that led to the birth of the city's iron and steel industries. People dubbed the new town 'Magic City' because of the pace at which it evolved, as labourers and ironworkers flooded in looking for work.

Today, there is still a rushed feeling to this large southern city. Despite a layering of finesse – of the occasional early Art Deco buildings and upmarket dining establishments, where the leisured few congregate – the city's origins are, like its British namesake, undeniably industrial. Small pockets of sophistication dazzle with detail in the same way that an artist might labour over one aspect of a painting, but then ignore the rest of the canvas. Opulent homes with sculpted driveways, dogwood trees and magnolia-laced lawns boom affluence next door to poverty. Downtown Birmingham still exhibits bald patches of bad planning. Empty, pockmarked streets with straggly trees bear scars from one too many highway exits and entries which transport the city's commuters into the ever-growing suburbs. The effect is to transmute progress into ugliness. Throughout downtown Birmingham, the hum of the shunting carriages can be heard as the railway line dissects the city centre. Steam rises periodically in the sultry distance with the quenching of super-heated metal. Faded signs mark the remnants of industry, and isolated chimneystacks hug the horizon. But there is also pride in this heritage. One of the old factories is a national historic landmark and these days, suburbs such as Irondale are named for the past.

Around the hills of this industrial city, the main highway arteries dissect the plentiful forests, snaking through greenery that shapes the two ridges on either side of the city. Greater Birmingham is located at the convergence of four interstate highways: Interstate 20, Interstate 59, Interstate 65, and Interstate 459, which creates a southern belt around Birmingham.

Alabama has a long-established desire for showmanship. When British actor Stephen Fry came to Alabama on his road trip around America in a London taxi, his cameraman caught the extravaganza, pageantry and fantasy of the place by filming a football game at the University of Alabama in Tuscaloosa. Drummers in scarlet tunics and white pants moved to the beat in the university stadium with the grand spectacle of an Olympic event. Alabama does not have a team in the National Football League, hence university football is the biggest sport in the state and southerners are fanatically loyal to their teams. The War Eagles, from Auburn University with its navy-and-orange colours, is by far the most popular football team. In Alabama, spectacle and theatrics have become part of the city's cultural identity.

Birmingham's history, however, is inextricably bound to the violence of the Civil Rights protests in the mid sixties. Martin Luther King penned his famous Letter from Birmingham Jail as a treatise against black segregation. As men scrambled for nature's industrial treasures, brutality and wealth lived side by side. In the early twentieth century, smiling at a white woman could mean death for a black man; juries were all white; baseball teams were segregated into black and white; and streetcars, buses and taxis had the same divide. After all of the bloodshed, it is hardly surprising that there is a death penalty for heinous crimes. The lethal injection, after it was introduced in 2002, is a preferred choice of death to the electric chair. If you are found guilty of murder in the state of Alabama, the biblical adage of 'an eye for an eye and a tooth for a tooth' applies. By the twenty-first century, after more than a hundred years of racial angst and inequality, there is an even split between black and white on death row. With such a bloody past, nowadays it takes an unusual crime to be noticed in Birmingham. Something out of the ordinary.

The Watson family were like many other Birmingham residents. They had sought a future life in the uneasy, haphazard growth of a city that welcomed opportunists. Gabe Watson's family stretched back decades in the south on both sides. His grandparents, U. G. 'Watt' Watson and Geneva 'Jenny' Estelle Hood Watson were both born in 1923 in Arkansas. Gabe's grandfather had the foresight to choose an industry that had clear growth: the merchants of Birmingham needed packaging materials for the expanding number of goods ready to transport. In the 1970s he started the Packaging Materials and Supply Company in Birmingham, supplying a large range of packaging materials including corrugated boxes and later bubble packs for mailing, which were ecofriendly. David Watson, his only child, slipped into the mantle of manager after Watt suffered a heart attack, putting in hard hours with the help of his mother, Jenny, to grow the business. He adapted it over the years to more specific packaging such as hazardous-material transport supplies. Glenda, David's wife, the matriarch of the Watson family, is a primary school teacher.

David Watson and his sons are lofty folk. Gabe is the tallest, but his brothers Daniel and Michael (known as 'Mook') also top the 1.8-metre mark.

Like the decision to continue in the packaging trade, the Watsons' choice of a home base also showed foresight. They settled in Bluff Park, which today is part of Hoover, Birmingham's largest suburb but also, since the 1960s, a city. Since the 1990s, it has expanded to a thriving population of around 70,000. The Watsons bought the family home in October 1986 after major highways began to link outlying suburbs with greater Birmingham, but before the real estate prices began to steadily rise.

The house where Gabe Watson spent his adolescence is

a two-storey Dutch colonial-style house with two dormers set in the dark blue gambrel roof, vinyl clapboard siding, a covered front porch and a garage entering into the side of the basement level. The house is built on a steep hill in one of the modern housing developments of Hoover. White balustrades lead up to the front door. Like many American boys, the Watson brothers grew up with a basketball hoop beside the double garage. Gabe attended the primary school at Bluff Park where he met one of his closest school buddies, Michael Moore.

Throughout his high school years, Gabe was a lanky teenager who played basketball. As the population of Hoover grew and more schools were built, his school, W. A. Berry High, became Hoover High School in 1995 during his last year. That same year he won the All Tournament Player in the basketball competition. Taylor Hicks, who was in Gabe's 1992 and 1994 basketball teams, went on to win the fifth season of *American Idol*. Gabe also had the occasional girlfriend. Ten years after buying the family home, the Watsons made another sound real estate decision, purchasing a condominium in nearby Homewood to provide for their sons as they entered adulthood.

In the summer Gabe turned fourteen, he worked for the family company during school holidays. It was a predictable route for him, as he and his brothers were expected to one day inherit the business. At the end of 1998, the twenty-one-year-old Gabe began working at the family packing materials company full-time. He had a few other odd jobs, at the supermarket chain Bruno's, and Vance Sikes Sales, a customer of his family's company. His father wanted Gabe to broaden his knowledge and learn about the company's client base.

Gabe, like his parents, was brought up in the Baptist faith. Around a third of the population in the state of Alabama are

Southern Baptists who separated from the main Baptists in the mid 1800s, initially over issues to do with slavery. The Watsons are committed to their faith. When life is tough, their pastor at the Shades Crest Baptist Church can be relied upon to guide them through. Gabe grew up immersed in the idea that he was one of the people of God and it was his job to scatter the seed of the gospel.

The Shades Crest Baptist Church was built in 1954 by a group claiming to be led by the Holy Spirit. Practitioners proclaim themselves as 'good news people in a bad news world'. Gabe's youth, protected within the safety net of the religion, was shaped by weekly meetings and social gatherings aimed at warding off evil. The multitude of activities put on by the church consumes young parishioners' daily existence: fellowship dinners, prayer meetings, children's choirs, cross-training and Sunday school ensure the followers a passport to Heaven.

As you pass through the front door into the small vestibule of the Watson home, an embroidered pincushion contains the words in cross-stitch: 'Bless this House'. To the right of the front door is the parlour, little changed from the days when Gabe Watson was an adolescent. Each Baptist, he was taught, is part of the body of Christ. He also learned that no matter how bad you might be, you can always expect salvation, if you accept Jesus Christ. This fundamentalism provided Gabe with a dual perspective on his existence, creating friction between dark and light, truth and untruth.

By twenty-one, Gabe was nursing the break-up of a relationship with a young woman from the church. He moved to his parents' condo and started at the University of Alabama, Birmingham (UAB), hoping to finish at some stage with a major in public relations. But it was a predictable life.

On cable television, program after program showed fearless divers battling the elements: prodding giant tentacles, swimming with huge manta rays and approaching, with daredevil bravado, the razor-sharp incisors of open-jawed sharks. This excitement contrasted sharply with the humdrum routine of study-related tedium and the inevitability of life. One ordinary weekend in March 1998 Gabe and his old school buddy Mike Moore, who was also studying in the city, passed The Dive Site store in suburban Birmingham while they were out having lunch. The Dive Site sign, with two distinctive inverted 'i's, caught Gabe's eye as they walked by.

'Hey, it'd be cool to go diving,' Gabe said.

The Dive Site was one of four such dive shops around Birmingham at that time. Traditional sports of Alabamians were fishing, boating, hunting, hiking and biking as the lakes, rivers, mountains and forests of north and central Alabama were tailor-made for the recreationist. But the Gulf of Mexico is only a 5-hour drive away from bustling, landlocked Birmingham, so from the late 1980s, scuba diving had grown as a sport. Inside the store, the colours were bright and the equipment shiny. Large posters adorned the wall as goggled, suited forms floated past, caught by the camera lens. This was a mysterious, silent world beneath the surface, where conversations had no place; a hobby that was at once masculine and daring.

The shop assistant took their tentative enquiries seriously: 'You can do group scuba diving lessons here. We don't just sell the gear. Or you can do private lessons – an accelerated course. That's kinda if you're fixin' to get there quickly.'

Gabe and Mike left the store with a buzz of excitement. They decided to share their hobby, expensive though it would be. Soon afterwards they enrolled in the open-water certificate, the course for entry-level divers.

They turned up on a Wednesday evening, 1 April 1998, for their first classroom-based lesson, kitting themselves out with the necessary equipment. That first night they impatiently watched a video. Reading a textbook and sitting dry on a chair watching others slide past on the screen was too removed from the real thing; it felt too much like school again.

Tom Jackson, their dive instructor, was a thirty-two-year-old native of Ohio who had moved to Alabama. He was shorter and darker-haired than the towering Gabe and the 1.8-metre, 86-kilogram Michael Moore. Aiming for his 2000th dive at that point, Jackson was an enthusiastic and patient teacher.

They were shown how dive equipment worked, taught proper breathing techniques, and learnt about potential problems such as decompression sickness known as 'the bends' and nitrogen narcosis.

'To prevent the bends,' Jackson told Gabe and Michael, 'you should not ascend more than 30 feet [9 metres] per minute. And no-one should stay longer than the set time limit for a certain depth unless they want big problems.'

He introduced them to dive tables used to work out the optimum wait period between dives. This was necessary, Jackson explained, so they would not have to rely entirely on a dive computer.

They learned about safety stops on ascending, about heat exhaustion and hypothermia, over-expansion injuries to the lungs from improper breathing and having air trapped in the lungs.

Jackson moved on to locating a lost dive buddy. If a wide sweep above and below does not locate a missing buddy, a diver should ascend at the prescribed rate with a 3-minute safety stop and then yell to the dive boat for help if the dive buddy has not surfaced.

'Don't drop back below the surface,' Jackson warned, 'unless you are the only other person present. You should also remember that if you don't continuously equalise your ears as you descend,' he demonstrated by pinching his nose and gently blowing to move air into the sinuses and ears, 'the unequal pressure with the outside pressure from the water might cause pain.' If ear problems occurred, he told them, stop and try to equalise, or ascend a short distance, equalise and start going down again slowly.

At the end of the instruction they were tested. Gabe scored 100 per cent.

The following Monday night, the young men had their first confined-water lesson. As private students, Gabe and Michael trained in the blue-striped lanes of the large Lakeshore Rehabilitation Facility pool in Homewood. Gabe squeezed his 100 kilograms into a thick wetsuit, while adjusting to the initial tight feeling. Tom Jackson first made them prove their swimming ability. Gabe and Mike trod water for 10 minutes without any of the gear, which sat poolside. After dutifully completing laps totalling 182 metres they were declared fit. They began basic scuba diving skills including breathing underwater, mask clearing, clearing the regulator or mouthpiece, and activating the inflator buttons on their dive jackets or vests known as buoyancy compensator devices (BCs) for buoyancy control. Once in the water, Gabe felt the heavy equipment miraculously lighten. Mike, likewise, was enjoying himself. The skills had to be performed in both the shallow and deep ends of the pool, followed by various entry and exit methods, learning to ascend and descend and then sharing air with the dive buddy's 'octopus', or back-up regulator attached to their cylinders. Their few days of confined-water training, completed on 25 April, included learning how to remove their equipment on the surface as well as underwater and to replace it – in case of entanglements underwater – and the proper techniques for emergency ascents.

The following day, Gabe and Mike arrived at Alabama Blue Water Adventures, a flooded 10.5-hectare former limestone quarry about 20 minutes' drive from Hoover, used by The Dive Site to conduct open-water classes. The old quarry was an ideal site for divers because it had varying depths down to 45 metres, some accessible by wooden platforms plus some underwater attractions including a school bus lying 21 metres under the surface.

Only a week later, the boys completed their training at Morrison Springs at Ponce De Leon in north-west Florida. Listening to Tom Jackson tell of his escapades, of the teeming underwater life and the unpredictability of each day on his dive trips to Mexico, made Gabe and Mike long for their first open-sea experience. The very next day, newly certified, they undertook their first wreck dive on the USS *Strength*, a former minesweeper deliberately sunk for navy diving and salvage training in the waters off Panama City. Accompanied by Jackson, Gabe and Mike entered a magical underwater world descending to about 22 metres – more than double what they had experienced at Blue Water or Morrison Springs. The visibility was good to 9 metres and the dive along the 54-metre vessel and up again lasted about 25 minutes.

'Fantastic,' Gabe said, grinning at his equally beaming friend as they surfaced. With an eye to going on some of Tom's small group trips to Mexico, they decided to do as many courses as they could.

On 18 May, a fortnight later, when buying a screen protector for his top-of-the-range Oceanic DataTrans Plus dive computer at The Dive Site, Gabe inquired about starting dates for advanced open-water dive courses. He and Mike chose one beginning at the end of August, when the weather was warmer. By the end of September they had completed three evenings of classwork, and in October, they each got an advanced open-water certificate.

Cozumel, Mexico, is an island in the Caribbean Sea off the east coast of Yucatan. Jacques Cousteau discovered Cozumel in 1959, declaring it the best place in the world to go scuba diving.

Early in July 1999, soon after they had completed the classroom portion of their next course to train them in rescue diving, Tom Jackson organised a dive with Gabe and Mike on the offshore side of the island. Here the boys saw another aspect of the underwater fairyland that could only be manufactured at Pelham. The coral toadfish, only found in these waters, hid timidly under outcroppings. The coral was so bright that it hurt your eyes even in the muted sunlight. At the docks, where a deepwater pier had been carved out of the reef in the 1990s, the regular cruise ships stop en route around the Caribbean. Stores sold Cuban cigars, jewellery and tequila and, at the southern end of the island, there were a number of brothels. But it was the drift dives that really captured the imagination of the young men: the current that sapped their strength if they tried to swim against it, the mighty pull of the ocean that rendered them as meaningless as a bobbing champagne cork. Gabe had bought an underwater camera to capture their escapades. During each dive, he insisted

Mike strike an adventurous pose. Then he took his turn as the model.

Once, while they were diving at 20 metres, they chased some fish behind a coral outcrop. Their eyes widened as they saw a weight drop out of a pocket on Mike's dive belt. Gabe was only a metre away. Within seconds, he grasped Mike's BC to hold him there; they both knew that surfacing too quickly from this depth was highly dangerous. Luckily, Tom was nearby and dived to the ocean bed to retrieve the weight. Mike trod water, firmly held by Gabe, while Tom placed the weight back into his pocket. Mike signalled an 'O' with his thumb and forefinger, the universal sign from a diver that he is okay. They continued the dive, thrilled with their encounter against the elements.

During another dive, Gabe signalled to Mike that he wanted to swim back to capture a large fish lurking under the rocks. They pushed their heads against the current, kicking their fins with thrashing legs, but try as they might, they made little headway. For the first time, Mike felt concerned, knowing they had become separated from Tom, Tom's girlfriend, Shelley, and the accompanying dive instructor. He knew, even before they surfaced, that they had drifted away from the small dive boat that they had chartered. When they finally reached the surface, the others were nowhere to be seen. They trod water, feeling the beginnings of panic. Fifteen minutes later, they saw the small boat heading towards them and raised their wetsuited arms, gulping shakily with relief.

During one of the last dives, Gabe witnessed firsthand one of the textbook descriptions Jackson had given him: nitrogen narcosis. They had dived much deeper than either of them imagined: about 47 metres. Jackson swam towards Gabe and pointed back at Michael, who was spinning through the water like a piece of flotsam. Gabe watched, fascinated, as Jackson swam to Mike and slowly guided him up until he seemed to be himself again.

All up, they did around a dozen dives. By the end of the short holiday, both felt more confident in their abilities.

Soon after Cozumel, they started back at Blue Water on the open-water portion of the rescue diver's certificate course with Jackson, to qualify under the National Association of Scuba Diving Schools (NASDS) credentials. It allowed them to go on to become dive masters if they chose. Gabe had been toying with the idea of making a living as a commercial diver, a far more adventurous living than graduating from university with a PR major.

They learned how to identify and help stressed or panicked divers, and the recommended actions of how to grab them from below and behind and control their inflation to help them ascend safely.

'It's better to put air into a panicked or unconscious diver's BC than your own in a potential rescue situation,' Tom warned them. 'If the other diver does break free or rises in an uncontrolled state they are better off being on the surface where medical attention is a possibility than going to the bottom where death is certain or the chance of other help is greatly reduced.'

It was back to Blue Water and the car park and the duckboard platforms with lots of theory and talk.

'Now, if you're going to rescue someone, there are many types of stress. Physiological and psychological,' Tom told them. 'People show stress in strange ways. These guys that are quiet . . . well they begin to talk a lot. Folks who never shut up are quiet. That kinda thing. If you're going to be dive masters, you have to look for that stuff before they even get into the water.'

Tom advised them to circle around the panicked person to work out their problem. If they were flailing under water, the rescuer was not to approach from the front at the same level or the panicked diver could knock their mask off or rip out their regulator – potentially putting them in danger. By deflating the BC slightly, they were taught to approach the panicked diver from lower down, push them up, spin them around and clamp onto their tank with the knees so the rescuer was out of flailing arm's reach. Stay in control, Tom stressed, and then do a nice, slow, safe ascent.

In the murky depths, Gabe could just make out the diver feigning unconsciousness on the bottom. He was one of Tom's dive master candidates. His skin was waxy, although tiny silver bubbles like mercury betrayed his real condition – he was breathing. Gabe swam down and turned him around, locking his knees onto the air tank. He reached around and pressed the button on the hose attached to the BC and they began to rise. He checked the man's regulator with his fingertips. Then, his fingers around the chin, he raised the man's head up. His airway was now clear. Any air that was in his lungs, which would be starting to expand, could be released. Then, Gabe checked his dive computer, making sure they would not ascend faster than 30 feet per minute.

Then it was Tom's turn. He lolled around, playing distressed, waiting to be rescued. As Gabe approached, Tom's arms began moving with alarming speed. Tom fought Gabe off as he tried to approach him and Gabe had to battle his flailing arms as well as try to remember all of the other instructions, turning him around, locking knees onto his tank, heading slowly, triumphantly, for the top.

After their two days in the quarry, Tom Jackson was pleased with Gabe and Mike's performance. He certified them as competent in stress and rescue diving.

If Gabe wanted to go on and train for his dive master certificate, he had fulfilled all that was required.

'One of the world's famous dives?' Bill French, a salesman at The Dive Site store repeated Gabe's question when he turned up to get his rescue certificate. 'Now, let me see. There's the Galapagos. You've done Cozumel. Wait . . . There's some good dives in Australia on the Great Barrier Reef. The *Yongala*, for one . . . ship like the *Titanic* – mainly intact – lying not that far under the surface. I haven't done it myself, but heard it's really something.'

Diving had filled the empty space in his life left from a broken relationship, Gabe would say later. Now he had mastered those skills, perhaps it was time to go looking again.

CHAPTER 2

In winter in Landstuhl, south-west Germany, snow settles on the picture-postcard churches and the steeply sloping roofs of the old town. Since 1953, Landstuhl has been home to the largest American hospital outside the United States, catering for more than 100,000 US troops and their families stationed in Europe, a number swelled by wars including those in Iraq and Afghanistan. A community accompanies the military and the war-torn casualties. The hospital caters for them too, conducting 400 operations each month. And there are other routine occurrences: births. Today, about three babies are born there each day. On 13 February 1977, Christina Mae Thomas was one of the new arrivals.

William Edwin Thomas III was born in Alabama, served in the army in Germany and was more commonly known as Tommy to distinguish him from his father, who was called 'Bud'. He was handsome in a beatnik kind of way with trademark long hair, dark moustache and eyebrows over soulful eyes. In contrast to his brooding looks, his wife Cynthia (Cindy) Waddell Thomas had the fair ethereal beauty of a Victorian heroine although she hailed from Midland, Texas, flat country known for its oil wells and ranches. She was the youngest of three children after big brother Gene and sister Billie. Cindy embraced the role of motherhood with a fierce delight.

Perhaps the most endearing characteristic of their elder child, 'Tina' as she was known, was her smile. Tina's mouth was Tommy's. It had a life of its own, rubbery in the way that clown's mouths are. As early as eighteen months of age, Tina communicated through her smile, but it was her eyes that connected even with strangers who experienced a strange sense of familiarity upon meeting her. Tina would openly welcome everyone like a flower turning to the sun. Her hair was fair like her mother's, although later in life the layers underneath darkened to brunette. When she was tiny, Tina's tresses would curl so she would resemble a Botticelli angel, but once she was past toddlerhood, Cindy cut Tina's hair in a like-mother-like-daughter straight fringe. She would plait it and tie it in bunches, smoothing it behind Tina's ears, dressing her up and telling her all about how she would grow up to be a southern belle like the famous belles back home. For Cindy, Tina was a daughter and friend, and a natural progression of the strong relationship she had with Tommy.

Tina Mae was the apple of Tommy's eye. Even before she could walk she was adored by all and doted on by grandmas Retha and Louise. She seemed blessed.

One of her favourite toys was a green and yellow turtle, a makeshift pouf in the lounge room of the family home. Tina would sit astride its neck, her chin cupped in her hands. And there was Mickey Mouse and a rag doll with ginger hair. Even when older, she wore her hair in pigtails which would stick up like a dog's ears. Being playful was her way of connecting with people. As a child, her infectious warmth won her praise and affection. The mixture of devilment and happiness she innocently displayed as a toddler remained with her as an adult, her bright smiles and jokes aimed at deflating any arguments.

When her sister, Alanda Michelle, was born in November 1980, Tina welcomed her enthusiastically. Despite their nearly four-year age difference, Tina and Alanda would happily play dress-ups in cowboy hats and jeans with handkerchiefs jutting out of their back pockets. Alanda, with rounder eyes and straighter hair, would squeeze into passport booths with Tina, sitting on her big sister's knee and giggling her way through poses. They often wore matching colours. As Alanda grew taller, she, too, wore her hair in pigtails. They were best friends even before Alanda could talk.

Alanda could not remember when she first became aware of her sister's ailment as they progressed through primary school. Tina's tiredness was simply part of her. Cindy and Tommy knew there was something wrong with their elder daughter. She couldn't be like other children, outside all day throwing balls and playing hide and seek, or skipping from one adventure to the next. Instead of growing through her younger years like a healthy, normal child, Tina, despite her childish energy and boundless enthusiasm, was constantly monitored and checked. There was an unvoiced concern that Tina may be taken from them if she tried too hard. The worry over the illness or condition, for no-one really knew what it was, dogged Cindy. The pleasure from her elder child was always undermined by that nagging sense of 'what if'. Cindy was steadfast in her efforts to get to the bottom of Tina's mysterious problem, all the while trying to hide her fear from her daughter.

When Tommy and Cindy were finally given a diagnosis of sorts, after Tina turned five, they were devastated: their child had a heart problem. The heart specialist declared it was minor, but Cindy and Tommy were still worried. From the age of five to eight, Tina was prescribed Inderal to stop palpitations. Cindy worked even harder to protect her daughter from stress and exertion, but like many little girls, Tina wanted to join in activities. She played T-ball for a time, but she was never involved in after-school or team sports. In the water, though, Tina was like a fish: 'Watch me,' she would say, twirling as she jumped into the pool, screaming with glee. Tina was Tina. Her love of life was limitless.

When Tina was eight, Cindy took the advice of her doctor and stopped giving her the Inderal medication. It was making Tina too lethargic and affecting her school-work. Meanwhile Tommy had left the armed forces and had been selling insurance. He had an easy rapport with people and selling came naturally to him. His real concern for clients' needs was conveyed through those soulful eyes. He sold life and health contracts as well as group insur-ance, steadily working his way up the corporate ladder at the same company through several takeovers. The family moved through various southern states including Georgia, Louisiana and Alabama, taking the occasional family holi-day in Cindy's home state of Texas.

Every long summer vacation the girls' cousin Krissie, Cindy's niece, would come to stay. She was like a big sister for Tina, eight years older. Krissie moved in with the Tho-mases when she was 17, while they were in Georgia, and stayed until she married Tom McCampbell in 1989. Alanda, meanwhile, grew up watchful from a young age, in the way that mothers are watchful. Tina's condition set the rules of the sisters' relationship. Alanda wasn't overly bossy, but she was a natural leader. She loved her big sister like a best friend. It was them against the world. Their joke was that because they were so close, they would end up room-mates in the same nursing home, bashing each other with canes.

By 1991, the Thomases had moved again. Tina started as a fourteen-year-old freshman in Grade 9 at Mandeville High School in Louisiana. Mandeville is on the north shore of Lake Pontchartrain, along Interstate 12, across the lake from the city of New Orleans and its southern shore sub-urbs. In middle school in Conyers, Georgia, Tina had played the flute in the school band. On the first day of band class at Mandeville, she sat next to Amanda Lorenz, a tall, slim, dark-haired fourteen-year-old. There was an immediate connection. Ready to perform they posed for band photo-graphs in their stiff royal blue boleros with silver brocade trim over long pants with a wide silver stripe down the side, caring more about their appearance than the music. They knew they were not the greatest flautists, but the bandmas-ter also knew it was not worth separating them. Mandeville in early autumn was still warm. The rainy days that some-times came with outdoor band gigs held less and less appeal as the girls marched through adolescence. Tina would laugh over Amanda's complaints about the sticky polyester band uniform and the white top they wore underneath, with its long ruched material spilling from the neck.

'You know I hate this ruffle, dicky type of thing,' Amanda would say crossly in anticipation of the sweltering temperatures.

Tina and Amanda performed in school concerts and in winter they played in mardi gras parades, which appealed to their sense of showmanship. Tommy became band escort to keep a watchful eye on his daughter. He would cajole Tina into taking breaks, much against her wishes; she concealed any tiredness well so it wouldn't overtly affect her school life. In the autumn, during the university football season, they would parade at the Mandeville High School game at half-time, dressed in outfits crowned with visored helmets and white-feathered plumes. Afterwards, they would have dinner and go to a movie or watch a video at home.

Amanda and Tina loved dressing up, modelling each other's clothes, applying make-up, pouting at themselves in the mirror. With her girlfriends, including one called Nicole Lyons, Tina would giggle through the long summer afternoons, sometimes striking poses for the camera. Then, Nicole came up with an idea that made them almost faint with excitement. Rather than try clothes on for fun, why not try something more professional? Nicole even had a place in mind. So they all travelled from Mandeville across Lake Pontchartrain to the huge Lakeside Shopping Centre, and the JC Penney store just off the causeway in Metairie, a large suburb next to New Orleans.

Over the clatter of stacking the dishwasher one morning, Tina announced to Tommy that she, Amanda and Nicole were going to enter the JC Penney sponsored modelling competition.

There were a staggering 120 entrants in the competition, and as the night drew closer Tommy prayed that all three girls would be accepted.

Cindy and Tommy attended the judging night. And Tommy, who truly believed in the Lord, had his prayers answered. All three girls were named among the sixteen finalists and went on to win. So began Tina's part-time modelling career that was to last four years, including her last three years of high school. She began modelling JC Penney's fashions in the store, where even the juniors had their own lingerie section. The models got to choose from several jeans lines, deciding which shirt to match with what. Every third weekend, they strutted the runway in the shopping centre, modelling everything from gowns to back-to-school outfits. Tommy, with his tall stature and easy style, as well as a desire to please his daughter, was talked into being in a Father's Day fashion show. Tina fell in love with the colours and fabrics, rarely tiring of any one outfit. Her dedication to grooming began. One weekend, the girls dressed as brides, taking turns to be bridesmaids and then the focus of the show: the bride in gleaming satin and veils accompanied by the boys in tuxedos. One day, Tina thought, she would dress up like this for real.

Cindy had always said Tina would grow up to be a southern belle, so it was no surprise that Tina was a born romantic. Her favourite story, *Gone With the Wind*, was about the most famous of all southern belles. She would luxuriate in the costumes and the finery; the landscapes and the drama of the Civil War. She had a framed movie poster, a Scarlett O'Hara stand-up figure and a Scarlett Barbie doll in a red dress which she kept in the box. She also had a *Gone With the Wind* book and movie collection. Most of all, she revelled in the romance, the declarations of love from Clark Gable to Vivien Leigh, the way that Rhett's masterful words cut Scarlett to the core. She and Alanda would fantasise about the Rhett Butlers in their own futures. The towering musical theme moved them every time, as the sweeping epic of loss and love played out against the fall of Atlanta. Once she got her own car, Tina drove her younger sister there to visit the museum dedicated to the Pulitzer Prize–winning novel by Margaret Mitchell.

But the harder Tina sought love, the more it eluded her. For Tina love was not to be found in those staged occurrences where it was supposed to grow – those end-of-year formals where broody boys would pose for photographs and she would smile as though her heart would burst. Some boys were too short. Some had acne. All were too young. If Tina was wild and 'whipped up fun' like Scarlett O'Hara, she needed to meet her own Rhett Butler, someone who was not afraid of being eclipsed by her energy and her love of life.

Like Scarlett, Tina would plan meticulously for her outings, including the guest list, the location and what she would wear. Seeing her girlfriends have their turn to walk down the aisle or watching Vivien Leigh's upturned face on the screen waiting to be showered by Clark Gable's kisses, fanned her desire for her own permanent partner, someone who also wanted a house with a white picket fence and children, and who would grow old with her. While Alanda never seemed to have any trouble finding serious suitors, Tina would take refuge in the latest Stephen King book, listen to her old Prince songs or a big favourite, the American Christian band MercyMe, where she was walking by the side of Jesus.

In May 1995, Tina graduated from Mandeville High School, her white pumps matching the sash draped around her shoulders over the blue cloak and mortar board. No more juvenile antics like nicking road cones from traffic detours as she and Amanda had done one night, or joining as many school clubs as they could to ensure their pictures were plastered through the yearbook. Her senior picture, in which she wore pearls over a plain ochre blouse, showed perfect white teeth, now minus the braces she'd worn for several years, and long, straight honey-blonde hair falling almost to her waist. She still experienced heart palpitations three times a week – sometimes they lasted over an hour and she would become short of breath, light-headed and begin to sweat. Her chest would feel weighted down.

Tina chose to study mass communications, a very popular course, at Southeastern Louisiana University (SLU) in the city of Hammond on the north shore of Lake Pontchartrain. Amanda enrolled in an engineering degree at Louisiana State University, an hour's drive away in Baton Rouge. There were no friends at SLU to replace the kind of camaraderie Tina shared with Amanda, but the girls talked every week and visited each other during holidays. For a year, Tina kept up her modelling, but then began working, instead, as a pharmacy technician at Eckerd Corporation, the oldest of America's drug-store chains. Pharmaceuticals, after all, had been a familiar part of her life from an early age.

Meanwhile the girls revelled in the culture of Louisiana, its French beginnings, Creole traditions and the world-famous New Orleans Carnival season held each January. During the Carnival tourists would sample the southern fare: spiced turkey necks, jambalaya, sweet potato pie and beans and rice. The population would almost double as crowds were lured by the sheer spectacle of walls of people in masks and costumes parading in their krewes (social clubs).

New Orleans was well known for its drive-up daiquiris, 'to go' cups from bars, and jello shots laced with hard liquor. Louisiana was the only US state in which the legal drinking age was eighteen rather than twenty-one.

By 1996, Tommy and Cindy were talking about moving back to Alabama. Tommy was always travelling with his insurance job and from there he could still commute from Birmingham to manage his career while being close to his mother, who also lived in Alabama. They talked about how this may be their last move for a while and how Tina should join them. She was reluctant but knew how important it was to them. As she moved around, she started her own bulletin board full of postcards she collected over the years from family and friends.

The city of Helena, once a thriving centre of steel production and coal mining, straddles the Jefferson and Shelby counties and is surrounded by mixed woodlands and semi-rural farming communities. In 2007, *Business Week* declared Helena number thirteen of the best places to raise kids in the United States and the number one place to live in Alabama. The village still has a Laura Ashley quaintness and a squeaky-clean country feel. Miss Harvest Pageants are a focus for the social calendar where girls from birth to seventeen parade their worth. The town manages to avoid the urban sprawl, retaining its rural identity despite the increasing service industry and industrial parks that have sprung up around it. People who live in Helena are committed to the slower pace.

Cindy and Tommy Thomas's house is on the downside of Seattle Slew Drive, named after the famous Kentucky Derby winner in the year of Tina's birth. It curves along the ridge of a steep hill not far from the main street of the historic township, in one of the fastest-growing areas in Shelby County. Sweeping driveways surrounded by towering oak and pine trees are common. American flags flutter in the occasional garden. The Thomas house is a Georgian-style, double-storey house with a teal-coloured, raised-panel front door and pilaster surrounds, and double-hung divided-light windows. The front is brick veneer with vinyl clapboard siding on the rear and sides. White columns make the entrance grand. Topiary hedges neaten the edge of the lawn at the front of the house. Two flowering crepe myrtles stand next to the driveway. Down the steep slope at the side of the house where the weatherboard walls are painted a dove grey is a double garage leading into a basement.

In the autumn of 1996 Tina, now nineteen and part-way through her degree, moved into this space. She decided to transfer from SLU to the University of Alabama at Birmingham (UAB), but to defer her enrollment to have a break. Living in the basement was a mark of her independence. Alanda, about to enter her senior year at nearby Pelham High School, slept upstairs in the house in a room near their parents. She also worked some nights at the Pelham Winn-Dixie supermarket. While Tina drove the cherry-red Honda Civic she had bought herself, Alanda inherited her two-door Honda Accord. Tina loved small, sporty cars.

Alpha Omicron Pi is a women's sorority popular among university students as a social club with charitable intentions. Tina had joined in Louisiana while at SLU, attending the weekly pledge meetings, pledging to the values of the society. Throughout her life she'd been supported by her girlfriends, and she liked the sorority's motto 'Women Enriched Through Lifelong Friendship'. And she loved the sorority's red flower emblem: to its founders, three formidable women from Columbia University, New York, the colour of the rose represented courage and vigour. The group's mascot, the panda, an animal the group considered had no natural enemies, instantly became Tina's favourite. She bought toy pandas and had a porcelain baby dressed as a panda. Entry to a sorority is by invitation. Interested applicants are sized up by members. As soon as she pinned on the badge as an initiated member with the letter 'A' clearly showing, Tina had entered a sisterhood for life. The stated values coincided with her own: promoting integrity and trusting and respecting each other. Boyfriends could come and go, even a fiancé, like Scott McCulloch, but Alpha Omicron Pi would always be there for her. She even used the letters for the registration plate on her red Honda Civic, but at Cindy's suggestion added QT between the AO and the Pi to show she was a self-declared 'cutie pie' of Alpha Omicron Pi. Once at UAB, she joined the local chapter. It made the transition from one university to another much easier. Get-togethers with other fraternities, charity functions and dances took up Tina's spare time in between her jobs.

By the time Tina was twenty-two, she had neither decided on a career nor found a permanent boyfriend. Dates came and went, but no-one new had arrived in her life to make her heart beat faster.

She was still working full-time as a pharmacy assistant, having managed to get a transfer with Eckerd's, and toyed with the idea of studying pharmacy part-time at UAB. At school she had wanted to be a pharmacist. It seemed like a sensible occupation, one that would provide a future, less ambivalent than communications with clear trajectories into the workforce. But Tommy and Cindy were always concerned about her over-taxing herself. With a strong work ethic, she would attend many night-time university classes in between her two jobs, then return home utterly drained.

It wasn't until 1999 that a doctor at UAB's Faculty of Medicine finally put a name to Tina's cardiac problems. She was suffering, he believed, from supraventricular arrhythmia. This caused the periodic rapid beating of her heart. It was not, the doctor said, life threatening. He ordered an echocardiogram. The results came back as normal. Surgery was possible.

As the 1990s drew to a close Tina also worked as an on-call pharmacy technician at Brookwood Medical Centre, the largest private hospital in Alabama, not far from downtown Birmingham. She spent long hours in the basement of the 568-bed hospital, following the doctors' imperfect scrawls on prescriptions, mainly for antibiotics. Tina sometimes delivered the medication to be dispensed by the nurses, donning a white lab coat, a managerial requirement in public areas. She would usually tie her blonde hair in a ponytail, a company regulation. She brought a sense of cheer to the workplace, brightening the dullest day with her smile, cracking jokes and playing the fool.

Despite this outward show of congeniality, she found the measuring and packing mind-numbingly predictable. Also, as a recipient of drugs for her heart condition, she was wary of their effects. She knew that for all the good brought by the medication that she was dispensing, there was always a downside for those who took it. Communications soon seemed more enticing. Working in public relations she could wear beautiful clothes and employ a different talent, one she was good at: talking to people. The UAB had a communications degree that was all about 'human interaction', with specialties in journalism, broadcasting or public relations. It had been her first choice after leaving school and she wanted to finish it.

Alanda, barely eighteen, was setting the pace for milestones. She was getting married. Her fiance's name was

Alex Eastman. For her wedding on 20 November 1999 Alanda chose a mulberry silk for her bridesmaids' outfits. The bridesmaids had their hair in ringlets and parted in the middle. Tina hammed it up in the lead-up to the reception. Looking like a Victorian heroine in her long gown, during a break before the reception began, she pulled the dress up slightly for a photo to reveal that she was wearing stark white and blue sneakers. Alanda followed the Cajun tradition, common at Louisana weddings, where those who wanted to dance with either of the happy couple would pin money to the bride's veil or the groom's suit so they had cash to start their married life. Following another Cajun tradition that poked fun at older, single siblings, after the bridal couple's slow first waltz, Tina, barefoot, seized a new stringy white mop complete with goggle eyes and felt eyebrows, mouth and nose. Pouting for the camera, clown-like with prominent mulberry lipstick, she held her skinny partner close. The mop was meant to represent the missing spouse. She was the older sister. Her younger sister had beaten her down the aisle.

CHAPTER 3

With his experience in the family business, sales and public relations was a more conventional career for Gabe Watson than commercial diving. As 2000 progressed, he continued to flirt with the unknown, still drawn to the world that represented excitement and adventure. Public relations was familiar territory, where he could gain useful skills for the family's prefabricated packaging company. Besides, it had the seal of parental approval, and was the kind of degree in which Gabe could comfortably dawdle. His lecturers knew he had the ability to be an A student, but he could just as easily achieve a B average by performing to the required standard without overly exerting himself.

Gabe formed an easy, bantering rapport with Dr John Wittig, director of the undergraduate public relations program. Wittig taught and conducted research in public speaking, political communication, propaganda and public persuasion, argumentation and debate. Congenial and softly spoken with an offbeat sense of humour, he was the kind of man you could imagine in a woolly dressing gown and slippers. Wittig became something of a father figure to many of the students. 'The coach' is how he described his role. Gabe was one of the students he would spar with, exchanging jokes in the corridor, chewing the fat over school, sport and politics or listening to his complaints about tuition fees, a favourite student topic. In those years around the turn of the century, before the Student Centre was built, Wittig would accompany his night class students after class to a Mexican restaurant nearby to 'shoot the breeze' as he called it. Mass communications remained a popular choice for students, whatever the economic climate. PR students at UAB did passably well, sometimes winning the student component of the Chapter of the Year competition against their rivals: Auburn University, the universities of North Alabama and South Alabama, and the University of Alabama, Tuscaloosa. The prize-giving was usually a grandiose affair organised at a designated hotel where winners posed for group photographs. Wittig would stand in the middle, the coach with the winning team.

Girls outnumbered boys in the field of communications. The discipline attracted pretty girls. Showy girls. Knitted together by their sorority sisterhood, they dressed to please and giggled frequently. They were the sorts of girls Gabe Watson aspired to be with, but they seemed unattainable. Smart. Confident. Appearance was part of the package for their future careers. Tina Thomas seemed kinder than the rest, even though she was a sorority girl. She didn't ignore him like the others may have. She bantered with him in a way he enjoyed – even flirted, but he knew she was flirtatious by nature.

Tina had been dating Stan Marks Jr, almost ten years her senior, since mid April of 2000. They'd been introduced at a bar by Amy Sullivan, a mutual friend. Stan was immediately captivated by Tina's smile and her outgoing personality. Within a month he'd taken her to the zoo in Atlanta so she could see her favourite animal and sorority mascot, the panda. Standing outside the enclosure, she turned to him, her eyes glistening with tears, and thanked him for taking her there. They'd driven to New Orleans one weekend where they'd met up with Amanda and her boyfriend, Jimmy Phillips Jr. Several times, they'd stayed at beaches in Florida, a 5-hour drive away. But Tina turned down Stan's invitations to go hiking as she didn't like strenuous exercise or activity. She preferred shopping, movies, hanging out with friends, long chats with Alanda, keeping up with her sorority sisters. And there was another reason for her dislike of physical activities. Once, Tina had pointed to her neck. Stan could see a pulse beating. She told him it was a palpitation episode coming on and that they occurred several times a week, usually when she was tired or stressed.

The Riverchase Galleria was one of those shopping malls built in the 1980s, with over 175,000 square metres of retail floor space and 5000 parking spots. It was built as Alabama's largest enclosed centre when money was no object. It had weathered with the times, the spacious nine-storey glass atrium creating the impression, for shoppers, of being suspended in time in a large glass bubble. The Parisian department store took up a sizeable portion of the second level, one of two Birmingham-based chains to open in the massive complex. Founded in 1877 by two Alabama sisters, Parisian was a long established name in Birmingham when Tina Thomas joined its payroll in 1999. Alanda had joined the company about six months earlier and was working as a sales associate in the juniors' department. She encouraged Tina, still at UAB, to join her. When designers like Tommy Hilfiger came to the store to promote his latest collection – Tommy jeans for juniors – Alanda invited Tina to the event. They crouched on either side of the man himself, who sat, hand cupped under his chin, smiling for the camera. The job, for Tina, was a contrast to measuring medicines. She began in the shoe department and later moved to childrenswear. Night and weekend hours suited Tina's university commitments.

On her break, there was always the Grand Atrium food court on the ground floor. She would walk past the nineteenth-century Dentzel carousel where thrilled children rode rabbits and giraffes and, at Christmas time, reindeers for $3 a ride. Tina had confided to another sales manager that she might never have children, but other than 'women's problems' she'd given no details.

Tina's best friend Amanda was to be married in May 2001 to Jimmy Phillips Jr., her beau of three years. Tina, like her other friends, had been expecting the announcement. Amanda and Jimmy had met at LSU while she was studying civil engineering. The girls had stayed in regular contact, with Tina visiting Louisiana in the spring and Amanda mostly visiting Tina each autumn.

'As maid of honour, you can stay at Mom's house with me,' Amanda had told Tina on the phone when the engagement was announced. 'There'll be six other attendants. Can you come early and help? I need to think about colours . . .'

With Tina's help, in the months leading up to the wedding, Amanda finally chose the dresses from a bridal store in Mandeville. They were baby blue with a long skirt and sleeveless top with clear beading work and little capped sleeves that could be taken off.

Tina arrived in Louisiana early in the week of the

wedding. Stan Marks drove down for the rehearsal. Tina had booked him into a hotel room, but after Stan realised she wouldn't be with him, he was hurt. Ever the peacemaker, Tina organised a couch for him to stay on at Amanda's mother's house.

On the morning of Amanda's wedding, the girls had breakfast together at one of their favourite haunts.

'Our last hoorah,' Amanda grinned.

'Our last hoorah,' Tina repeated. 'The last time you are single.'

They laughed into each other's eyes.

'And when are you and Stan going to tie the knot?'

'Aw, you know,' Tina said, her voice trailing off. 'He's talked about it. Maybe after I graduate.'

The reception was in Mandeville, at Amanda's mother's place, on 3 hectares. There was plenty of room and the party went on into the night. Amanda had to unpin $100 from her new husband's lapel, bestowed upon him in 'the Money Dance' in true Cajun tradition by guests, to pay the DJ so he would stay for another hour. Jimmy and Amanda then left for their honeymoon in Cancun, Mexico.

Despite her diagnosis in 1999, Tina hadn't followed up the doctor's recommendation for surgery. Soon, she would finish her degree and if she was working full-time, finding time for surgery and recuperation might be difficult.

Finally, in 2001, she made an appointment with a cardiologist at the Princeton Baptist Hospital in Birmingham. Dr Farrell Mendelsohn undertook a Luke Monitor Test, a stress test and an echo test. Examining the test results, he confirmed what she already knew.

'You have an arrhythmia called supraventricular

tachycardia,' he said. 'That means you get a loss of the normal rhythm in the heart resulting in those episodes of rapid heartbeat you've been getting for years. There's also a minimal abnormality in your mitral valve, but it's otherwise normal. As it's arrhythmia, I'm going to refer you to one of the best experts in the field here. He has a very good record in fixing this problem.'

'Is that serious?' Tina asked.

'It's not going to kill you, put it that way. You've lived with it all your life. But it can be fixed.'

Cindy said she had always believed that God was listening. Her prayers had been answered.

In July 2001, not long after Amanda's wedding, Tina had her first consultation with Professor Andrew Epstein, a cardiologist and a Professor of Medicine at the University of Alabama. She was surprised when he suggested an immediate operation after so many long years waiting. It gave her no time to think.

'I don't want to have the operation until I've finished school,' Tina said, alarmed.

'Well, we can do it in August – say mid August, that's during a big break from school?'

'I'll talk to my parents about it,' Tina replied.

Cindy and Tommy said it was probably best to go ahead and, finally, she agreed to the day surgery procedure. When she awoke from the anaesthetic, Cindy and Alanda were standing by her bed. Professor Epstein appeared later. Tina looked pale, but managed a groggy smile as he approached. The waiting had been most stressful for Cindy, who had always dreaded the day her elder daughter might have to face surgery. Now, here was Tina, propped up in bed, with the doctor telling them that it was over. She would not need another operation.

Cindy had to sit down. Her lower lip trembled.

'As I explained to you before, you had dual AV nodes between the upper and lower chambers of the heart, which were causing your symptoms,' Professor Epstein said. 'It occurs in about 30 per cent of the general population, but only a fraction of those people get the arrhythmia.

'What I've done is performed a slow pathway ablation – which just means burning or sealing the extra AV node. That's the extra node that has been causing the palpitations by sending electrical activity circling around the heart . . . instead of from the top to the bottom as it should. What I've done today is to set up a roadblock which will stop the palpitations.'

Stan came to see Tina in her tiny hospital room, bringing a dozen red roses. He was there when she was discharged in a wheelchair later. He noticed a change in her within weeks.

Tina told Dr Mendelsohn in September: 'I'm so much better. I've got energy . . . I can feel my heart racing sometimes at night, but it's not nearly as fast as it used to be.'

'That'll settle down in a couple of months,' he said. 'Your heart is structurally normal. The operation has a success rate of 99 per cent and if there were going to be any problems, we would have known by now.'

Afterwards, Tina had a more positive attitude. She told Stan she had feared that her heart condition would affect her ability to have children. Now, able to keep up with her social life, work and study, she even said one day she might go jogging with him. To her family the change in Tina was miraculous. For 24 years Tommy and Cindy had worried and constantly urged her to slow down. But now, there was no more having to take stairs slowly. She was free.

***

By the autumn of 2001, as fate would have it, Gabe's goal of dating Tina was made relatively easy. CM311 Organizational Communication was a core subject for students in communications, whether majoring in PR, communications management or mass communication. The subject examined theories and models of communication in organisational settings. Gabe juggled his timetable to coincide with some of Tina's classes.

He gradually got to know her routine and easily recognised her confident stride from across the campus. She had the studied carelessness of someone who was used to being watched; her blonde hair, if it wasn't tied, was always brushed and flicked over her shoulder. Their interaction was more like sibling banter: jocular, light-hearted, put-down kind of stuff, rather than a serious attempt at courtship. Even Dr Wittig was susceptible to Tina's charms. He would provoke her the same way Gabe provoked her, two lions playing with a lioness, delighted when they got a haughty reaction and she would turn on 'a Hollywood moment' where she would toss back her ponytail and turn her back on both of them as though following a well-worn script.

The Watsons' condo was one of many in Woodland Village, Homewood, just up the hill from the Homewood High School. It was an upstairs apartment in a group of bluey mauve-coloured, two-storey wooden buildings surrounded by small hedges. Close to the main highway, the clustered buildings were tucked away in a peaceful woodland setting which made it easy to forget the hum of continuous traffic speeding in and out of Birmingham. Car parks surrounded the various wings and small cement pathways dissected and linked the condominiums. The upstairs apartments had small wooden balconies to make up for the lack of garden.

Gabe Watson lived in one, sharing over the years with a friend, Jeff Bradford, and his youngest brother, Michael. It was an easy arrangement and one that gave him independence without costing him too much. It was also closer to the university campus than his parents' home. Inside the doorway was the same 'Bless this House' pincushion his parents had in their front hallway. He had left the nest but had not flown far from it.

Gabe now had four dive certificates including his rescue certificate and spear-fishing certification. Mike Moore, while attending a community college in the city, had regularly dropped in, staying the night at the condo on a Thursday or Friday when they talked late into the evening. But as the new millennium dawned their friendship had waned. Mike had turned down Gabe's invitations to go diving at Blue Water. He had a serious girlfriend. For Gabe, the dwindling companionship meant more time to focus on Tina.

The assessment in CM311 Organizational Communication was a major group project. This was the opportunity Gabe Watson had been waiting for. The banter that was their trademark continued, but this time he had an excuse to meet Tina Thomas outside of class.

One morning, she'd seemed down. She'd told him her boyfriend had come back from New York and he hadn't bothered to get her a designer purse she'd asked for. Instead, he'd bought her something from the airport. Kate Spade, she'd said, was more than just a designer. She helped women all over the world and her purses were 'so cool'.

'Bright colours,' she was saying. 'You can't get these purses in Alabama. In Texas, maybe. There's a store there.'

'So, there's a store in New York?'

'Yeah. A couple in New York . . . I know there's definitely one on Fifth Avenue . . .'

Another silence.

'I'm going to New York,' Gabe said.

'You are?'

'Sure. I can get you one.'

'Ah, it's okay,' she recovered herself. 'I mean . . . I just meant that it's disappointing that Stan forgot. You know?'

'Up to you. I'm going there, so I can get you one. Just let me know.'

One evening in mid November, he struck gold when his phone rang. He could tell she had been drinking.

'My sister's twenty-first,' she answered when he asked what all the noise was in the background.

'We're at Dave's on Southside. I've got a coupla' girls you should meet, friends of Alanda.'

'Alanda?'

'My sister, dummy.'

'I've got a friend with me,' he said.

'Oh . . .' she squealed. 'Is he good looking? Bring him too. I trust it's a "him", right?'

He turned up at Dave's with Jeff Bradford in tow. The group was near the long bar with the large array of beers on tap. Alanda seemed nothing like Tina. Her eyes were a different shape. She was a little frosty. But Gabe didn't have much time for Alanda's friends. He only had eyes for Tina.

Weeks later, sitting around the family dining table, Tommy began his familiar quiz about boyfriends.

'So, it's all over with Stan?'

'Well . . . I don't know.'

'That means, no.'

'There's some guy in my class who's always trying to get me to go out with him . . .'

'And?'

'He's a little weird, that's all.'

'Well, that doesn't sound like a selling point,' Tommy chuckled.

'Not at all,' Cindy drawled.

CHAPTER 4

Tina graduated from university on 15 December 2001. The day before was cold and wintry and the trees were stripped of leaves. The houses in Seattle Slew Drive stood stark against dry lawns when Tina posed for photos outside the family home with Cindy and Tommy. Her mortar board with a tassle was placed so that it was pulled down on the right of her forehead, a practice session for the official photographs. That night, Stan Marks came over for the graduation party. Stan couldn't help noticing that Tina seemed to have changed towards him. It was a big party. Tina had made Tommy proud, the first on his side of the family to graduate. The following day, with her shoulder-length hair loose, wearing small earrings and a paler shade of lipstick than her customary dark colours, she posed for the official photographs. She felt a sense of accomplishment. The awarding of the degree was the culmination of juggling a variety of jobs, night classes, handing in assignments, often late, and, of course, her beloved sorority functions. The black robes of graduation marked a change in her status with her sorority sisters, although she would still have a role through the UAB Alumni.

After graduation Tina confided in her sister, as she always did about the issues in her life. The relationship with Stan Marks had come to an end as far as she was concerned. But she waited until three days after Christmas to tell him. Stan was devastated. They'd talked about getting married, possibly after she'd graduated and got a job.

On New Year's Eve Tina turned up to a party with a girlfriend and Gabe Watson. Here was someone who appreciated her. Gabe had returned from New York with the Kate Spade purse, which was red, her favourite colour, and presented it to her just before Christmas. She lifted up her glass to him and watched the tiny bubbles sparkle in the yellow liquid. Gabe had been one of the people to urge her to break up with Stan. That night they had their first kiss.

'I was born in the wrong century, you know,' Tina sighed, putting down her dog-eared copy of *Gone with the Wind* on the poolside table next to their sun lounges. She and Amanda Phillips were visiting Miami, Florida. They were back at the hotel pool after visiting Amanda's friend, Jennifer.

'But instead of a horse-drawn carriage, you've got your Mazda Miata,' Amanda chuckled. 'Your mid-life crisis car . . . You've only been talking about it since high school . . .'

'That's why it's my mid-life crisis car,' said Tina, lying on her stomach, her hands under her chin. 'That's how long it's taken. After breaking up with Stan, I had to do something to mark the occasion. And besides, I'm twenty-five.'

'Hey, that's *way* old,' Amanda said, laughing. 'You are quite the southern belle with all these beaux, Tina. Trouble is, a southern belle is the sort of girl that puts up with the crap and takes it with a spoonful of sugar,' Amanda teased. 'That's never going to be me.'

'Scarlett didn't put up with crap,' she retorted. 'She got exactly what she wanted.'

Tina, slipping onto her back, placed a large hat over her face. Her legs were sticking out under the umbrella. Her hand groped blindly on the table beside her until she found her paperback and her page again.

'I can't believe you're still re-reading that – after how many years? You must know it by heart.'

They made a striking couple as usual, the dainty blonde and the 1.8-metre tall graceful brunette. They might have been two models doing a fashion shoot.

'What about this Gabe guy? Are you serious about him?'

'Well,' Tina drawled, 'he did bring me a Kate Spade purse.'

'So, he does what he's told?'

'Well . . . not exactly, and he still has to finish his degree, but his parents have this packaging business . . .'

Amanda snorted.

'You're not saying he's a prospect, are you? I know you, Tina. That's why you need to text him on the half-hour? You haven't stopped since you got here.'

'Amanda, it's all very well for you to talk. You're married. Alanda is married. Have you got any other spinster friends left?'

'And when am I going to meet him?'

'Whenever.'

'Has he met Mr Tom and Mrs Cindy yet?'

'Not exactly.'

'That means, no.'

'There's no rush. We're taking it slowly. We're not exactly going out.'

'What does that mean? He's been after you for so long. What happened with that?'

Tina jumped up and ran to the edge of the pool, slipping

into the water. Then, scooping the water in her hands, she splashed it towards Amanda's long tanned legs. Amanda squealed.

'Watch my magazine, you goof.'

But Tina had already begun her 'funky dog paddle' as Amanda called it. In spite of herself, Amanda grinned. There was something peculiarly Tina about the theatrical air of the stunted freestyle strokes, her head at an over-extended angle above the water, her hair piled high.

'Oh, oh, oh, oh!' she squealed, half cooing, half grunting, in an effort to get to the other side of the pool without getting a single hair wet. It was a sound that never failed to make Amanda laugh.

After one little lap, Tina returned to the sun lounge.

'I thought this guy, Gabe, liked diving,' Amanda said. 'If you call that swimming, how are you fixin' to be a scuba starlet?'

Tina took off her towel and flicked Amanda with it. She squealed in mock protest.

'Have you told him you'll be spending all night drying all that fine cornsilk hair, 'cos it takes so long? Might not want to hang around if you tell him that.'

Tina sighed heavily.

'He played football, you know, and he loves the Auburn Tigers. We're going to see a game of basketball together.'

'So maybe we can go see a game when I come to Birmingham next?'

'Mmm.'

'And he loves diving,' Tina continued. 'He's been to Cozumel and Panama City. And he loves fishing!'

Amanda rolled her eyes. 'Come on, Tina. Fishing! You, Miss city girl. This I gotta see. When can I meet him?'

***

'When're we ever gonna meet this boy of yours? This Gabe?' Tommy wanted to know as they sat in the lounge room at Seattle Slew Drive.

Gabe's weekends were often taken up with fishing expeditions. Tina put it down to him preferring to be with his own crowd. He didn't like being the centre of attention, and was reserved and quiet when it came to meeting her friends. But Tina knew that when her father put that voice on, he was serious.

'When you were going out with all these other guys . . . Scott, James . . . we'd watch movies together. You know, what do you guys call it – "chill"? They'd come over. We'd hang out. *Meet the Parents*. But we haven't seen this one . . . you *are* going out with him, aren't you?'

'Oh Dad, that was years ago and Stan wasn't here much. Everyone's at college now and working and busy. There's no time to, um . . . chill.'

Tina picked up a magazine from the coffee table and crossed her legs. Tommy and Cindy exchanged glances across the bar stools.

'You've got so much more energy now, darling,' Cindy changed the subject, smiling. 'There was a time not so long ago that you couldn't have gone out after work, or school, you'd be so tired. We barely see you now.'

In May 2002, when Gabe finally arrived at Seattle Slew Drive, he sank his large frame into the comfy beige armchair, positioned in front of the paintings of racehorses, antique vases and table lamps. Tommy tried his best offbeat humour to engage him in conversation, but Gabe seemed reluctant. Tommy's first priority, as always, was to make Tina happy, so he kept quiet about his feelings. Tina, always respectful and sensitive to her father's moods, noticed his reaction. After that first visit, her parents did not pressure her so much to bring Gabe over.

Amanda Burchell, a co-worker at Parisian who, like Tina, had also been promoted to the position of sales manager, was used to spending time with Tina, particularly since Tina had started dating Gabe and her weekends were free when Gabe went fishing. Tina also hung out with another sales manager called Robert Collins.

'I tell you Amanda, when Gabe found out that Robert wasn't gay, he said I couldn't hang out with him. I mean, we're just friends. We'd go to a basketball game together . . . that's it.'

Sometimes, on Monday mornings, Tina had asked Amanda Burchell: 'If my mom or anyone asks, I was with you this weekend, okay?'

During a break in October, Amanda Phillips came to visit. It was the usual Saturday night where the girls settled down with a box of blush wine to watch a movie – this time it was *Practical Magic*.

'You know, you're Sandra Bullock,' Tina said, giggling, after several glasses of the semi-sweet pink alcohol.

'And you're Nicole Kidman.'

'Only we're both better looking.' Giggles.

'Sure we are.'

'We'd better hope life doesn't imitate art then, after what happens in that movie. What about the guys we're marrying?' Tina joked. 'We don't want them to end up dead.'

'Oh, "we're" marrying now, are we?'

'No . . .'

'My Jimmy . . . he's so sweet, Tina. I'm dying to meet Gabe tomorrow,' Amanda giggled. 'S'the whole reason I'm here – apart from seeing you and the family, of course.'

'Tomorrow morning, if we're up to it,' Tina said, and then suddenly reached for her phone. 'I'll ring him,' she said. 'See what he's up to. See if he's missing me.'

She handed the phone to Amanda, already a little tipsy.

'You talk to him. Don't let on who you are.'

They were giggling loudly when Tina lost her nerve and wrenched the phone from Amanda just as she'd started to speak.

'That'll teach you to talk to strange girls,' she sniggered to Gabe on the other end.

'Now we're going to see you tomorrow morning, honey,' she hiccupped, and he laughed at her.

'And then there's dinner?'

But the two girls stayed up far later than they'd planned. Amanda quietly cursed Tina the next morning, groaning each time a coffee cup banged too loudly in the kitchen. Nursing a hangover well into the afternoon, all good intentions of meeting with Gabe were long gone.

'Cheap wine and me don't get along that well, you should know that, Tina.'

'And who made you drink it?'

'Mr Tom, it's your daughter's fault I feel this way.'

Tommy laughed.

They were still laughing and goofing around hours later when they entered the Cracker Barrel restaurant. Gabe was sitting at the table already. Amanda saw a quiet, tall man, a little overweight, but not the retiring type, she decided. It was evident from his monosyllabic answers and general demeanour that he was in a foul mood. Amanda was surprised that he paid her so little regard, considering that she was Tina's best friend and they were meeting for the first time. But no matter how hard Tina cajoled him, she couldn't snap him out of it.

The girls headed for the restroom. Tina spoke first.

'Aw, don't worry about him. He's got sinus troubles and he's always Mr Grump when that happens.'

Amanda washed her hands in silence.

'I mean . . . I know he doesn't come across like he really is. When he's alone with me, he's different. He's handsome, don't you think? And his family are so welcoming. His mother, especially.'

But Amanda prided herself on her knack of judging character. She knew that something didn't sit right with this guy. Making excuses to your best friend wasn't right. She felt uneasy. Tina was a closer confidante in some ways than her own husband, yet she didn't want to tell her best friend that her new boyfriend had been a disappointment.

Tina was first up the stairs and had pushed open the door to Gabe's condo, carrying some groceries. It was November 2002 and getting colder by the day. As well as being warm inside, everything was neat and tidy. Perhaps that was why, she later told her family and friends, she immediately noticed a small jewellery bag on top of the entertainment unit. She put down the shopping and walked across to the bag, glancing sideways at Gabe. He did not appear to be looking. She busied herself putting things away in the fridge. Then she caught him looking at her almost expectantly.

'What's that?'

'What?'

'On top of the TV.'

'If I catch you looking at that, you won't be getting it.'

'Oh Gabe,' she wheedled. 'What is it? I bet I can guess by the size of it and what it says on the bag.' She recognised the name of a jewellery store. Her eyes shone with expectation.

He did not reply.

'You can't keep secrets from me. Is it for me?'

'Now, you heard what I said, honey. You look anywhere near it and you'll never get to find out what it is. I'll just take it back to the store.'

Tina bit her lip, unsure how to respond. If he was joking, he didn't let on. As the night wore on and it was obvious that he wasn't joking, she tried to work out how to deal with his challenge. She sat quietly. She couldn't tell Amanda or Alanda. What would she say anyway? She imagined different ways of starting the conversation, but gave up. Besides, she had already sensed their verdict on the man she hoped to marry. She wondered whether he would change his mind. Maybe he was cross with her for some reason. Maybe he'd ask her the following night. But Christmas came and went. So, too, did New Year's Eve. Maybe, she had hoped, he'd ask her on her birthday in February, or perhaps save it for Valentine's Day. Soon it would be the first anniversary of when they'd started dating. Later, she would complain that he would use the ring to get her to do things, knowing she would comply. But no proposal was forthcoming. She was in a strange half-state, with a ring provided but not bestowed upon her. She imagined her friends and family confirming that all along they'd been right. Then, Tina would feel protective of him again. He just didn't realise. But, as the months dragged by, she felt more and more paralysed. Gradually, she began to confide in her family and friends, relieving herself of the burden she carried. When Tina had told her father about the ring and the lack of a proposal,

Tommy had told her: 'Tell him to take the ring and shove it. Why would you be with someone who treats you like that?' He had been pained that she had so little regard for herself.

'Because I love him,' she had said, looking into her father's eyes. 'And I hope one day he will ask me to marry him.'

Tommy sighed.

'He said he wants a short engagement.'

And what he says goes, Tommy had thought, but he didn't tell Tina that. How could he argue against love? He knew how important it was.

It was in February, three days before Tina's twenty-sixth birthday, that Tommy had received an unexpected call from Gabe. Tommy was in Greensberg, Pennsylvania, on business. Gabe had said bluntly that he wanted to ask for Tina's hand in marriage. Tommy insisted they meet face to face. That was the right thing to do. Perhaps, Tommy reflected, the fact that he hadn't warmed to Gabe was no more than him being a protective father who was losing his daughter.

The meeting with his prospective son-in-law on his return to Alabama was uncomfortably formal in the coffee shop of one of the Books-a-Million stores closer to Gabe on Montgomery Highway in Hoover. It was Saturday, 15 February. Already Valentine cards had been reduced. Crowds of Saturday shoppers thronged the aisles of books, magazine and toys in the huge retail space. It was just the two of them launching into the age-old conversation every father has with a man who declares he wants to spend a lifetime with his daughter.

Tommy sat opposite Gabe, still struggling with what it was that he wanted to say. He wanted to begin diplomatically. Tommy Thomas was known for his deep sense of humanity, of fairness and integrity. These were the same qualities that made him a good salesman, and later on a successful management training consultant, because his clients sensed correctly that his trustworthiness wasn't just skin deep. He carried a responsibility to those he encountered in his daily job. That responsibility was even more deeply felt when dealing with issues concerning the people he loved.

He became more certain, after the pleasantries were over, of what he was going to say, realising what it was that bothered him.

In the few times Tommy had met Gabe Watson, Gabe had never demonstrated to him that he loved Tina, not in the way that Tommy and Cindy were in love when they were first engaged – smiling into each other's eyes, touching hands, physically aware of each other. Tommy was prepared to accept that Gabe was a reserved sort of guy, and perhaps undemonstrative in front of his girlfriend's parents. Everyone was different. The issue of the ring, and tormenting Tina, however, did not stem from that kind of personality.

Sitting across from Gabe, Tommy knew that the teasing, controlling element behind Gabe's actions was not the sort of behaviour one would have expected from someone in love. Nor had Tina ever said that Gabe had told her he loved her.

Getting straight to the point, Tommy said in an even tone, 'Why do you want to marry Tina?'

'Sir, I think the relationship we have just feels right.'

'Gabe, do you love my daughter?'

Gabe paused, sipping on his coffee, before looking back at Tommy.

'Well, Mr Thomas, I feel that's a little corny, if you don't mind me saying so.'

'Corny?'

The word jarred with Tommy who had been waiting, he realised, to be reassured.

'Well, I mean, I feel right with Tina and that's what matters, isn't it . . . ? We're comfortable together. She would have told you that.'

Tommy nodded.

'Most people who get married are in love, that's why they get married,' Tommy said.

Gabe shrugged his shoulders.

'Well, as long as we're right for each other . . . I'm just not too sure on how or when I'm going to ask her . . . you know?'

'Well, whatever you do, you should make sure it's something very special, because Tina will expect that.'

'Yes, sir. I understand.'

And there was another thing troubling Tommy.

'You should also know that Tina hasn't been well throughout her childhood. She's mentioned about going scuba diving and learning new stuff. Well, I don't think that'd be good for her. She's had her operation, but . . .'

'Yes, but she's cured now and it's not going to be a problem. And if I am going to do things that Tina likes to do, she has to do those things that I like to do and scuba diving is what I enjoy doing.'

Afterwards, driving home, Tommy puzzled over why Gabe had refused to admit to loving Tina. Far from being reassured that his daughter was about to enter a loving union, the episode left him even more uneasy, but there was nothing he could do. After all, it wasn't his relationship. It was his daughter's and she had to make her own choices. He and Alanda had raised their concerns with her about Gabe but she was either unable or unwilling to listen.

***

Everyone knew that Tiffie really belonged to Tina. She was the first dog the family had owned. Tiffie had pointy ears and brown eyes like buttons. She was allowed to sit on the couch and was treated like a member of the family. It was usually Tiffie who heard of Tina's romantic woes. Tina would fling her arms around Tiffie's neck and burrow her nose into the dog's curly, soft hair. Tina adored her. The dog starred in many family snaps. But Gabe would tease Tiffie. At first, Tina started to complain, but Gabe ridiculed her so that, over time, she stayed silent, uncomfortable that Tiffie was clearly unhappy. Alanda, though, visiting at the same time as Gabe one day, and never one to mince her words, would have none of it.

'Stop it,' she said initially as a low-voiced request, but as he continued and she saw Tina's pain and the look of bewilderment on the dog's face, she spoke more sharply.

'Stop teasing the dog. She doesn't like it. You can see that.'

Gabe erupted in a way that shocked her, swearing and stomping, telling her to mind her own business. Tina said nothing. Alanda was glad that Cindy and Tommy hadn't seen it.

On other occasions, Alanda noticed how quickly Tina's mood changed when they were out on a social or family gathering and her phone rang. She knew right away it was Gabe from her sister's usually open and happy face. Tina would walk quickly away from the group, phone pressed to her ear, and Alanda would hear her raise her voice in protest. Sometimes, she would return distracted and defeated, no longer the Tina she knew.

'He's doing this, you know, deliberately,' Alanda said. 'He hates you having anything else in your life except him. He hates you being around me. He knows how close we are and he doesn't like it. Every time we're together, he rings you up. He's so possessive. Look what he does to Tiffie. What are you doing with him, Tina? He makes you unhappy. He's trying to ruin your relationships with other people. I just don't get it. You've had lots of boyfriends.'

'He's got the ring, Alanda.'

'But is he ever going to give it to you?'

Tina looked down.

'And you're putting up with this? The guy acts like a jerk.'

'No. You just don't know him like I do.'

When the story circulated about the ring, the family and friends Tina had reluctantly confided in were concerned. Tina's cousin Krissie McCampbell had never met Gabe, but it seemed to Krissie that Tina exaggerated her feelings for him. Tina always talked about what Gabe liked, what Gabe thought, what Gabe wanted. This wasn't like the Tina she knew.

'Yes, there's tensions, Krissie, and I need to keep the peace,' she confided on the phone one evening, 'even between the families – you know, Thanksgiving and Christmas. And then there's Mom and Gabe. They just don't get on.'

'Maybe,' Krissie advised brightly, 'you should write things down in a journal. You know, it helps to sort through things and keep your sanity.'

'I keep a journal already. I've been going to a counsellor because of all of this stuff and she told me to keep a journal.'

'Good. That's important. And what's this about the ring? He won't give it to you?'

'He tells me I have to really show him I love him before I get it.'

***

Cindy bailed Tina up one evening.

'I can't believe you put up with this, you of all people. You wouldn't have with anyone else.'

Tina said nothing.

'You know, I've just got a really bad feeling about him,' she said. 'I don't like him. And I cannot believe you are starting scuba diving lessons just because he wants you to. I've been thinking about it since you first brought it up. It sounds like a very strenuous sport and even though your heart condition is cured, you have never been the real physical, sporty type. Although I must say,' she said, giving her daughter an appraising look, 'you do look better since the operation. Your face has filled out a bit.'

'But, Mom, I've told you before. You're not giving him a chance. Gabe wants me to scuba dive and I want to make him happy, so I'm going to learn to dive so we can spend more weekend time together.'

'Okay,' Cindy sighed, 'I will try to give him a chance, for your sake, but we need to get to know him better. We hardly know him at all.'

'Let's go get a pizza after work,' Tina said to Alanda on the phone. It was a cold winter's afternoon.

They were running through the menus when Gabe showed up. Alanda looked at Tina, wondering why she hadn't told her he was coming. She smiled cautiously, but Gabe ignored her. Nor did he say anything to Tina. He glared at her instead. Tina tucked her head down as he sat opposite her. Alanda tried small talk, but nothing worked. Whatever Tina said, which was little, Gabe would come up with a retort. If the pizza hadn't been about to arrive, Alanda would have got up and left. She wished it had just been her and Tina. That's why she had come. Alanda was never prone to pretence. She turned her large eyes to Gabe in disgust, trying to block out his angry outbursts. At last, the pizza arrived and was placed on the table. They could soon call this night to a close.

Gabe reached for a piece straightaway, the cheese melting onto his fingers, but instead of lifting it up to his mouth, he hurled it towards Tina. Then he stormed out.

Alanda was left to hold Tina's hand and try to stop her sobbing.

'Has he given you the ring yet?'

Tina shook her head violently.

'Then leave him.'

Tina continued to cry.

'And you're putting up with this?'

'Would you rather I was an old maid with a bunch of cats?' Tina sobbed.

CHAPTER 5

Tina's induction into the world of scuba diving began in the classroom on Friday, 6 March 2003 with brand new gear and an Oceanic Versa Navcon dive computer she had bought for $1854.15 the night before on hire purchase. She had 4 hours of tuition finishing with the compulsory test and scored 86 per cent. The following day, it was still dark when she got up to begin her first class in water at the heated pool in HealthSouth Rehabilitation Hospital in Vestavia. Despite the tepid water and wetsuit, it took a few minutes for her to adjust to the temperature.

'We won't be starting the open-water sessions until the last weekend in April – at the Blue Water in Pelham. As y'all know it's too damn cold even this far south in Alabama,' Tom Jackson told the group. 'Unless we go to Florida where the water temperature is around 68 degrees.' It was decided to stay local and begin earlier to suit a class member who was getting married.

Inside the swimming pool, Tina wondered why she had made such a fuss. It wasn't that hard. Tom Jackson repeated the instructions so many times that even though she found herself tuning out to begin with, the sheer repetition meant she knew what a regulator was, how to find it and what BC stood for. Gabe would be pleased. Whether she would remember it underwater in a real dive setting, she was not sure about.

When she visited the condo after her weekend of diving instruction, the small bag was still on top of the television. She told Gabe in detail about the weekend, how silly she'd looked in the mirror with her mask on and how hard it was to tell people apart, how they looked so different kitted out in their gear; why didn't The Dive Site sell purple fins? She had saved some funny anecdotes about some of the people in the class. But the ring stayed where he had placed it.

Tina was crying on the phone to Amanda Phillips, who took a break from pump stations and pile drivers to offer solace. It was mid March 2003, four months since she had first seen the bag containing the engagement ring and about two weeks after she'd started dive classes.

'Gabe and I . . . We're having some time apart. I'm sick of looking at that bag with the ring in it at his place. I'm sick of all the excuses. First, he was waiting for a pay rise. Then he was waiting to catch up with Dad for "the talk". Now I don't know what it is, but I am over waiting,' Tina said, relieved at last to be speaking the truth.

Amanda was sympathetic. 'Is this guy really who you have been waiting for?'

Tina remained silent as she put down the receiver to blow her nose.

'You need to think about this,' Amanda went on. 'Are you settling for second best?'

'Oh, I don't know,' sighed Tina despondently. 'I'm sick of looking for Mr Right. And Mom is always on at me about

Gabe and worrying about scuba diving. I need to get away from all this . . .'

'I told you that wouldn't work . . . diving and fishing, that's not you. Now cheer up. You're usually the one telling me to cheer up.'

'Honestly, Amanda, if I don't finish the scuba course my life wouldn't be worth living.'

'Well, maybe it *is* worth living if you pack your bags and leave him for good. None of your other boyfriends made you this unhappy.'

'You know I was thinking of Xander the other night,' Tina said, changing the subject. 'I always thought we could have made something of it, you know? We had lots of laughs. I don't have so many of those at the moment.'

Alexander Lorenz, 'Xander' to the family, was Amanda's cousin. He was living in Atlanta.

'Oh yes, the emails,' Amanda said. Amanda had recently copied Tina in on a group email and Xander had been in the group. Bantering back and forth, they had easily returned to their old flirting ways from high school.

April Fool's Day was looming. Xander and Tina decided to play a joke on Amanda by pretending that after secretly dating for some time, they had been married. Tina sent her the email containing the 'news' on 1 April.

Amanda had fallen for it immediately in a way that neither of them expected. She had rung Xander to say how happy she was for both of them and how much she'd always wanted them to be together. They had to remind her what day it was and that the whole thing had been a joke, but the seed had been sown. It was as if they were kids again, planning and scheming, just the diversion that Tina needed. The banter continued and with it the dares. Xander said that Tina would never come to Atlanta and Tina responded that she might.

Xander asked whether the relationship with Gabe, whom Amanda had told him about, was serious. Tina emailed back that things weren't as good as they could be. Meanwhile, she would rush to check her emails, captivated by this new flurry of excitement in a life that was otherwise a waiting game. The thought of a liaison in a strange place with someone other than Gabe was tempting. Here was someone who was straightforward, who said what he thought and who clearly cared for her. He knew her family. They had hung out as teenagers.

'I'm thinking of going to see him,' Tina said.

'It's a short plane flight away,' Amanda replied.

'Aw, right, Miss Smarty Pants, and what do I tell Gabe? He knows I don't know anybody in Atlanta. Besides, he's been asking me to do stuff that weekend.'

'You don't have to tell him anything. You don't owe him an explanation. You're not engaged to him and you're having a break anyway. If he were decent in the first place, he would propose, not half-propose and put you into this situation. He's the one that's muckin' you around.'

'I'll tell him I'm spending the weekend with a girlfriend. But, what if a relationship does develop with Xander? What do I tell Gabe?'

'So, why not follow the advice you always give?' Amanda started humming the Johnny Rodriguez song. Whatever she did today, she'd have to sleep with tonight.

Tina left Birmingham on Friday, 4 April in her beloved Mazda Miata, driving east into Georgia. She said goodbye to Alanda before leaving Parisian.

'You have a wonderful day tomorrow. I know you'll look gorgeous,' Tina said. Alanda was getting ready to be a bridesmaid for her friend and co-worker, Kelli Duke.

'Where are you off to?' Alanda asked.

'I'm going to go visit Xander Lorenz, you know, Amanda's cousin who I had that big crush on back in school?'

Alanda had raised her eyebrow.

Later, on the Interstate 20, Tina rang Alanda to explain.

'I am totally fed up with the way things are with Gabe. And you want to know the biggest problem? I am darn sick of looking at that bag on top of the TV. I'm going to see what else is out there.'

After filling the car she rang Alanda again.

'I've told Mom I'm going to see Amanda who is visiting her cousin Xander!'

But Alanda knew Amanda wasn't going.

Nearly 3 hours later Tina arrived at Xander's house and met his roommate, Chris. She had one glass of wine but she seemed nervous to Xander. The further away from Birmingham she had driven, the more unsure Tina had become over what she would say to Gabe about this impulsive decision to drive off to meet up with someone from so far back in her past. After going out for dinner, they had returned to the house and watched TV with Chris, before going to Xander's room to watch TV in bed. They were expected to behave as if all of this was normal. Xander turned to kiss her but she responded stiffly. Both of them felt awkward and decided to just go to sleep. Tina checked her mobile phone. A missed call from Gabe. The next day she accompanied Xander to a golf tournament, standing on the sidelines watching the white-clothed golfers tee off, but by the end of the day, she was sunburned and tired. Gabe had rung several times but she'd ignored the calls.

'Will we go out to dinner, or do you want me to cook something?' Xander asked.

'Oh, Xander, I don't know. I don't feel well. You know, too much sun.'

They sat in the lounge room for a while.

'Look, do you mind if I just drive home? I mean . . . I really appreciate everything and I've had fun spending time with you, but I really should go home.'

On the drive back Tina rang Alanda several times needing to talk.

'How did it go?'

'Well . . . things didn't go quite the way I had hoped. I just couldn't do anything. It wasn't that he wasn't great or anything. But we ended up just talking.'

The phone rang again. It was Gabe. She told him bluntly where she had been. She had been weighing up this decision. Alanda always said she was no good at telling lies and anyone could read her like a book. It was much better she 'fess up now rather than him find out later, she had decided.

They had a big argument and Gabe hung up. Tina rang Amanda.

'Well the weekend was not what you'd call an unqualified success. He was very nice but there was just no spark. Gabe kept ringing and I finally took his call just now. He is so mad, Amanda. I think this might be the end. Wait. He's ringing again now.'

Tina rang Xander when she arrived back just to say she was okay.

What had seemed like a series of good jokes with old friends now seemed silly and ill-considered.

'Nothing happened,' she had reassured Gabe later.

'Well, you picked the right guy, then, after all, didn't you?' Gabe said softly.

***

On a clear, sunny Saturday spring morning, 12 April 2003, the 1.8-metre tall dive coordinator Craig Cleckler stood waist-deep in water. His arms were folded across his expansive chest which was encased in clinging black rubber neoprene, bristling with hoses and buttons and mouthpieces, all connected to the scuba tank harnessed to his back. Cleckler was used to noticing things that were out of place. It was part of his police-academy training from his fifteen-year career as a police officer and in his recent shift to lawyer in a small Hoover firm. He would note body language and the telltale signs of someone not acting in tune with their environment. These skills suited perfectly his weekend role as a voluntary dive coordinator in certification classes for his friend Tom Jackson.

Alabama Blue Water Adventures was known to the locals as 'Blue Water'. The limestone quarry had morphed over the past two decades into one of the premier inland dive training facilities in the south-eastern United States. It had multiple underwater attractions: cars, trucks and boats lying 6 to 21 metres deep, a 5.8-metre wooden sailboat with sails up, a 7.5-metre sailboat, the school bus, concrete pipes 4.8 metres long with a 2-metre inside diameter plus ten underwater training platforms. And there were natural distractions too: bass, sunfish, catfish, bream, bluegill, Japanese coy, carp, rainbow trout and turtles that roamed the quarry.

Here, in the often chilly, murky waters of the manmade lake, Cleckler, with his mask lying loose around his neck and large rubber fins planted on a metre-deep pressure-treated wooden platform, would watch as the class members readied themselves for their first dive session in open water.

The platform occupying half of the pool-like enclosure was surrounded by sun-bleached wooden decking that was used by the divers to train. It was a startling contrast to the azure blue of the other half of the enclosure, where another platform, about 3 metres deep, was dimly visible below the surface.

When Cleckler first noticed the slim blonde with the purple mask, it was as if she was illuminated by a halo, despite the three student divers between them. Not only was she not moving freely like the others on the confined space of the platform, she was clutching the wooden decking as if hanging from a helicopter instead of standing with her chest rising out of the water. He noticed that her tight, white fingers never left the decking even though the other divers were already moving a hesitant few steps to the left. Some were even playing at being carefree, splashing about. One, with an especially loud kerplunk, had not heeded the 'slippery when wet' sign at the steps leading into the water.

The students began elementary tasks: adjusting their masks to get any hair out, blowing into their regulators, grinning at the ease with which they could inflate and deflate their buoyancy compensator devices (BCs), the dive vests that could be filled with air when they wanted to ascend. Most of them were looking forward to deeper underwater practice. It was beginner fun to bounce off the 6-metre platform and swim around in their first open-water experience. They loved to press each button on the front of the BC – inflating to ascend and become positively buoyant, and deflating to become negatively buoyant and sink. This was known in the dive game as 'riding the elevator'.

After the classroom and heated pool, this was the first of two full days set down to practise and pass final skills testing in open water. Now it was up to them to prove they could master some of the skills necessary to stay alive underwater while breathing highly compressed air. Today's tests, which included simulating an emergency ascent while buddy breathing with a partner and swimming around off the 6-metre platform several times, would lead to their first 'C' card, their open-water dive certificate.

The other students had been there since just after eight o'clock that morning, assembling their gear and listening to Tom Jackson's dive plan for the day. To prevent any of the excited class members inadvertently stepping off to the second, deeper half of the pool without a regulator in their mouth, Cleckler stood near the edge of the short platform. Patience being a virtue honed during his police years, he took his time studying the mob before him, satisfying himself that the anxious young woman in front of him did, indeed, have object fixation. Helping her was obviously going to be his 'major task for the day'.

'Tom,' Cleckler called to the master diver who had also taught him. 'We've got issues.'

Cleckler turned away from a student who was performing a slow solo waltz fighting the flipper that refused to attach to his foot and jerked his head towards the young woman, now inching her way back towards the steps.

'Ah, yes. Tina,' said Jackson, nodding, as he prepared to arrange the class in a U-shape in front of him. Jackson looked up the steep wooden stairs leading away from the pool decking to the spacious gravel car park, the dive office and store and the shower block.

'I taught her boyfriend all the way up to rescue diver,' Jackson said to Cleckler. 'That's him up there.'

Cleckler followed Jackson's gaze. He could make out a good-sized man propped up on the wooden railing at the edge of the car park right in front of the picnic tables that divers used to assemble their gear after donning their wetsuits. Cleckler recognised the same man that he'd noticed watching the earlier dry-land session from above the trees that grew all the way down the steep slope to the water's edge.

Cleckler would learn, only much later, that Tom Jackson had specifically warned Gabe Watson not to come near the class. All too often enthusiastic, well-intentioned but interfering family members or close friends of novice divers tried to instruct loved ones. Their expectant hovering in the water, in plain view of the other students, was the bane of many an instructor's open-water teaching time. It was unnecessarily distracting to both class members and instructor, who only had an allotted time to get through a packed curriculum.

Tom Jackson was a great believer in the students deserving a hassle-free first open-water dive after completing their theory and three sessions in the heated indoor pool. Anxious students, like Tina, were not uncommon. They either fixated on objects, like the deck in Tina's case, or on their equipment, known as 'equipment fixation', constantly adjusting their masks, regulators or checking their inflator buttons. They were generally fearful in an unknown environment, sometimes claustrophobic because of the confining wetsuit, loaded down by tanks and regulators. Then there was the cold water, the constant unfamiliar feel of water on the face while breathing, followed by trepidation about descending 6 metres underwater for the first time. Sometimes it was the loud and constant Darth Vader–type breathing sound made by the air from the scuba tank whooshing through the regulator mouthpiece that caused concern, or even the compressed air drying out the mouth. Despite being surrounded by nature, the act of diving was paradoxically unnatural.

'I need you to stay on her shoulder today,' Jackson said

to Cleckler before turning back to the class. The students were getting ready to step off the edge of the metre-deep platform, and sink to the 3-metre platform at the other end of the enclosure. He told them to swim one by one over the waist-high railing to the open water beyond, before hovering and deflating their BCs to help them sink to the 6-metre platform immediately outside and below the wooden superstructure.

As he continued to watch Tina, Cleckler realised that he'd never seen anyone as ill prepared to dive. She was virtually frozen among the waving arms and bobbing heads of the other excited students. When she moved it was with jerking steps, all the while gripping the decking that separated the pool from the deep blue of the open water in the rest of the quarry beyond. Cleckler honed in on her.

In such a class with first-time open-water divers, it was incumbent upon the instructor to keep all the divers safe. If one or two were slower than the rest, one of Cleckler's tasks was to work with them and separate them from the group so as not to slow the whole class, then patiently go through multiple repetitions of the specific skill that confronted the student. It might be the 'partial flood' of the mask, which Jackson would indicate underwater with a tap of the finger to the top of his mask. While submerged, all students had the task of letting water into half of their mask and then clearing it by pressing on the mask with one or both hands. They then had to expel air inhaled from their regulators through their nose to force the water out of the rubber seals that keep the eyes and nose clear. Another skill taught was the 'full flood', which meant taking the mask off underwater, waving it around and putting it back on and clearing it of water. This was only able to be done with both hands so the vital air pocket around the nose and eyes could be re-established. Without a mask underwater, a diver is virtually blind.

The big difference between practising these skills in a pool and in the quarry was that instead of being in a metre of water and progressively moving down to the deepest part of the chlorinated pool, they started in the murky quarry at the 3-metre platform where the fish were visible flitting past the wooden beams of the superstructure.

After flooding their masks, the trainee divers would take out and re-insert their regulators, feel around by making a sweeping motion with an arm underneath the scuba tank for their 'safe second', another regulator and alternative breathing source. Without a mask it's harder to breathe through the regulator. Water tends to go up the nose. Newer divers are more likely to panic, as they are unaccustomed to breathing with water on their face.

'Don't panic and don't hold your breath as you ascend,' Jackson had repeated, 'otherwise air could become trapped in your lungs and explode.'

'Stop. Think. Breathe.' The last instruction was crucial to prevent an embolism. The word sounded fearsome.

Cleckler's sheer size was reassuring to the students as they made their way past him from the metre-deep platform and stepped off to fall downwards for several seconds to the 3-metre platform. There was worse to come. They still had to descend a further 3 metres. Jackson signalled with the universal 'okay' sign to each student as a question. They signalled back with the identical thumb and forefinger. Tina mimicked them automatically. Above her was the sky and fresh air. Jackson began moving the short distance over the low railing. Several bream and bass and the occasional catfish scuttled around the poles embedded in the sloping muddy terrain away from the side of the quarry.

Slowly she followed the group, Cleckler behind her. Again she freefell, down and down. On the 6-metre platform, the students sank to their knees and formed a circle at a signal from Jackson, who positioned himself in the middle. The students began removing at first partially, then completely, their regulators from their mouths, putting them back in, then removing their BCs, sitting the diving vest in front of them, and then putting it back on and buckling it up properly. These were skills that might one day save their lives. Tina was trying, in this silent world, to remember Tom's words. He went methodically around the group, waiting while each, in turn, took off their mask, put it back on and cleared the water around their eyes and nose so they could see underwater.

It was Tina's turn next. She began breathing more quickly. It sounded loud and hoarse. Underneath the pool the quarry disappeared into velvet blackness. Even the fish flitting by added to her anxiety as she thought how ludicrous it was that humans were expected to swim around like creatures that had gills. She was sure that there was not enough air coming through her regulator. The student next to her was groping in the water, having momentarily dropped his mask, and she imagined such an event. Jackson turned to her and motioned with his fingers in a circle against the side of the mask. What was it she had to do? Was it a partial flood, or was that the signal indicated by Tom tapping his mask? Confusion added to her panic. Or was this when she was supposed to take her regulator out? When she pulled her mask off, the cold water hit her like a slap. Suddenly she knew she had to get out, get up. Terror gripped her and she longed to gulp real air. Oblivious to the teaching of the past two days, she forgot Tom Jackson's oft-repeated mantra. Without warning, she pressed down on her feet, bent her knees and pushed herself straight upwards in an uncontrolled ascent.

Cleckler had positioned himself outside the circle behind Tina, and was a second behind her. He grabbed the back of her tank as she went up. Using his 108-kilogram bulk as a dead weight, he dragged on her to slow her too-rapid rise. In the short distance to the surface there was no way he could stop her. And, in total self-rescue mode, she was going to the top, that much was clear. He checked whether or not she had spat out her regulator – the panic-stricken, illogical response from some divers desperate to get to the air above – but it was still in place. Deflating his BC to make himself even heavier, Cleckler noted that Jackson was also right there by her side. Tina's BC was fully inflated so she would temporarily float on the surface. They were so close to the decking, there was no need to swim. She should have felt comforted by the expansion of her vest and the realisa-tion that she was not going to drown. Normally Cleckler would then talk quietly and slowly. Calm her. Make sure she was all right. Help her to the deck so she could feel the solid wood under her arms, and see if she wanted to continue with the course that day.

'Talk to her. Calm her down,' Jackson mouthed from behind her, satisfying himself that she was not in immediate danger. 'Don't let her back in the water.' Then he descended to continue with the rest of the novice class.

Cleckler, in slow, soothing tones, said: 'Tina, it's okay, everything is okay. Are you okay?'

But Tina, still breathing heavily, looked straight through him and began dog paddling frantically towards the decking just metres away. She was what Cleckler called 'functioning in pure, basic survival mode', looking right past him, her eyes like saucers. He had never seen anyone in such a state.

Grasping her arm above the elbow, he pulled her towards him, kicking backwards a few times. They both reached out to the deck, grabbed on to the solid planks of wood and hung there for some minutes as Tina's breathing gradually slowed and she lost her glazed look.

'Tina, you've got to really want to dive to do this. *You've* got to want to do this,' he said, concerned at her response.

She lifted her head towards the car park above and then turned to face him.

'Is this what you really want to do?' he asked.

'You don't understand,' she said, in a resigned, even defeated tone, her face showing exhaustion. 'I have no choice. If I don't do this, my boyfriend will kill me.'

Cleckler didn't think she meant a literal threat, but he was concerned nevertheless about the coercion the statement implied.

'Now, Tina,' he drawled, each word carefully enunciated in the unhurried way of the south. 'Peer pressure is one of the things that we have talked about in class. Everyone has the right to say, "No. I do not want to do this dive."'

Cleckler recalled what Tom had told him earlier about Tina's boyfriend. By the look of her brand new gear there was obviously financial, as well as emotional, pressure for her to be certified.

Cleckler told her calmly, 'You have to make sure that you're doing this because you want to, not anybody else. Now put your mask back on and we'll swim under the deck, back into the pool enclosure, and over onto the shallow platform where you can stand up again. There's no easy way to get out of here, but we'll have you on firm ground very soon.'

Once on the shallow platform, Cleckler turned to Tina, who answered his question before he had time to ask.

'I'm done,' she said, struggling with her fins and mask. With his help, she hauled herself up out of the pool. He watched as she trudged up the steps to the car park.

A week later, on Easter Sunday, two weeks after the weekend in Atlanta, Gabe arrived at Tina's apartment. Finally she'd moved out of home. He was carrying a small box. Without much ado, he asked her the question she had been waiting for him to ask for so long. Tina had screamed so loudly that anyone in the vicinity outside might have been alarmed. Gabe had even put his fingers in his ears. She stood on tip-toes, flinging her arms around his neck. Later, he would joke that he'd never actually heard her say: 'Yes.'

'When?' she said, tears in her eyes.

'I've always said a short engagement. October.'

'Mmm,' she said uncertainly. 'But there's so much planning to do. I want it to be perfect.'

'And you've still got to finish your open-dive certificate, as we're going to Australia for our honeymoon.'

'But there's shower teas . . . and dresses and wedding registries and we have to book the church. It will have to be at the Southside Baptist Church downtown . . . we'll have to book.'

'Don't you worry. And my grandmother's graduation present will pay for the trip.'

They were to be married. He would do the right thing, after all. But, when she rang to share the news, somehow she couldn't bring herself to sound elated.

Craig Youngblood, a school friend of Gabe's, was pleased he'd finally popped the question to the bubbly blonde who made him laugh. When Alanda found out she was very surprised, thinking that the last she had heard, the relationship was all but over. The weekend after Easter Tina arrived at Seattle Slew Drive sporting the diamond ring, finally able to prove to her parents that Gabe intended to marry her. She had rung Amanda a few days after the proposal. Amanda thought Tina sounded as though she had got first prize, but was cheated along the way.

'Yeah, he proposed on Sunday,' Tina told her in a matter-of-fact voice.

'Congratulations, Tina. That's what you've been waiting for, isn't it?'

CHAPTER 6

Tina was making preparations for the wedding, engaging in half-conversations, jotting down notes, zipping between her apartment and the family home. She would disappear down Seattle Slew Drive in a flash of blue convertible Mazda Miata, her hair flying behind her in the summer sun.

Gabe's mother, Glenda Watson, extended an invitation to the Thomas family to come over for dinner. Glenda recalled later that Cindy had asked: 'Why? Tina is marrying into your family. We're not.'

Meanwhile Tina was preparing for her dive certification. After the incident at Blue Water, Tom Jackson had rung her, reassuring her that it was common for students to panic while taking off their masks underwater. She had agreed to come back for some more confined water skills practice in May when the water was a little warmer and, perhaps in June, re-attempt her certification.

There was one black cloud. Tiffie died suddenly. Her beloved Tiffany. She hadn't even reached ten years old. Everyone was baffled. The vet, too, was at a loss to explain her death, saying that the actual cause was kidney failure and she may have got into some poison.

There was also some good news. Alanda, at twenty-two, was pregnant. Holding her little sister's hand tightly, Tina was the first to listen to the heartbeat of Alanda's child during her first ultrasound appointment. For the next few months, it was their sisterly secret. But when Alanda's marriage ended and Alex had moved out, Tina gave notice to her landlord. She spent the last three months before her wedding at Alanda's house in Helena.

On 13 May, Gabe had received an email from Mike Ball Dive Expeditions, the company in Australia that was to take them diving on the Great Barrier Reef. The email from an employee, Shelley McLaughlin, read:

Premium cabins are only available on three of the eight expeditions in the two months you want to go. The first is available October 21–28.

A summary sheet was attached and a rate and date sheet listing the berth rates in US dollars per person.

'We're going,' Gabe told Tina that night at dinner. 'And we'll need to try and fix the church for October the eleventh, which is the Saturday, and then we'll have about a week in Sydney or Cairns before we go scuba diving.'

'It's so close,' Tina sighed, frowning. 'And I'm still not qualified.'

'I've told them we don't want bunk beds. This *is* our honeymoon . . .'

He showed Tina the twin-hulled catamaran, *Spoilsport*, and the pictures of coral reefs on Mike Ball's website.

Gabe emailed Shelley McLaughlin on 20 May asking how to pay the deposit:

I would also like to know about the Yongala dive. I have up to my rescue cert, however Tina only has her beginner cert. I notice on the booking form it says anyone with less than 15 logged dives in the past 12 months must pass a wreck orientation. Is this something you guys do on the trip so she would be able to dive it? Also is trip cancellation insurance purchased through you (MBDE) or an independent agency? I have never dealt with that type of insurance before.

Shelley replied promptly:

Should we visit the Yongala Wreck on the way out to the Coral Sea, Tina may need to sit out the first / second dive if she has not done enough dives to qualify her to dive on the wreck.

However, she mentioned that the *Spoilsport* was likely to return to the *Yongala* at the end of the expedition, depending on the weather. She named two travel insurance companies but added that he should check those policies because, she warned, 'we do adhere to our cancellation policy'. She also recommended two insurance companies, 'one called Travel Ex'.

Gabe paid the deposit the next day, adding in an email: 'Also Tina would like to know if there is a good chance we will get to see sea turtles on the dives? She loves those things!' Shelley assured him she would. *Finding Nemo* had reached cinemas all over America that month. During the summer and autumn of 2003, many Americans were heading to eastern Australia, where the movie is set, to 'find Nemo'.

On Sunday, 8 June, seventeen days after Gabe booked the honeymoon stating that Tina was already certified, Tina was whooping loudly on the decking above the platforms at

Blue Water, having successfully completed her open-water certificate. In her excitement, she was doing high-fives with anyone who cared to be included. Tom Jackson grinned, happy at her accomplishment.

Meanwhile, Glenda Watson had been planning a trip through her travel agent, Freida Gammill, at Get Away Travel to Torino, Italy, coinciding with the 2006 Winter Olympics. Gabe also visited Freida in August to book the flights and accommodation for the honeymoon.

'You know with this honeymoon costing as much as it is, you should look into travel insurance,' Freida Gammill advised, and handed him some brochures.

'This is a good one,' she said, pointing to the one he eventually chose, 'because it covers everything, even if there was some type of terrorist attack.'

The brochure had a list of limitations and exclusions online, but Gabe claimed later he was busy and did not check the website. Instead, he tore off a number for the insurance policy and placed it in his wallet.

He and Tina went for a dive in the quarry at Blue Water. It was Gabe Watson's fifty-sixth logged dive, but he had barely dived in the last year. They descended to 9 metres, trying to imagine in the gloom of the quarry what the Great Barrier Reef might be like. Tina seemed more relaxed, three months after qualifying. The water was warmer, which helped.

Tina's pre-nuptial list was growing longer. On top of the wedding plans, she and Gabe were looking at houses in Hoover. Gabe paid off Tina's $12,000 debt which included university fees so that she qualified for a housing loan. The house they finally decided on had a beautiful street name: Oak Leaf Circle. It wasn't the best street in Hoover; it had few established or well-cared-for gardens like many of the other houses in the neighbouring area, but there was a park nearby. Around the corner there were stately homes, some backing onto a lake filled with ducks. On their side of the street, there were tall trees and little letterboxes. Their new home was a suburban split-level house with brick veneer on the first level and vinyl clapboard siding. Down the side was a basketball hoop on one wall. It had a cream front with an alcoved entrance and replica shutters either side of the four windows facing the street. Small brick steps led up to the front door. The garden was mainly lawn with some sparse shrubs up against the wall. At the back was an above-ground swimming pool.

The house had cost them US$188,500, which meant a large mortgage, but Gabe's parents had paid the deposit. It was only 10 minutes away from their place and about 25 minutes from Cindy and Tommy.

Tina's upcoming nuptials was the talk of Parisian. There was nothing quite like a wedding to get the girls chattering. Christmas decorations were appearing even though it was only the beginning of autumn. Snowmen and Santas and baubles were stacked on centre aisles.

One lunchtime in September, as Tina walked off the floor to her desk behind the children's department on the first floor, a colleague, Sonja Jordan, stopped her.

'Hi Tina,' she said. 'How y'all doing with the wedding preparations?'

'Oh, they're coming along. It's a busy time and so much to do . . . And we've bought a house in Hoover.'

'That's just great! . . . Hey, I was hearing the other day about some kind of mortgage insurance policy that actually ensures the house would be paid off if your spouse or signatory to the title was to die.'

'Oh yes, I know about that,' said Tina, launching into an explanation of how Gabe had been talking to an insurance agent. 'He's a friend of one of Gabe's buddies,' she said.

On 15 September, Gabe posted his signed and dated travel insurance policy for the honeymoon.

Tina's life was turning upside down. Not only was she becoming Mrs Watson and moving into her first house, but her dog had died and she'd had to ditch her beloved Mazda Miata. Gabe had insisted she get another car.

The new Jeep Cherokee that Tina leased was smaller than Gabe's SUV. She was entering the phase of many newlyweds: mounting debt.

Gabe bought a black labrador puppy which would have to be kennelled during the honeymoon. Tina told Amanda she was not keen on the new dog. It wouldn't replace Tiffie.

There was always going to be more than one bridal shower: Gabe's mother, Glenda, threw one; Tina had one with her sorority sisters and co-workers; and her cousin Krissie gave her one. Even Bob Austin, a Birmingham lawyer and close friend of David Watson's, and his wife hosted a 'tool and gadget' shower, where the Thomases met the Watsons for the first time. The main shower was to be held at Seattle Slew Drive. The forecast rain, common at that time of year, held off as Amanda Phillips flew in from New Orleans on Friday, 19 September and waltzed into lunch with Tina and Gabe at the Olive Garden at the Riverside Galleria. Alanda's pregnancy was a major topic.

Tina mentioned that she would need to help her sister after the baby arrived.

'Well, that's Alanda's problem,' said Gabe flatly. 'You're certainly not going to be spending all your spare time over with her.'

Tina and Amanda exchanged glances over the table.

'That's just how families work,' explained Amanda, herself one of five children. 'We all look after one another.'

'Yes,' Tina piped up. 'That's just the way it's going to be.'

'After the wedding things will be different,' he warned.

The girls laughed and rolled their eyes. He just didn't get it.

At the shower at her parents' house, Tina wore a bright red top and a black, patterned skirt with black high heels. Her hair was loose and tucked behind her ears. Amanda was wearing her favourite high-heeled shoes, a little black dress and pearls. The girls howled with laughter as the gifts were paraded one by one through the air by Tina. Tina cried with delight after unwrapping each of the many kitchen items she would need.

'What's this?' she said, lifting a strange phallic object above her head.

There was muffled giggling until Amanda jumped in to save her.

'A turkey baster,' she cried. Tina was never known for her cooking prowess.

With the shower still in progress, Alanda drove Amanda back to the airport at breakneck speed, shaving a substantial slice of time off the usual 45-minute drive. Amanda was so flustered she got on the wrong plane.

***

Gabe moved into Oak Leaf Circle after the house was settled. Tina moved her belongings into the garage and they
spent time doing some maintenance, including painting.

On her next visit to Seattle Slew Drive, on Friday, 26 September, Tina broached the subject of life insurance with
her father. Under Tina's employment package with Parisian
and the usual group insurance benefits including medical,
dental, vision and accident insurance, there was a basic life
insurance benefit which had cost her nothing to enrol for.

'Dad,' she said, leaning over the island which stood in
the middle of the kitchen. 'Gabe says I need to change my
benefits at work and increase my group life insurance benefit to the maximum and make him sole beneficiary. What
should I do?'

Tommy looked across at Cindy who was preparing something on the bench. He saw her shake her head slightly.
Tommy had expected he would cease being the sole beneficiary of Tina's life insurance after the wedding. But during
his twenty-five years in the insurance game, starting out as
an agent selling life and health contracts, Tommy had never
come across a situation where a young soon-to-be-married
couple was concerned about these matters.

'Did Gabe say why he wanted you to do this?'

'He said that now that we were getting married, any policies
I have should have him as the sole beneficiary,' Tina replied.

'Well, Tina, I know you've got a lot on your plate right
now,' Tommy said in his considered voice. 'I don't know
that this is something you really need to be worrying about
at the moment. You're going to be doing re-enrolment of
your benefits in November anyway, which will be right after
you come back from your honeymoon.'

Tina mulled this over.

'I'm surprised that Gabe is even thinking of such a thing,' he added quietly.

'I know,' she sighed. 'I am just so busy with all the errands and running around and work and all, that I haven't got time to fool around with all that kind of stuff. What do you think I should tell him, Dad?'

She pushed her dark spectacles up the bridge of her nose.

'We can do it in November when you get back. Just tell Gabe that it's been taken care of.'

When Tina left, Tommy waved her goodbye from the steps of the family home. Cindy was gathering up the coffee cups in the lounge room when he returned.

'You know, Cindy, I've worked with couples who've been married for several years without having taken out life insurance. That's the strangest damn thing I've heard in a long time. I've had couples in to talk about insurance who haven't even thought to check the beneficiary designations on their insurance – long after they were married.'

'I think it sounds strange, too,' Cindy agreed.

Four days before the wedding, Gabe again emailed Shelley McLaughlin at Mike Ball Dive Expeditions, asking what kind of wetsuit was needed and whether the company supplied weights.

Shelley McLaughlin replied promptly: The water temperature would be around 25°C/77°F. Their 3-millimetre wetsuits would be adequate. Weight belts were included, she added.

On the Wednesday night before the wedding, Amanda Phillips arrived on the 30-minute hop from New Orleans. She and Tina were up early the next morning. The first stop was The Dive Site shop. Gabe's dive watch wasn't working, Tina explained, and it had to be picked up.

'Hi y'all,' said Tina as they headed for the counter. Amanda milled around the store. 'I'm here for the dive computer I left the other day. Did you find out what was wrong?'

'Oh,' the attendant said, rummaging around under the counter and bringing out a package. 'It turned out it was just the batteries were in backwards.

'See,' he said, turning the watch on to demonstrate; they saw the rectangular screen on the watch light up. 'It works now the battery is in right.'

He handed it to Tina over the counter.

'I feel bad even having to charge you for it, but here it is. It's working fine.'

They both laughed. Tina paid with her debit card. It was one more chore to tick off her list.

Outside, the girls hopped into Tina's Jeep and drove to a second dive shop, the only one in Birmingham with the right type of pages for Tina's dive booklet that she needed for the trip.

'As if it's not enough worrying about dresses and make-up and shoes without all this diving stuff,' Amanda said.

After a third chore – collecting Tina's going-away outfit – the girls had lunch with Tina's parents before Tina took Amanda on a tour of her new house in Oak Leaf Circle. They found Gabe in the garage. He was in charge of packing their dive equipment for the honeymoon.

'You're always making fun of me about being a ditzy blonde – and your batteries were in backwards. How silly can *you* be?' Tina said as soon as they saw him, holding out his dive watch.

Gabe looked sheepish as Amanda saw him inspect the watch. Tina and Amanda began going through the boxes.

Amid all of those yet to be unpacked, the girls had to find Tina's wetsuit, BC, fins, mask and dive computer and stash them all in one spot on the floor of the garage ready for Gabe to pack.

'Oh, and here's the dive pages for my dive book, honey,' Tina said as she handed them to him ready to be packed for the long trip to Australia.

CHAPTER 7

The Southside Baptist Church at Five Points South, Birmingham, built in 1911, resembles the fairytale church on the wedding cake where the married couple stand forever embedded on thick white marzipan. Despite its Grecian Revival style it is a modern church, with jazz vespers and church picnics. From the nondescript bare footpath, twenty-five curved marble steps lead up to a marble flagstone entrance. Two imposing wooden doors with brass handles are surrounded by ornate carving, but it is the six Ionic pillars at the top of the steps that form the building's most dramatic feature.

The wedding rehearsal was the night before the wedding. There had been friction between the families from the start. The pastor, the Watsons' friend Craig Greer, who had been involved in pre-marital counselling with the couple, was later to recall that the tension at the rehearsal was the worst he had ever encountered. The Watsons were to claim later that Cindy had threatened not to pay for the wedding unless certain things were to her liking.

Tina had chosen a simple maroon dress and a string of pearls for the occasion. She had been to so many weddings where she was part of the crowd; now it was her turn to shine. All eyes were upon her. Craig Greer looked plump and boyish as he went through the familiar routine, plucking out the agc-old words that they would use the following day.

'I do,' Tina spoke, too quietly.

'And now you may kiss the bride,' the pastor was saying.

Gabe raised his hands, fluttering them, with mock theatrics, pretending there was a veil. Then, as if he couldn't resist it, he made a comment Tina guessed was aimed at Cindy.

Cindy stormed up the aisle towards the front door. Tina sighed. The moment was ruined. And this was just the rehearsal. It was like a sport Cindy and Gabe played with each other, and she was in the middle.

They began walking up the aisle, Tina's eyes darting about to see what harm had been done by the outburst, and then Gabe suddenly grabbed her hand and they began running.

The next day, Tina was up early, unable to sleep. There was so much to do. Her cousin Krissie McCampbell was helping her get into her wedding dress. Krissie's daughter Shali was to be Tina's junior bridesmaid and her son Reid was to be the ring bearer. Krissie looked at Tina's reflection in the mirror. She made a beautiful bride, but the expression in Tina's eyes was not one that Krissie recognised. Krissie always knew what Tina was feeling; her eyes said it all. For a moment, they were alone and Krissie seized the opportunity.

'This is the wedding of your dreams, but if you're not entirely happy with it, you don't have to go through with it,' she said in a rush.

Tina looked at herself in the mirror. The dress was as beautiful as she had hoped. The slip straps were beaded, as was the bodice, which was sculpted in a classic line, coming in at the waist and then flowing out in the skirt. She was wearing a small tiara and her hair was piled on top.

'No, I have to do this,' she said as much to her reflection as to Krissie.

'Okay, if you feel that, that's fine,' Krissie said, recognising the rebuff. 'Just remember I love you and will always be here for you.'

Tina nodded. Once dressed, she came downstairs slowly into the lounge room, her long skirts flowing down the stairs behind her, a turban veil leading from her hair to the ground. She looked radiant. She sat carefully, smoothing out the dress on the same yellow couch with imprints of flowers that she knew so well from her years at Seattle Slew Drive. Soon, like Scarlett O'Hara, she would be her own mistress. Ready for the photographs, Tina picked up her flowers: pale lilies that matched the flowers in the lapels of the grooms-men. Behind her, Cindy – in a long peacock-blue jacket and matching dress – also clutched a bouquet of flowers as she stood next to Tommy, who was standing proudly in a black suit and white shirt with a carnation in his lapel.

As she stepped into the limo with her father, Tina looked up at Amanda, one of her six bridesmaids, who waited on the footpath.

'I'm a princess bride,' she said, smiling.

'You sure are,' Amanda said through a veil of tears that seemed to last all day. Tina was the last of 'her girls' to marry.

Outside the church, Tina posed on the flagstones behind the pillars. Veils like white ribbons were attached to the brown doors behind her. Krissie's husband Tom was videoing the event. He had begun with the lead-up to the wedding, even filmed the shower teas, then the rehearsal and now, finally, the ceremony.

All eyes were on Tina as she walked down the aisle on

Tommy's arm towards the 3354 pipes of the massive church organ. Several pews were empty. Behind them, the wedding photographer and Tom McCampbell scrambled for the right shot.

As she walked down the aisle the space between her and her husband-to-be closed. Gabe stood facing the altar, hands clasped together, but as she approached he half-turned towards her, looking handsome in his dark suit, with a grey silk button-up waistcoat and a white rose in his lapel. He smiled.

Alanda always said that from her early twenties Tina talked about already being old, and with a sense of urgency, how much she'd like children and a white picket fence around a family home. She'd wanted to love someone and for someone to love her so they could grow old happily together.

Tom McCampbell, his camera rolling, stood behind the minister facing Tina and Gabe so he could get a good view of the nuptials. Apricot roses filled the altar. The brides-maids were in purple, the junior bridesmaid in pale orange. Alanda, her pregnancy hidden under the swathes of skirt, had her hair piled high above her customary fringe. She was maid of honour, as Tina had been for her. And here was Amanda, gracious, as she always was, with a big smile.

The ceremony passed quickly, the vows exchanged without any of the awkwardness of the previous night, and then Tina was on her new husband's arm. Tommy stood at the end of the well-wishers, throwing confetti and clapping enthusiastically. As they reached the door ready to leave the crowds behind, Gabe, holding Tina's arm, ducked, bending down to pat a little boy on the head, so Tommy was unable to catch his new son-in-law's gaze.

The reception was nearby, at the Pickwick Hotel in South

Birmingham. In the low-ceilinged reception room, Gabe serenaded his new bride with one of her favourite Hank Williams songs. He hand-fed her nibbles, his cuff links visible as he stretched to put food in her mouth for the camera. Tina opened her mouth like a baby bird. Then Gabe went down on his knees to roll the garter off her leg, stretching it like a schoolboy playing with an elastic band for effect. Tina sat for the ritual, high heels on display on a stool. There were speeches and toasts.

When the festivities ended, Tommy and Cindy walked the newlyweds to the elevator to say goodbye.

'I'm sorry, Gabe, about what happened in the rehearsal,' Cindy said quickly, loudly enough for Amanda, standing nearby, to hear.

Amanda watched Tina's features soften. Tina knew how hard it was for her mother to say this. As they stood inside the elevator, the doors held open, Tommy reached in and took his elder daughter's hand.

'I love you, darling.'

'I love you too, Daddy.'

'Have the time of your life, y'hear?'

Then he turned to Gabe, who had his finger on the open-door button.

'You take good care of my baby girl.'

'Sure, Mr Thomas. I will.'

And then the elevator doors closed, shutting Tina off from her family, closing a chapter of her life. It was the last time they were to see their daughter alive.

Back at Oak Leaf Circle, Tina and Gabe finished packing for their honeymoon. Tina was to spend only one night there. She would have plenty of time to get to know their new home now the wedding was over. Tina had dragged her hair back into a ponytail, which showed her darker roots underneath. She bent over the honeymoon suitcase, wearing her prescription glasses and a pale brown round-necked pyjama top, almost ready for bed.

She had organised everything in her suitcase into neat piles, her toiletries carefully on one side. She had put some of the sleepwear in the lid for easy access. She imagined it being searched by Customs officers in the post 9/11 world. Well, if they were checking out this honeymooner's suitcase, they'd find it neat and tidy.

Gabe walked up the stairs talking to himself. The video camera preceded him around the corner. She looked up, knowing he expected a reaction.

'Tell the camera: "Bye",' he ordered.

She turned back to the suitcase, her voice muffled.

'Bye, camera,' she said.

'Blow the camera a kissie.'

She blew half-hearted kisses towards the camera.

'Smile at the camera just in case we get eaten by a shark or something.'

The honeymoon journey began at the Birmingham-Shuttlesworth International Airport. Tina had flown from this airport many times on family holidays, but never as far away as Australia. The distance was inconceivable. She could only imagine how tired she might be at the other end after so many hours of flying and waiting for connecting flights at other airports.

They reached Sydney just after dawn. Australia was such a big land mass, not quite as big as the United States, but emptier and full of the unknown.

After recovering in the hotel, the Watsons headed out armed with information from the woman at reception. The Sydney Opera House was like a gigantic soft white shell on the foreshore of Sydney Harbour. Tina sat on a small wall on the waterfront. In front of her were the Royal Botanic Gardens. Behind her a mass of steps led up to the interior of the Opera House. This was *her* part of the holiday. She enjoyed every bit of it. It might not be Paris, but she liked the breezy, bright city with the backdrop of the harbour. Outside the Chinese Gardens in Darling Harbour, she posed for a photograph in front of a large fern and wooden pagoda backing onto a stream. Wearing a turquoise top, camera dangling from her wrist, a small brown day backpack and a jacket around her waist in case the weather turned, she looked every bit the tourist. Gabe wanted to visit the Sydney Aquarium, where they saw sharks being fed and he spoke excitedly about the upcoming dive and the Great Barrier Reef.

But it was Taronga Zoo that captivated Tina. The zoo was a ferry ride across the busy harbour, in which green and cream ferries cut pathways between the bouncing yachts and speedboats. The Sydney Harbour Bridge straddled the whole scene. October was the zoo's birthday month. It was just after the school holidays. The newlyweds posed for a photo in front of some koalas up a gum tree. Gabe wore his favourite navy blue cap and green T-shirt; Tina was in a red sweatshirt and trademark brown glasses. There was so much to see. The first lion cubs born at the zoo in twenty years were starting to venture out for an audience. The young male chimpanzee, three-month-old Shikamoo, performed antics with his family. But most of all, Tina wanted to see the tiny red pandas. Later they dressed up for the Opera Australia production of Benjamin Britten's operatic version of *A Midsummer Night's Dream*, directed by Baz Luhrmann.

By the time they flew to Townsville, almost six days later, they were rested. Compared to their epic journey from America, it was a short flight.

They arrived in Townsville around 11 a.m. on Monday, 20 October and drove briefly through an industrial land-scape into the city. Their hotel, The Plaza, opposite the police station, was a puce-green besser-block building not far from Flinders Mall, an empty dead space in the city centre that looked like a construction from another era, forgotten in the developers' rush to build out in the suburbs where the real population growth was happening.

Townsville on the north-eastern coast of Australia is one of Australia's fastest-growing local government areas and the largest city north of the Sunshine Coast. During World War II, the city was host to more than 50,000 American and Australian troops and it was bombed by the Japanese. It boasts sprawling suburbs and expensive houses clustered around a mass of red granite, Castle Hill, which at 985 metres high dominates the town. Locals barrack for sports teams with names like the North Queensland Cowboys and the Townsville Crocodiles. In the CBD, new and old build-ings jostle for space. The mining boom fuels Townsville's economy. It is also Australia's strategic military base and a university town, so it often weathers economic downturns better than the rest of the country. Down from the hotel on Flinders Street East is a row of heritage buildings, where geometric poles and bright colours proclaimed a new space, a contemporary layering over the historical. It is home to bars that were once banks and millineries in a bygone era, some with original signs in faded letters.

Even in October, the days were hot, although in the

evening the temperature dropped. Gabe and Tina were only there for one day and spent it happily enough without an itinerary.

'Ready to go. Love you all,' Tina wrote on her second card home, mailing it from the post office, which backed on to the mall.

They spent some time on The Strand, a pleasant promenade looking across Cleveland Bay to nearby Magnetic Island, just 8 kilometres across the water from Townsville. Restaurants, ice-creameries and activities for families were scattered along the 2.2 kilometres of the Strand. It was at the southern end of this promenade that Tina and Gabe would board their vessel, *Spoilsport*, that evening and meet the crew from Mike Ball Dive Expeditions.

At 6.25 p.m., number 88 cab from Townsville Taxis arrived at their hotel. The taxi driver lifted the luggage and dive equipment into the boot.

'So you're going diving?' Steve Lawlor, the taxi driver, asked, immediately picking that his two customers were Americans.

'Yeah, we're on our honeymoon and we're off scuba diving for a few days on the *Spoilsport*. Don't know if you know it. Big boat . . .'

'And how long you been married?'

'A few days.'

'So how long you been diving?'

'Oh . . . a while.'

Gabe did all the talking. Tina, silent, gazed out of the window at the passing cars as they headed down Flinders Street.

'And what about you?' Lawlor nodded in the mirror in Tina's direction. She was tiny compared to her husband.

Gabe answered for her.

'Oh, she's not as experienced as I am.'

The couple sat on opposite sides of the taxi, barely touching. The trip was under 10 minutes. Lawlor had done his best to fill it with chat, but he reflected later that it seemed strange behaviour for two people just married. The image of the silent dainty blonde, as he would later describe her, was to stay with him for some time.

The Quarterdeck on the Marina, then a popular waterfront eatery near Jupiters Casino, was right next to the marina where they were to board *Spoilsport*. There were only a handful of people eating at the small plastic tables: some looked like they were joining the same trip after dinner, from the large dive bags lying near them. Tina ordered grilled chicken and they both had a Coke, deciding that they would not drink alcohol as they may well be offered some on board. The evening had become unexpectedly chilly compared to the heat of the day. Gabe and Tina left their luggage on the wharf in their line of sight.

After dinner, they sat on a bench on the wharf, waiting to board. An older couple approached and introduced themselves as Ken and Paula Snyder, from the state 'next door', Florida. The talk immediately turned to diving – and of course, college football.

'Are you a fan of the Tide or a War Eagle?' Ken asked as soon as he heard they were from Alabama, knowing the intense rivalry between teams from the University of Alabama at Tuscaloosa, known as the Crimson Tide, and the War Eagles, or Auburn Tigers, from Auburn University.

'War Eagle, of course,' Tina drawled.

The Snyders had done more than 800 dives between them, but then they were in their fifties. A specialist doctor from Chicago, John Downie, also introduced himself. Tina recognised him from the Quarterdeck restaurant.

'I just got certified in the spring,' Tina told them.

'Oh, I'm trying for an advanced certificate this trip,' Downie volunteered. 'But I haven't been diving for about a year, so I'm a little nervous.'

The *Spoilsport*, a 100-foot (30-metre) purpose-built aluminium catamaran, was docked nearby. A gangway reached from the dive deck across to the wharf. As the Watsons walked on board, to leave land behind for seven days, the entire uniformed crew of twelve was lined up to welcome them. Every passenger got a name tag. The first mate, David Lemsing, stood just beyond the gangway, crossing the passengers' names off his list and asking their occupations to help identify those who were medically trained in case of an emergency.

'Passengers in even-numbered cabins go upstairs for an interview with the trip director and take your luggage into your cabins,' Lemsing directed, 'and odd-numbered cabin occupants stay on the back dive deck and set up your equipment into the stations with your name on it.'

BCs and regulators were attached to tanks and placed in the tank racks, masks on shelving above the tank racks and fins in bins underneath. Upstairs, the trip director, Wade Singleton, a slightly built master scuba instructor in his thirties, had already met the passengers as they milled around the marina. Now he began circulating among the divers, following up on the dive experience summary forms that had already been sent, by conducting lengthy interviews with each person about their dive experience and certification, checking insurance and medication and assessing their abilities as a diver. Singleton also wanted to know if they were diving on air or nitrox and whether they had their own dive computers or wanted to hire them. Then, he would get down to buddies. Did each diver have one? Did he need to find them one? If they were inexperienced, they would need an orientation dive.

Singleton was later to recall the first meeting with the Watsons after the introductions, and remembered Tina producing her open-water certification card.

'So, you've never done a night dive?'

'No.'

'And you've only done eleven dives in the last twelve months.'

'Yes.'

'In the US.'

'Yes.'

'Well, if you haven't done a night dive before, your first dive should be completed with one of our dive instructors. You should also probably do an initial orientation dive with one of our instructors as you haven't logged that many dives.'

'I think I should be okay with that, but I'd like an instructor for the night dive.'

'Yeah, she'll be fine. We're only going down to 45 feet,' Gabe added. 'Just to the top of the wreck. She mainly wants to see the turtles and Nemo . . .'

'Right?' Wade smiled at Tina. 'And you have your own equipment?'

'Yes,' Gabe answered. 'We'll need weights, though, and tanks.'

'Sure. And no medical conditions or injuries that I should know about?'

'No,' Gabe said.

'No,' Tina answered too.

'So you've both got to complete this questionnaire, which covers a history of dives and medical matters and an indemnity.'

'Sure thing.'

Gabe took the paperwork and handed the form to Tina

as Singleton moved on to the next passenger. In spite of their reassurances, he noted Tina's name down on the list of six other divers to be split between himself and another dive instructor for orientation on the following day's dive.

They began filling in the paperwork, Gabe writing on his release form that he had done twelve dives in the past twelve months. His log book, which he had with him, recorded fifty-six dives altogether but only listed three dives in the past year. He filled out a duplicate form to the one he had already sent Shelley McLaughlin, ticking the box that gave a thirty-day Divers Network Alert insurance coverage.

Tina and Gabe went up on deck to see one of the large ships that was in port refuelling. Then the twenty-five passengers assembled at 9.30 p.m. in the saloon. Blue cushioned lounges with wicker supports were on the starboard side of the vessel. In keeping with the ocean theme for the rest of the vessel, Harlequin tusk fish graced the walls in gold frames along with bright orange and blue coral cod.

On the port side, there were benches and tables for dining, and closer to the dive deck were the eatery hatch and galley, which had a cold-water dispenser, freshly brewed coffee, herbal tea and Milo. The cups were all stacked one above the other in wooden slots. Next to the galley was a bookcase with fish-identification books, Coral Sea reef guides and a compendium of seashells. There was also an area to download movies and pictures taken under the water. Opposite this bookcase, also on the starboard side but across from the lounges, was a huge TV screen and another bookshelf with novels. Seven days was a long time at sea. Tina eyed the collection.

Wade Singleton began his welcome and introduction briefing to all of the passengers. Crew members were individually introduced. He handed a bottle of champagne to

Tina and Gabe and to another couple Tina had noticed at dinner at the Quarterdeck.

'Hey, they're on their honeymoon too,' she said, nudging Gabe.

Dawn Asano and Gary Stempler, from northern California, had been married exactly a week after Tina and Gabe. Unlike Tina and Gabe, they had flown directly from the United States to Townsville. They were both tired, like many of the other jetlagged passengers.

Gabe and Tina allowed themselves two glasses of champagne each. After the welcome, Gavin Docking, the ship's master, provided a general boat briefing, advising the passengers of the proposed itinerary for the following day and week, and then the general housekeeping rules – information on meal times and bar rules including alcohol consumption before diving.

Reading from a Mike Ball Dive Expeditions manual, Wade Singleton gave a general expedition briefing. Uzi Barnai, an underwater photographer/videographer and master diver, then told them what to expect. After that it was time for the video of the SS *Yongala*. By about 10.30 p.m., already well under way, Tina and Gabe retired to their cabin. Theirs was the first cabin in the hallway off the dive deck on the starboard side, beneath the galley. Like the rest of the cabins, it had wood-panelled walls. There were two windows, turquoise carpet and curtains and a single bed, parallel to their double, where they had put their luggage. There was a separate bathroom and toilet and a Nemo print on the wall in a gold frame. Tina had squealed at this. On the other wall was a mauve and green turtle framed as though the artist, Maria Watson, was beneath the creature looking up as it swam through the water.

CHAPTER 8

The *Spoilsport* took 3 hours to reach the SS *Yongala*. By the time the vessel reached the mooring, most of the crew was asleep. It was around 1.15 a.m. Peering into the darkness in front of him, the ship's master, Gavin Docking, checked the radar and the GPS. He was used to these long stretches at sea. The twenty-five passengers on board had been warned about the sound of the anchor chain, which, after Docking got his position and turned off the revs, was released by the crew. Arriving so early, it was common for *Spoilsport* to stand off the wreck. It was safer to wait for daylight to assess the conditions and choose the best of the five permanent moorings, marked by fluorescent-orange inflatable buoys, for both the diving and the vessel. The anchor plummeted to the seabed about 30 metres beneath them, coming to rest not far from the graveyard of the 121 souls who had lain in their watery tomb for almost a century. As the anchor descended, Dawn Asano, a light sleeper at the best of times, awoke lying next to her husband of four days, Gary Stempler. Their cabin, one of four premium cabins, was in the bow where the clanking was the loudest, but she soon settled back into slumber. The trip director, Wade Singleton, had gone to bed around 11 p.m. There had been only one minor quibble from a passenger about accommodation. Once that was resolved, he headed for his cabin ready for rest. Tomorrow was the first of the seven-day expedition. Everyone would be up early – expectant, as they always were – for the first dive.

The next morning, using the first rays of the tropical spring sun, Docking searched for the best mooring position. With first mate David Lemsing, he noted the prevailing conditions: the current was running virtually north–south towards them. Docking manoeuvred the *Spoilsport* towards mooring point 905. Lemsing's duties included anchoring, berthing and mooring. The buoy marked the position of the heavy, knotted rope that led, far below, to the stern of the *Yongala*. As the sun began to climb over the horizon to the east, Lemsing used a grappling hook to retrieve the mooring, then threaded the *Spoilsport*'s berthing line through the metal eye of the mooring as well as back onto the vessel, securing it firmly. Docking had breakfast, then headed to the wheelhouse to complete the ship's paperwork and do the radio schedules.

Paul Crocombe, manager of Adrenalin Dive, another Townsville dive company, and one of the three commercial divers on board, had risen at daybreak to begin his work before the passengers entered the water. The divers were conducting regular maintenance and repairs on three of the five permanent moorings at the *Yongala* site. They hoped to be finished that morning and then planned to transfer to Crocombe's day boat, the *Adrenalin*, for the return to Townsville in the early afternoon. *Spoilsport* would stay the night moored above the *Yongala*.

Gabe and Tina's cabin, at the stern of the *Spoilsport*, had not been as close to the anchor, but was under the galley.

Cutlery clattering against enamel, stainless steel pots and pans scraping over metal gas rings and footsteps overhead was its own alarm system. Soon after 6 a.m. chef Steve Wells was chopping fruit and assembling the jugs and cereal containers to be put out in the saloon. Claudia Petersen, a nineteen-year-old German backpacker who worked on the *Spoilsport* in exchange for free scuba diving, had been the first into the galley after waking at 5.45 a.m. She was joined by Rebecca Hayllar, a hostess with Mike Ball Dive Expeditions. Shortly after 6 a.m., they began setting up the dining area for breakfast.

At 6.30 a.m. Paul Crocombe and two other divers took a new mooring line out to mooring point 901 in one of the two inflatable Zodiac tenders that belonged to the *Spoilsport* for short runs from the main vessel. Crocombe, fit from years of physical exertion even as he approached middle age, descended into the sea with the big, heavy rope and attached the shackle to replace the older one that was hauled to the surface. He had no trouble changing the mooring on the seabed and after a 20-minute dive he was back on the *Spoilsport* by 7 a.m., before the passengers had even begun to arrive for breakfast. He grinned to himself; they had judged the day well, anticipating these conditions from the weather forecast – even a moderate current would have made it difficult to change any of the moorings that were due for replacement that morning, and in a strong current it would have been virtually impossible.

Wade Singleton was happy, too, that the weather had lived up to the forecast. The day, he decided as he stretched and yawned on the deck before breakfast, was sunny and clear and the surface of the water was relatively calm. At around the same time, volunteer deckhand Lou Johnstone was about to log her 187th dive. She would help master scuba diver instructor Brian Fotheringham start the early morning recreational dive set-up and conditions check, an important prerequisite to any dive. They would then report to Singleton, the trip director, on the all-important strength of the current, visibility and other factors before he made a decision as to how the dive would run.

Fotheringham, a New Zealander and veteran of at least sixty *Yongala* dives, went over the procedure with Johnstone as they checked their gas tanks.

'We place the buoys and hang the emergency tanks and a regulator each at 5 metres under the surface from the drop lines at either end of the wreck,' Fotheringham said. 'Other lines run off those lines to the wreck itself at the stern and the bow. We do these conditions checks to see if the wreck is "diveable" and God knows I've seen it in all sorts of conditions,' he chuckled as she tightened her BC straps. 'It's the sort of dive that you wouldn't want to send people down without knowing what it was going to be like.'

At twenty-six, Lou had attained dive-instructor level in the recreational diving hierarchy since learning to dive in a quarry in England four years earlier. This was her first day on the *Spoilsport*, and her first dive of the day. Lou was thrilled just to be there.

She sniffed the slight breeze, knowing that the overcast conditions were set to clear into a fine morning. But half an hour later, as she wearily climbed out of the second tender that brought them back from the drop lines, she felt weak. Her mouth was dry and she felt the start of a bad carbon dioxide build-up headache from her extended rapid breathing. She was later to write in her diary that the current under the water was 'savage'.

Climbing back on board *Spoilsport*, she told others: 'It was so tough. We couldn't get to the line on the first attempt. We had to come back on board the tender and do the backward roll off again and go straight down. The current was that strong it was the only way to get to the line.' She rubbed her temples. 'I was kicking as hard as I possibly could and I could see the line in front of me and I was really struggling to get to it.'

Fotheringham's report, noted on the vessel log, was that the current was 'strong'. That meant a reasonable amount of effort was needed to make headway against it and a moderate amount of effort to maintain position facing into the current. He felt that it was moving generally from the direction of the bow to the stern of the *Yongala*. It might have been just slightly off the port side of the wreck, or about 10 degrees to the left of the bow.

'Yeah, that's what the *Yongala* is all about. A strong current is fairly normal,' he grinned at Johnstone as they stripped off their gear. 'The worst I've dived is a 2.7-knot current. You can't do a 3-knot. It's impossible. What you felt down there,' he told her, 'was at least .5 of a knot to my mind, but everyone has different perceptions and it depends on your experience. Also, once you're down on the wreck itself, the current drops right back.'

They were back in the tender at 8 a.m. heading for breakfast. After being briefed by the dive crew, Wade Singleton noted that the only adverse condition was the strong current and made the decision to take the passengers to the far end, at the bow of the old steamer, by tender so they could drift back, using the current, to its stern and the *Spoilsport*.

Jazz II was a 53-foot (16-metre) fibreglass dive boat owned by Tropical Diving, based in South Townsville. The company ran a scuba dive business out to the SS *Yongala*, picking up extra passengers from nearby Magnetic Island. Barton Painter, the ship's master, chugged out of Townsville at around 7.15 a.m. His only passenger was Dr Stanley Stutz, an emergency doctor based at Townsville Hospital; the *Yongala* represented the best opportunity to complete the deep-dive component of the advanced water certificate he had signed for the previous day. On the way they stopped at Magnetic Island to collect dive master Rob Webster and his eight other divers.

The dive instructors on the *Spoilsport* dive deck that morning included Fotheringham, Lou Johnstone, Lemsing and Uzi Barnai. They carried out more morning check procedures. Although everyone's BCs and tanks had been checked when the passengers boarded the previous evening, it was procedure for the specialist crew to carry out systematic double-checks, including that the gas tanks were full, the air gauge wasn't flickering and that everyone had a safety sausage, a 2-metre orange balloon that meant any diver could be spotted if they were swept away by a current. Under Australian standards, every diver was required to have two air sources – primary and 'safe second' regulators attached to their BCs. Everything appeared to be in order.

At about 7.20 a.m. the passengers in the fifteen cabins on board *Spoilsport* began arriving in the saloon deck for breakfast. When Gabe and Tina arrived 10 minutes later, only one of the three bench tables of ten had spare seats. Almost everyone was in shorts and T-shirts over their bathing suits. Tina re-introduced herself and Gabe to those sitting closest: Jacqueline Sherman from Guatemala, holidaying with her parents and sister Jamie, and Dawn Asano and Gary Stempler, the other honeymooners.

'How y'all doin' this morning? asked Tina, sitting down at one of the vacant seats after helping herself to toast and jam and chocolate crispy cereal. Everyone was wearing name tags, so engaging in chat was made easy. '. . . My husband, Gabe. And I'm Tina.'

With a wink at Gary and Dawn, she drawled, 'We're the *old* honeymooners.'

Everyone smiled at the joke. Dawn, a physiotherapist whose smooth auburn hair and clear skin belied her forty years, and Gary, a youthful-looking forty-five-year-old engineer, were clearly the elder pair.

'Oh, I must ask you,' said Jacqueline Sherman, who was the same age as Tina. 'I'm getting married next year and already I'm so overwhelmed by everything. And I've got fourteen months to go. Did you both have a long time to prepare everything?'

Both new brides answered at once, then stopped and giggled.

'I had six months, that's all,' Tina said.

'And I'd been engaged since February,' Dawn said. 'We were going to be engaged for a year, but I found out that the best time for diving in northern Australia was October, so we brought the wedding forward.'

'Ooh,' Tina cried. 'We planned our wedding around this trip too.'

Dawn leaned over the table towards Jacqueline Sherman conspiratorially. 'You will never get everything done that you would like. But it doesn't matter,' she told the young woman. 'Just enjoy the day.'

They both spoke about the details of their weddings. Dawn talked about hers at a winery in San Jose. Their husbands, heads bent, were engrossed in breakfast, avoiding the wedding chatter.

While they were finishing breakfast, Wade arrived and told the passengers more history about the *Yongala* before moving on to briefing details of the dive.

'Those of you wanting a nitrox dive briefing should meet me on the dive deck after breakfast,' Singleton advised. 'Anyone who has hired Mike Ball dive computers should remain in the saloon for the dive computer briefing. It's also open to anyone who has recently bought a new computer and you want to go over the instructions. That briefing will be followed by a short exam so you can show what you know.'

Then Singleton gestured towards the windows lining each side of the saloon, through which clear blue sea and sky were visible.

'It's shaping up to be a great day. I'll give you a conditions report on the dive deck during the general dive briefing that everyone who is diving today must attend. That'll be at 8.30. The dive deck will be open today from now until . . . midday. You should all know there's a mandatory 20-minute surface interval between dives with a recommendation to allow an hour between dives.'

Gabe and Tina headed below to their cabin to change. Tina put on a floral bikini which was to go under her wetsuit and Gabe wore bathers.

At 8.30 a.m., everyone gathered on the back deck. Wade Singleton began the compulsory briefing with a roll call of the twenty-four guest divers. One passenger did not dive. The serious part of the day had begun. Singleton spent about 40 minutes explaining general diving safety procedures, standing in front of a chalkboard diagram that outlined the stern and bow of the wreck. He gave details of the site, the anchor ropes, the conditions and the strong current the divers might expect. He also went through emergency procedures and basic signals, which he read from the procedures manual. Singleton described the dive as a 'red dive', explaining that 'it requires more thought processes; it'll be deeper and there may be currents, so you have to be aware of them'. Jacqueline Sherman, who had already done around ninety-five dives and had an advanced open-water certification, was impressed. Tina Graves, who had a rescue certificate, later recalled that it was the best dive briefing she'd ever had. Singleton went on to talk about how the 1958 discovery of the wreck had contributed to it being ranked among one of the world's top ten dive sites and that it was protected under the Historic Shipwrecks Act, meaning no-one was permitted to enter it.

Protected by the mass of the old steamer, the divers would drift with the current to the stern line hanging from the surface, where they would ascend and pull themselves the short distance on a surface rope to the dive platform of the *Spoilsport*. Alternatively, they could hail a tender to pick them up. Singleton then described the best way to enter the water and how to roll off the tender.

'It is a drift dive, so there is no need to swim or fight against the current. Just let it take you along to the far end of the wreck and grab on to the stern line when you see it.'

Singleton looked around the throng crowding the dive deck.

'Today the current is strong – and that's both on the surface and the wreck, I am advised. We're going to make it easy for you by taking you to the diver access point in the tender. Your chauffeur today is our eminent engineer, Craig Haslet. He's that handsome guy over there,' Singleton pointed to the designated tender driver, who was leaning casually against a railing. 'The water temperature is 77 degrees Fahrenheit – that's 25 in Celsius for any locals.'

'There will be a lookout stationed on the top deck of *Spoilsport* at all times. There's six divers to a tender . . . Craig will get you out there pretty smartly, and help you with anything that crops up. He will have weights on board for anyone with buoyancy issues.'

Flicking over the page in the manual, Singleton continued: 'Mike Ball's policy is to allow standard buddy diving. There is no requirement for a dive master or a guide to accompany you. But I want to stress that there are guides available.'

He looked slowly around the group.

'If there is any dive you feel uncomfortable about, or you want to explore in more detail, all our dive masters,' Singleton gestured to the four crew members lounging on the outskirts of the group, each certified to dive master or the higher dive instructor level, 'would be more than happy to help and point out the many items of interest. All of them are very familiar with each dive we will visit on the expedition.'

He smiled.

'I know they would much prefer to dive with you and show you around than clean the toilets, wouldn't they, Dave?' He motioned to Lemsing, at the back of the crowd. It was obviously a much-used line.

Briefly consulting the manual again, Singleton reminded everyone to maintain contact with the access line while both descending and ascending so as not to be carried too far by any current. He then began his wind-up.

'And before I give the individual briefings to those taking an orientation dive – remember these dive masters really would rather *not* be cleaning, so make use of their skills.'

Then he turned his attention to the list of orientation divers to be split between himself and Simon Smith, another of the dive masters among the crew.

'Okay,' Wade Singleton called to the divers in the melee

that signalled dive time was starting. 'I'm going to buddy up those doing orientation dives now.'

Three divers would be guided by Simon Smith. 'Dawn Asano. Gary Stempler. Tina Watson,' Wade called out loudly. 'Can you all make your way upstairs for the orientation briefing with me, please?'

He looked around as the Californians mounted the stairs. Where were the other newlyweds?

By 8.30 a.m., the *Jazz II* had left Magnetic Island and was heading south-east. On board were nine divers and four crew members, including trip director/second mate/coxswain Alana McMahon and dive instructor Rob Webster, a dark-haired, nuggety man with crinkly smiling eyes, weathered from years in the tropical sun. Webster, who ran Pleasure Divers on the island, brought his own students and Danish dive master candidate, Kasper Brodersen, who was to assist him with the recreational divers. Jarrod Fisher, a thirteen-year-old Magnetic Island local, was the youngest passenger. He already had his advanced open-water dive certificate as well as thirty dives and was keen to gain further experience. Webster's seven other divers, from Korea and Britain, moved around the boat as it left Nelly Bay Harbour on Magnetic Island, sunglasses on against the glare, taking in the brilliant blue of the water sparkling in the sunlight.

Wade Singleton was quite clear about what happened next. He said he found Gabe and Tina on the dive deck, checking out their gear, and he remembered the conversation.

'Hi Tina. Thought you might like to do the guided dive?'

'No,' she shook her head, frowning. 'Remember we

discussed it last night? I'm going to do the *Yongala* dive with Gabe. And I'll do the night dive orientation with you, because I've never dived at night and that definitely sounds scary.'

Gabe nodded his head, looking at Singleton, who studied his list.

'We're only going to dive along the top of the wreck – you know, about 45 feet,' Gabe said.

'You might have put it down the wrong way,' Tina said.

Wade looked down at his sheet again.

'You know,' he said, with the beginnings of recall from the night before, 'I think you might be right.'

He gave her a spontaneous hug. She was that kind of girl, open and friendly.

'You don't have to wait, enjoy your dive, okay?'

She smiled widely showing lovely, straight teeth.

'We sure will.'

'Okay, thanks,' Gabe said.

Tina bent down to pick up her mask and fins. This was it.

Walking upstairs from the deck, Singleton mulled over the conversation he'd just had with Tina and Gabe. The dive had been set up to make the current a so-called 'nil factor' for the *Spoilsport* passengers. Both of them had declined the offer of an orientation dive several times, saying they were comfortable diving together. Tina had agreed that she was happy too, in spite of only being certified this year with just eleven dives. At least it would be fresh in her mind, Singleton thought as he walked across the sun deck. Having logged more than fifty dives – twelve that he'd written down in the past year – Gabe was more than qualified to be Tina's buddy. But it was Gabe's rescue diver status that was the clincher that helped Singleton make the decision that she could dive the *Yongala* without a crew member on her first outing.

'Hey Wade!' Tina sang out, cutting through his reverie as he reached the top of the stairs. 'I want you to remember now,' she said, sticking her finger up in mock schoolteacher pose, a teasing grin on her face. 'If you get scared on the night dive, you can always just hold ma hand.'

She delivered the last phrase in a deliberately drawled southern twang. He laughed. Still smiling as he joined Dawn and Gary for their orientation briefing, Dawn recalled that Singleton had commented: 'They didn't want to come.'

Lou Johnstone's job as general deckhand involved filling dive cylinders, sorting out equipment and signing divers in and out of the water. It was only natural that she was watching everyone from the moment they got on deck and began getting into their wetsuits before approaching the cool blue ocean. Tina, she had been told, was graded green, the least-experienced rating for a diver. A red flag fluttered on the dive deck in the slight breeze, signifying the site was graded red. Because of this, Lou was keeping a special watch on the Watsons. It was 9.30 a.m. Gabe and Tina were working through the range of tasks leading up to the dive.

'Let's wait a while,' said Gabe, surveying the crowd of wetsuited divers edging towards the dive platform below like giant crabs. He hated getting into his wetsuit until it was almost time to go. His large frame grew warm inside a wetsuit very quickly, especially in this tropical sun. In October, the average temperature in Townsville hovered around 25°C.

They laid out their equipment in order and Gabe started to hook up his tank to his BC vest. As Gabe worked steadily through the tasks, Tina clearly had more trouble remembering how to set up her dive gear. Lou watched as Gabe, who clearly had little patience, grabbed bits and pieces of equipment and began fitting them on for her. It irritated Lou that this man was so dogmatic. Instead of instructing his new wife on how to use it, he did it himself. Lou moved closer, seeking eye contact with either of them, but Gabe made it clear through his body language that he did not want help. Mike Ball Dive Expeditions had advertised an 'independent diver scenario', so dive-deck staff, especially volunteers like Lou who were aboard for the free diving, were not expected to jump on guests and correct their every move. So she watched intermittently from a distance as they put defog on their masks and put their snorkels in their BC pockets. Then they put on their wetsuits, boots and gloves. Tina sat down on the bench and Gabe helped her get into her BC while she held his fins and camera. Fins were put on last because they restricted movement. Jamie Sherman, whose sister Jacqueline was going to get married, helped Tina put on Gabe's fins.

Gary Stempler was more concerned with his camera and how Dawn would cope on the dive. He had taken a few pictures during Singleton's dive briefing, fine-tuning the camera settings and recording the start of this dive. Neither of them had been inside a wetsuit for fourteen months. Dawn was quite anxious about being so far from land and diving so deep on a wreck. Gary was hoping that Wade Singleton would concentrate on Dawn so he would be free to experiment with his new camera, which had a bulky housing around it to enable underwater photography.

On the far side of the dive deck portly insurance executive Ken Snyder was chatting to his old buddy and fellow dive master Doug Milsap, a dentist also from Florida, as they prepared their gear. They had about 850 logged dives between them.

'That was one of the best dive briefings I've ever heard,'

Snyder said. 'I've almost got a Polaroid shot in my head of what it'll be like down there.'

'Yeah,' grunted Milsap, hoisting his BC with tank attached over his left shoulder. 'He seems to have covered pretty much everything that might get us into trouble.'

Paula Snyder, a short-haired blonde, 53, and her best friend Ginger Milsap, 52, were also accomplished divers like their husbands. They had, over the past twenty-five years, dived together as a foursome all over the world. Paula and Ginger both had advanced open-water certifications and had also logged hundreds of dives, although fewer than their spouses. Paula had called the Great Barrier Reef their 'ultimate dive trip'. As the crew began ushering the two couples to the back of *Spoilsport* and the steps leading down to the dive platform, Paula looked back and saw Gabe and Tina on the back deck. Gabe had spotted a turtle on the surface just off the boat and pointed it out to Tina, who screamed in delight. Craig Haslet had the tender idling as the first names were checked off. It was about 9.45 a.m. The Snyders and Milsaps, along with others, were the second crew into the water. Despite their recent exhausting 30-hour trip from Florida, they were here and on their way to a fantasy land.

CHAPTER 9

Paul Crocombe and his two fellow commercial divers had finished breakfast and were unloading the old mooring from position 901 and placing another heavy lump of knotted rope and shackle aboard the tender. Knowing the divers would soon be getting into the water, Crocombe jerked into life the 25-horsepower outboard motor. It roared into the quiet of the morning. Then, throttling slightly, he pointed the tender to position 902 in the south-west corner of the *Yongala* site. With the *Spoilsport* at 905, that left positions 903 and 904 free for any other dive boat that arrived. Paul's day boat, the *Adrenalin*, which was expected to arrive later that morning, would take one. Crocombe stayed aboard the tender while one of the other divers took a turn at replacing the 902 mooring. The sun was warm and sleep-inducing after the cold of the seabed. Crocombe settled in for a wait as the other diver hooked up the new mooring, attached the rope to the subsurface float to keep it taut in the varying weather conditions and tethered it to the orange buoy.

***

As guests prepared for their dive, the nearest dive master carried out the ABCDE safety checks on all departing divers.

A for air: check that the cylinder is completely open and back slightly so the valve can't stick, that both regulators work and the contents are full at 3000 psi (pounds per square inch) or the alternative measurement of 200 bar.

B for buckle or weight belt: ensure the belt is threaded properly through the buckle, or weights are distributed fairly evenly around an integrated belt and the diver doesn't look too over- or under-weighted.

C for the compensator or BC: this must be secure on the tank, the buckles and straps adjusted well and fitted evenly. A quick inflation/deflation test is performed to ensure air floods in and out of the vest when each button is pushed.

D is for the diver's experience: it should match the dive site.

E ensures the diver is marked on the sign-off sheet with a buddy.

The Snyders and Milsaps were well used to all of this preparation, but perhaps because of the jetlag, Paula Snyder felt crowded, like a million people were behind her as she waited for the tender to nose against the stern of the *Spoilsport*. It was her first time on a boat where divers didn't either roll off, do a backflip or take a giant stride straight off the main vessel, and she was not happy. Instead she had to lumber down the steps from the dive deck wearing her BC and tank and step into a small inflatable dinghy that was not terribly stable. She had almost 300 dives logged around the Florida Quays, the Bahamas, the Cayman Islands and the Virgin Islands, Honduras, Jamaica and St Lucia in the Caribbean, but this morning she was feeling her age, aware that if she moved the wrong way, she could sprain an ankle getting into the dinghy.

Finally, their group was seated and the tender took off under the stewardship of Craig Haslet, cruising slowly along the length of the wreck beneath to the diver access point at its bow. They rolled off the sides of the tender together, grouped at the buoy, and then descended one by one into a new world.

Paula immediately felt lighter and her cares from the world above dissolved. She noticed the cold first, then the visibility, which was about the length of two cars. A strong swimmer, Paula thought the current was brisk, and it took her a moment to take stock, but it was manageable. Certainly it was mild enough for her to later contemplate a second dive. She was overawed, though, by the size of the fish. The divers lowered themselves down the drop line, then began swimming as directed along the length of the wreck, beginning at the bow about 26.5 metres down and heading for the stern, the current aiding them all the way.

There is something confronting about the 363-foot long (110-metre) dark shape of the steel wreck lying on its starboard side, the promenade deck exposed, rising from the bottom of the ocean where it came to rest a century ago. Ginger Milsap and Paula Snyder, eyes wide like the majority of the *Spoilsport* divers, drifted past the ghostly coral-encrusted deck in amazement. For the next 30 minutes they were suspended in the wonderland they had come halfway round the world to see.

Gropers, some weighing up to 300 kilograms, floated past, once almost hunted to extinction but now protected. Giant stingrays, up to 100 kilograms, flapped rhythmically like strange terrestial spaceships. Everything at this depth seemed larger as the divers were embraced by this silent world testing their courage, relying only on their eyes to guide them. On the Great Barrier Reef, the colours of the corals are breathtaking. Both soft and hard varieties compete with algae for space and life on the wreck. Weighed down by its natural burden, the SS *Yongala* weighs three times as much as it did when it was turned out of the shipyard. Inside the wreck, out of bounds to divers, are mementos of a past era: lifebuoys, a cribbage board, a cedar trunk and four farthings – and the remains of those who died all those years ago. The wreck teems with life: parrotfish and angel-fish play among gardens of soft red corals; fusiliers swim in silver streaks like lightning movements. Even further, 27 metres down on the wreck itself, swim Venus tusk fish, evolved over millions of years. Seemingly suspended in mid air are sea turtles, some around fifty years old, the males evident by their long tails and claws.

Ken Snyder thought it was a pleasant day. The current was, in his 500-odd dive experience, 'doable . . . even for an old fat guy'.

It was Craig Haslet's job to maintain the compressors that filled the dive tanks with air as well as driving the tender for passenger drop-offs and pick-ups. He kept a UHF radio with him that was in contact with the lookout stationed at the top deck of *Spoilsport*. After dropping off the group of Americans, Haslet returned to the *Spoilsport* at about 10.05 a.m. Tina, then Gabe, sweating already in his 3-millimetre-thick wetsuit but cooled slightly by the mild sea breeze on his face, had been standing in line. They were the last to get in the tender, joining the Sherman family, Dr John Downie from Chicago and another male passenger. Facing each other in the bow of the tender, Gabe and Tina listened as Craig shouted over the noise of the engine.

'I'll take you up-current from the white diver-access buoy that you can see about 110 metres – I mean 300 feet – away to the north,' Haslet shouted.

Once they reached the buoy, Haslet tied the tender to the safety line and turned off the engine. All eight divers rolled off their respective sides, swam to the buoy and signalled to each other that they were ready to descend. The two men went first, followed by the Shermans. Gabe and Tina were the last to go under.

Adriana Sherman realised right away that she would have to go back up: she did not have enough weights on and, instead of sinking, she was bobbing back up. Her daughter, Jacqueline, had the same problem. They began to swim upwards and Jamie, her other daughter, followed, perplexed by what was going on.

Gabe and Tina too were having problems. Down only 1.5 metres, Gabe was later to claim that he heard loud beeps emitting from his dive computer watch, a top-of-the-range Oceanic DataTrans Plus, the same watch he asked Tina to have checked back in Birmingham just before the wedding. He motioned to Tina with the thumbs-up signal to ascend.

'What's wrong?' asked Tina when they surfaced.

'My computer's not working. It was beeping. Hang on,' said Gabe. He took hold of his regulator. 'I'll try again.'

Later he was to claim that he did this because he thought the water pressure might kick in and activate the computer.

Again he came to the surface, joining Tina and the Shermans on the safety line.

Craig Haslet was still in the vicinity and he pulled up beside them.

'What's up, mate?' said the engineer, peering at the dive computer on Gabe's arm, which he held out of the water.

'It's not working.'

Haslet peered at the screen and saw it was blank. He heard nothing either.

'And we need more weights,' Adriana Sherman said. 'Both Jacqui and I are finding it hard to get down.'

As she bobbed around, Adriana noticed Brian Fotheringham on the sundeck, the highest point of *Spoilsport*, in the identifiable orange jacket and remembered Wade Singleton had said that there would be a lookout.

'No worries. Can fix you up,' Haslet said.

Provided with more weights off the tender, the Shermans returned to their dive.

'Hop in,' Haslet said to Gabe and Tina. 'You'll have to go back to the *Spoilsport*.'

The Mike Ball rule was that if a problem could not be rectified in the water, the diver must be taken to the *Spoilsport* to solve it there. Buddies had to return too.

Once they were in the tender, Haslet asked: 'So did you see anything under there?'

'Oh yes, we saw a really large fish, but because we had to come back up to the top, we didn't see anything else,' Tina said, a little bit woebegone.

Wade Singleton was surprised when he saw Tina and Gabe back on board *Spoilsport*. David Lemsing helped them out of the tender, directing them to put their tanks back in the tank rack. One of the crew began topping them up with air in line with the policy that no diver was to leave the vessel without a full tank.

'So what happened, mate?' Lemsing asked.

'My computer's not working. That's why we came back,' he later recalled that Gabe had said. 'The battery's flat.'

'Do you want me to see if I can find another battery?'

Gabe nodded.

Tina was sitting next to him.

'I think I might be underweight,' Tina said. 'It's a bit hard to go down.'

'Oh, right. The weights bin is just over there,' Lemsing replied. 'That's common when you start off diving, to get your buoyancy right. Let me know if you need some advice.'

Waylaid by other duties, Lemsing forgot all about the battery. Soon afterwards, in the busy to-and-fro on the dive deck, Uzi Barnai passed Tina.

'You tired?' he asked. He thought she had been among the first divers off the boat who had completed a full dive. Tina was still puffing from the unaccustomed exertion of heaving herself and her weighted dive gear from the dinghy up the steps from the dive platform.

'No,' she grimaced. Pointing to Gabe behind her with one of her fins she added: 'The computer isn't working.'

'Hi,' said Gabe to Uzi as he turned around. 'My computer's not working. It usually starts to work in about 1 foot of water.'

'Did you dive?'

'No. The computer wasn't working, so we came straight up after a few feet. Can you fix it?'

'No way,' Uzi replied. 'I'm not certified to fix those things. I'm not allowed to touch them. We have plenty for hire. If you need one, take one.'

'No, no, no,' Gabe rejoined, shaking his head in refusal. 'Can I have a coin?' he asked Uzi.

'Sure.'

Still busy with the few last divers preparing to leave, Barnai came back with a five-cent piece, thinking that Gabe wanted it as a souvenir. But Gabe casually handed it back after a short while. He hooked his regulator back onto his tank, turned the air on and checked that his computer indeed registered the 3000 psi of compressed gas that it held. He winked at Barnai.

'Don't tell anybody,' he said conspiratorially, 'but I had

my battery in backwards. Just so you know that problem was solved.'

Tina and Gabe were heading back out for their first dive when John and Tina Graves left the *Spoilsport* on one of the last tenders. Both experienced divers from Colorado, the Graves realised straightaway that they were underweighted. By the time Tina Graves inserted the extra weights provided by Haslet into their integrated dive belts – pockets in their BC vests – she noticed that they had drifted around 50 metres away from the descent-line buoy and the safety line. After a quick conversation, the Graves decided to swim back to the descent line, a distance almost the size of an Olympic pool, instead of struggling back into the tender again. Battling against the surface current back to the diver-access point, they were breathing hard from their unexpected exertion. Thank goodness, Tina Graves thought, that she had conditioned herself with three visits to the gym every week as part of her pre-holiday training. Inflating their BCs to act as temporary flotation devices, the couple hung on the safety line for about 5 minutes to relax and get their heart rates down.

Jazz II had finally completed an uneventful two-and-a-half-hour trip across from Magnetic Island, arriving at the *Yongala* dive site at about 10.10 a.m.

'Beauty, we'll take that one,' thought Alana McMahon as she saw that mooring point 904 was unoccupied. From here, it was a very short surface swim – roughly 20 metres – to the diver descent line, which made life easier for the divers who could then use the drop line to go both up and down to the wreck.

As *Jazz II* chugged towards the mooring line, ship's master Barton Painter saw that *Spoilsport* was already moored. He also noticed the deck watch at his station and could see that the Alpha – the internationally recognised dive flag – was flying. A dive was in progress. Dive master Rob Webster began to organise the divers and give the briefings. Webster was to lead two English backpackers, Karl Diggins and Christian Bennett, and another Englishman Neil Joslin, who was buddied with Dr Stanley Stutz, on the deep dive to the sandy ocean floor near the wreck for their advanced certificates. Joslin's wife, Leanne England, had chosen to remain on board, taking photographs and relaxing. Teenager Jarrod Fisher was looking forward to this big adventure. Also diving were Kasper Brodersen, buddied with Ashik Shah, a London-based IT specialist, and two Koreans, Sun Min Jeon, an international business management student and Han Gyu Kim, in Australia on a working visa. Sun Min thought the water was clear and the weather perfect. Alana McMahon took Rob Webster to the diver access point in the *Jazz II*'s tender. She too noted that it was 'a lovely day', bright, sunny, with a 5-knot wind that barely 'ruffled the cheek'. A slight current showed from a rippling on the surface of the water. She could clearly see other divers below as they made their way down the bow descent line.

About 10.15 a.m., Rob Webster took the *Jazz II* emergency air tank, also known as a hang tank or deco (decompression) tank, and descended from the tender to clip it to a stainless steel shackle on the descent line. He positioned it at 5-metres depth, just like the hang tank put there earlier for the *Spoilsport* by Brian Fotheringham. Alana McMahon noted that the mooring line of the *Jazz II* was not taut at all, as would be expected in a strong current. It was just lolling around. About 10.25 a.m. the *Jazz II* dive group was readied with last-minute instructions. Their dive was about to begin.

Once Tina Graves was underwater, she forgot all about the exertion on the surface. Although she thought the current was very brisk, she settled into what was indeed a beautiful dive. John Graves, an advanced open-water diver with at least fifty dives to his credit, also thought the current was strong until they reached the floor of the ocean near the *Yongala* wreck. Even 2 or 3 metres out from the wreck, he felt it tug at him again. For the whole dive, they saw no-one except for the Ladors, a Swiss couple who were similarly experienced and were the last of the *Spoilsport* divers to enter the water. After Wade Singleton's briefing, the Ladors had retired to their cabins for a sleep for about an hour. When they finally entered the water, some of the early divers had already returned to *Spoilsport*.

On their way back out in the tender to restart their dive, Gabe and Tina found themselves in the same seating positions. This time, ironically, they were with Wade Singleton's orientation group: Dawn Asano, Gary Stempler and Claudia Petersen, the German backpacker volunteer.

'So what happened to you two?' Wade asked.

'Got my batteries in back to front on my dive computer,' Gabe answered.

Haslet motored slowly, on the lookout for divers who might pop up unexpectedly away from the drop ropes at either end of the wreck. Gary sat next to Dawn, nursing his new Olympus camera. Having made the switch to digital, he liked the camera being small, but it had a bulky lucite housing he was now inspecting closely. One loose part could flood the camera. He was hoping to take a lot of pictures on this first dive – at least a few of them memorable. The sea life on the Great Barrier Reef was vastly different from the Caribbean where he had dived before.

Dawn, seeing Gary absorbed in his camera, kept her eyes firmly on Wade Singleton and mentally ran through what he had told them that morning. She really only wanted to think about the moment when it would all be over and she would be hauling herself back on board *Spoilsport*.

Tina sat at the bow of the tender. Dawn thought Tina seemed far calmer than she herself was, as she was sitting upright and looked confident. Dawn presumed that Tina must have done enough dives in the past twelve months not to need the orientation dive. The only wreck diving Dawn had done before was in Honduras, at more like 14 metres. Contemplating twice that depth, Dawn was scared and still unsure of her diving skills, acquired back in 2001.

As they approached the buoy, Dawn began to pull on her mask.

It was about 10.32 a.m. when Haslet cut the engine and tied the tender to the safety line. On the count of three, the six divers rolled off the boat simultaneously, disappearing into the aqua-blue of the ocean. It was dangerous for divers to roll off a tender while others were already in the water.

Gabe and Tina were ahead of the pack and the first to reach the safety line. Gabe had almost 13 kilograms of weight in his integrated weight belt, preferring, he would later say, to over-weight himself so that when he released his BC he could get down quicker. Tina went down the rope first, followed by Gabe. After Wade attended to his group, they began to descend a few minutes later. Claudia Petersen led the way. Stempler was next, with a firm grip on his Olympus. Dawn followed, lagging behind a little, her eyes never leaving Singleton. When her descent slowed, Singleton reached over and pressed her deflator button; air was immediately released from her over-inflated BC and she began to go down a little faster. Only 20 metres away, the divers on *Jazz II* had taken a giant stride off the stern of the vessel, but, as yet, the divers off *Spoilsport* were unaware of their presence. Dawn Asano was concentrating on Wade Singleton's constant signals asking if she were okay, which she found very reassuring. Below her, Claudia Petersen saw the Watsons until they reached the hang tanks at the 5-metre mark, and then she lost sight of them.

The SS *Yongala* was the fifty-fourth dive recorded on Gabe's high-tech Oceanic dive computer. Holding on to the descent-line rope, Tina looked this way and that as she went down. Here were these big fish again, bigger than any she had seen at home. Gabe's dive computer was registering a steady descent of about 3 metres per minute. Leaving the rope at about 13 metres, the Watsons swam out.

Barton Painter jotted down the time each diver from *Jazz II* entered the water on the dive roster. He and Rob Webster both signed the document. Webster had dived the *Yongala* many times and judged the dive conditions that day to be perfect.

Ashik Shah was first in.

'I don't like boats,' he had said on the way out to the wreck. Now, at least, he was in the water. His buddy, Danish dive master candidate Kasper Brodersen, was leading the four divers who were not part of Rob Webster's advanced open-water class. The nine divers off *Jazz II* swam about 20 metres, holding on to the surface line leading from their boat to the diver access point. Alana McMahon took up her designated lookout duties with two watches on her arm: one told the time, the other was her dive watch, which would tell her all sorts of useful facts about her depth and nitrogen load and rate of descent – but not in real time. It was there if she needed to look for any diver from the *Jazz II* who stayed underwater for more than the allotted hour. After photographing the divers on their way off the boat and along the drop line, Leanne England stayed at the stern with Alana McMahon and Barton Painter.

Making his way down the descent line, Ashik Shah felt crowded. As thirteen-year-old Jarrod Fisher began to descend, the boy felt a shooting pain in his jaw at around the 3-metre mark. Painfully, he went down a further 4 metres to let Webster know he had a problem, before heading to the surface after his dive instructor acknowledged the problem with a thumbs-up. Webster had been watching his class above him as they came down the line at staggered intervals of about 1 metre apart. It had taken him less than a minute to descend the 16 metres to the end of the descent line.

It was about 10.39 a.m. Wade Singleton and his orientation divers, as well as Tina and Gabe, had been under the water for 5 or 6 minutes. To Brian Fotheringham, from his lookout position on the sundeck of the *Spoilsport*, the current seemed to have reduced considerably since his 7 a.m. dive check. He could tell from the way the tender approached the drop-off point and how the divers reacted once they got into the water. Like the changeable weather patterns, the current around the SS *Yongala* could differ from one half-hour to the next.

***

Dr Stanley Stutz, the thirty-year-old emergency doctor, had been greatly looking forward to this dive that he had heard so much about. Stutz was pleased with his decision to upgrade his ten-year-old PADI open-water dive licence while he completed his post-residency term in North Queensland. He and British tourist Neil Joslin were among the last to descend in Webster's depth dive class. Stutz slowly followed Joslin down the drop rope, thrilled by the good visibility that revealed his first coral sea fish even though he was a little distracted by the divers all bunched together on the rope. At one point, Stutz let go of the line to test the current, but he had to make an effort to swim back and grab hold again, and decided not to risk it a second time. As he descended, with a diver just above him and another just below, he swivelled around and noticed that a bunch of divers appeared to be going up to the surface. He had just passed the hang tanks indicating 5 metres in depth. He knew the top of the wreck was in front of and below him, although he couldn't see it yet. Suddenly, 7 or 8 metres down and to his left, in his peripheral vision he noticed a female diver. For a moment, he could not believe what he saw. As a trained accident and emergency physician, he immediately noticed her limbs moving in a disorganised way. He looked at her face, and blondish hair that trailed behind her head. Her mask was still in place and her regulator in her mouth. She looked petrified. Her arms were outstretched to the sides, which reminded him of Jesus outstretched on the cross before his crucifixion. Her arms and legs thrashed without purpose and her eyes were wide, a classic sign of panic.

Uncharacteristically for a diver, she was lying horizontally, her feet closest to him. It seemed, from his higher position, and perhaps distorted, as things tended to be underwater, that she was nearer a group of other divers about 3 metres from him. His immediate thought was that they might save her. What alarmed him, though, was that they seemed to be unaware she was even there. Stutz knew that the woman was in trouble. He had a sense of foreboding. As with catastrophic events, time slowed. As Stutz was digesting what was happening and deciding what to do, about 10 seconds later he noticed another diver, obviously male, bigger in both height and width, approach the woman from the left from about 3 metres away. The man swam over the top of the woman as she lay facing upwards. Mirroring her position, facing the seabed, he lay along her and put his arms under her armpits, encircling her. At first, Stutz thought the other diver was helping her, trying to bring her to the surface. It seemed that this cradling motion, or bear hug, as it was later described by police, lasted about 30 seconds. It was probably less, but the moment played out in time. He couldn't see if the full length of their bodies were touching because the man's body blocked his view. He did not look at his watch. Then, he momentarily looked away. When he looked back, the two divers had split apart and the male diver swam towards the surface, leaving the woman. On the woman's face was a look of abject terror. Her limb movements seemed to progressively weaken as her legs flapped slowly up and down, without any power. She was sinking.

Stutz could see that the other four or five divers were still reasonably close to her, but they were spread apart. He couldn't tell whether they were on the same plane as the stricken diver, or 3 metres higher or lower. They either didn't see her, or were too far away to help. No-one from the *Jazz II*, not even his buddy, now about 1 metre below him, appeared to have seen any of it. He held the woman in eye contact as long as he could, wondering if she could see him. He was still at a depth of 5 metres and his only point of reference was the bow descent line disappearing into the depths to the wreck below, which was still not visible. He pushed himself down the line, feverishly, skipping other divers in his haste, to alert Rob Webster to the scene he had just witnessed. The last time Stutz saw Tina Watson she was sinking into the blackness.

Han Gyu Kim, the 24-year-old Korean diver, also saw a female diver about 8 or 10 metres directly below him when he was about 5 to 10 metres underwater. Kim and his friend, Sun Min Jeon, had been close to Stutz when the divers from *Jazz II* entered the water. The female diver was lying flat on her back looking straight up at him and not moving at all, he would say later. Someone was holding on to the top of her tank. This diver was pulling her up and across at the same time. He was to say later that he thought she hadn't equalised properly and that she was being rescued.

CHAPTER 10

Gary Stempler had noted on his dive computer that it was 10.37 a.m. at the start of their descent. From the minute the four divers – Singleton, Gary Stempler, Dawn Asano and Claudia Petersen – had done the backwards roll off the tender, Singleton had been watching his group carefully. When they got to the bow of the wreck about 15 metres down, Singleton beckoned to them and led them down over the deck side of the wreck to what was known as a calm zone where they were shielded from the worst of the current above. Within 5 minutes they had descended further, down to 22 metres, and in a slow drift parallel to the hull towards the stern, Gary could make out the hold. He noticed some debris lying on the ocean floor towards the bow. They all watched a couple of sea snakes swim vertically like ribbons with the help of their paddle tails. Returning to the air periodically to breathe, each snake, with no natural predator, had enough venom to kill three adults.

Wade, routinely taking in his surroundings as part of his duties, looked away from the wreck, searching for more interesting fish or sea creatures to point out. Claudia was slightly ahead and Dawn was still at his side. Gary fiddled with his Olympus, focusing, ready to take another picture of his wife. As she tentatively looked around, Dawn thought for a moment that she saw something below. But it was Wade, more attuned to the unusual, who first noticed the diver lying on the seabed. He thought, at first, it was one of the *Spoilsport* guests looking up at the fish. He looked back at Dawn. Still anxious, she was unaware that her husband was framing her for his next shot. Even this early into the dive, she was monitoring the depth and how much air she had left. As she turned to look for Singleton's reassuring presence, Singleton again looked back to the seabed, years of training guiding him to the diver: a woman, he decided, from her shape and long hair. There were no fish flitting by. Far more worryingly, he could see no air bubbles coming from the diver's regulator. She hadn't moved.

About 7 minutes into their dive time, Gary held up his Olympus, pointed it at his wife and pressed the camera shutter. Looking up from the viewfinder, he got a surprise to see that Singleton was swimming down to the seabed, strong scissor kicks with his splayed fins propelling him towards the prone figure Gary now noticed on the sandy bottom.

Wade reached the diver, who was lying predominantly on her right side, her left arm and head angled upwards and her legs straight out. He recognised her right away. Tina's eyes were open underneath the mask, which was still in place, as though she were staring at him, but she made no response to his touch. He looked around for her buddy Gabe. He'd seen them such a short time ago when they'd parted ways, leaving him with his orientation divers. In full rescue mode, he quickly assessed the surroundings. No hovering sharks, no protuberances. She was in clear water with nothing between her and the wreck. Her regulator was still in her mouth.

Bubbles discharged as he purged her regulator to clear it. She still had air in her tank. He noted there was no air in her BC. On a cursory inspection, everything else appeared normal. So why was she was lying there, her eyes unseeing, staring upwards? All of this was going through Singleton's mind, as, with a single click, he dropped his weight belt to the ocean floor. It was quicker than removing the weights from Tina's integrated BC pockets to get them back to the surface. Turning, he quickly signalled to Claudia Petersen to stay with the honeymooners and to continue the dive.

To help him off his knees, Singleton inflated his own BC slightly. Then, without difficulty, he inflated Tina's BC to propel them both upwards. She was semi-cradled against him as he held the regulator in her mouth with one hand, keeping her head tilted to provide an airway while, in classic rescue position, he kicked up using his fins to rise at an angle, heading straight for the surface. All these actions took just seconds.

Purging her regulator, Singleton made a rapid but controlled ascent, to what he hoped was the diver access point. Fotheringham, the designated *Spoilsport* lookout, would be monitoring the whole wreck site, so Singleton knew they should be sighted as soon as they surfaced.

Later, Singleton's dive computer would tell him they had only been about 8 minutes into the entire dive when he saw Tina. He was not concerned about the levels of nitrogen absorbed into his tissue, or risking the bends by not stopping to decompress, or he or Tina developing an embolism. Years of training had prepared him for this. He breathed normally through his regulator, exhaling the air in his lungs, which were rapidly expanding the higher, and in turn, faster they went. The question was, was Tina? He had no time to stop to check, heading for the surface and fresh air, ignoring the alarm on his dive computer that registered an ascent that flashed the words 'Too Fast'. Halfway through the ascent, he noticed Rob Webster hanging from the bow descent line on his way down with the passengers from *Jazz II*. Webster signalled a question, one of the most used diving signals, circling the tip of his first finger on to his thumb making the sign of an O. Singleton shook his head, continuing his ascent.

At about 10.45 a.m., Stanley Stutz finally caught up with Webster, who was waiting for his students at the end of the line. He could now see the SS *Yongala* beneath him.

Communicating rapidly with his hands, Stutz tried to explain what he had seen: 'Did you see that? Did you see THAT?' As they eyed each other in the silent, underwater world, and he tried to make Webster understand what he had seen, Stutz was later to recall seeing Wade Singleton rise virtually straight past them, taking Tina to the surface.

Stutz's medically trained eye battled with his emotional response. He noted that the regulator, held in the woman's mouth by Wade, was trailing vomit, and that vomiting from 30 metres down was a bad sign. Blood was also seeping out of her mouth. Nor was it a good sign that she was limp, not moving at all and was slumped back, held under the armpits by her rescuer. Her eyes were still open, but she was not looking at anything. As his professional eye made a clinical assessment, there seemed, he was to recall later, little hope for her. She looked, to him, to be dead or dying. 'Not save-able', a medical term, flashed into his mind as he grappled with the fact that he had been a helpless witness to her final moments. Stutz began again making frantic signals to Webster that he, too, should go to the surface to offer medical assistance.

This is terrible, Stutz thought, making guttural sounds

through his regulator. There is a young girl. And she's dead, he kept thinking. But Webster, not realising Stutz was a doctor and concerned for the welfare of his own group, signed in diver-speak: 'Stay with the group.' Webster kicked off, heading towards the surface behind Singleton, whose angle and speed defied whatever current there was.

Closer to the surface, and looking up, Webster realised right away that Singleton would surface within metres of *Jazz II*. He knew that Singleton would have immediate help, so he returned to the group of divers undertaking their advanced dive certificate. They descended to about 16 metres to the junction where another rope branched off to the bow of the *Yongala*. From there they would drift along to the stern and complete the return trip swimming against the current from the stern to the bow. One of the divers, Christian Bennett, had no idea there was even a rescue going on; he only noticed Tina's long blonde hair flowing behind her as she was taken to the surface by Wade Singleton.

Singleton had risen 27 metres from the ocean floor in just 92 seconds. In diving terms, he and Tina were flying.

Craig Haslet was lying back in the tender, his eyes closed to the bright sun after dropping off the last passengers of the session. Yawning, he'd allowed himself a break of around 10 minutes. He crouched over the engine, yanking on the starter cord and began idling back to the *Spoilsport*. All the divers had descended, but he still needed to exercise caution in case any of them unexpectedly bobbed up. Some, like Paula and Ken Snyder and the Milsaps, were already hauling themselves up the dive platform at the stern of the *Spoilsport*, excited and chattering about the dive.

Suddenly, a diver erupted out of the water between the

Spoilsport and the *Jazz II*, closer to the latter. White water sprayed everywhere. Haslet recognised the diver right away as Gabe Watson. Brian Fotheringham, on the *Spoilsport* sundeck, also spotted the diver and made a radio call which was picked up by the *Spoilsport* master, Gavin Docking. Only 15 metres away, Alana McMahon and Barton Painter, on the stern of the *Jazz II*, noticed him, too, as did Leanne England, standing on the back deck. She had just put her camera down when she heard the words, 'Help! Help!' and saw the *Spoilsport* tender going to the panicking diver's aid.

Haslet asked the first question all crew were trained to ask: 'Where's your buddy?'

'She's gone to the bottom and she's disappeared. She's in trouble,' gasped Gabe.

Haslet reached across and immediately grabbed Watson's BC, concerned he would try to go to the bottom to find her. He kept hold of the vest firmly so Watson couldn't fight him off, but he was a big man and seemed quite distressed.

Haslet grabbed for the *Spoilsport* radio on his belt. 'We need rescue divers urgently. A diver's in trouble.'

By this time Crocombe's boat, *Adrenalin*, had arrived, but Haslet could see the *Jazz II* was closer to him. He turned and saw Painter and McMahon, repeating the directions: 'I need a rescue diver. We have a diver in trouble. The diver is on the bottom and I don't know what condition she's in. We need somebody now,' he shouted. 'Get ready to prepare back-up.'

Paul Crocombe, on the foredeck of the *Spoilsport* getting ready to haul up one of the old moorings, had also heard Gabe Watson yelling. He ordered one of the commercial divers, driving the *Spoilsport*'s other tender, to go around to the stern and then raced downstairs to alert the designated emergency diver on the dive deck.

David Lemsing was in the wheelhouse of the *Spoilsport* when Craig Haslet's radio call came through. He sensed immediately the urgency in Haslet's voice. Moments later, Craig repeated the call: 'We definitely need two divers in a hurry.'

Docking was running from the wheelhouse. As he ran, he yelled to the hostess, Rebecca Hayllar, who was halfway through preparing morning tea in the galley. 'Rebecca, can you get the oxygen and the first-aid kit down to the dive deck?'

Lemsing grabbed his gear and his tank and alerted Uzi Barnai. They both jumped into the second tender being used by the commercial divers.

Haslet, with radio in hand, was directing Gabe into the tender, thinking he might go into shock. He shouted several times to Gabe: 'Where is she? Whereabouts is she?'

Gabe didn't answer him coherently. Finally he shouted: 'She's panicked. I've tried to help her. We tried to swim against the current back to the ascent line and surface there. I couldn't help her. So, I had to let her go and surface and see if I could get some help . . . I think she's halfway along the ship.'

Uzi Barnai, still not clear on what the 'emergency' entailed, saw Gabe pointing down into the water and screaming to Haslet: 'Quickly, quickly. We were together. One minute she was there and the other minute she went down and I went up.'

Barnai and Lemsing took off in the direction of the bow of the *Yongala* and *Jazz II*.

Meanwhile teenager Jarrod Fisher, still suffering pain in his jaw, was arriving on the surface and heading for *Jazz II*.

'Out of the water, mate. Quick,' Barton Painter motioned as soon as the boy pushed up his mask. 'We've got a missing diver.'

It was Fotheringham, at the rear of the *Spoilsport* sundeck, who first saw Singleton and Tina break the surface close to *Jazz II*. He had moved to the top deck to see how progress was going with the rescue divers and returned to the front of the vessel to begin recording details and times for the investigation that would follow.

'There! There! There!' he shouted to the tender.

Barnai heard the directions from Fotheringham.

'About 5, 6 metres off the stern.'

Later, Singleton was told that it had taken 92 seconds to get Tina to the surface. They emerged 2 or 3 minutes after Gabe Watson, close by, but closer to the right side of the wreck and the descent line. Fotheringham could still not make out the identity of the two divers who had just surfaced but right away it was obvious that one was in trouble. Singleton, having removed Tina's mask and regulator, began water assisted breathing.

Watching from the stern of *Jazz II*, Leanne England also saw Tina being brought to the surface. Jarrod Fisher, scrambling on board, saw them too, about 6 metres off the left side of the stern. Barton Painter jumped in to assist Singleton and pull them towards his vessel, but not before he radioed Docking on the *Spoilsport*.

'This is serious. We are going to need helicopter evacuation,' he said.

Haslet dropped Gabe at *Spoilsport* and, hearing yelling and shouting on the *Jazz II*, concluded that the missing diver had surfaced. This was confirmed by Docking, who told him Rebecca was fetching the oxygen.

Uzi Barnai began ripping off his equipment as soon as he saw Singleton surface with an unconscious diver. Lemsing dropped Barnai and, noting the experience of Barnai and Singleton as well as the crew on board the *Jazz II*, returned to the *Spoilsport*. As he approached Singleton, Barnai recognised Tina Watson. Reaching *Jazz II*, Painter, Singleton and Barnai grabbed the dead weight of Tina, her heavy BC and attached air tank, and dragged her clumsily over the edge of the rear diving platform. Wade pulled off his dive gear, quickly discarding it on the deck. Barnai had taught medical first aid when he was in the Israeli army and had been a scuba diving instructor for almost ten years. He and Alana McMahon both removed Tina's dive gear. While McMahon put the gear to one side, Barnai tilted Tina's head sideways, cleared the foam and blood from her mouth and immediately started mouth-to-mouth resuscitation. Now that she had a hard surface beneath her, Singleton began chest compressions. Tina was not breathing. She had no detectable pulse. Now her mask had been pulled off, her blue eyes were still open, unseeing.

By 10.55 a.m., few of the guests on board *Spoilsport* knew anything about the drama that was unfolding only 80 metres away. Ken Snyder, on the dive deck at the rear of *Spoilsport*, paused. He had contemplated a second dive before taking off his dive gear. Perhaps because he was a seasoned diver and qualified with one certificate beyond rescue diver status he began to sense that the rhythm of the day had changed. The crew members appeared to be talking more loudly than usual, striding around purposefully rather than at the steady pace of quiet professionalism. Instead of the usual idling speed, the tender roared away as though on urgent business towards *Jazz II*, which was moored at the other end of the *Yongala* site. Doug Milsap, at his equipment station next to Ken, saw some of the crew communicating on handheld radios. They were looking across from the starboard side of *Spoilsport*. It was clearly an emergency.

'Please move away from the side,' one of the crew members told him. 'There's been an accident.'

Ken had gone upstairs to the sundeck to get a better look. He heard radio communication about a diver in distress and saw Wade Singleton helping to put a body on the stern of the other boat. He had no idea who it was. He and Doug told a crew member that an emergency physician, John Downie, was on board. Snyder raced down the stairs again to get him. Doug then peered from the starboard side of the vessel and saw Gabe Watson, returning to the *Spoilsport* with Haslet. Gabe was on his knees, his vest ripped off and wetsuit pulled down to his waist in the tender, thumping the side of the inflatable as it approached the larger vessel.

'Oh my God, I've lost her. I don't know where she is. I couldn't find her. I don't know what happened.'

On the *Spoilsport* the news was out: Tina was missing. From then on, events sped up, overlapping each other in the confusion. Rebecca Hayllar, the hostess, had collected the first-aid kit from the wheelhouse and had run downstairs, giving it to one of the crew. Then, she rushed into the hallway past the cabins and into the crew rooms. Here, she grabbed the oxygen resuscitation gear and the DAN 02 kit from a cupboard and brought it all up to the dive deck. The cylinders were heavy. Haslet helped her to place them into the dinghy. Ken Snyder had found Dr John Downie, who stepped hastily into the tender.

Ken went on to the back deck and found Gabe standing there.

'My God. What happened?' Ken asked.

'We were into our dive – and at around 30 feet – Tina started to panic because she was over-weighted. I couldn't control her. She was too heavy and she started flailing. She knocked my mask and regulator off and by the time I'd got myself organised, she had descended 10 feet below me and was sinking. I had to make a split-second decision to help her or go and get help.'

Snyder eyeballed him.

'Bullshit, Gabe. That didn't happen.'

Gabe looked at him. He repeated what he had said, this time in more detail but it still sounded illogical to the 52-year-old who had been diving all over the world for years.

'Gabe, you need to think that through,' Snyder said. 'That didn't happen. Something happened but that didn't happen.' Snyder felt himself getting angry. Far from comforting the young man who stood before him, he became more and more irate. This diver had deserted his wife when he was only a couple of kicks away from saving her. Surely, what he was saying couldn't be true? Snyder didn't believe that Tina had panicked 7 minutes into a dive – it was the sort of thing that happened straightaway. But even more disturbing to Snyder was the fact that Gabe – clearly more than 1.9 metres in height compared to Tina's 1.67 metres – couldn't control her. If she had reached out and grabbed his mask, surely Gabe could have easily held her in check. He was a rescue diver and would have known how panicked divers behaved. Besides, even if she had knocked his mask and regulator off, it would have taken a few seconds to fix. To Snyder, the timing didn't fit with the way Gabe described how Tina had gone from a struggling, panicked diver to suddenly being obviously unconscious. And even then, why, if he saw her clearly in need of help, did he go to the surface? None of it made sense.

Doug Milsap had heard the raised voices, but he hadn't

heard exactly what Ken had said to Gabe. Ken stalked away, saying, 'Doug, you talk to Gabe, 'cos this doesn't make sense to me.'

'What happened?' Doug asked.

'We were into the dive, Doug,' Gabe said. 'All of a sudden, Tina panicked, went for my regulator, dislodged my regulator and mask. I got my regulator back in my mouth and cleared my mask. I grabbed hold of her BC and she was too heavy and I couldn't hold her up. I lost my grip and she started to sink.'

'Gabe, that's bullshit.' Doug, a veteran diver with thirty years' experience, unwittingly mirrored his mate's reaction. He, too, was a trained dive master and had completed his rescue certificate.

Gabe stared at him.

'Gabe, underwater, there's no sensation of weight. She couldn't have felt heavy.'

'I was trying to hold her up. I was kicking and she was too heavy. I was trying to hold her up and I lost my grip on her.'

'Gabe, that's bullshit. There is no sensation of weight underwater,' Doug Milsap repeated.

Snyder returned from his dive station, hearing his usually mild-mannered dentist friend also raising his voice.

'Doug, this is not the time,' he said. As angry as he was, he was aware, too, of the emergency resuscitation attempts on the other boat.

'Listen,' Paula Snyder heard her husband say to Gabe as she walked over from the other side of the deck. 'John is going to be there doing everything he can for Tina.'

Gabe, in the face of such a strong reaction to his tale, looked bewildered.

'Is there anything I can do for you?' she asked.

'I need a hug. I need a hug,' Gabe said.

Paula Snyder reached up to embrace this large man she barely knew and he hugged her back as though she was his own mother. She understood that need and patted the bench on the back deck, urging him to sit. He did, but not for long. Gabe was restless and left the dive deck. Paula left, too, following her husband. Ken and Doug had headed upstairs to the sundeck to get a better view of what was going on.

'Why isn't Gabe over there?' Doug asked the group. 'To be with her . . .'

CHAPTER 11

Ginger Milsap passed Dr John Downie as she went towards the stairs to the *Spoilsport* sundeck. She recognised him from drinks the previous night. He seemed to be in a hurry. After a few minutes some of the passengers began to gather on the top deck.

Ginger's husband, Doug, and Ken and Paula Snyder soon joined her, forming one sombre group. Ginger looked enquiringly at her husband.

'What's going on?'

'I told John . . . he should be on the other boat helping her,' Ken Snyder answered, moving his head in the direction of *Jazz II*. 'Gabe's just told Doug and me some story that doesn't make any sense about what happened when they left the drop line. He left her to go to the bottom while he came up for help.'

Ginger looked across to where Ken Snyder had gestured and saw another boat about 80 metres away. A body lay on the back deck and she could see two people performing resuscitation on it.

'Tina?' she gasped.

Doug Milsap nodded slowly. He put his arm out and she

147

moved next to him. Everyone looked across at the other vessel.

Ginger saw John Downie boarding it.

Imagine if that was Doug over there, Ginger was thinking – I'd be swimming across to get to him. They wouldn't be able to stop me. Where was Gabe?

Paula Snyder overheard one of the crew saying that it had been 19 minutes since they started resuscitation procedures. She turned to her husband.

'She's not alive, is she?'

'No, she's not,' Ken said soberly.

'Do you think Gabe knows this?'

'You'd better go and find him, honey, and see if he's okay.'

Paula Snyder went back down to the dive deck but couldn't find Gabe anywhere. So, she opened the door off the dive deck, which led into the cabins. Gabe was leaning against the wall in the hallway opposite cabin 9, which he and Tina had left only hours before. As soon as Gabe saw her, he began to cry. Paula could see right away that he appeared not to know that his wife could be dead.

He was still going through events.

'She panicked going down. She was too heavily weighted . . . She knocked off my mask and tried to grab my regulator. I tried to get her to inflate her BC shortly before she panicked.' His sentences ran one into the other as though he was addressing anyone who would listen. 'She was sinking. Her arms were outstretched upwards.'

In the tight fit of the hallway, Gabe raised his arms upwards. Paula Snyder imagined Tina, still conscious, floating halfway down to the seabed gasping for breath.

'She was looking up. I was looking into her eyes. She blinked. I just hoped that she didn't think I was leaving her there to die and she knew that I was going for help. I just had to make a split-second decision whether to stay and try and save her or go and get help and I decided to leave her and go and get help and come back.'

Paula shuddered. Tina may have panicked, but surely he had panicked more and left her there. Why? As soon as Gabe had turned and left her, Tina had no hope. He must have known that. Paula looked closely at the man in front of her. She hardly heard what he was saying. She did not know what to do. From what Ken had said, Tina was dead, but what was she going to tell Gabe?

John Downie, although only thirty-six, had extensive experience in emergency medicine. He had been practising medicine since he was twenty-five, completing his residency in paediatrics at the University of Rochester and finishing his critical care fellowship at Johns Hopkins University in Baltimore in 2000. Before joining the *Spoilsport*, he had been holidaying in Australia for two weeks.

Downie had been in the same tender as Tina and Gabe when they attempted their first dive. Like Snyder, Downie, too, had become aware of the increased urgency of activity on board the *Spoilsport*. After Gabe had got out of the tender, the doctor had brought Gabe a drink of water to calm him down. Downie, having been told that Tina had been found, had assumed she was okay, but when Ken Snyder approached him and asked for his assistance, Downie feared the worst. Rushing down the stairs to the dive deck and platform where Craig Haslet waited in the tender, he had called out: 'Has Tina got any medical conditions, Gabe, that I should know about?'

'No,' Gabe had said.

As soon as he was settled in the inflatable, Downie asked Haslet what was happening.

'They're doing CPR on Tina,' Haslet replied.

Downie asked Haslet what medical facilities there were available and later said that Haslet told him there was no defibrillator on board. Downie sighed, knowing this would be tough. After reaching *Jazz II*, he stepped off onto the duckboard, immediately approaching the body lying on the deck. Only 3 hours ago, he had greeted Tina at the breakfast table. She had no pulse. Her eyes were fixed and dilated, indicating a major problem with her brain stem. She had no heartbeat and wasn't breathing.

Downie inserted an oral airway, a piece of curved plastic that kept her tongue depressed and provided an open airway directly into her lungs. Then, he hooked the oxygen tubing up to the bag valve mask, or pocket mask, so he could bleed in more oxygen. This would give Tina a better chance of getting the oxygen – without the carbon dioxide produced by straight mouth-to-mouth resuscitation.

After he completed each action, Downie repeated what he had done out loud. Paul Crocombe stood behind the doctor awaiting directions.

'Go back to our boat,' he told Haslet. 'Get into my room – it's Berth 11 – and grab my epipen – it's in a toilet bag.'

Downie had an idea. It was a long shot but worth a try. In his toilet bag he had an epipen containing a measured dose of epinephrine, which is a powerful heart stimulant administered in a spring-loaded self-delivery 'pen' tip needle. He kept it for his own use because of serious food allergies. Ordinarily it would be injected into the thigh in a massive dose to break an allergy. But with little else on hand, Downie planned to administer it into Tina's jugular vein.

Haslet motored back to the *Spoilsport*, retrieved Downie's toilet bag, some spare medical grade oxygen and Rebecca

Hayllar, the hostess, and was back within minutes. Rebecca climbed on board and took up a position behind the doctor awaiting directions. She had been shocked when she saw the body. Rebecca had served Tina a glass of champagne the night before. A new bride, so happy and bubbly. She had even taken a photo of her with her new husband.

Downie was handed his epipen medication and attempted to open it to expose the needle so he could deliver the dose, but the spring mechanism forced the syringe. The medication was discharged pointlessly into the air.

Ship's master Gavin Docking was busy in the *Spoilsport* wheelhouse across from *Jazz II*, setting up communication with lookouts and tenders. He had made contact with Townsville General Hospital's Hyperbaric Unit. Amid the busy radio traffic between *Jazz II* and *Spoilsport*, those working on Tina advised that a helicopter was required for evacuation. He finally reached Dr Webb from Townsville General Hospital on the ship's phone and began a verbal report on what had happened.

'I'm afraid the helicopter is on a tasking and it'll be an hour before it can be re-tasked to your position,' Dr Webb told him.

'I'll put you in touch with one of our passengers, a Dr Downie, who is with the diver now. I can relay conversations between you,' Docking said.

Tina's new dive gear had been dumped on the duckboard at the back of *Jazz II*. Paul Crocombe was asked to check her air supply and to access her dive computer to get an accurate picture of how long she'd been underwater, to what depth she'd gone and how fast she had been brought up. This would assist in working out whether she may have developed an embolism from a rapid ascent or decompression illness more commonly known as the bends.

Without detaching it from its console, Crocombe turned Tina's Versa dive computer on and waited for the normal checks to complete. *Spoilsport* hostess Rebecca Hayllar took notes. Crocombe checked the pressure gauge to see how much air was in Tina's tank.

'Plenty of air left,' he said out loud.

Crocombe pressed the button again and the computer's dive log showed in the illuminated glow of the dial. Initial data indicated the history of the computer starting with a test dive going to a maximum depth of 197 feet [60 metres] during 16 minutes dive time. Crocombe thought that such a depth would surely not be part of a novice's dive history.

'Probably a test dive from the time of its manufacture,' Crocombe thought as he read out the numbers. He pressed again and the computer returned to the last dive it recorded.

'This is more like it.'

He nodded.

'Maximum depth 89 feet.'

A 10-minute dive time had registered and the flashing red indicator on the right-hand side of the screen revealed a rapid ascent, emphasised with the glowing words 'Too Fast'. On the left-hand side of the screen there was an identical colour-coded bar graph to that on the right-hand side, starting with green on the bottom, yellow in the middle and red on top. It was flashing, but not in the red zone. The flashing of between just two and three bars meant that Tina's nitrogen loading – the amount of nitrogen in her body – was still well and truly in the green, thought Crocombe. She was unlikely to be suffering from the bends.

So what was the problem?

Frustrated, Downie was sitting back on his heels, reluctant to make the call.

'I can't do anything more without further equipment like an IV access,' he said, looking helplessly at Painter.

'We've got one of those on the *Spoilsport*,' Barnai told him.

Neither Barnai nor Singleton had let up in their resuscitation efforts. Barnai had left Tina twice for only seconds at a time, while he washed away the foam from his face. In between the exhaustive process of trying to tilt her head and holding up the mask, the only change Barnai could see was that Tina's chest was slowly turning blue. Each time he tilted her head more foam came out of her mouth.

Craig Haslet and Rebecca Hayllar returned for one last time in the tender, bearing more medication from the ship's first-aid kit. Rebecca positioned herself as lookout on *Jazz II* to redirect all its divers to the *Spoilsport* tender.

Downie had set up an IV of 1 litre of normal saline and placed a 16-gauge IV catheter into Tina's right external jugular vein. He gave her a rapid intravenous dose of 500 ml of normal saline and two doses of epinephrine from an epipen. Even after the other half of the saline had gone into Tina, there was nothing to indicate any change, so Downie gave her another dose of epinephrine. He looked meaningfully at Barnai and Singleton. Nothing.

As a last resort he attempted needle decompression. He inserted a needle into both sides of her chest cavity to drain any potential air or gas that had escaped out of her lungs – but nothing came out.

On board the *Jazz II*, Docking's voice could be heard relaying his conversation with Dr Webb at the hyperbaric chamber. It was after 11.20 a.m.

'Dr Webb said you should cease CPR.'

They were the words Downie had been expecting to hear, but he continued, in spite of this advice, for more than 5 minutes.

No matter how hard he tried, Dr Stanley Stutz could think of nothing but the distressed diver during the 10 minutes of drills on the ocean floor for his advanced diving certificate. One of the divers swam down to pick up a weight belt from the sandy bottom and brought it back to the safety line. It was later confirmed it belonged to Wade Singleton, the man Stutz had seen rescuing the other diver. Stutz was surprised to find that the whole dive had only taken 38 minutes. It seemed that he had been down there a lot longer.

As he surfaced, Rob Webster immediately asked Stutz if he was a doctor.

'Yes,' Stutz said, fearing the worst. They swam back to *Jazz II*. Stutz handed up his flippers before climbing onto the duckboard and then up to the deck. Someone helped him with his tank and he handed over his mask. At the back of the boat on the port side, a group was standing around the stricken diver. He could see they were still performing chest compressions and someone was ventilating her with a pocket mask.

'What's going on?' he asked.

Downie introduced himself.

'She's been pulseless for about 40 minutes. Her pupils are fixed and dilated. She's had five rounds of epinephrine and two rounds of lidocaine. She's had IV access in her EJ [external jugular]. That line blew and she's had another line in her left EJ . . . Oh . . . and two needle decompressions.'

'Has she had any return of pulses?' Stutz asked, all the while looking into the same lifeless face of the girl he had seen far below.

'No.'

Stutz saw that the girl's skin was blue and mottled. There was vomit around her mouth. He could see where the vein had burst on the right side of her neck. Despite obviously aggressive efforts with the drugs and equipment available, the fact that she was not breathing by herself indicated brain injury. Her fixed and dilated pupils were a sign of severe neurological impairment, probably brain death.

Stutz began the perfunctory process of finding out what he had already known under the water, feeling the carotid artery in her neck and the femoral artery in her groin for any indication of circulation. He then stood up and addressed them all in a flat tone.

'She's gone and there's nothing more you can do.'

Forty-one minutes after they began resuscitation attempts, Stutz called the time of death: 11.27 a.m. Stutz helped another diver to move Tina out of view of the rest of the passengers on board *Spoilsport*. Someone gently placed a towel over her.

'Are you all right?' Stutz asked those nearest to him, knowing well how these emergency situations taxed those unaccustomed to them. He, himself, felt shaken.

Barton Painter ordered his crew to begin packing away the medical equipment. Wade Singleton stopped to check the level of air in Tina's tank: it contained 2000 psi, ample air for her to dive with. He also checked the air valve to see if it was open: it was. No problems there. He placed Tina's gear into the tender to take back to *Spoilsport*. Painter and Singleton went over to the *Spoilsport* on the same tender, where they went up to the bridge to meet the master of the vessel, Gavin Docking.

'Best to inform our passengers and crew what's happened,' Docking said. 'I've been in contact with the police on shore. We'll also have to wait for the Water Police and their instructions before we move the body and decide which vessel she will return on.'

Singleton took Tina's gear up to the wheelhouse. Later, another dive master handed him Gabe's computer and it was placed with Tina's gear. Then Singleton rang Craig Stephen, Mike Ball's operations manager, to give him an update. Painter then returned to his own vessel.

'We will need to prepare her for the arrival of her husband. That means making the main deck and the deceased as presentable as possible,' he told his crew as soon as he arrived back on *Jazz II*.

John and Tina Graves had returned to the *Spoilsport* and removed their BCs and wetsuits oblivious to the commotion that had gone on while they were under the water.

Tina decided to return to their cabin to rinse off, leaving her husband cleaning his camera. She was unprepared for the scene in front of her when she arrived at her cabin, number 13. Paula Snyder was standing close to Gabe Watson, opposite Tina and Gabe's cabin. Gabe was leaning against the Graves' cabin door. He looked distressed, but Tina noticed he was not crying. Paula, too, was quiet.

'Hey, is everything okay?' she asked.

'No,' Gabe replied. 'There's been an accident and they're working on Tina on the other boat.'

'Oh, my gosh,' Tina Graves said. 'Let me get you something to drink.'

She returned along the corridor and opened the door to the back deck. John Graves was still there unpacking from the dive.

'There's been an accident and they are working on Tina on the other boat,' she told him.

'What other boat?'

'I don't know.'

They had thought they were alone out in the middle of the ocean. Tina went over to the water cooler in the middle of the dive deck and poured two cups of water. Carrying the cups, she went to the port side of the *Spoilsport*, but dive equipment blocked her view. She could see a mooring line, however. She returned to the hallway.

'What happened?' she asked, handing Gabe a cup, not seeing Paula's hand motion that signalled: 'Don't ask'. Gabe, looking in her direction, spoke quietly.

'She grabbed my regulator. I got a mouthful of saltwater and I grabbed my regulator back and I pushed her away,' Gabe told her.

There was a long pause as the two women took stock of what he had said.

Gabe hung his head down.

'I can't believe I pushed her away.'

Tina could see the cups were empty.

'Let me get you some more water,' she said for want of something better to say.

She returned to the dive deck and the port side of the boat. This time she moved forward until she could see another boat. Tina's body had been covered with what looked like a blanket. Two people stood on the starboard side of the boat. One looked very upset with his hand to his head. As Tina

Graves returned to the cabins with refilled water cups, she passed her husband again.

'I think she died,' John Graves said. His wife nodded.

Gabe was still leaning against the Graves' door but was now crouched down on the floor, opposite the cabin he had shared with Tina.

He was speaking so quietly that she had to lean closer to hear him. 'I tried to hold her but she got so heavy I couldn't hold her up any more . . . She just slid out of my hands.'

'I'm so sorry,' Tina Graves said. Slowly she got up and unlocked her cabin door. 'If there is anything I can do, please let me know.'

Paula Snyder had been in the corridor with Gabe for about 20 minutes when Dr John Downie returned. After Tina Graves had entered her cabin, Ginger Milsap, Paula's best friend, had also joined them. As they were in the main corridor to the cabins, it was a busy thoroughfare. People came and went, which made conversation difficult, but no-one seemed to know where to go. Gabe kept repeating what he said over and over – as if to himself.

'She has her eyes open. And she is looking at me,' he said for the umpteenth time.

Paula was concerned. Gabe seemed to think that Tina was alive, but he still made no move to see or check on his wife. When John Downie appeared in the hallway with a serious expression on his face, both Ginger and Paula looked straight at Gabe.

'Tell me she's okay! Tell me you have good news,' he implored.

'I did everything I could to save her.'

'You're kidding, right? John?'

'No.' Paula Snyder thought he looked defeated.

'We worked on her for a long time, but we couldn't revive her.'

Gabe stumbled onto Downie's arm and Paula placed her arms around him. All three fell to the floor crying.

'Can you take me to her?' Gabe asked.

'Can you give me a moment?' Downie said wearily.

Wade Singleton appeared silently in the corridor.

'I'm very sorry, Gabe,' he said. 'I'm sure the doctor has told you we worked on her for a long time and everything that could have been done was done.'

Gabe nodded mutely, red-eyed.

'If you don't mind I need to call all the passengers to the saloon to advise them of the situation.'

Gabe nodded again.

'Do you want to come into your cabin?' Singleton suggested. 'You'll have a bit more privacy.'

Inside, Gabe sat on the bed and launched into another lengthy explanation of the events.

'We went down to about 45 feet [15 metres]. We'd started the dive along the wreck. At some point, Tina signalled that she wanted to turn around and head back. Her eyes were wide open. We turned around to start heading back and I grabbed her hand. She seemed to relax, but then she suddenly tried to grab my regulator from my mouth and to grab my mask. I couldn't tow her any more and I let her go. She sank to the bottom.'

'Yes, Gabe, we'll sort it out. All in good time,' Wade Singleton said, shattered by the morning's events. He was still seeing Tina's face before him when he shut his eyes.

'Dr Downie is taking me over to see her,' Gabe said.

'I'll come with you, if you like,' Wade said.

Uzi Barnai and Craig Haslet had done their best to clean

Tina up. When Gabe arrived, Alana McMahon on the *Jazz II* immediately offered her condolences.

Once on board *Jazz II* and confronted with the incontro-vertible proof that she was dead, Gabe Watson sobbed. He could see the mark on the right side of her neck where the IV line had been inserted. Bending over, he removed Tina's hair band from her hair, then sat beside her.

They had only been with Tina for a few minutes.

'I want to go back to the *Spoilsport*,' Gabe told Single-ton. Almost in tears himself, Singleton was plagued by the thought that he had failed to bring her back.

Inside her cabin, washing off the salt from the Coral Sea, Tina Graves could not stop thinking about what Gabe had said. In the cramped quarters of the corridor, she had been standing so close to him that there was no doubt in her mind about what she had heard: he'd said he had 'pushed' Tina away when she tried to reach his regulator.

One question kept reverberating in her mind. Like many of the Americans on board, Tina Graves had completed her rescue dive certificate. She knew that if Tina Watson had grabbed Gabe's main regulator because she needed air, Gabe could have used his safe second regulator, also known as an 'octopus'. Why didn't he breathe out of his octo?

'Why would you grab a regulator out of any panicked person's mouth? That's just not done,' Tina thought. In res-cue certification the training was to do the opposite – that's why divers had second regulators: to assist those in distress. Rescue divers were trained to deal with this. Gabe was a qualified rescue diver.

***

Craig Haslet remained on board the *Jazz II* to look after Tina's body and to keep in radio contact with the bridge at the *Spoilsport*. At 11.45 a.m. the Water Police gave permission to Gavin Docking for Tina to be moved back to *Spoilsport*, which meant that the passengers from the *Jazz II* could now return to their vessel. After Gabe Watson, John Downie and Wade Singleton left, Tina's body was placed in a body bag and taken over to *Spoilsport*, where it was laid on the top bunk in the air-conditioned cabin 14 on the starboard side of the vessel. Haslet collected all of the medical gear used in the emergency and stored it under the same bunk. Water Police orders were that no-one was to be allowed access to the cabin until police boarded the vessel in Townsville. Likewise, Tina's equipment was to be isolated and left as it was found. The rest of the passengers congregated in the saloon for Singleton's announcement.

Wade Singleton entered the saloon alone, bowed, looking older than his thirty-four years after the day's events.

'There's been an accident,' he said quietly. 'Despite lengthy efforts by staff and Dr John Downie, a fellow passenger from the *Spoilsport* and specialist in emergency medicine, and another doctor from the *Jazz II*, unfortunately, Tina Watson has passed away.'

Wade provided a short account of the details.

'We will be returning to Townsville with Tina's body . . . You will be able to continue with your dive trip if you wish, or cut short your holiday. That will be up to you. We will have a further meeting as we get closer to Townsville.'

Up until Wade Singleton's announcement, some passengers had been unaware that Tina had died. Dawn Asano, seated on her husband's lap due to the shortage of seating, gasped at the finality of Wade Singleton's words. The exuberant bride who at breakfast had shared her wedding day tips with Jacqueline Sherman; the girl who had seemed so confident in the tender before they all rolled off backwards only hours before. It was incomprehensible. She had seen Wade Singleton's rapid ascent with Tina, but up until he spoke, she had somehow thought it would be okay. Her husband gave her a sympathetic squeeze.

'I want everyone to stay in the saloon for the next little while as Tina's body is brought on board. We'll be heading back to Townsville shortly,' he said. 'We'll have lunch soon.'

People started to look at one another, then around the room to see if Gabe was there but no-one could see him.

'Now be mindful that there might be reporters when we get to Townsville,' Singleton continued. 'We've had to notify the police, of course. Somehow, the media seems to find out about bad news very quickly. Please, we need you to stay on the boat because the police will want to speak to everyone on board and take statements.'

Lou Johnstone accompanied Gabe Watson back to his cabin. She sat on the single bed thinking that, having signed up as a volunteer, the day had dished up some peculiar duties. Gabe restlessly paced the small room, clearly distressed. Johnstone had worked in child protection, and made a decision not to question him about what had happened. She would let him decide when to speak and what to say.

'I can't believe it,' he began, walking back and forth.

He clearly wanted to talk, stopping in front of their luggage on the bed and grabbing an object. At one point, Johnstone didn't know where to look as he fondled one of

Tina's bras, seeming to have forgotten her presence. Tina was only a year older than Lou. She felt uncomfortable, an intruder on his grief.

The honeymoon suitcases, lying next to her on the spare bunk, were a stark reminder to Johnstone of the excitement and noise of the passengers boarding the previous evening. She remembered Gabe and Tina smiling with the other passengers as they came off the boarding ramp to be greeted by the assembled crew.

Johnstone sat quietly as Gabe told her how he was a trained rescue diver, how he'd talked Tina into diving, how they'd met at UAB and how they'd just bought a house before they got married. Finally, he stopped pacing and sat down on the double bed. His voice had become more measured and controlled.

'Do you mind if I tell you what happened?' he asked her suddenly. 'I need to talk about it.'

'Of course not,' she said gently.

'I think I'll feel better if I tell you what happened,' he said.

'That's fine.'

'We hadn't descended far – we weren't that far from the surface when Tina . . . Tina grabbed my regulator and I grabbed it back. She then grabbed my mask and pulled it and it . . . it flooded with water. By the time I cleared my mask of water . . . I had to let her go and by the time I cleared it, I couldn't see her.'

'What happened then?'

'I came up right away to raise the alarm on the surface yelling: "I've lost my wife. I can't find my wife."'

Lou knew that a rescue diver should know how to deal with a panicked diver. If they grab your regulator – that's the most likely event – you keep blowing bubbles and get your alternative air source. God, she was thinking as she looked at Gabe, that's crazy.

'What am I going to do? What's going to happen to my life? What . . . I just got married.'

Later, she pondered the obvious gaps in his story. He hadn't said why Tina had panicked. He didn't say he had reached out to touch her, nor did he say he had tried to help her at all. For that matter, he didn't mention whether he had panicked either. He didn't mention any obstacle that prevented him from going after her. The basic steps to help anyone in Tina's situation had been ignored. Besides, even while still in the cabin, listening to him, she was struck by how calm he was. Not everyone was emotional, she reasoned. And she wasn't a psychologist, even though her job prepared her for traumatic situations. But she felt that there was something odd about his reaction. That feeling stayed with her.

In professional listening mode, she uttered soothing words when needed.

'You've got to take it one day at a time,' she said.

By the time she left, Gabe had settled into what she could only describe later as 'a strange calm'.

In the quiet of her cabin, in the early hours of the following morning, Lou began her diary entry for 22 October 2003: 'I feel sick about the thought of this day's conclusion. The girl that died on the *Yongala* today was nearly the same age as me. It's such a waste of a life. The scariest thing is that it could have been me . . . I'm unsure about Gabe. I sat with him for an hour and he made me very uneasy. He seemed agitated, then just came over so calm. I didn't feel threatened or anything, but I just don't believe a guy could push his newlywed wife away, especially as a bloody rescue diver. Why didn't he help her?'

***

As the *Spoilsport* motored through the waves and early afternoon sunshine on the way back to Townsville, Ken Snyder and Doug Milsap had the first of many conversations about what Gabe had told them.

'Wade said she had her regulator in when he found her, air in her tank and her BC was not inflated,' said Ken, relating details from Singleton's announcement. 'How's that possible? Why on earth is she dead then?'

'Look,' said Doug, leaning forward in his wicker chair in the saloon, 'Gabe could have done far more than he did. All right, if she had an integrated dive belt, there's no time to fish all that out and dump it, but he could have leaned over and inflated her BC himself. Then all he has to do is go up quick but make it as controlled as possible by venting the BC all the way to the top so they both don't become ballistic missiles.'

Doug shook his head, trying to clear the murky, illogical picture in his mind.

Snyder nodded. 'The fact that he said that she panicked and knocked his mask off, you certainly don't need a mask to scuba dive in that situation. That's not a priority in . . . an emergency situation, to me at least . . .'

Doug interjected: 'But it might be to someone who hasn't done more than 500 dives like you . . . Putting your regulator in your mouth is a priority and if she panicked, he certainly was significantly larger than her and – this was going through my mind as he was speaking – that in a panic situation, had it been my partner, I would have grabbed the panicked diver and given them the thumbs-up sign: "We're going up." Most of the time a panicked diver will calm down, you know, when you just tell them: "We're going up." '

Ken thought of Tina telling him proudly outside the Quarterdeck the previous night that she had just been certified in the spring. The girl who had said she was a War

Eagle, an Auburn University fan, when they'd talked college football.

He could see her smiling at him. 'I've already done eleven dives, and there'll be more to add from this trip,' she'd said.

'Oh my gosh, aren't they cute,' Paula had remarked.

But, still he niggled away at it. He and Doug. Two old friends who shared a passion for their sport.

'It was only two fin kicks down to her, if he was only 10 feet [3 metres] above,' Ken said. 'Why didn't he stay with her? She had no hope after that. She was his buddy – and his new wife, for Chrissakes.'

Doug winced, recalling Ginger's reaction and how, despite her more than twenty years of diving experience, she had rounded on him, accusing him of lacking compassion for a grieving young man who'd just lost his wife in such tragic circumstances – and on their honeymoon.

'You know very well how panic kills divers,' Ginger had said. 'They were such a lovely young couple. And Gabe is just devastated. How can you talk about something not being right at a time like this?' she'd blazed. 'It's a terrible, terrible accident and we need to give him support and solace, not accusations.'

Doug well understood his wife's mothering instincts, but his was a more analytical approach. He probed for smaller details. There was too much that didn't add up. A panicked diver who didn't struggle? Tina could not have been conscious if she was sinking – that's if what Gabe had said was right.

When is the only time that you abandon a buddy?

When they're dead, a voice in his head whispered back.

'Yeah,' rejoined Ken, breaking his friend's reverie, squinting through the window. 'There's something he's not telling, all right.'

Tina's death left a gloomy pall over the boat. Only the night before, it had contained the buzz of passengers excited about a seven-day diving adventure. Her death was a reminder of the potentially dangerous activity they were engaged in. Snyder thought of Tina lying somewhere on the boat – cold and wet, in a body bag. This morning her whole life had been ahead of her. Now, her destination was the morgue.

CHAPTER 12

Gabe Watson stood in front of the assembled guests, his head bowed. They had gathered again in the air-conditioned saloon, the second time in as many hours. Wade Singleton had promised to provide more details on what to expect when they docked, but there was more. Gabe, he had told them, had an announcement to make.

The guests either sat in the wicker chairs or the fixed bench seats adjacent to the dining tables.

Gabe seemed to be searching for words.

'I want to thank those people who have been supportive of me in the past hours,' he said. 'As you know . . .' Gabe paused. 'As you know my wife died today.' Everyone waited. 'This just really sucks.'

Some of the guests looked at each other, perplexed. Tina Graves glanced over at her husband and those nearest her: 'I can't believe he just said that.'

After Gabe's departure, the conversations in the saloon continued. Ken Snyder and Doug Milsap were niggling away again.

'Panicked divers never calm down,' said Ken. 'And they don't sink. Their one aim is to go up – not down.'

'I would never have left Ginger in that scenario,' said Milsap. 'None of it makes sense. None of it, Ken. Someone is lying.'

Snyder looked back from the window, where he'd been watching the white caps on the waves.

'Look, there's no indication of foul play here,' Doug reasoned. 'It seems to be a tragic accident. But there has to be a better reason for what happened than what we've got so far. Gabe said that she was sinking underwater. You and I both know that any rational person would have put air in the BC to raise her. Either Tina herself, or Gabe, should have put air in her buoyancy compensator.'

It was a no-brainer. They both knew it. Dropping weights was optional. Inflating the BC was not.

'Now,' said Doug, 'if that air was on, she would have been able to . . . fill up her BC.'

They debated the merits of her not having air. That raised further points. Could she have been so over-weighted that inflating her BC had little or no effect? Or, was her air not getting through for some reason?

Doug continued: 'Wade tells us that when he found her on the bottom the regulator was in her mouth and air was in her tank and functioning. All right. Now, the only way she could not have been able to put air in her BC was if the air was off on the bottom of the ocean. But Wade found her with air on there.'

'Someone would have got her computer and downloaded the dive profile by now,' Ken said. 'We'll find out later how long they were down or if it happened straightaway.'

'You know, I still think somebody's lying here,' Doug surmised. 'Either . . . she went into the water with no air on and she sank directly to the bottom of the ocean . . . [or] the air was *not* on when they found her on the bottom of the ocean, or the air was turned off during the dive and then turned back on. That's the only way she could have had no air to put in her BC.'

Ken Snyder stared. His jetlag and the glaring sunlight outside made it all seem surreal. But here they were – going back to Townsville, no more dives that day, a girl dead, and her new husband telling them at least three versions of events that barely made sense. He pushed back his chair.

'I'm going to try and lie down . . . But I think you're right, Doug. At this point, either Wade is wrong or Gabe is wrong. If it turns out she was diving normally for only a few minutes, and that'll be clear from the computer log, then Wade is not wrong and Gabe has more explaining to do.'

The *Spoilsport* chef, Steve Wells, had been in the galley during the morning's dramatic activities. He had helped Rebecca Hayllar to bring the Oxy-Viva kit to the back deck, but his more pressing job had been to prepare meals. He, too, thought that when they brought Tina to the surface there was hope for her. Around the time the guests began coming back, he was preparing coffee. He was surprised when Gabe Watson appeared at the bar in front of the galley and began to tell Steve what had happened. Steve nodded, at a loss for what to say.

Later both of the Graves noticed Gabe on the back deck with John Downie.

'She seemed really agitated and she had a strange look on her face,' Gabe was telling him. 'Then she panicked. She was thrashing about and pulled my mask and regulator off.'

'It might have been hypoxia – a lack of oxygen . . . that causes that kind of behaviour after a very short time.'

'Oh,' Gabe said.

'We did all we could to save her, that's for sure,' Downie said, giving him a hug.

As the *Spoilsport* neared the end of its 3-hour trip back to Townsville, Tina Graves was amazed to see Gabe in the saloon with two other passengers. A card game was in progress.

'That's extremely inappropriate, John,' Tina Graves said to her husband. 'Don't you think?'

John nodded slowly.

By 3 p.m., Dawn Asano and Gary Stempler were sitting at one of the long tables in the saloon area reviewing Gary's on-the-job photographic prowess with his new camera. They peered at the small screen, flicking through the shots of Singleton's general dive briefing that morning, which had included the detailed chalkboard drawing of the *Yongala*. Stempler pressed the forward display button to view the shots of butterfly fish and coral, but he was a bit disappointed in some. He realised he needed to get the knack of the timing, the strobe light and adjusting the settings in only moderate visibility. There weren't many in the sequence of more than twenty photos that he would keep, he decided. He had a nicely framed close-up of Dawn to show everyone at home. He was sure he had taken one with Dawn and Wade Singleton when they'd finally started the drift after getting close to their orientation depth plateau of 25 metres next to the wreck. But all he had captured once he pressed the shutter was Dawn half-turning as she looked for Wade and checked what depth they'd reached. This random shot of people, instead of fish, was actually one of the best in terms of exposure, quality and lighting.

On the second run through the photos, Dawn saw something in the background of the shot.

'What's that?' she said, pointing to something blurry that couldn't be made out on the small screen.

'Was that a coral formation?'

'Don't know,' said Stempler as he zoomed in on the spot in the picture.

Dawn breathed in quickly. Gary stared.

'Oh my God,' she cried out. 'She's there. It's Tina.'

'I think you're right,' he said.

In the photo, Tina lay well beyond the wreck, pinned down by the weight of her dive tank, one arm still reaching upwards. Gary remembered he'd been within 3 metres of the *Yongala* and around the 22-metre mark, sheltered from the current by the wreck, when he'd taken the shot. Tina was at least 6 to 8 metres out from him, so about 9 metres away from the *Yongala* itself.

It all fitted with what Singleton had briefed them about a few hours earlier. When he pressed the shutter Singleton was right next to Dawn, but in that moment of the shutter opening and shutting, Singleton had dived deeper, with powerful kicks from his fins, to carry him to the ocean floor.

'Look,' he said to Dawn, pointing at Singleton's blue and black fins disappearing over her right shoulder. 'That proves he went to assist her. I wonder if the police will need this picture?'

Wade Singleton's incident report would be sent to the headquarters of Mike Ball Dive Expeditions in Cairns as well as the Queensland Department of Workplace Health and Safety. Amid his fragmented afternoon under ordinary blue skies that included briefings, calls from police and liaising with Gabe Watson, passengers, the skipper and other crew, Singleton used the ship's log – where all pertinent information and times about any dive expedition was entered – to guide him in his report. Snowed under, he merely copied what had been entered earlier on the log in blue ink by Brian Fotheringham reporting on the conditions after the 7 a.m. set-up. Fotheringham had written that the current was 'strong'. The *Yongala* dive was known for its currents that ebbed and flowed, often changing within the hour. The issue of the currents was to play an important part in what was to come.

Shortly before docking at Townsville around 5 p.m., Wade Singleton tapped Paula Snyder on the shoulder while they were in the saloon.

'Gabe has asked if you would be his support person at the police station tonight. Would you mind?'

Paula was startled. It was one thing to give this poor man a hug and comfort, but quite another to get involved in what he might tell the police. She hesitated.

'But I don't even know what that means, or what it involves.'

'Just someone to be with him, I think,' Singleton replied. 'Just . . . you know, provide him with some emotional support. He's all alone now and it might help him. You were there at a crucial time earlier and he probably feels comfortable with you.'

'Well, okay,' Paula replied.

As they approached the busy port, the sun was sliding towards the west over Townsville. It was around 5.15 p.m. The *Spoilsport* motored into the harbour between the gap in the manmade loose stone breakwater, into the shallow channel in front of Jupiters Casino where the other yachts congregated in the marina. Two crew members jumped onto the berth and began to tie up the vessel. Three other men stood waiting on the wharf. Two were in police uniform: Senior Constable Glenn Lawrence, the lead investigator, and Senior Constable Paul Campbell, both from the Townsville Water Police. The third man was Leon Thomas, a Workplace Health and Safety inspector. The men introduced themselves to the ship's master, Gavin Docking, then addressed the crew and passengers in the main saloon area. They needed information on all of their dives, the equipment they used and safety measures in place that day. Other uniformed police officers also began to arrive to take photographs and assist with the onboard investigation.

Lawrence asked Docking to supply him with a passenger manifest and crew list and requested that everyone on board separate into two groups: those who had witnessed anything or had any involvement in the incident, and those who had no involvement. The passengers and crew were quiet. Gradually, the passengers were taken to the Townsville Police Station for the lengthy procedure of obtaining statements. The crew would come later.

Senior Constable Campbell went through a commercial and fishing vessel in-service checklist relating to manuals and safety equipment. He physically checked that each item was locatable and in good working order. Docking then handed over the ship's log, operations manuals, dive operation manuals – everything that related to the operation of the vessel as well as the diving operation. He also provided full sets of Gabe and Tina's dive equipment, including their dive logs and personal dive paperwork. It was all placed in the Townsville Police Station's property office. Campbell issued receipts for everything.

A couple of TV crews and a newspaper photographer from the local newspaper, the *Townsville Bulletin*, were on the dock as Singleton had predicted. The official police activity on the back deck in the fading evening light provided them with plenty of footage and photos for the next day's news.

Gabe was wandering around the boat, not doing much. Senior Constable Lawrence had been with the Water Police for the past two years and had an advanced open-water dive certificate. After being introduced by one of the crew members, he spoke with Gabe briefly on the dive deck. Formal questions would be asked later, but Lawrence wanted a précis of events so he could coordinate the relevant investigators and specialists who would form part of this investigation into a death at sea.

'Can I ask you what happened?'

Gabe appeared cold to Lawrence as he gave a brief sequence of events. The police officer put it down to shock. Lawrence made notes in his notebook, improvised from an old alphabetic address book. He had to keep moving. It was part of his role to uncover any quality-assurance problem and to find out whether all procedures and regulations had been put in place by the master and crew and that all equipment used was of the correct standard.

Lawrence and Leon Thomas, the safety inspector, combed the boat looking for systemic problems. Lawrence went across the saloon and into the wheelhouse to interview Gavin Docking and collect statements from the crew, and then was taken to cabin 14 where the body bag was unzipped for his inspection. Tina was still wearing her two-piece black wetsuit, black dive boots and bikini. A blue towel was wrapped around her head. Lawrence saw right away that there was significant swelling on her face and neck as well as dark bruises on both sides of her neck. A small amount of blood was in and around her mouth and nose. Photographs were taken by a female constable. A uniformed police constable then brought Gabe into the cabin to formally identify Tina. Lawrence rang general duties police to arrange for Tina's body to be collected as soon as possible by Morleys Funerals, the government undertakers, and taken to the Townsville Hospital morgue.

He returned to the wheelhouse and the dive deck where the police photographer was taking pictures of Tina's dive equipment.

By this time, Lawrence was satisfied that all possible measures to prevent any incident had been undertaken by the master as well as the company. The crew members, including the volunteers, were all suitably qualified and experienced and interacted well with one another. The overall operations of the venture, he concluded, were successful.

Gavin Docking had been unable to say what had caused Tina's death. Thorough safety briefings had been conducted and all dive equipment and associated systems had been operating normally. The vessel itself was clean and tidy. Equipment was stored appropriately and in good condition with the exception of the expected wear and tear of dive equipment. Docking presented a CD to the police of Gary Stempler's photographs, including the one of Tina lying on the bottom of the ocean.

Lawrence was impressed by the fact that the documentation was produced as soon as he asked for it. It corroborated everything he had been told by the crew about safeguards and briefings. His initial conclusion was that there were no suspicious circumstances.

By the time this had all been done, the sun was slipping behind the craggy citadel, Castle Hill.

***

Craig Stephen, a no-nonsense Scotsman from Edinburgh in his thirties, was the company's operations manager. After receiving the news about a fatality on board the company's vessel, Stephen immediately searched for the earliest flight from Cairns, where the company was based, to Townsville. He and Stan Kielbaska, the company's general manager, touched down in Townsville on a Skytrans Airlines flight the afternoon of Tina's death and arrived at the dock at about 5.45 p.m. After meeting with Docking and the crew, and receiving the all-clear from police, the company decided to continue with the expedition the next day. Even though Mike Ball had offered to reimburse the passengers for the trip if they opted to leave, everyone had decided to stay. For most of them, abandoning ship was not an option as they had come from so far away.

The only passenger who departed the *Spoilsport* that evening was Gabe Watson.

Townsville Police Station is a flat-roofed affair with two sets of steel grilles lining the front of the building. It sits at the northern end of the mall on the corner of Sturt and Stanley streets, one of the main thoroughfares in town.

The thirteen *Jazz II* passengers and crew, who arrived in Townsville ahead of those from the *Spoilsport*, were first to be interviewed beginning at around 4 p.m. About thirteen officers, the majority of them Criminal Investigation Branch (CIB) detectives but also Water Police officers, crime scene police and general duties officers employed to transport Tina's body to the mortuary, were called in to take statements from among the fifty passengers and crew on board both vessels. Detective Sergeant Gary Campbell, a shrewd man with close-cropped grey hair and a quiet no-nonsense attitude, was working for the Break and Enter Squad when he got the call to provide as many police as he could spare. Carloads of the *Spoilsport*'s passengers were transported from the Quarterdeck marina to the Townsville CIB during the evening.

As the officers came and went, Gabe Watson sat on a sofa with Paula Snyder in the reception area waiting to be called.

'We had so much fun at the wedding,' he told her. 'Tina had all her close friends as bridesmaids. She looked so beautiful. I even serenaded her with a Hank Williams song that she liked.'

Gabe went on to describe the church and the reception and then the long flight to Australia.

'We did everything she wanted to do, we saw *A Midsummer Night's Dream*. We went to the Opera House and Darling Harbour, and it was awesome. We saw sharks and crocodiles and sea wasps and Tina even saw Dory and Nemo at the Sydney Aquarium . . . We caught a ferry to the zoo – you get off at the wharf and catch an aerial gondola to the entrance because the hill down to the water is real steep . . . Tina had the first week of the honeymoon to do what she wanted. Then it was my turn on the second week . . . This week . . .'

He trailed off.

'I'm scared to death of telling her family. I don't know how I am going to tell them.' Gabe was running from one issue to the next, thinking out loud. 'Tommy, her dad, travels a lot and I don't want to call and tell her mom without Tommy being there.'

'You need to call somebody,' Paula Snyder said firmly. 'You should call your parents.'

'I'll call them later. I don't want to wake them up.'

'You need to call somebody. You need to call your parents,' she repeated, concerned not for the first time by the amount of responsibility she had unwittingly inherited.

'Your parents can give you guidance,' she added. 'You probably don't need me any more. You don't need me from here.'

Gabe looked alarmed.

'No, I need you here. I would like you to stay with me.'

To Paula he seemed defenceless. She imagined what it would be like if it were one of her own children and decided, then, to stay.

Detective Senior Constable Kevin Gehringer arrived from the CIB and ushered Gabe and Paula into a room.

Sitting in front of a computer, Gehringer began filling in the Queensland Police Service Statement of Witness form and typing in Gabe's answers, which were recorded on four C90 cassette tapes. The interview began at 6.30 p.m. Gabe was cooperative, Paula thought, answering all questions put to him immediately and thoroughly. He outlined what happened after they boarded the *Spoilsport* leading up to the fatal dive.

After aborting the first dive because, he told police, the battery in his computer was in backwards, Gabe then told the officers that he and Tina took off their equipment and their tanks were refilled.

They were back in the water within 10 minutes, he said. 'Tina went down the anchor rope first with myself following.' He said they were not descending fast, and left the rope to head out over the wreck at about 15 metres. They could barely see the divers on the drop line.

'We were around the 45 feet mark [14 metres] or something like that,' Gabe said. 'We swam out. I don't know – if I had to guess – I'd say maybe 30 yards [27 metres], I don't think it was that far. That would be the farthest away we were. And we were right over the top of it and the current was coming over pretty good, so that's when Tina motioned to me to go back up. We started to swim back and I noticed she was going down a little bit so I grabbed her hand and started pulling her back . . . towards the anchor line. Uh . . . and I think we were still at the same height, I mean the same depth . . . I was pulling her and at some point, she went and she quit swimming with me . . . It was like she just panicked or something . . . so I let go and turned towards her to try to see what I could do and motioned to her . . . like she grabbed her inflator hose on her BC. I grabbed mine to motion to her to put some air in it . . . I thought that's maybe what's . . . what the problem was. She squeezed the hose, but I don't think she'd get . . . I don't think she put any air into her BC. I don't know if she hit the wrong button . . . or . . . you know . . . who knows? Um, that's when I guess . . . realised something was going on so I grabbed hold of the strap on her BC. And I kept swimming back towards the anchor line. Pretty much floated back to where we started from. At this time, when I held on, she wasn't swimming, she was just kind of back there . . . I was the only one doing the kicking.' There was a long silence apart from the sound of Gehringer typing. Gabe coughed, sounding upset. Gehringer advised him to take his time.

'We were pulling hard and she reached up and you know . . . she knocked my mask off. I don't know if she was reaching for my regulator. That was my first thought. She was reaching for my regulator instead like she had lost hers. When she did it . . . I don't know if it was me or her . . . one of us knocked my regulator out, so I grabbed my mask. I still had enough air in my lungs to clear my mask – and I got it back on, but when I did that, I had to let go of her . . . so I grabbed my safe second and I was breathing off that, and I turned around to see what was going on and the next thing I noticed, she was down below me . . . so I started swimming down to see if I could grab a hold of . . . grab her hand or grab whatever and . . . um . . . um . . . that's when I realised, you know, that I don't think there's anything I could do . . . I just realised . . . so I swam back over to the anchor rope and I don't know, I don't know how shallow it was, probably somewhere around 20 feet [6 metres] or so when I got to the rope. I saw some people that were hanging on. I thought they were from my boat so I was tapping on and pointing in her direction just to see if somebody saw some bubbles. I had no way to tell them what I needed.'

It was then he had gone to the surface, he said, and 'started yelling'.

Gehringer went through the dive insurance and asked Gabe some general questions about Tina and her dive experience. He was with Tina, Gabe said, when she collected her newly purchased dive gear. She was an average swimmer. Gabe said he had been on dives with Tina while she was doing her class and also about 'four or five' times after she was certified, all of them at Blue Water.

'Tina would always get a little nervous before diving but once she was in she was okay,' her new husband insisted. 'I have not known her to have panicked in the water before.'

Asked whether he had done routine dive buddy checks such as checking Tina's air, he said they had each checked their own.

After the statement was completed, Senior Constable Gehringer organised for Gabe to call his parents from the Townsville Juvenile Aid Bureau Office.

'I'll leave you alone to speak with your parents,' Paula said, relieved.

'No, stay with me,' Gabe insisted. This was the only phone call he had made that day. It was 7 a.m. in Birmingham.

'Hello, Dad? You sitting down? Hey Dad, Tina's gone. We went for a dive. Tina didn't make it . . . Dad I'm not kidding. I'm not kidding. Can you call her dad's cell phone and tell him what happened?'

Paula Snyder then heard Gabe talking to his mother.

'Hey, Mom. I tried to help her. I went up too fast and it bothered my ears and disorientated me. My ears are really hurting. I am really in pain. I am really in pain . . . need to go to the hospital.'

Paula was perplexed. This was the first time she had heard Gabe mention any problem with his ears.

Dr Downie was one of the passengers who was still at the police station. Before leaving he looked briefly into Gabe's ears and said: 'I can't see any problem. I am not saying that you don't have a problem. It's not my expertise, but if you continue to have a problem, go to a hospital or an ear specialist.'

After Gabe Watson's statement was complete, he and Paula returned to the reception area. There Gabe approached the counter and spoke with Senior Constable Paul Campbell, who had been responsible for seizing the diving equipment for examination.

'I'd like the dive computers returned to me,' Gabe said.

'I'm afraid we will need to keep them for testing.'

'They're worth a lot of money. I want to know when I'll be gettin' them back,' Gabe raised his voice.

'Senior Constable Lawrence, in charge of the investigation, will let you know when you can have them back, when he returns,' Campbell said.

'I want to know when I can have them back.' Gabe was getting louder.

'I don't know how long. You will be contacted and told when you can have them back.'

'I want a receipt for these belongings,' Gabe shouted.

'You already have one,' Campbell said. 'The dive computers, along with all your other equipment, [are] on another receipt altogether. I gave it to you when you arrived.'

'I don't have a receipt. I don't know what you're talking about. I want these computers,' Gabe yelled, beginning to shuffle through his wallet, which he threw onto the counter.

To calm Gabe down, Campbell pulled out a pocket-sized Field Property Receipt book and began writing out a duplicate receipt.

The *Spoilsport* was due to leave again in the early morning. The *Jazz II* was also leaving with a different load of passengers the next day. The police needed to collect the information while the eyewitness recall was fresh, which proved stressful for some of the tired, shocked, jetlagged and overwhelmed witnesses to the dramatic events of the day.

Ken Snyder's statement had been taken by a young female constable. Her questions, he believed, left no room for providing any sort of detail or sequence to events. In his opinion, the questions were very general and jumped around in time. He did not know what police considered important or irrelevant in a situation he found so foreign himself. Nothing was mentioned about his heated retort to Gabe earlier in the day after he came back on board *Spoilsport*.

Doug Milsap had also been waiting for hours to give his statement. Finally, a precious computer was free. He took his seat opposite a young plain-clothed female constable.

'Your full name and date of birth please, sir?'

He found the sound of her slow tapping out of his response, with not much more than two fingers, excruciating. He rubbed his hands against his roughened chin and up over his eyes. He was exhausted. After such a dreadful day, he was feeling every one of his fifty-three years. She needed facts about the day: times, equipment, diving briefings and what he actually saw. She asked what seemed to be random questions, then typed his responses.

'Could you please read over this statement,' she eventually said, returning from the printer and handing him the statement, 'and tell me if you want something included or deleted, and if not, please sign at the bottom.'

Doug scanned several sheets of paper, but the words swam on the page. The constable hadn't asked if anything unusual had happened, nor had he been asked his opinion about Tina's death.

'What could you say about such a terrible accident?' he thought. He signed the statement and rose wearily for the short drive back to the *Spoilsport*. There was nothing in his statement about him shouting at Gabe, nor the reasons why he had been so angry.

Around midnight Dawn Asano and Gary Stempler were finally collected from the *Spoilsport* by a female officer who drove them to the police station to give their statements. For some crew members it was even later. It was well after 1 a.m. when Lou Johnstone began her statement. By then it was so late that every time she tried to give more than a general answer to a question the exhausted young officer, Glenn Lawrence, asked her, she didn't seem to have time to finish. She didn't even talk about her conversation with Gabe in his cabin, which she felt was important. Nor were some of the other exchanges Gabe had with passengers on board *Spoilsport*, such as those with Doug Milsap and Ken Snyder, recorded in police statements. Some passengers and other divers were not interviewed at all, including Tina Graves and dive instructor Rob Webster. Their accounts would not be followed up until much later.

CHAPTER 13

In 2003, the Holiday Inn towered above every building in Townsville, before a development craze led to other apartment blocks competing for the horizon. Still a major landmark in the city today, the Holiday Inn, known to locals as 'the Sugar Shaker' because of its shape, was the Mike Ball company's designated hotel and the place where guests on *Spoilsport* tended to leave their luggage while away diving.

Earlier, during one of the breaks in the lengthy interview process, Gabe had said to Paula: 'I want to stay back on the boat tonight. I don't have anywhere to stay tonight. Do you think they would let me stay on the boat?'

Paula had thought this request was strange, but replied: 'I will go and ask Wade and see what he has to say.'

She'd found Singleton in the police station and relayed Gabe's request.

'Well, I'll ask somebody, but I think we are going to head back out and I don't think that will be possible,' Singleton had answered. Gabe spent the first night without his wife at the designated company hotel.

It was after midnight by the time Gabe Watson arrived at the hotel with Mike Ball's operations manager, Craig

186

Stephen, and general manager, Stan Kielbaska, who he had met earlier while on *Spoilsport*.

Paula hugged Gabe goodbye with a mixture of relief and sadness. She and Steve Wells, the *Spoilsport* chef who had also been providing a statement to police, then continued in the taxi for the short trip back to the *Spoilsport*.

In the bar on the first floor, the three men – strangers until that evening – congregated for drinks.

'What will you do?' Craig said in his lilting Scottish accent.

'Well, I've rung my parents from the police station and . . .'

'Look, I'll stay with you tonight in the same room if you like,' Craig said quickly.

Gabe shrugged.

Stephen had booked room 1511 on the fifteenth floor with views out across the Ross River. Almost immediately, the TV was switched on and they sat on the comfortable armchairs to watch Rugby World Cup replays.

'This was going on during our honeymoon,' Gabe told Craig. 'In Sydney. We caught one of the games at a pub there. Pretty much every channel on the TV had rugby going on in Sydney.'

Craig, settling into one of the other armchairs, nodded. He was there for moral support and to look after his company's interests. If this fellow wanted to talk, that was fine with him. He intended to take notes of any conversation they might have.

As the night moved towards dawn, the phone rang a few times. Stephen also heard Gabe make a few calls: one to his mother, who, it seemed, was en route to Australia, and one to his preacher. Gabe was still dressed in his khaki shorts and polo T-shirt.

To Stephen, Gabe appeared upset, but he didn't cry.

Later, with the TV humming in the background, Gabe slowly began to talk.

'She was below me. I turned around and showed her how to inflate her BC. Then I continued to swim upwards towards the drop line at a 45-degree angle.'

'Did she still feel negative – as in sinking?' Stephen asked.

'No. We could both still see the drop line at that point. Then, she was no longer swimming. I turned around again and this was when she knocked my mask off and pulled my regulator out. I had to let her go. I cleared my own mask and put my safe second in my mouth. By then, I looked down and she was falling backwards. Her eyes were wide open and her arms extended up and she did not appear to be moving.'

'Were there any bubbles?'

'No. I don't think so, but I'm not sure . . . I started swimming towards her and I felt this terrible pressure in my ears. I couldn't equalise . . . I didn't know what to do . . . I was worried that if I went to the bottom, I wouldn't be able to bring her to the surface, so I thought I'd better go up to get help. If she was on the bottom and couldn't move, somebody could help her up off the bottom.'

'So have you dived in currents before? I mean the *Yongala* is a dive with lots of currents.'

'Yeah. I dived in Cozumel – that's in Mexico – and that was strong. It was difficult to stop and look at things.'

Before long Stephen fell asleep. Gabe's face flickered in the light from the TV as the Rugby World Cup replays continued. Eventually, he fell asleep, too. The noise from the TV soothed him. He could not face turning out the light.

The next morning, Craig Stephen joined Stan Kielbaska in the dining room for breakfast; Gabe said he was going to stay in the room and shower. There, alone, under the jets of warm water, he broke down sobbing for 15 minutes, succumbing to the events of the day before. It was final. She wasn't coming back. It wasn't a dream. He sensed her presence so strongly. What was he going to tell her parents? He couldn't imagine what he was going to say. His father would at least break the news; he had said he would.

He looked at his watch. Back home it was dinnertime the night before. In Bluff Park, the tight-knit community where he had grown up, news was spreading fast. He walked out of the shower in his robe into the kitchen, waiting for something to happen, but he couldn't bring himself to pick up the phone to ring the Thomases. It sat silent, accusing, on the bedside table. Out of the window, the Ross River shone in the early morning light. The suburbs of Townsville were waking up to another ordinary day. Gabe Watson's day was anything but ordinary. After breakfast, Craig Stephen gave Gabe the name and number of a counsellor from Relationships Australia. The company had used her before. Her name was Candia Bruce.

On the *Spoilsport*, heading back to sea, Lou Johnstone continued her diary from where she had left off in the early hours of the morning: 'Everyone's gone back out to sea, except Gabe. It's weird to be going back out to enjoy the diving after such a sad day but life (+business) goes on I guess. I can't imagine what it must be like for Tina's family.'

At 8.36 a.m. US time on 22 October, Tommy Thomas's phone rang. It was almost 12 hours after Tina's death. Tommy was in Tallahassee, Florida, on business. It was Gabe's father, David Watson.

'Tommy, are you still at the hotel or the office?' David Watson asked.

'I'm at the office,' Tommy replied. 'Why?'

'Are you alone or are people around?'

'Well, there's people around, but I can talk.'

'I don't know any other way to say this, but there's been an accident and Tina has drowned . . . Here's my preacher.' David Watson handed over the phone.

'Is there anything I can do for you?' a male voice, Tommy later learned belonged to Craig Greer, said.

Tommy fell to his knees. Later, he was only able to recall that he had asked for the news to be kept quiet until he could get home to Cindy and Alanda. He wanted to be the one to tell them.

'I'll do my best,' Greer said.

Tommy rushed to his motel to get his clothes and pack, before heading to the airport. He presumed, at that stage, that Tina had only just died.

Meanwhile, Alanda arrived at Parisian at 9 a.m., her usual start time. At first she thought she was imagining it, but then she realised that everyone *was* looking at her strangely. Someone finally came up to her and took her to the store manager, Caesar Lamonaca, who told her that her sister had been in an accident and that she should call her parents.

Alanda began to cry hysterically.

'Tina. I want Tina,' she screamed.

At the airport, Tommy rang David Watson but got his voicemail. The preacher rang Tommy back instead. When Tommy asked how Tina had died, Greer said all he knew was that she had drowned. He also told Tommy the news was getting around.

Tommy breathed quickly. He knew Alanda was going to work. He tried to ring her at home, but there was no answer. Then he tried to ring her at work but the phone was continually busy. Just as he was about to board the plane, his mobile phone rang.

'What happened to Tina?' Alanda asked right away, crying.

'How do you know?'

'I got to work and everyone already knew.'

Tommy told her as much as he knew.

'Don't leave work alone. I want someone to go with you. Put me on to Caesar.'

Just as the doors of the plane were closing, he spoke to Alanda's boss and insisted that someone drive Alanda home.

After landing at Atlanta to change planes, Tommy had two messages. One was from a friend who already knew about Tina's death. The other was from Alanda. When he rang her back, she had surprising news. She had spoken to Gabe's mother, Glenda Watson, who was already packing to fly to Australia. Glenda had arranged her ticket and visa and was waiting for Gabe's father to take her to the airport. Glenda had repeated to Alanda that she knew nothing except it was an accident and that Tina had drowned. Tommy wondered how Glenda Watson had managed to organise everything so quickly if Tina had just died.

He and Alanda then agreed that Alanda would be the one to tell Cindy – at least it was better than her finding out some other way.

As soon as Tommy got back to Birmingham, he rang Alanda. She was at Seattle Slew Drive with her workmate Kelli and Kelli's parents. She told him she'd gone upstairs and woken her mother to tell her that Tina was gone.

When Tommy spoke to Cindy she was hysterical.

'What happened? What happened to Tina?'

But Tommy had no answers for her. Cindy refused to

believe the news. Thirty minutes later, at 2 p.m., Tommy arrived home.

Alanda rang Amanda Phillips, Tina's best friend. Amanda called her husband immediately and left work traumatised. For Amanda, it was like losing another member of her own family. Alanda tracked down the police in Townsville, unable to settle to anything and more and more disturbed about the lack of information, even confirmation of the events. They confirmed the worst: Tina was dead. Alanda was provided with Senior Constable Glenn Lawrence's name and contact details.

During the afternoon, Tommy made several calls to David Watson, at home and work as well as on his mobile number, leaving messages each time. He did not reply.

One of Tommy's friends contacted the US Consulate in Sydney. Around 5.30 p.m., a woman rang from the consulate and Tommy explained that he was desperately trying to obtain information about his daughter who had died in a diving accident.

The woman rang back an hour later and said she had Gabe on the line. Cindy, Alanda and Tommy each picked up one of the phone handsets. It was after 6.30 p.m. and growing dark outside when they went down to the basement, Tina's old bedroom, so they could all hear the conversation.

'Gabe? Is that you? Are you okay?' Cindy asked.

'Yes, I'm okay,' he said.

'Are you sure you're okay? Are you hurt?'

'No . . . no, I'm fine . . . Well, I've got an earache, and it hurts.'

'Gabe, what happened to Tina?'

'Do you want to know what happened?' Gabe asked.

'I want to know exactly what happened. Tina is our daughter. We need to know everything.'

Gabe explained there were two people in the room from the dive company.

'Give me a moment. I'm going to ask them to leave.'

They heard him telling them to leave, explaining he had Tina's parents on the line. They heard the door shut.

'Do you want to know everything that happened?'

'Yes, yes Gabe,' Cindy and Tommy spoke together. 'She's our daughter. Of course, we want to know.'

Tommy was exasperated.

'Well . . .' Gabe spoke quickly. 'We were on our first dive at the *Yongala* wreck site. We'd gone in the water. We were down about 40 feet [12 metres], I guess, but I'm not the best judge of distance. We were swimming along. Tina tugged at me and she gave me the thumbs-up signal. That's the signal to go to the surface. I took her hand and started swimming back towards the anchor rope – which I guess – again I'm not good at judging – but might have been about 40 feet [12 metres] away. We made it halfway and then . . . she was sinking below me . . . At that point, I stopped, spun her around, then went down in front of her to maintain eye contact. I looked at her and blinked and she blinked back. Then I squeezed my BC as a signal for her to tell me she was getting air. She squeezed her BC back and let me know she was getting air.'

'And then . . . ?'

'Well, I was about to go back to the anchor rope when she just reached out and knocked my mask loose. It filled up with water. I had to let go of her then to clear my mask, which I did and got it back in place. I looked for her and she was about 10 feet [3 metres] below me. So I started to go down after her, but she was falling faster than I could go down. She had her arms stretched up towards me and I could see her eyes. She was looking at me. She was falling so fast I had to make a decision whether to go up for help or go after her. I thought it was better to go to the surface and I went up ripping my gear off on the way and when I broke the surface, I realised that I'd come up at the wrong boat. So I began swimming towards the *Spoilsport*, our boat, screaming for help. Then two divers went into the water to get her.'

'At least Tina knew you were going for help,' Cindy said through her tears.

'Did you hold her and talk to her when they were trying to revive her?' she asked gently.

'Yes, I did.'

'Gabe, I'm so sorry for you,' Tommy said.

'Me too,' Alanda said. 'It must have been awful.'

'If you need anything at all – anything at all, make sure you call us,' Tommy said.

'Yes, I will, sir.'

'Do you know what's happening with the police and everything?'

'No, they haven't told me what's happening.'

'Just keep us informed. And can you please bring Tina home as soon as you can?' Tommy asked.

'I will,' Gabe said.

'Well, Gabe, we love you,' Cindy said. 'We're so very, very sorry.'

Once off the phone and back upstairs in the lounge room, Tommy relayed the conversation with Gabe to Alanda's friend Kelli and their next-door neighbours, Mike and Kim Brashier, who had called in for support. Kelli was a scuba diver.

'That just doesn't sound right,' she said straightaway.

***

Craig Stephen and Stan Kielbaska bid Gabe goodbye in the potted-palm-and-cane foyer of the Holiday Inn. Gabe went upstairs to his room where he spoke to his mother, who was in transit. As he hung up from the call, the TV news was on. A banner ran across the bottom of the screen proclaiming that an American diver had died. It was only a matter of time, he thought, before the news reports would reach the United States.

Gabe's old friend Craig Youngblood rang. He had heard about Tina's death.

'So what happened?' Youngblood asked, concerned.

Gabe briefly outlined the events of the previous day: how Tina had ripped off his mask and that he'd had an earache and was in quite a bit of pain; he had raised the alarm; at first he hadn't panicked because he thought they were doing CPR and that Tina would be okay.

At about 1 p.m. reception rang to say Candia Bruce was in the foyer. She told him she was here for a 1-hour counselling session. Gabe began explaining yet again the events of the day before.

'Well, I'm here to help prepare you as much as I can for the emotional landslide you'll be going on,' Candia said. 'This is day one.'

It was Wednesday afternoon. His mother wouldn't be there until Friday.

That evening, Candia Bruce returned to the hotel on her way home from work. She was doing this on her own time, she told Gabe, but she knew he shouldn't be left alone that night.

'It'd look a bit odd if I stayed, so I've called my husband Greg, and he'll stay the night with you.'

'Thanks,' Gabe said.

Candia and Greg took Gabe to dinner. That night, the ocean was calm and there was a light breeze, so they chose to sit at a table outside. Gabe, normally reserved, sitting here with perfect strangers, the day after Tina died, felt surreal. At first, he said nothing, but the Bruces gradually won him over with their friendly approach as they told him about their life. After dinner, they strolled down to the beach and along The Strand, walking along a pier which had a cabana at the end of it. When they'd reached it, Gabe leant against the railing and gazed out to sea. Nothing was familiar.

Back at the hotel, Candia dropped off Gabe and Greg, telling Gabe she would take him to a lawyer in the morning to get a next of kin affidavit filled out. That night played out much the same as the previous night. Greg was a stocky man who looked to Gabe like a rugby player. The Rugby World Cup was still on. One channel showed continuous replays of the day's games. It was a typical bloke's evening: not much conversation but comforting nonetheless. At least he wasn't alone. Greg didn't ask much and Gabe didn't say much. At some point, Gabe flicked the remote on the TV to mute so Greg could get some sleep. He couldn't bear to turn it off and face the dark. It was in the dark that Tina's face would appear everywhere.

Senior Constable Lawrence was checking his handwritten notes jotted down in the old address book. They were in no particular order. Over the frenetic few days after *Spoilsport* docked he had scribbled wherever he could find space. There were a few things that puzzled him. In his notes, he had placed an asterisk next to where he had written about the day of Tina's death: 'Bart (the skipper on *Jazz II*) stated no person (divers) mentioned anything to him about being approached by another diver whilst on the shot line.'

Lawrence had a list of all the divers on the descent line and had begun working through the gruelling task of collating all the evidence. He'd noted that Tina had finished sinus decongestion pills on 15 October, and the dates she and Gabe had arrived in Townsville as well as the wedding date. He had also written a note stating: 'Husband ringing 501's parents. Ring Craig to confirm.' 501 was a Queensland police radio code for a sudden death.

At 9 a.m. on 23 October, before many of Tina's friends knew of her death, someone called 'Jason' posted an entry on an online scuba forum website.

Sad day: We lost a beautiful friend who died on Mike Ball Spoil Sport [sic] . . .
Jason – Not certified/Retail
October 23, 2003 at 09:00:57
Please forgive my ignorance on the subject of diving. I am not a diver and have no interest in it. My reason for visiting this site is that I just lost a very dear friend today. She drowned while on a diving trip aboard the Spoil Sport [sic]. *All I know is that she was certified and had done numerous freshwater and at least a couple saltwater dives. She may have done more . . . I am not sure. My question is this . . . how safe is Mike Ball's diving trips and are they any more dangerous than other diving charters? This is a sad day to many people who lost a beautiful friend in such a tragic manner. Thank you.*

At noon the same day, Australian time, at the Townsville Hospital the post-mortem examination had begun. Senior

Constable Lawrence attended the autopsy as the police officer who had identified the body. Tina was marked autopsy number TN03J201. Lawrence continued his handwritten notes, writing down the findings from Professor David Williams, the consultant forensic pathologist, who spoke aloud as he examined Tina's body. Her neck had swollen to almost twice its normal size because of the frantic attempts to resuscitate her; her lower legs showed abrasions; and the whites of her eyes were congested. There were no obvious congenital abnormalities of the heart or any other illness, such as deep vein thrombosis. A CT scan had been conducted 22 hours after her death. Gas had been present in all four chambers of her heart and in the arteries of the arms, but it was difficult to work out whether, like the abrasions and neck swelling, this had been part of the resuscitation efforts and the extended period spent on CPR.

'This 26-year-old female demonstrated no evidence of any significant natural disease,' Professor Williams wrote later in his report. 'There was florid evidence of air embolism, but this appeared to be a complication of her rescue.'

Lawrence had written in his notes: 'Nil evidence of foul play. Nil suspicious injuries.'

At 2.30 p.m. he rang police media who were awaiting the results of the post-mortem examination. He organised someone at the undertakers to liaise with Tina's father. Both Tina and Gabe, he noted, were insured.

That morning, a small story appeared in the local newspaper, the *Townsville Bulletin*:

The Spoil Sport [sic] *last night docked at the Quarterdeck where the woman's body was removed and taken to Townsville Hospital.*

Detectives last night interviewed 50 people – all of the passengers and crew – from the dive boat.

198

Police communications coordinator Sergeant Nick Sellars said there were no suspicious circumstances with the death and a report would be prepared by Water Police for the Coroner.

At 11 a.m. on Friday, 24 October, Glenda Watson landed at Townsville airport jetlagged but anxious to see her son.

Gabe was at the hotel with Candia Bruce. Glenda didn't cry as she thought that would upset him and he seemed to want to stay strong for her.

That same day, Senior Constable Lawrence organised a viewing at the mortuary for them. The mortuary was part of the hospital, but had a separate entrance.

Detective Kevin Gehringer was there, as was Marika Vanderklugt from the Forensic Pathologist's Office. They met the Watsons in the waiting room.

'What happened at the post-mortem?' Gabe immediately asked the mortuary attendant.

'Well . . .' she hesitated. 'A possible cause of death is an embolism. If it was an embolism, it could have been pre- or post-mortem.'

'Oh, really? So there's no way to know if . . . ?'

'No, but we haven't got the official report yet.'

'At some point, before we went down, she knocked my mask off,' Gabe said. 'Whatever happened, happened before she hit my mask.'

Marika was used to traumatised relatives who just needed to talk. Gabe went on to talk about his and Tina's regulators.

'We had 'em both set where you wouldn't have to suck much,' he said.

'I see.'

There was silence.

'I hope whatever happened, happened fast,' he added.

Still Marika did not venture an opinion.

Gabe approached Gehringer. Senior Constable Lawrence stood nearby.

'I'd like to clear up a couple of things, especially since I read something in the newspaper about the currents on the day,' he said.

'Okay,' Gehringer replied. 'What about you come in on Monday?'

'Sure.'

Gabe looked at his mother, who nodded.

The viewing room in the mortuary was beyond the small reception area. It was impersonal, the sort of room where no-one lingered long. It contained some seats and a large viewing window with curtains drawn. Gabe's mother left her son and stayed in the waiting area with Gehringer. Lawrence accompanied Gabe but stood respectfully out of sight, just outside the viewing room.

Gabe slowly approached the window. Lawrence heard Gabe speaking even though he couldn't see him. Gabe was clearly addressing Tina. He waited until Gabe and his mother left the mortuary a short while later before he wrote down what he had overheard Gabe say:

'I am so sorry.'
'I never meant to hurt you.'
'I shouldn't have kept taking you down.'
'I'm sorry. I couldn't stop it.'

Each point was written in his notebook on a separate line in his backward-sloping handwriting. Senior Constable Lawrence wasn't quite sure what to do with these notes. Gabe's words to his dead wife didn't sound terribly significant.

Besides, he had other things to follow up: clarifying statements from Han Gyu Kim, who had been diving on *Jazz II* and had seen a female diver – face-up with eyes open and blood coming, he thought, from her nose. And there was a diver called Stutz who had said he'd seen two divers together, who inexplicably split apart before one sank to the bottom. Lawrence wrote a big question mark in the margin next to a précis of Stutz's comments.

There seemed to be a muddle of conflicting reports.

Gabe and Glenda visited Tina at the morgue several times before her body was transferred to Morleys Funerals at The Lakes, 4 kilometres from the city centre. Through Morleys Gabe selected a coffin and organised for Tina's body to be transferred. Morleys also obtained the death certificate and registered the death with the Registrar General's Department on Gabe's behalf. Gabe had provided one of the funeral directors with the phone numbers for the Divers Alert Network, Old Republic Insurance, and his private health insurance company, Blue Cross.

The following day, Saturday, 25 October, Gabe, accompanied by his mother, visited Dr Kerry Gillespie, a local Townsville GP across the road from the Holiday Inn. Mindful that Gabe's departure date was five days away, Glenda Watson was concerned about her son's ears. Dr Gillespie examined Gabe's ears but found nothing wrong except a slight redness on his eardrums. She did not recommend treatment, believing the problem would resolve itself.

Over the next few days, Gabe and his mother did some sightseeing around Townsville. Candia Bruce decided on a whim to take the week off work to chauffeur Gabe and Glenda around. They visited the aquarium around from

The Strand, where Glenda bought a book called *Top Dive Sites of Australia*. The section on the *Yongala* described the currents on the dive.

Among the many friends who tried, usually at night, to call from Birmingham, Gabe heard from his old roommate, Jeff Bradford, who asked what happened. Gabe went into further explanation as to why Tina had died. This time, he blamed the conditions: 'You know, Jeff,' he explained, knowing Jeff had recently been certified, 'had they said . . . "Gabe, go down, check out the dive, come back and let us know what you think," . . . there's no way I would've let any beginner do it. *I* probably wouldn't have done it.'

Gabe emailed Craig Youngblood and asked him to pass on a message to friends about what had happened on the dive and how it was affecting him. His old school and diving buddy Mike Moore also rang.

The next few days at Seattle Slew Drive passed in a haze. Alanda kept playing a message on her answering machine that Tina had left the day after her wedding, asking if Alanda knew where her debit card was.

The Thomases had heard no news about when Tina's body was coming back to Birmingham. Tommy had not received a call from Gabe or his father. Craig Greer and his wife, Suzie, also a minister, visited up until the day of Tina's funeral, which was planned for 5 November.

On Sunday, 26 October, David Watson finally called in with the Greers.

'I'm sorry I didn't return the calls and haven't been to see you before this,' he said as soon as he walked in the front door. 'I've been a bit uncomfortable about your loss. I didn't really know what to say.'

After a cup of coffee, Tommy said: 'I'd like to pay for Tina's funeral and I'd like to go to the funeral home and start making some of the arrangements if that's okay?'

'I'd like to get four plots,' Cindy said. 'One each for Tina and Gabe – if he wants to be beside Tina – and one for Tommy and me.'

'Well, that's up to Gabe,' David said.

There was silence.

'How are Gabe and Glenda going?'

'Oh, they're going fine . . . as could be expected. I'm in regular contact with them.'

'That's good . . . Well, we'd just like to know what's going on and to be kept in contact,' Tommy said.

David Watson left after reassuring the Thomases he would keep in touch and let them know what was going on.

CHAPTER 14

The interview room was bare, but to introduce cheeriness the grey walls were offset with modern colours: a yellow door, blue L-shaped desk and maroon chairs. Gabe Watson's official record of interview didn't begin until 5.21 p.m. on 27 October. A clock was on the wall. As the videotape rolled, the time was also logged on the screen. Time, in any police procedure, is always of the essence. The interview would take two hours and twenty minutes. Gabe and Glenda Watson sat at one end of the desk. Glenda, in a blue cardigan, her hair dyed a golden brown, sat on Gabe's left, her sympathetic noises, interjections of 'sweetie' and the occasional tut-tuts scattered throughout the lengthy interview. Occasionally, she would lean over to rub between her son's shoulder blades, her face turned towards the desk. Gabe, seemingly oblivious to this show of affection, was dressed in a pale grey T-shirt with his alma mater, UAB, emblazoned across the front. His yellow cap with a green visor sat upturned on the table in front of him next to his sunglasses. Lawrence was on the other end of the desk writing notes, his forehead resting on one hand as he wrote. Gehringer, looking every bit the professional detective in white shirt, dark suit and tie, had Gabe's first statement in his hand. He leafed through it, apparently relaxed but all the time watching the witness carefully. Gehringer began asking questions. Avoiding eye contact with both officers, Gabe alternately slumped forward, with his head in his left hand, or placed both elbows on the table. Sometimes, when he became animated, he waved his arms to emphasise his account. His words were disjointed, punctuated frequently with 'you know'. Many sentences trailed off, incomplete.

He wanted to tell the police he had miscalculated the distance that he and Tina had been away from the anchor rope. Instead of the '30 yards' (27 metres) he had mentioned, he said it should be '25 to 30 feet' – or 7 to 9 metres. 'We had the anchor rope in sight,' he said.

Gehringer admitted that he was not a diver, suggesting that Gabe provide as much detail as he could to describe what happened. Gabe continued to venture more ideas, almost immediately bringing up what was to become a recurring theme in the interview: the current.

'I had to write this down, so that I'd be able to remember . . .' he explained. 'I do know that from what we were told of the current . . .'

'Mmm,' Gehringer said.

'. . . and how the current was . . . we were not told to prepare for how the current truly was . . . from . . . the type of diving that we're used to . . . [it] would not have been considered a drift dive. It would've been considered, you know, pretty much [a] severe current and you know, like I said I . . . we still don't know, we don't know what physical thing happened with her . . .'

Gehringer asked why Gabe had concerns about the newspaper account he had mentioned at the morgue.

'Yeah well that, that's what brought this up about the

current was because . . . one of the people from Mike Ball said "conditions were near perfect" . . . and, you know, I don't . . . feel that it was "near perfect" . . .

'You know when we go out in the Gulf, most of the time, there's just there's no current and I've gone on some down there where they've said there's a pretty big current and it was, you know, not even a third . . . as strong as that one was.'

'Mmm,' Gehringer said. The current hadn't been mentioned as an issue relating to Tina's death when Gabe's first statement had been taken.

'Yeah . . . I guess at first I was . . . afraid they were going to come out and say stuff about her. You know saying she was an idiot or she had no idea what she was doing 'cause . . . you know, she did but just kind of at the tail end [of the newspaper article] he [the person quoted from Mike Ball] said "we don't feel that it's diver related because it was near perfect diving conditions".'

Gabe said it was those words that had 'set me off' and that 'maybe the medical thing' could have happened at that time 'no matter where we were but I think because of that struggle, you know, against the current caused, you know, whatever to happen just to happen . . . we may never know but I just had to get that off my chest . . . would hate myself if I left not saying what I think I need to be said.'

He described the first aborted dive and how his dive computer started beeping before he and Tina even got to the drop line, how he had gone down a few feet and it kept beeping 'gas alarm' so he put it back behind his head next to the transmitter on his tank to see if it wasn't getting a signal [about the air pressure]. When it kept beeping he had ascended and gone with Tina back to the *Spoilsport*.

His immediate thought, he said, was that his battery in

the receiver was wrong or dead, so Uzi had found him a coin to help get the battery out and he had pulled it out, swapped it around and put it back on.

'After the tank fill was done I screwed the transponder back on [the tank] and turned my air back on, held my computer next to it and it showed the pressure . . .

'I, you know, casually told Uzi . . . "Here's your quarter . . . don't tell anybody but I had my battery in backwards," ah, so, you know, that problem was solved . . .'

Gehringer asked him if he'd put a battery in wrongly before.

'Yeah,' Gabe replied, '. . . the computer goes in one way, the . . . transponder goes in the other way and I changed both the batteries before I left and I basically just stuck them in . . . 'cause there's really no way at home other than turn on the computer. I turned on the computer and it worked so, you know, I didn't think anything else of it but you know I mean I have done it before.'

Asked if he had done any 'buddy checks' Gabe said: 'I did her [BC] strap across the front and pulled it tight.' He said they had gone through some hand signals but: 'I guess we didn't go through an official buddy check.'

The original plan, Gabe said, was to swim across the top of the wreck, look at the turtles, try and find the 'Nemo fish' they were told were there and go up the other shot line at the stern to the surface.

'. . . the reason when the problems happened that we didn't keep going with the current was 'cause we couldn't see the other end . . . and that was one of the things I was saying about the misconception about the visibility . . . had we been able to see a significant amount of the wreck to know where we were going, chances are I probably would've gotten her, and we would've gone quickly to the other side . . . but you know something I'd never been on, didn't know anything about the dive . . . you couldn't see that far of a distance so I thought you know well . . . we may start swimming the wrong way and then we have no idea of where we are and that's the reason . . . when we got in the current that we turned to go back to the anchor rope, 'cause we . . . had a focal point, we knew, you know, where to go . . .'

He began outlining the events of the day, saying that Tina had gone in front of him and that he moved out of the way of her bubbles.

'Basically, we got right to the top of the wreck and we decided before . . . we went on our dive that . . . since we're gonna be there all day, the first time we dove it we would just go across the top . . . check everything . . . there are plenty of other dives later on to go down to the bottom and all that so, yeah we went down and I remember I reached down and tapped her on the shoulder and kind of, you know, motioned out and, ah, we floated out and she was on my left, I was on the right . . .'

Around 20 feet (about 6 metres) from the rope, he said, was when they had both realised the current was a lot stronger than they felt 'comfortable diving in'. Tina had thumbed a signal to go back to the anchor rope and he had held her left hand in his right hand. It was then that she seemed to be falling behind and was dropping down and was almost vertical. He had pointed to his BC inflator button and indicated for her to squeeze hers like he was with his.

'She squeezed, I know she squeezed it; whether she squeezed it hard enough or didn't squeeze the right thing, or, it wasn't working, I don't, I don't know.'

He had gone down, he said, and realised she was

frightened. He grabbed the left side of her BC, pulled her towards him, then turned and started swimming back to the anchor rope.

'I didn't look at my computer any more. At that point I was just getting her back and I thought, well, her BC didn't inflate so we obviously can't ascend to the surface, so we were swimming back to the anchor rope and I . . . thoughts were going through my head were – I'm gonna get her . . . back to the anchor rope and she can either pull herself up it, or she can hold it until I can go get somebody, um, you know, I even thought . . . I still had my clamp on my BC that I use, you know, when I would go spear fishing . . . I can clamp that to her BC, the other to the rope and she can't drift off.'

It was then that he noticed other divers on the anchor rope and he ventured that they may have thought they saw something unusual. He said: '. . . I know at that point I was breathing hard. I could feel the heat on my face just from being hot, so I know I was probably blowing bubbles all over the place. I was thinking these people are going to see us, or at least see something odd's going on.

'At some point, you know, obviously before we got there, ah, her hand hit my mask, um, it knocked my mask sideways so, ah, I had to . . . let go, ah, let go and kind of turn back so that I would have some, you know, that I would have some space 'cause at that point I didn't have a mask, didn't know if she was still flailing . . . ah, didn't know what she was doing, so I let go and I remember I kind of, I don't know if, I, I think I may of kicked with my fins back, you know, to give myself a little bit of space . . .' He said he was 'scared as hell' as he couldn't find his mask and he knew Tina was in trouble.

He said then that he had cleared his mask. On reaching

for his regulator to breathe, he realised it wasn't there, so he had grabbed hold of his 'safe second'.

'Grabbed it and I remember the thought going through my head as I put it in my mouth, you know, I had no air so I knew I wasn't going to be able to breathe and I hit the button to push the air in and I remember thinking if I hit the wrong button you know, um, it's probably too late for me also . . .'

Hitting the right button, he got some air, then turned around and saw that Tina was 'going down'.

'I don't know if she was still kicking or not, ah, but she was looking up – had both her arms out, you know, reached, stretched up almost like looking at me, reaching her arms up to grab.' Gabe raised his arms above his head, his fingers splayed, to demonstrate how her arms had reached up to him. There was silence in the room. 'So I kind of, ah, I upended myself, you know, head first, um, and I remember going down, you know, reaching . . .'

He continued: 'At this point I was thinking, you know, I'm gonna grab a hold of her, I'm gonna yank off either her weights or, you know, just do whatever I could and I'd even thought at this point if I could grab a hold of her I'm just gonna fill my vest up, grab a hold, let it pull both of us up to the top or whatever, ah, and . . . she was . . . out of arm's reach . . .

'Just from me inverting myself, you know, I couldn't grab her hand 'cause she was, you know, maybe 5 feet [1.5 metres] below me or something like that, I don't really know . . .

'I went down, started kicking down and I was kicking down, but as fast as I was kicking down to go get her, um, she was . . . going down just as fast and, ah, I just remember, I mean it's . . . it still shocks me now . . . how clear some of the stuff, some of the thoughts were going through my head, but I just remember thinking, ah, you know, I can chase her down to the bottom, get down to the bottom and either . . . dump her weights, let her . . . dump everything, let her rocket to the top 'cause at that point I knew something's going on.

'And I thought, well . . . hell, you know, busted lung, or whatever's better than what in my mind I was thinking was [going] to happen and . . . I just knew I wasn't going to catch her.'

She fell, he said, 'like that statue in Europe – both hands up . . . it worried me that she was wondering why I was leaving. I made eye contact with her. I don't know if she was even still with us at this point. But I saw her eyeballs. I saw her eyes when she was going down.'

'Do you think she was alive at this stage?' Gehringer asked.

'Yes,' Gabe replied.

Gehringer asked: 'You never saw an indication that she needed air?'

'Right. Right,' Gabe answered.

Asked if rescuing someone was part of what he had learned during his rescue training, Gabe replied: '. . . most of the training I've had is taking care of yourself, there was nothing as far as taking care of somebody else . . .'

Knowing the ocean floor was around 30 metres down and that he could still see the hull of the *Yongala*, he guessed they were still at around 15 metres. Going to the bottom would prove problematic, he decided. If Tina was unconscious, other than dumping her equipment, he didn't know what else he could do. He had considered, as he was halfway down, that if he went all the way down he couldn't come back up quickly because of the depth. So he had turned, swimming back to the anchor rope where he saw another diver.

'I probably never swam so fast in my life 'cause it just seemed like from the time she went down to the time that I realised I couldn't . . . get to her that I was at the anchor rope and you know 5 or 10 seconds and then could've been longer, I don't know but it, you know, it just, I know I was moving.'

When he reached the drop line, where some divers were descending, he remembered shouting through his regulator – 'Tina, Tina, Tina, tapping 'em, I know the guy turned around and looked at me, and I was pointing, you know, where she went down thinking, you know, if it's people from my boat, maybe they'll make out that I said "Tina", and if they're not, maybe they'll realise I'm pointing, and I'm distressed, and maybe, you know, they can get a visual 'cause I didn't know if people would be able to see her still going down and . . . . they just kind of looked at me, and, ah, so from that point I just, I pretty much turned and, pretty much just rocketed to the top . . .'

Later he told them the person he tapped was an Asian male and that he had recalled seeing an Asian male on the *Spoilsport*. He said it was only later that he was told that the divers on the drop rope had come from another boat that he had been completely unaware had turned up.

Gabe said that later he was amazed that he didn't end up with the bends. He said he made sure he wasn't 'going up quicker than the bubbles were . . .'

'I remember getting to the top, ah, yanking my mask off, you know spitting out my regulator . . . and just yelling, you know, "Tina's gone down" er, you know, "I need help".'

When Haslet had arrived in the tender he repeated, 'Tina's gone down, Tina's gone down . . . I just remember telling him . . . that she went down within sight of the anchor rope.'

Once back at the *Spoilsport* he had seen divers getting into the other tender. He took off his fins and wetsuit, leaving the underlayer. It was then he noticed the other boat, *Jazz II*.

'I remember they asked me, you know, what was she wearing . . . I just remember yelling out she's got a purple mask and purple snorkel, she's got blonde hair . . .'

He remembered that Paula Snyder had given him a hug. He was aware, at around that time, that John Downie had gone over to the *Jazz II*.

He made no mention of conversations with either Ken Snyder or Doug Milsap.

'I was just outside walking round . . . I remember some guy . . . said: "Have they told you anything?" and I said: "No," and he said: "Well, you know, they've got her on . . . one of the other boats and they've got an IV in her." And I just remember thinking well, you know, there was just a huge relief because I thought, you know, that they were rehydrating her or something. You know, at that point, you know, my worst fear was when I came back up leaving her, was that she was just going to float off, um 'cause I knew that, you know, I was thinking back to that current and I was like "My God she's going to be lost." And that was probably the reason why I didn't want to leave her too . . .'

He detailed how he had gone up to the bridge where the ship's master was, had provided Tina's age and weight, and listened to information relayed back and forth to the doctor in Townsville.

'. . . I remember after I heard that he said . . . she didn't have a pulse . . . and wasn't breathing . . . when they brought her up and . . . when I saw them doing CPR I had to turn and leave . . . I remember I went back down to the deck for a few minutes then went and . . . went back outside where my room was and Paula and Ginger were both there . . .'

Gabe went on to describe how John Downie had approached him while he was with Paula and Ginger in the corridor.

He put his hands up to his eyes, his long fingers rubbing his eyebrows. Glenda leant in closer, an elbow on the table covering her own face with one hand, increasing the physical contact with her son.

'Sweetie . . .'

'I knew, you know, when I saw him that he wasn't coming to tell me, you know, everything's fine she's just got a headache or something . . . and he walked over and said: "I don't have good news, and I did everything I could, but we lost her."'

They had all fallen to the floor, Gabe said.

He told the two police officers conducting the interview that after he was taken to see Tina on the *Jazz II*, he hadn't realised until they got back into port that Tina's body had been transferred back to the *Spoilsport*. 'The worst thing I've ever experienced,' he told them.

Gabe asked for a glass of water. Gehringer agreed to a break, but the tape kept rolling. Without the police presence Gabe fell to pieces. Glenda kept rubbing her son's shoulders.

'And it's like, you know, want to just lose it but . . .' he sniffed.

'Just lose it,' Glenda said.

'I just . . . I, well . . . I just, I want to, I want to get [it] over with. I want everybody to have all the information . . .'

'I know you do,' his mother said, comfortingly.

'. . . don't want to be here any more.'

'That's okay, sweetie.'

Unlike Gehringer, Senior Constable Lawrence was an experienced diver with an advanced open-water certificate.

He began the questions after one break, checking whether Gabe had been offered an orientation dive. After several attempts, Gabe finally answered the question: 'No, there had been no orientation dive offered.' Until he had read the book from the aquarium about Australia's greatest dive sites, he said, he had little knowledge about the *Yongala* dive.

Gabe described how, during the second dive, they had both deflated their BCs and Tina had descended on the anchor rope before him and her bubbles had got in the way, so he had moved to one side.

Later Lawrence asked if he saw Tina stop at any time and equalise.

He did, he said, but then digressed momentarily to his own ears. '. . . the last time I shot down for her I ended up messing up my ear . . . I have to equalise more than the average person . . . until I get down to, you know, about under 130 feet [40 metres] . . .'

Lawrence wanted to know what sort of facial expression Tina had when Gabe indicated to her to inflate her BC.

'Well, I think – you know – panic's not the right word, but, I know, you know, we made eye, you know, we were making eye contact and all that and I'd . . . maybe scared's not the word, concerned just 'cause we tried the first time and we didn't make it . . .'

He continued, stopping and starting through his answers, beginning one line of thought and then changing to another.

When Lawrence asked why he didn't just grab Tina while she was still close to him and inflate the BC, Gabe answered, 'because I didn't know what the problem was'.

'My thinking was, ah, you know, like, didn't know . . . if it was her inflator hose or something else . . .' Rather than dumping her weights and risking her not exhaling properly as she ascended from a depth of about 15 metres, or her not going up slower than her smallest bubbles, he was taking her back to the rope. He said that having been trained by the same instructor with the same signals, if Tina had been having trouble breathing she 'might've asked' but that there was 'never any indication from her that she was needing air'.

However, asked at another point how he felt when Tina pulled down his mask, he replied: 'Scared as hell . . . I knew that she did that 'cause something was going on that, you know, she was in trouble . . .'

Throughout the whole interview Gabe made only the briefest mention of any trouble with his ear, but did not mention grabbing back his regulator or pushing Tina away like he told Tina Graves. Nor did he give any indication that he was the diver seen by Dr Stanley Stutz cradling a horizontal, weakly flailing Tina. None of those factors would become clear to police until much later.

Four tapes were used in the interview. Later, Lawrence pinpointed several discrepancies and police circled back around the key points. Wade Singleton had been adamant that an orientation dive had been offered to Tina. Lawrence was also mystified as to why Gabe would assert that he'd done a rapid ascent – he said he had 'rocketed to the top' and 'swum faster' than he ever had before – when his dive computer hadn't registered that sort of pace.

In his notes, Lawrence had circled a sentence in the margin: 'Why wasn't he watching her?' Then he'd written: 'She squeezed her hose' – then 'What hose?' In the margin of one of the pages, he had doodled a boy wearing a baseball cap, reminiscent of the man he was interviewing. In the cartoon Gabe had his cap facing to the right and his face was looking straight ahead. The head was perched on a rectangular block.

On Monday, 27 October, Tommy and Cindy visited the Southern Heritage Funeral Home not far from their Helena home.

'We'd like to make arrangements for our daughter, Tina,' Tommy told the receptionist.

'I'm afraid that's not possible. The Watsons have already contacted us and made arrangements,' the receptionist told them. 'You will need power of attorney from her husband.'

Tommy immediately rang Gabe at the Holiday Inn in Townsville. The receptionist put him through to Gabe's room.

'Hi Gabe.'

'Oh, hi Tommy.'

'How're you going?'

'Oh, goin' fine . . . as well as can be expected.'

'And how's your mother. Is she staying with you?'

'Yes, she is. It's good to have her here. She goin' fine too.'

'I'd been hoping to hear from you. I've been waiting to hear how Tina was going to be brought home. It's been nearly a week.'

'Well, there's been police interviews, an autopsy and a heap of other stuff and I've been waiting until we organised everything till I rang you.'

'I see. Well, how is Tina going to be brought home?'

'DAN [the Divers Alert Network] is taking care of everything from . . . the time of the incident to . . . the time that Tina gets off the plane in Birmingham . . .'

'I hope that's happening as soon as possible. I can take care of everything else as soon as she gets here,' Tommy said. 'We've been to the funeral home – Cindy and I – and we were told that arrangements had already been made. I'm more than willing to take care of all that. It'll give us something to do – while we're waiting for her to come home. But, in order for us to do anything, Gabe, the funeral home told me that we will need a power of attorney to do anything, to make any kind of arrangements whatsoever.'

'Well . . . there's no way I could get a power of attorney to you from over here. There's only one or two notaries here and it's impossible for me to get that done.'

'One other thing, Gabe, it's been preying on my mind . . .' Tommy paused. 'I want to make sure that – that Tina isn't alone coming back . . . Will you be – with her all the way back?'

'Yes, sure, Mom and I will be on the same flight.'

'It's just . . .' Tommy felt at a loss for words to describe how much this meant to him, 'it's just that if you can't be, for any reason . . . for some reason . . . if you can't be on the flight with her, please let me know, because I'll come over myself and come back with her.'

'I won't let her come home alone,' Gabe said.

In Louisiana, Amanda Phillips, who had been waiting for a response from the US Consulate in Sydney since she had first spoken to Tommy on the night of 23 October, finally received an emailed reply on 28 October. It contained a contact phone number for Gabe. She rang him at about 7 a.m. Birmingham time, which was around 10 p.m. in Townsville.

'Yeah, I'm doin' fine, considering,' Gabe said after the introductory chat. 'Yeah, I switched rooms. Couldn't bear being in the same honeymoon suite . . . Yeah, Mom's here. We've been around town seeing different things.'

'So what happened, Gabe?' she asked. 'I just can't believe she's gone. I just can't believe it . . . What happened?'

Gabe began yet another version of events.

'There was something wrong with the equipment, Amanda, and the current was really strong. We got out because the equipment was wrong and I put additional weights on Tina as the current was so strong. It was so strong that when she got down there, she started to panic and when I was trying to bring her up, she knocked my mask off and reached for my regulator and then when I'd gotten my mask back on, she'd sunk about 10 feet [3 metres]. It was a choice of getting help or going after her . . . If I'd known what was going to happen, I'd have gone after her . . . I can't believe all this is happening to me.'

'It must be terrible,' Amanda said.

'I had the happiest time of my life before her death. Tina was on cloud nine. You should have seen her. We went to the Opera House and . . . we had an awesome time in Sydney.'

He told her snatches of the honeymoon, emphasising how much Tina had enjoyed it.

'Her body should be released on Monday and then I can take her home. I'm going to need every bit of help I can get, Amanda. You're Tina's best friend. I'll need your support.'

'Sure, Gabe. I'll be there for you. What you need I'll get for you. Sure.'

She asked him: 'They don't know what happened?'

'Well, the autopsy isn't conclusive. They're waiting for further tests,' Gabe answered.

They chatted for about an hour. Amanda gave him her email address and asked him to email any pictures through to his dad, or his friend Craig, and she would send them on to her friends.

'There're some pictures that are going to be in the

newspaper from the honeymoon. You should know about that, and they're the same ones that are on the emails that they had – that I've forwarded on,' Gabe said.

It wasn't until she had time to reflect on the conversation that she realised Gabe had never stuttered. Nor had he cried. And there was another thing that struck Amanda. He had looked out the window and said what a nice day it was.

A couple of days later, Tommy met David Watson for coffee to talk about the funeral arrangements. It was an awkward meeting. Both men spoke about their children, but it was not the kind of conversation either imagined they'd be having, after a wedding that should have marked a beginning, not an ending. Tommy stated, again, that he would like to have a role in the arrangements for Tina.

'Well, Tina is Gabe's wife too,' David reasoned. 'My concern is Gabe first of course. I am sure he'll include you in funeral arrangements.'

'I don't know about you,' Tommy shifted the subject, trying to avoid the irritation he felt. 'But I knew nothing about this scuba diving before this. Now, I'm starting to learn about it.'

'Me too.'

'You know, I told Tina that she shouldn't scuba dive as it's dangerous, but I knew that I couldn't tell her not to do it.'

'That's kids for you. Yeah. I know what you mean.'

They finished their coffees, shook hands briefly and left.

Everyone in Birmingham was waiting, helplessly, for Tina to come home.

Alanda spoke on the phone with Gabe.

'Could you pick an outfit out for her, Alanda? She only packed a nice skirt and blouse for the Opera House, the rest is just casual.'

'Sure,' Alanda said. Like Cindy and Tommy, she was desperately looking for something to do. But when she went to look through Tina's clothes she broke down sobbing, unable to do anything. A friend had to pick something out for her.

On 30 October, Gabe rang Tommy while the family was gathered for the evening meal. Tommy put the phone on loudspeaker. This was the call they had all been waiting for.

Gabe's voice sounded hollow in the room. Travel arrangements had been finalised. He read out the itinerary.

'We're flying from Townsville to Brisbane, then Los Angeles and then Atlanta. We'll have to spend the night in Atlanta because the flight's so late and then we'll catch another flight to Birmingham.'

'So when will you leave Townsville?' Tommy asked.

'This morning.'

'And you'll be with her all the way?'

'Yep, Mom and I will be on the same flight the whole way home. I've got to go back to the police station to drop off some contact information and our itinerary for the travel home . . .'

He paused. Then he laughed, a chuckle that reverberated around the room.

'I tell you what, they'd have to drag me kicking and screaming before I'll ever come back to Australia.'

There was silence. No-one knew what to say.

Alanda pushed her plate away. She had lost her appetite.

When the *Spoilsport* had returned to port on 28 October, some of the passengers were surprised to see two people standing on the wharf waiting for them as they walked up the small pier onto land. It was Glenda and Gabe Watson.

Gabe approached Paula Snyder and introduced his mother.

'I just want to let you know that I am okay,' Gabe said. 'The officials and the police department have been wonderful and we have got Tina onto a flight. We are still waiting for the body to be released and we are going back in a couple of days. I need to get everyone's emails so I can keep in touch,' he said. He spoke as though Paula had asked for a report.

'Are you sure you are okay? Is everything all right?' Paula asked, still unsure as to what he wanted her to do.

'Yeah,' replied Gabe.

'I will touch base with you once we get back to the States,' said Paula as she and Ken began to collect their luggage.

Tina Graves also saw the Watsons as they disembarked.

'I'm sorry for your loss,' she said.

That night, some passengers from the *Spoilsport* who were staying on in Townsville and some of the crew congregated at the Hog's Breath Cafe in Flinders Street. Someone told Tina Graves about a newspaper article in the *Townsville Bulletin*. She returned to her hotel and found a copy. The more she read of the story, the angrier she became.

The husband of 26-year-old American scuba diver Christina Watson, who died during a dive near the Yongala wreck a week ago, told yesterday how the pair would not have gone in the water had they known how strong the currents were.

Gabe Watson, speaking publicly for the first time since his wife's death, said the wind had whipped up white caps on the surface on the day of the dive and 'they were not ideal diving conditions'.

However Mr Watson said he entered the water with his wife

222

and decided to abort the dive after a matter of minutes when they realised just how strong the current was.

'After the incident one of the female volunteers on the Spoil Sport *[sic] told me that as they were on the anchor line after setting up the site, the current was so severe it pushed them horizontal,' he said.*

'Had we been told exactly what the conditions were like before the dive we never would have attempted it.

'From what we were used to in the [United] *States, the current was very strong.*

'Tina got into difficulty as we turned back. It is my belief that whatever physical problem took Tina's life was triggered by our struggle with the current as we tried to abort the dive.'

Gabe went on to thank family and friends for their support.

'In a time like this, no words can heal the pain, but knowing how much people care helps.'

The article continued:

The body of Mrs Watson is expected to be released this week and will be flown to Alabama for her funeral.

'Hopefully we'll be on the same flight,' Mr Watson said.

Stan Kielbaska, the Mike Ball company's general manager, had also been quoted in the article, stating that the divers had been well briefed on the conditions as well as advised about the current. He pointed out Mr Watson had been able to make headway against the current even while towing his wife.

Tina Graves showed the article to her husband. 'Those dive briefings were spot on,' she said. 'I've never seen them done any better than I did that day. If they were uncomfortable diving in currents, they should never have entered, or remained in, the water.'

Gabe and his mother also dined out that night, discussing the trip and Tina's death and attempted resuscitation with Dr John Downie.

Glenda Watson hadn't expected to spend the second day of her fifty-third year in New Zealand. As the plane was descending into Auckland on a scheduled stop en route to the United States, Gabe claimed that he had difficulty equilibrating his right ear. An ambulance was dispatched at 6.57 p.m. to Auckland International Airport and the Watsons boarded it about 15 minutes later. It was 1 November 2003.

Gabe's chief complaint, given to Dr David Scott, was 'earache'. He told Dr Scott that he'd been diagnosed with barotrauma. Dr Scott's handwritten notes state: 'History of painful ears post diving trip 10 days ago in Australia – advised by Dr not to fly then for 5 days – [patient] took advice – today on descent into Auck, sudden onset of excruciating pain bilateral ears – once landed pain eased – still uncomfortable – Pt elected not continue journey to USA.'

On the electronic discharge summary, the doctor had noted that on the scuba diving trip Gabe had been 'unable to equalize ear pressure at ~18m. Felt water "rush in" to right ear. Seen by doctor – labelled barotrauma. For 2 days after, throbbing ache right>left. Felt slightly decreased hearing in right. Flew to NZ. On descent difficult to equilibrate right ear with pressure feeling. Since landing intermittent throbbing in ear.'

His ears, however, were intact, Dr Scott found, with no evidence of fluid in the middle ear or perforation.

'Some small burst capillaries on surface – looks old,' he added to his discharge summary.

In Townsville, Dr Gillespie had not noted that she had given Gabe any advice about when he could fly. And Gabe had barely mentioned anything to police about ear problems.

The same day, the Watsons' preacher, Craig Greer, dropped around to Seattle Slew Drive.

'I've got some news,' Craig Greer said as soon as Tommy opened the door. 'The plane had to make an emergency landing in New Zealand to let Gabe and his mother off. Tina is still on her way home.'

'What was the problem?' Tommy asked, incredulous.

'Gabe had problems with his ear. It was medical[ly] related.'

'So when will our daughter be home?' Tommy said, his voice catching.

'Well, she'll be in Atlanta for the night as we planned. But Gabe won't be able to catch up. But,' he rushed on, seeing the look on Tommy's face, 'she'll land in Birmingham on Sunday morning and Gabe'll be there by Sunday night.'

Tommy left the preacher with Cindy and Alanda in the lounge room. He could not bear to stay in the room. Instead, he rang the Southern Heritage Funeral Home and was told that as soon as Tina arrived, she would be taken to a downtown location where she would be 'prepped' and then taken to the funeral home.

'You won't be able to see Tina or her coffin at the airport. It's best to wait until she arrives at the funeral home,' Tommy was told.

For the Thomas family, it was yet another disappointment in a continuing round of disappointments.

'I would just like to let everyone know that I arrived back in the US with Tina on Sunday November 2,' Gabe began in an email to friends. He spoke of her funeral, scheduled for 5 November, and how life with his wife of just ten days was 'the happiest 10 days either of us had ever experienced'. Tina, he wrote, was a truly remarkable woman who would 'forever hold a special place in my life'.

CHAPTER 15

The Southern Heritage Funeral Home on Cahaba Valley Road, Pelham, is tucked between Highway 65 and Indian Spring Lake, hidden from view from the interstate commuters on the major artery that links Alabama with Tennessee, Kentucky and Indiana, ending up south-east of Chicago, Illinois. The cemetery lies in pastureland surrounded by forests of cottonwood trees and myriad oaks: blackjack, post oak and eastern red cedar. Once into the cemetery parkland, studded with willow oak and hickory trees, the continual hum of the highway traffic can still be heard, but there is a sense of peace upon entering the sweeping driveway that leads up to the funeral home.

A cemetery gate off to the right separates the funeral home from the rest of the land. Once through the gate, the road passes the crematorium area marked by isolated bunches of flowers and individual memorials. There is a lake and a crematorium garden with benches, and then the road sweeps up the hill to the burial sites, passing some of the family mausoleums on the higher ground.

On the afternoon of Sunday, 2 November, the Thomases had a private viewing of Tina's body. The event was for immediate family and some close family friends. For Alanda, the reality of seeing her sister lying there was a shock from which she thought she would never recover.

They returned the next day at 11 a.m.: Cindy, Tommy, Alanda, Cindy's brother Gene Waddell and Krissie McCampbell, Cindy's niece, who had helped dress Tina on her wedding day. It was the first time Tommy had seen Gabe since he shook his hand in the elevator at the reception and asked him to look after his 'baby girl'. Tommy nodded to David and Glenda Watson.

Sam Shelton, the funeral coordinator, was officiating. They had a preliminary conversation before talking about what would happen at the funeral ceremony.

'I'd like to release some doves,' said Gabe. 'She would have liked that.'

'I don't think she would've liked that, Gabe,' Cindy exclaimed. 'We were going to do something like that at the wedding and . . . Tina was dead against it, as she hated birds being kept in a cage. She thought it was cruel to animals and anything that was cruel to animals was a bad thing for her.'

'She was a member of the World Wildlife Fund and they are against any caging of animals,' Alanda added.

Gabe stood up to make his point.

'I think y'all got to realise that this is not about you. This is about me. I might as well let y'all know that Tina already told me what she wanted for her funeral, on the plane on the way to Australia . . . I mean I could have had her cremated and buried in Australia if I'd wanted to.' He paused. 'You should be thankful that I even brought her back here.'

Gabe stormed out of the room, his eyes flashing. His father, David, followed.

Tommy was angry under his calm demeanour. He

thought back. Never, in all of the years and conversations he'd had with his daughter, even when she was ill, had they ever discussed her funeral. Why would she be talking about a funeral on her way to her honeymoon? Tina was always uncomfortable with that kind of talk. When Tommy had the annual conversation with his eldest daughter to discuss her work-related insurance, she never seemed to take it seriously. Even more alarming, though, was Gabe's last comment. It hung in the air and sat uneasily with him.

Glenda Watson was the next to speak.

'Well,' she said. 'I have to say something. Y'all need to realise that Tina was Gabe's wife and that he's going through a difficult time and he thinks you're blaming him for Tina's death.'

Cindy's eyes widened. She got up immediately and walked out of the room to where Gabe was sitting in a chair. Her brother Gene and Tommy followed, perplexed at the turn of events. Gabe was sitting with his elbows on his knees. Tommy couldn't see David Watson anywhere.

'We don't blame you,' Cindy said as Gabe leaned away from her and avoided her gaze. 'We don't blame you,' she repeated when he did not reply. She felt sorry for this man whom her daughter had chosen to marry. He was suffering too. 'Your mother says you believe we do, but we don't. Why would you think that we do?' But Gabe kept his head down and would not look at Cindy.

After a while, everyone returned to the room. Arrangements had to be made.

'I think Tina would have liked a horse-drawn carriage,' Cindy said. 'She loved *Gone with the Wind* . . . how many times did she see that movie, Alanda? . . . and remember when you and she went to the museum in Atlanta? She loved Scarlett.'

'Is that okay, Gabe?' Tommy asked, adding: 'I'll pay for all the arrangements for that.'

'Yes, that'll be okay,' Gabe said.

The atmosphere became a little less tense. Gabe, Gene, David and Tommy went into the next room to choose a vault that would enclose the coffin. In the end, it was Gene who chose one. Gabe and David Watson agreed. Tommy was relieved there were no arguments. Then there was the matter of plot selection. They went back into the original room. This was more important to Tommy because it would be Tina's final resting place. They drove up the hill behind the funeral home to the part of the cemetery that overlooked Oak Mountain. Sam Shelton pointed out various plots en route that were vacant and the different sections of the cemetery. Then, they stopped at one of them.

'The view is lovely up here and Tina liked Oak Mountain, that's for sure,' Tommy said, the emotion evident in his voice. 'It's also far enough away from the main road and more peaceful.'

'Yep, I agree,' Gabe said.

David Watson nodded and so did Gene.

They returned to the funeral home and Tommy made arrangements, in front of Gene and both Watson men, to pay for the funeral. Sam Shelton told him it would be fine to pay afterwards.

Before they left the funeral home, though, tempers flared again. Tommy brought up a donation account that had been set up by Gabe for donations in lieu of flowers to the World Wildlife Fund. Things had been changed so that Gabe had sole access and discretion to disperse the funds for the payment of the funeral, or whatever Gabe wanted. What upset Tommy most was that as far as he was concerned, he and Cindy were paying for the funeral. No-one else needed to pay for it, so the donations from others might be given under a misapprehension. Gabe refused to budge on that point, simply shrugging.

As they were leaving, David Watson approached Tommy. 'We need to get Tina's Jeep.'

'That's fine. Can we wait until after the funeral, out of respect for Tina, and I'll be happy to take care of that?' Tommy answered.

'Well, I'm afraid we need to get it as soon as possible.'

Tommy decided to act immediately to avoid any more confrontations. That night, he drove the Jeep to the house that would have been Tina's marital home and parked it in the driveway. Alanda followed in her own car to take him home. Tommy decided to give the keys to Gabe at the funeral.

The last time Alanda had been at Oak Leaf Circle, Tina had been excitedly talking about her plans for 'fixin' up the house'. Now, Alanda and Tommy pulled up outside the home, stark against its bare lawns. This had never been Tina's home.

The following day, 4 November, a notice was published in both the *Birmingham News* Memorial Page and the *Times-Picayune* in New Orleans, Louisiana.

WATSON, CHRISTINA MAE THOMAS 'TINA', age 26, of Helena, died October 22, 2003 in a diving accident of [sic] *the shore of Townsville, Australia while on her honeymoon, after which they planned to return to their new home in Hoover, AL. She was a graduate of the University of Alabama at Birmingham, where she was a member and an alumni of AOPi Sorority. She was a Manager in the Boys and Girls Dept. at*

Parisian's Riverchase Galleria Store. Funeral services will be held on Wednesday, November 5, at 2 p.m. at Ridout's Southern Heritage Chapel with burial in Southern Heritage Cemetery. Rev. Craig and Suzie Greer officiating. Visitation will be Tuesday, from 5 to 8 p.m. at the funeral home. Survivors: husband, Gabe Watson; parents, William E. and Cindy Thomas of Helena; sister, Alanda Thomas; grandparents, Marcus and Retha Phillips of Jasper, Louise Thomas of Guin; aunt and uncle, Gene and Edna Waddell; cousins, Cheryl Rockwell, Clint Waddell, and Carol Rivas, all of Midland, TX, Krissie McCampbell of Conyers, GA. In lieu of flowers, the family requests donations be made to the 'Tina Thomas Watson Memorial Fund' that has been established at the AmSouth Bank on Hwy 150 in Hoover, AL. Ridout's Southern Heritage directing.

That morning, Tommy was about to leave to go to the funeral home. He wanted to be alone to say goodbye to Tina and had organised a private viewing. He was running down the stairs when his mobile phone rang. It was David Watson.

'I want to touch base with you, Tommy. It's about getting Tina's Jeep.'

'Oh, you don't need to worry about that. I put it in Gabe's driveway the night before. Alanda and I drove over with it . . . I've got the keys and I'll give them to Gabe at the funeral home this afternoon.'

'What about the rest of Tina's things? The wedding gifts?'

'Can't that wait, David, until after we bury our daughter?'

'Not really. We need to get this done for Gabe as soon as possible.'

'Well, you could've brought it up yesterday, before I took the Jeep over. Now you'll have to wait until after I bury my

All dressed up… the closest of sisters, Tina and Alanda.

Below: Along with best friend Amanda, Tina played the flute in her high school marching band.

Gabe Watson's Year 11 yearbook photograph.

Gabe Watson's winning chapter in the Chapter of the Year Competition, 2002, a year before he and Tina were married. Gabe is in the front row. Dr John Wittig, director of the undergraduate public relations program at the University of Alabama, is in the middle towards the back. Dr Wittig is convinced the woman standing in front of him is Tina.

Gabe and Tina in their engagement portrait.

Below: The submerged dive platforms at Alabama Blue Water Adventures, the former quarry where Gabe and Tina were both certified as divers.

Tina with her father, Tommy Thomas, on the morning of her wedding day.

THE STATE OF ALABAMA

Jefferson

COUNTY

Marriage License

To any Licensed Minister of the Gospel in Regular Communion with the Christian Church or Society of which he is a member or Judge of the Supreme Court, Court of Criminal Appeals, Court of Civil Appeals, Circuit Court, District Court, Federal Court, Judge of Probate or Pastor of any Religious Society according to the Rules ordained or Custom Established by such Society.

GREETING

You are hereby authorized *to solemnize Marriage between*

Mr. _____ DAVID GABRIEL WATSON _____ *Birth Date* 03/05/1977 *and*

Ms. _____ CHRISTINA MAE THOMAS _____ *Birth Date* 02/13/1977 _____

and to join them together in Matrimony, and certify the same in writing to this office as required by law.

Given under my hand __7TH__ *day of* __OCTOBER 2003__

Alan L. King

This Certifies *that I have solemnized Marriage between*

Mr. _____ DAVID GABRIEL WATSON _____ *and*

Ms. _____ CHRISTINA MAE THOMAS _____

according to Law, at __BIRMINGHAM__ *in said County and State, on the* __11TH__ *day of* __OCTOBER 2003__

S CRAIG GREER REVEREND

The State of Alabama, JEFFERSON COUNTY, *I, the undersigned Judge of Probate for said County in said State, hereby certify that the above and foregoing transcript is a true and correct copy of the Marriage License and Certificate of Marriage of said parties as the same appears of record.*

Given under my hand and Official Seal this __1ST__ *day of* __OCTOBER 2009__

Alan L. King *Judge of Probate*

Gabe and Tina's wedding certificate.

Gabe and Tina on their wedding day.

Gabe and Tina at
Taronga Zoo in Sydney
on their honeymoon.

Below: The *Spoilsport*.

Wade Singleton gives the detailed dive briefing that preceded Tina's fatal dive. The chalkboard, showing the wreck layout, depths and measurements, is behind him.

Below: The back of the *Spoilsport*, with the sun deck on top, the saloon deck in the middle and the dive deck with steps down to dive platforms for boarding the tender.

SPOILSPORT   TOWNSVILLE

The *Yongala* wreck
on the day of the
dive, taken by Gary
Stempler, who shortly
afterwards unwittingly
photographed Tina's
body on the sea bed.

Below: The photograph
that shocked millons
around the world.

Gary Stempler and Dawn Asano, the other newlyweds, on a sandbar in the Coral Sea.

Below: From left, *Spoilsport* crew members Brian Fotheringham, Claudia Petersen, Uzi Barnai, Rebecca Hayllar, Wade Singleton (standing), Lou Johnstone and Simon Smith.

Above: The other passengers
who boarded the *Spoilsport*
with Gabe and Tina on
21 October 2003. Back row:
far left, Doug Milsap, fourth
from left, Ken Snyder, and
third from right, John Graves.
Middle row: from left, Gary
Stempler, Ginger Milsap,
Adriana Sherman, Jacqueline
Sherman, Paula Snyder. Tina
Graves is third from right
and Dr John Downie is on
the far right. Front row: far
left, Dawn Asano, and Jamie
Sherman is third from right.

Right: Tina's unmarked grave.

Above left: Wade Singleton on 20 November 2007, during the inquest. *Above right*: Uzi Barnai, a *Spoilsport* crew member who performed continuous resuscitation attempts on Tina and gave evidence at the inquest.

Tommy and Cindy Thomas at the resumption of the Coronial inquest into Tina's death, 21 January 2008.

The Thomas family and supporters watch via video-link from Texas as Gabe Watson's legal team of Rohan Armstrong (left) and Steve Zillman (centre), together with counsel assisting the Coroner, John Tate, wait to deliver final submissions on 19 June 2008.

Right: David and Glenda Watson bring pizza to Gabe's home the day the Coronial finding was delivered in Townsville.

Tommy Thomas after Gabe was
sentenced, 5 June 2009.

Right: Gabe's current wife, Kim
Lewis Watson, in Brisbane on
5 June 2009.

Amanda, Alanda and Tommy leave court together on 5 June 2009.

Detective Senior Constable Kevin Gehringer (left) and Detective Sergeant Gary Campbell, who each dedicated countless hours to investigating Tina Watson's death.

David and Glenda Watson continue to protest their son's innocence.

Tina's grave, finally marked with a gravestone more than
six years after her death. Tina's body is again the subject of
a re-interment application, this time by her father.

Alanda holds a framed picture of Tina.

daughter. I'm on my way to spend some private time with her and I don't really have the time or energy to deal with this at the moment.'

'Well, we need to get everything for Gabe as soon as possible. Is there any reason why we wouldn't get these things?'

'No, not at all. I just want to spend time with my daughter, right now. Goodbye.'

Tommy hung up the phone. He saw Alanda as he was leaving and told her what had just happened.

'We could have taken everything over in the Jeep and delivered it all and been done with it,' Tommy said.

'That's right, Dad. What are they playing at?' Alanda said. 'I'll call Gabe and explain how we feel.'

Tommy, impatient to be at the funeral home, nevertheless knew this had to be sorted out.

'Why are you doing this?' Alanda asked Gabe when he answered the phone, convinced that at least if she explained their point of view, he might understand.

'You have to understand I have already completed the grieving process and you are just starting,' he said coldly. 'Look, I want a mattress, some clothes, the wedding presents that are rightfully mine and everything that belonged to Tina.'

Alanda was too upset to hold the phone. Tommy took it from her.

It was about 11 a.m. when Tommy eventually arrived at the funeral home. Sam Shelton was there and came into the viewing room every so often to see if Tommy was okay.

While he sat with Tina, talking to her, being with her, Tommy felt strangely at peace. Every moment counted. It was his last chance to see her and tell her how much he loved her and that he'd never stop caring for her. His mobile phone vibrated several times. Tommy ignored it, used to persistent work-related calls. When he left the funeral home at about 1.30 p.m. and walked out to his car, he checked what the interruptions had been. A number of calls were from David Watson and Cindy. He rang Cindy right away. She was hysterical.

'David's rung me. He and Glenda are coming over to get the presents and Tina's stuff right away.'

'No, honey. I've got it all sorted. I'll be home real fast,' Tommy said.

He drove quickly, turning into Cahaba Valley Road and then Pelham Parkway before heading across to Helena. As soon as he came over the rise in Seattle Slew Drive, he saw the Watsons' SUV outside his house. Glenda and David Watson were standing in the driveway with Cindy and her brother Gene.

He got out of his car and walked over.

'Please,' Cindy said, tear-stained and blotchy, unable to hold herself together. 'Wait until after the funeral. I can't deal with this now.'

'Show some respect,' Gene added, standing behind his sister.

'I'm sorry, but I need to get the things now.'

Tommy walked up behind them.

'David, I thought we had all this sorted. I told you we needed time to get ready for the viewing – so does the rest of the family. Please give us some peace to do that.'

Some friends who lived nearby turned up. Unlike Tommy, they showed little restraint. One threatened to call the police if the Watsons didn't leave.

'This is the last thing they need at a time like this,' the man said, turning on the Watsons who initially stood their ground.

There was silence, then the Watsons turned and got into their car and drove away.

***

The extended Thomas family arrived for a private viewing an hour earlier than the official viewing time, which was set for 3 p.m. Tommy walked through the heavy wooden doors and stood inside the foyer, waiting for directions. Sam Shelton and the funeral director approached.

Sam coughed.

Tommy looked at him, waiting.

'I've been instructed by Gabe and his family that if you say or do anything that they consider derogatory or inappropriate inside the funeral home, they expect us to call the police and have you removed from the viewing and the funeral later . . .'

Tommy's eyes widened.

'Look, we know this is a difficult time for you and your family. We don't agree with what's going on, but if the Watsons push it, we'll have to have you removed.'

'Are you trying to tell us,' Tommy spoke quietly, 'that you could have us removed from our own daughter's funeral?'

'Well, sir, we have every legal right to do that . . . If you could keep family members under control and be careful of your actions and what you say. I'd like to bring the situation under control and for you to meet Gabe before the viewing.'

'No problem. I've got the keys for Tina's Jeep to give to him,' Tommy replied.

Shortly after this, Tommy handed the keys to Gabe. Gabe gave him Tina's birth certificate.

'Look Gabe. I don't really understand what's going on. What's happening? Why am I being threatened?'

Gabe looked at him. He said nothing at first, then: 'I want Tina's stuff.'

They parted. After that, Tommy, Cindy and Alanda spent most of the time in the viewing room with Tina. The foyer was festooned with an overflow of the flowers that already filled an adjacent room and the hallway behind the viewing rooms. There were flowers from family and friends, of every hue. They brought splashes of colour to the cream walls inside the Georgian-style building.

Alanda had set up poster boards of photos on the right as mourners entered the viewing room. There was Tina with her trademark smile, in different poses at various stages throughout her life. In one striking picture, she was part of a trio, all dressed in elegant black, a big lipstick smile, with her arms around Amanda and her other girlfriend from Mandeville High School, Keather Pack. Tommy, taking a break from the viewing room, walked past, his eyes drawn again to his beautiful daughter. Gabe, his father and another woman were looking at the photos.

'She looks like a model,' the woman said.

'No, she just liked to dress up,' Gabe replied.

'Actually, she was a model,' Tommy interrupted quickly. 'She modelled for four years. Even at high school . . . She used to model for JC Penney's with her girlfriends.'

Gabe said nothing.

The foyer was full of people as everyone came and went from the small room where Tina lay. Melinda Kayton, one of Tina's bridesmaids and fellow pharmacy assistant, approached Gabe. She wasn't quite sure what to say to him as she didn't know him that well, but someone had told her he'd had problems with his ears while flying back from Australia.

'How are your ears?' she asked him.

'I don't know what you're talking about,' he said.

She explained why she was asking.

'Yeah, yeah, yeah. They're fine. I get what you're talking about now,' he said with a brief laugh.

Melinda stayed in the foyer, glancing at the casket

that contained Tina, unsure if she could bring herself to approach it. Gabe's mother Glenda came past and, seeing Melinda's hesitation, offered to go with her. Melinda stood looking down for a while at Tina's face. It was as though she were sleeping, but her face was pale.

'It's so important for Gabe that she be buried with her wedding and engagement rings,' Mrs Watson said, interrupting Melinda's thoughts.

'Mmm.' Melinda was remembering Tina as a bride, how beautiful she had looked. She had waited so long for that moment and she had been a wife for such a short time.

'Yes, Gabe won't have it any other way.'

Melinda Kayton thought it was a bit odd that Mrs Watson kept repeating this.

As soon as Amanda Phillips and her husband Jimmy arrived for the viewing, together with her mother Ellen, sister Karin, and brother Andrew, who was to be one of the pallbearers, the first person she saw was Gabe. Tears filled her eyes as she approached him. He began to cry too. But, even through her grief Amanda registered that his tears seemed showy. She brushed this thought away, thinking that she must be distracted. They both walked into the viewing room. Amanda gasped when she saw Tina lying there. She and Gabe spent about 10 minutes looking at her before going outside. Amanda then saw Cindy and gave her a big hug. Then, she and Gabe went into the back viewing parlour and sat down on the couch.

A man with dark hair and wearing a grey suit approached. Amanda thought she recognised him as the guy from The Dive Site store when Tina had collected Gabe's dive computer. That had only been four weeks earlier but seemed like an eternity. Tom Jackson, Gabe's dive instructor, was with his now wife, Shelley.

'I'm sorry for your loss,' Tom said to Gabe.

'Yeah, thanks,' Gabe said, standing up. 'Look, I want to talk some more with you. I did everything that you trained me to do but I could not save her.'

'What happened?' Tom asked.

Gabe explained how the dive master had said there was some current on the dive and what they had been instructed to do.

'When we got down to 45 feet [14 metres], we let loose of the line and swam towards the edge of the boat. We realised that the currents were too strong. So we both agreed to swim back to the ascent line. I turned and was kicking with everything I had but I didn't feel like I was getting anywhere, Tom. I turned and looked back at Tina and the current was pushing her away. When I turned back to help, I got to her and my mask was knocked off. I had to replace it and by the time I got the mask on she was pushed down and away from me and I was pushed up. When I tried to kick back down and help, my ear drum ruptured. All I could see was that she was reaching out to me. That's all I can remember.'

'This is probably not the time, Gabe. You need to grieve. I'll sit down and talk to you once everything's calmed down,' Tom Jackson said.

'Okay. I might come in on Monday,' Gabe said.

'Sure, that's fine,' Tom said, preparing to leave. 'Come by whenever you like.'

Outside, Tom and Shelley Jackson noticed the uncomfortable atmosphere that they had sensed on the way in. Tina's family seemed to be on one side and Gabe's on another. Tom remarked to his wife how strange it seemed to have such a divide.

The couple moved away. Gabe sat down on the couch with Amanda again.

'I can't believe all this is happening,' he said to her. 'Look at all the flowers. Look at all the people that loved Tina . . .'

'Yes, I know,' Amanda said. 'Everyone loved her. She was that kind of girl.' Her lip trembled and she began to cry again. 'Always smiling . . .'

'I have to tell you you'll be receiving a postcard,' Gabe said, 'that was mailed from Sydney from Tina, so don't freak out when you get it . . .'

Amanda reached for another tissue, smiling through her tears, thanking him for warning her. Then Gabe was called away. Amanda mingled with her own family, walking outside to check out the poster board that commemorated Tina's life.

At 9 p.m., after the staff tidied up, the large doors in the funeral parlour were closed. The viewing was over.

The day of the funeral dawned hot and humid. By lunchtime, the humidity had eased. Later, the scattered clouds of the morning had developed into an overcast afternoon.

Tommy arrived alone at about 1 p.m., the hottest part of the day and an hour before the ceremony was due to begin. Almost as soon as Tommy walked in, Sam Shelton approached. Tommy looked up, sensing more problems.

'David Watson has spoken to me and asked me to remind you if there's any type of disturbance or comments made, you will be removed.'

'The only type of disturbance will be if you try to remove us,' Tommy said curtly.

Amanda Phillips also arrived early. Before the ceremony started, Glenda Watson pulled her aside and pressed a coin into her hand.

'That's one of the last things that Tina held. I know she would want you to have it. There's only one other coin and Shali has gotten that one.'

Amanda looked at the gold coin: it was an Australian $1. Amanda closed her fingers over it, imagining Tina's presence.

David Watson approached.

'I hope Cindy behaves herself. I don't want a scene,' he said. 'I want this to be respectful. I'd like to thank you for your support of Gabe, Amanda. Also to say that it would be good if you and Jimmy can come back to our house after the ceremony.'

Well before proceedings began the large car park outside the imposing columns of the funeral home was full, and mourners had to park along busy Cahaba Valley Road. The funeral service went for about an hour. Craig and Suzie Greer officiated. Gabe read a poem and spoke about Tina for more than 10 minutes. Some of those listening were amazed at Gabe's relative composure so soon after the sudden loss of a new spouse.

Amanda, too, read a poem she had written herself. There were plenty of tears in the packed congregation inside the white chapel. People who had known Tina at various stages of her life had made the effort to attend. Stan Marks slipped in quietly to remember the girl he might have married. Steve Johnson, owner of The Dive Site, sat down the back. For others it was standing room only. Just as the curtains began closing on Tina's casket, with all of the finality that moment brings, Gabe got up and walked towards it. He placed an envelope inside.

Outside, the white horses and a carriage stood waiting. Tina's casket was carried out of the chapel. It was the first time Tina had got to realise her dream of riding in a carriage.

The thought wrenched at Tommy's heart as he watched her casket being placed inside the carriage. He walked beside it to the burial site. Cindy sat inside.

Straight after the ceremony, Amanda saw Gabe, who had driven to the gravesite.

'Your dad has asked us over after the burial,' she said.

'Yeah, great. Hey, I've got a video from our honeymoon. But I'm nervous about watching it,' Gabe said. 'You should watch it with us . . . I'm just worried about how I will react watching it for the first time since I've been back.'

At the gravesite, Tina's casket was lifted from the back of the carriage and lowered into the ground. Someone was circulating with flyers inviting friends of Gabe and Tina for a get-together later at Craig Youngblood's house to celebrate Tina's life. 'Bring your photos', the flyers said, 'and things to remember Tina by'.

As dusk fell, Amanda and Jimmy made their way to Gabe's parents' house about 20 minutes' drive away. They spent most of the journey up the Montgomery Highway talking about who they'd seen, Amanda describing various friends and family of Tina to her husband. Large neon signs for fast-food outlets, their lights bleeding down, merged with set after set of traffic lights as they whizzed past. Then the shops and small businesses became more spaced apart and rush-hour traffic clogged the intersections. Crossing over the multiple lanes of the 459, they passed into more residential territory along John Hawkins Parkway.

Jimmy parked their car on the steeply sloping street where the Watsons had lived for seventeen years. They walked up the steps to the front of the house. Inside, they met Gabe's parents in the kitchen.

'So, are you ready to see the video?' Gabe asked Amanda anxiously, almost as soon as they had crossed the threshold. 'I tell you, I'm glad you're watching it with me, 'cause I'm a bit freaked out. You know. Don't know what to expect.'

They walked into the den. The door was shut and Amanda and Jimmy sat on the couch. Gabe was holding the video camera, which was hard-wired to the TV.

Amanda recognised the location for the first bit of footage: it was inside Gabe and Tina's new home in Oak Leaf Circle. Gabe was carrying the camera and walking up the stairs and, although you couldn't see him, you could hear his voice. Panning around, Tina came into view, packing her luggage. She had her glasses on and was in her pyjamas. Amanda's heart lurched as she saw her.

'Smile at the camera,' Gabe commanded.

Tina obliged.

'Smile at the camera just in case we get eaten by a shark or something,' he said.

Amanda was puzzled. She felt a sense of unease.

'I can't believe that,' Gabe said.

There was footage of Taronga Zoo in Sydney. The footage was all time stamped and dated on the bottom of the screen. Then Tina and Gabe were inside a cabin on board a boat. They were both talking and the camera panned around showing the porthole and a toilet.

After the video, everyone walked out into the kitchen.

'Mom, where are those pictures – you know, the photos I took?' Gabe asked.

Glenda Watson disappeared, returning with four or five stacks of photographs placed in envelopes. Prompted by Gabe, Amanda flicked through them. There were several photos of Tina standing next to warning signs, mostly relating to potential drowning hazards involving water and currents. One was a danger sign on a beach.

After she looked at the third picture to focus on strong currents, Gabe, watching her, commented: 'This seems weird and seriously ironic. Doesn't it?'

Amanda had not had a good first impression of Gabe and this just confirmed it.

'Well, Amanda,' David Watson said as they took their leave. 'Gabe will be needing you in the future, now Tina's gone.'

Amanda made polite noises, agreeing to keep in contact and inviting Gabe to visit her. For Tina's sake.

Gabe, too, came out to say goodbye as they walked towards their car.

'You know, Tina – Tina obviously loves you and she wanted you to be part of her life, you know. That's very important to me, so I want to keep in touch with you, you know,' he said. 'We'd just gotten a black lab. He's really cute.'

Driving away, Jimmy spoke first in the car.

'Don't know about you, darling, but those pictures really disturbed me.'

'I agree. I'm real spooked by them . . . and the video.'

Jimmy hadn't been as concerned about the video. It was the photos of Tina that had unsettled him.

At the later get-together, Melinda Kayton and her husband Adam showed up with the little things that reminded her of Tina. She, too, had been shocked by the strange references on the honeymoon video, particularly the close-up of a plaque at the aquarium in Townsville which referred to the number of shark attacks in Australia. They left early. The gathering had consisted mainly of Gabe's friends having drinks and nibbles.

Gabe said goodbye in the hallway.

'You know Tina panicked and knocked my mask off,' he told her. 'All I remember was her floating away and I was looking into her eyes. I will always have to remember that. There was nothing I could do.'

The day after the funeral, Tommy returned to the Southern Heritage Funeral Home to pay for the service. He wrote a cheque, then asked about the flowers and plants – sent by friends, family members and people who worked with Tina – that had not been placed on the grave.

Sam Shelton invited Tommy into his office.

'Mr Thomas, we have been advised by the Watsons,' he said quietly, 'that your family are not to be given any of the flowers or plants regardless of who sent them. They were sent for Tina.'

Tommy walked slowly back to his car, his shoulders bowed. He was exhausted by grief and the strange series of events that had happened since Tina died. He was incredulous at what had been happening. He thought again that the Watsons were a domineering family. Even after the wedding, they had taken most of the flowers home, even though Tommy and Cindy had paid for them. Now, they would rather that the flowers left at the funeral home die instead of the Thomases being allowed to take them home as a reminder of their daughter.

Tommy had paid for Tina's funeral, but Sam Shelton strongly suggested he should not pay for a plot for Tina.

'The Watsons can move Tina from the plot even if you do pay for one,' he had told him.

Move her? Why would anyone want to do that? thought Tommy.

***

The same day, the *Townsville Bulletin* published a story on page five as a routine follow-up to a diving death: 'Grieving husband tells of life alone'. The article quoted Gabe Watson thanking the newspaper and community for its support, and blamed Tina's death on the currents. It was the sort of story filed for posterity.

The thought had been niggling away at Tommy for some time. It was about the conversation he'd had with Tina two weeks before the wedding, when she told him that Gabe had asked her to change her insurance policy to name him as sole beneficiary. Had she carried out Gabe's wishes?

He asked Alanda if she knew anything about it. His second daughter's pregnancy was showing, a distressing reminder to him that Tina would never get to see his first grandchild. He was only too aware that Alanda lived with that thought every minute of every day. She had told him that she continually expected to see Tina walk into the room and that she'd find out the whole episode was a bad dream. Each day she could see Tina, arms outstretched as she sank.

Tommy explained to Alanda the conversation he'd had with Tina back at the end of September and how odd it had been. He asked Alanda to contact the employee benefits department at Parisian to clarify whether Tina had changed the policy beneficiary.

A couple of days later, Alanda told Tommy she had spoken to someone who confirmed that Tina had not changed the policy beneficiary. Alanda helped Tommy with the paperwork and he made an application to the insurance company.

***

On 11 November, Gabe presented himself at Alabama ENT Associates in Southlake Parkway and consulted Dr Robert Sciacca, a Birmingham otolaryngologist who specialised in the ear and larynx as well as diseases of the head and neck. He conducted hearing tests to make sure Gabe's hearing wasn't damaged.

The following day, Tommy was en route to Jackson, Mississippi, to conduct a workshop when he received a message on his mobile phone.

It was Bob Austin, David Watson's close friend. He told Tommy that he was the lawyer for Gabe Watson. Gabe, he said, wanted anything that belonged to Tina turned over immediately.

Tommy had found it hard enough coping with being back at work and felt unable to ring Austin back. He would deal with it after he'd got through the workshop. A week later, while Tommy was checking in his luggage en route to Akron, Ohio, and finishing his second week back at work, Austin rang again and left a message. This time Tommy rang him back.

'Look Mr Thomas,' Austin began. 'I'm calling to set up a meeting with you and my client, Gabe Watson, and myself next Wednesday, the day before Thanksgiving. Does that suit you?'

Austin, a former president of the Hoover City Council, had a no-nonsense style, speaking in short forceful bursts.

The same day Tommy received the first call from Austin, the phone rang in the reservation office at Mike Ball Dive Expeditions. It was Tina Graves. Laura Waters, the US reservations manager, had made the reservations on the

Spoilsport for the Graves. Tina Graves wanted to tell Laura something that was worrying her.

'I spoke with Gabe in the corridor outside of my berth. I just can't stop thinking about what he said . . .'

'What was that?'

'Well . . . he said that his wife had grabbed his regulator out of his mouth and that he'd grabbed it back and he pushed her away . . . he was upset about that. The fact that he'd pushed her away.'

She went on to talk about other things that happened on the trip but she told Laura it was this particular conversation about Gabe pushing Tina away that concerned her the most. Tina had needed air and Gabe hadn't allowed her to have it.

'Well,' Laura said. 'Perhaps you should put it in an email and send it to me. And thanks for letting us know.'

Two hours later, an email arrived from Tina Graves. Laura forwarded it to Stan Kielbaska.

The following day, Gabe lodged a claim form with Travelex for reimbursement of the medical expenses he had incurred after Tina's death. After filling out his personal information in Part I of the form, he moved on to Part II, writing out his reason for the claim: 'Severe barotrauma to the ears during diving accident.' He ticked: 'Yes' he had been hospitalised in Auckland, New Zealand, but left the admission and discharge date spaces blank.

'Invoice is included but not paid,' he stated next to the address of the hospital. Gabe attached forms detailing the consultations in Townsville with Dr Gillespie who had not recommended treatment for his reddened ears. The total amount claimed was US$156.64.

Gabe also went to the Probate Court of Jefferson County where he was granted authority to wind up Tina's estate, which Gabe estimated was worth no more than $5000. He had to provide an inventory of her assets as she had left no will.

That same day Gabe's dive watch was inspected by Chris Coxon, the principal Workplace Health and Safety Inspector (Diving) of the Queensland Department of Industrial Relations. He had earlier inspected Tina's dive watch, noting from screen-based data that the fatal dive had commenced around 10.30 a.m. on 22 October and that she'd gone to a maximum depth of 27.1 metres. The total dive time was 10 minutes. Wade Singleton's Uwatec Aladin Ultra dive computer data was downloaded to show his dive began at 10.31 a.m., he went to a maximum depth of 27.6 metres and his total dive time was 9 minutes. Tina's dive equipment, along with her hired Sea Hornet scuba cylinder (which showed no evidence of surface corrosion), a safety sausage attached to her right-hand shoulder clip and a small bottle of aquaseal antifog found in one of her pockets, were all lodged at Operations Support Command. Tina's two integrated weight pouches had been placed correctly in their quick-release weight pockets. In total her BC carried a total weight of 9.7 kilograms, or 20 pounds.

Throughout the long, sad days after Tina's funeral, when everything seemed to remind her of Tina, Amanda Phillips remembered her promises to Gabe and to his parents and how insistent Gabe had been about needing help. She knew Tina would have wanted her to help Gabe.

On the middle weekend of November, the LSU, the alma mater for both Jimmy and Amanda, was playing the University of Alabama at its home stadium in Tuscaloosa. Jimmy had been trying to convince her to go with him. Amanda rang Gabe.

'So, how you doin'?' Amanda asked.

'Oh, okay,' Gabe said forlornly. 'I'm fixin' to go to Parisian tomorrow. My lawyer, Bob Austin, has asked me to work out Tina's assets so we can finalise her estate and I'm a little worried about getting everything.'

'That's understandable,' Amanda said.

'And I've gotta finish up the paperwork and finalise some insurance information. You know I need to get a copy of the death certificate, stuff like that.'

'Oh yeah.'

'Funny thing is, Tina and me had been talking about – you know – increasing insurances now that we were going to be married – it must have been early September. We'd joked that – you know – for ten dollars more we could have a – she could have a million dollar life insurance policy . . . Just as well we didn't get that policy as I'd be sitting in an Australian jail now on involuntary manslaughter charges.'

He laughed. Amanda felt uncomfortable and changed the topic.

'Well, look Gabe, there's a game this weekend,' she said. 'You know, we're big fans of LSU and it's between them and Alabama. Jimmy's really keen for me to go. If . . . we end up . . . coming to Birmingham, I'd love for you to come and meet us at the game. If I don't end up going, you know, Jimmy's still going to be there, you can still come and meet him for the game and hang out.'

Gabe took the elevator to Parisian on the first floor of the large complex in the Riverchase Galleria near Pelham. When Tina worked there, he had rarely visited the store. Once or twice, he had come into the cubicle within the office she shared with others.

Gabe approached Caesar Lamonaca, the store manager at Parisian, a man in his mid fifties.

'I'd like to know about Tina's life insurance policy that's associated with her employment package,' Gabe said. 'I'd also like to pick up any personal items belonging to my wife.'

Caesar nodded, directing him to the Human Resources Department across the room.

As it happened, Amanda decided she *would* go to the game. Tuscaloosa was home of the Crimson Tide. It had started as a tailgate party in the car park with people drinking and grilling food out of the boots of their cars. Then, they moved into the stadium to watch the football game. Gabe sat next to Amanda. He was laughing and seemed happy. She imagined being introduced to him. She would have found it hard to believe he had just lost his wife. She had lost her best friend and nothing could bring her joy. Neither of them brought up Tina's death. He stayed the night in their motel room, and the next day the three of them went to lunch and then Gabe headed off.

A few weeks after Paula and Ken Snyder returned from their trip to Australia, Paula rang Gabe, leaving a message on his answering machine. It wasn't Gabe who rang back, but his mother Glenda.

'Oh, hi Glenda,' Paula said. 'How's Gabe? I was wondering how he was going.'

'Well, he's having a tough time of it.'

Paula made sympathetic noises but was quite unprepared for what followed: the lengthy explanation Glenda gave about Tina's family withholding wedding gifts.

'While I remember, can I have Tina's mother's telephone number?' Paula asked.

'No, I don't think so,' Glenda said. 'I don't think you should be calling her . . . Look, Paula, Gabe's spending time with his friends and he's being consoled. He'll call you back when he's a little more pulled together.'

Paula never heard from Gabe or Glenda again.

CHAPTER 16

Tommy Thomas had been told that his elder child had been taken from him through a terrible accident and he had believed that was the case. He had no knowledge of scuba diving. As the months passed after Tina's death, his genuine feelings of pity and sorrow for his new son-in-law slowly eroded as he moved through exasperation, frustration, anger and then, gradually, a new emotion: suspicion.

Gabe Watson had always been hard to like. At first, Tommy put it down to a matter of personality. After all, Cindy was often critical of Tina's beaux, as many parents are. But it wasn't just Cindy. Everyone in the family and, it seemed, Tina's friends, had found it difficult to warm to the tall, bulky, reserved man who, when asking for Tina's hand in marriage, could not even declare that he loved her.

Alanda's friend and workmate, Kelli, had been the first to sow seeds of doubt the day after Tina died when Gabe rang from Townsville. She had asked how Tina could have been falling faster than Gabe was kicking down to her. 'It doesn't make sense,' she'd said. 'Tina would have been trying to get to him with everything she had.'

Kelli's dad, also a diver, had agreed – Gabe's account didn't add up.

Alanda, Cindy and Tommy were still coming to terms with Tina's death, not questioning *the way* she had died. It was an accident. That's what they'd been told. Why would they think that it was anything else?

Gabe Watson was not supplying any answers. In the days following Tina's death, Tommy rang the Townsville Water Police. Above all, as he tossed and turned in the master bedroom at Seattle Slew Drive, he had to know *what* had happened. He got hold of Senior Constable Glenn Lawrence who was heading the investigation. He began by telling Lawrence what his son-in-law had told him about the events leading up to Tina's death.

'Does that sound like the story you've heard?' Tommy asked, waiting for reassurance. He wanted an official, dispassionate voice telling him not to worry, that it was 'a horrible accident'.

Instead the senior constable surprised him: 'Well, that's one thing that we'll look at.'

Tommy wasn't sure he'd heard right. It shifted the ground from under him. Tina's death was the subject of an investigation.

It was kind of hard to catch it, he said to friends later, 'but it was like these guys are concerned about something, you know? And I just wish they'd tell me. And I couldn't pin him down to anything. He wouldn't really tell me anything . . .'

Tommy began what would become an ongoing exchange with Lawrence in the weeks following Tina's death. Tommy learned that Lawrence had been present at Gabe Watson's police record of interview on 27 October. By the time

Lawrence spoke with Tommy, he had already reviewed Gabe's first audio-taped police statement as well as sifted through other eyewitness statements taken on the night of Tina's death. He had also been slowly working through a seeming mishmash of thoughts, checks to be made and matters of concern.

Gabe's private words to Tina at the morgue remained in Lawrence's workbook, mysterious rather than conclusive, but not shown to anyone. Lawrence had noted that Gabe's ascent had been far slower than Wade Singleton's as Singleton rushed to bring Tina to the surface.

When Lawrence was first assigned to the case, he assumed that it was just another dive accident. He had expected no suspicious circumstances. Now, a few weeks down the track, there were a mounting number of unanswered questions.

The Helena Police Department, outside Birmingham, is a single-storey green-roofed redbrick building with a grand entrance on two pillars to an ordinary front door, which faces a car park. A stone table and benches sit outside.

Safety is an important value for the citizens of Helena. Helena has the eighth-lowest crime rate per head of population in the US. The crimes in Helena run the gamut from robberies and bag snatching to an occasional murder/suicide and child molestation. But these offences are far enough under the radar for the community to be able to prove the claim that it enjoys 'one of the lowest crime rates per capita in the Southeast'. The police department's vision statement echoes the importance of safety, stating its force is committed to making Helena 'a safe community in which to live and work'. In this small town, police are part of the community and police officers boast their hunting and fishing prowess on the department's website.

In the car park, lines on the bitumen mark the reserved spaces for the higher-ranking police officers. Lieutenant Doug Jones had been a member of the Helena Police Department for twenty-five years and Chief of Police for three-and-a-half years. Out of the many phone calls he received, he was surprised, one morning, to receive one from Australia. It was a Senior Constable Glenn Lawrence. He wanted Lieutenant Jones to act as a liaison for one of Helena's residents, a Tommy Thomas, whose daughter had died in a tragic diving incident on the Great Barrier Reef.

A week or two after Tina's funeral Tommy also received a phone call out of the blue. A man named Ken Snyder wanted to speak with him. He had been on the *Spoilsport* and had met Tina. He left a number for Tommy to ring him.

When Tommy rang, Ken explained that he and his wife, Paula, had met Tina when everyone was boarding the *Spoilsport* in Townsville.

'Look Tommy, I'm a father too,' Ken said. 'I have kids. And I have daughters. If I was in your shoes I know I would want to talk with someone who was there to find out what happened. I'll be in Birmingham on business the week of Thanksgiving. How are you placed to meet?'

Tommy said he would be off work all that week, and home in Helena.

'My wife, Cindy, might not be up to talking about all this,' Tommy ventured. 'She's devastated, quite emotional and . . .'

'I quite understand. This might be too much for her this soon. You choose somewhere and I'll meet you.'

At 4 p.m. on Monday, 24 November, they met in the coffee shop at the Barnes & Noble bookstore in Hoover. They chatted about jobs and weather and dive holidays. Tommy took a sip of his coffee, liking the man in front of him. He seemed to have genuine compassion, and he certainly knew about scuba diving.

'You know, Ken, the thing that just haunts Cindy and I the most is the thought of Tina going to the ocean bottom with her arms stretched up toward Gabe, looking at him, and him looking at her, and him turning to leave her . . . wondering what was going through her mind.'

'Tommy,' said Ken, leaning forward in his chair to emphasise his next words, 'You can rest assured, that was not her last sight. Because that didn't happen.'

Tommy stared at the man in front of him, startled.

'Tommy, I don't know what happened underwater, but *that* didn't happen.'

Ken then related what had transpired immediately after Gabe had surfaced, what Gabe had said to him, and the two different versions he had given Doug Milsap when Milsap had first challenged him.

'Something is not right with his story. Whatever happened, it's not what he said happened, Tommy. I've had over 500 dives and my buddy Doug has had around 350 . . . We've dealt with panicked divers, lifted bulky objects, dived in many different places. None of it makes sense. Her being too heavy, the sinking too fast for him to catch her . . . panicked divers just don't sink – if they're still conscious. Both Doug and I had the same reaction to what he told us – bullshit!'

Tommy swallowed the rest of his coffee quickly, disturbed

256

and alert. He told Ken word for word what Gabe had told them on the phone when the US consulate had finally helped them make contact. These words were seared in his memory.

'Cindy asked Gabe if he had been with Tina and holding and talking to her as they tried to revive her and he said he had,' Tommy related.

'Well, that's bullshit too,' exploded Ken Snyder. 'He never even went over to the other boat she was on. That would have been a normal male response. I would have jumped over the side of the boat and swam to my wife. Just as you would, I'm sure . . . I mean, if you deserted her once, you wouldn't desert her again . . . it was just unbelievable. Even our old friend Ginger said, if that happened to Doug, nothing, or no-one, would have stopped her swimming across there.'

'So when did he actually go over there?' Tommy asked flatly.

'Well . . .' Ken hesitated, watching the man opposite him. 'It was after she had been pronounced dead. After Dr John Downie and others had worked on her for more than 40 minutes and Downie had come back to personally relay the news to Gabe. My wife Paula was there. She actually felt sorry for Gabe.'

Tommy thought that nothing could be worse than the day he buried his daughter. But now, hearing this man, who had no motivation other than as one father to another, telling him these things – that Tina had died alone, had been abandoned; that what Gabe had told them wasn't true – was unbearable.

About 5.30 p.m Alanda and her friend, Leia Travis, joined the two men after Alanda finished work at Parisian. The cup of coffee stretched into a serious talk of more than 3 hours, during which time Tommy struggled to cope with another set of facts. He heard all about the first night on board the *Spoilsport*, the welcoming drinks, how his daughter had said she was one of the War Eagles and how that had made Ken and his wife laugh. For a while, everyone was smiling as Ken Snyder's memories filled the gap of how Tina had spent the hours leading up to her death. As the talk turned to what had happened underwater, however, Tommy was concerned how Alanda, now halfway through her pregnancy, would take it. But Alanda was strong. Besides, she wanted to know. She had been watching Ken, gradually warming to him. Alanda's resolve and strength were comforting to Tommy. He knew she would do anything for her sister.

No matter what, Tommy could not ignore Ken's conviction that there was much more to what happened than Gabe had let on.

Soon after meeting Ken Snyder, Tommy contacted Senior Constable Glenn Lawrence again and relayed what he had been told.

Lawrence recorded in his notes: 'Ken Schneider [sic] – concerns about Gabe's actions, attitude before, during and after, as did doctor and dentist.'

In the late afternoon of Wednesday, 26 November 2003, Tommy Thomas kept the scheduled meeting with Gabe Watson and Bob Austin at the lawyer's office. Taken into Austin's conference room, Tommy sat to Austin's left, near the door and directly opposite Gabe. Tommy appraised him carefully. Ken had given him much to think about. Austin sat at the head of the table with a legal pad and mini tape recorder in front of him.

'Now, this meeting is designed to get the parties together,

to clear up any issues and to ensure that Tina's belongings are turned over to Gabe,' Austin explained. 'Gabe here is the rightful owner since he and Tina were married at the time of her death.

'Now Gabe, as I said, is Tina's husband. Therefore under the law he has all rights to Tina, to her belongings, and to anything that might still be in your possession or the possession of others. Tommy, I hope that any damage in the relationships between your family and the Watson family can be resolved, any misconceptions cleared up. Can I ask if there are issues that are causing you concern?'

'Well, I might start with my concern about the threats that the Watsons have reportedly made against the funeral home,' Tommy said. 'And then what about the threat against Parisian after Alanda and I were allowed to clear out Tina's desk at work? And the group insurance?' Tommy continued, his voice rising. 'I just want them to stop threatening to sue people.'

Austin responded in the firm voice of a man who was accustomed to smoothing ruffled feathers: 'I can't guarantee that. It may be necessary to bring legal action against liable and/or responsible parties concerning Tina's death and the surrounding events following her death.'

He repeated again that anything that belonged to Tina now belonged to Gabe.

'Tommy, is there anything we can do for you?'

There was a silence. Bob Austin's words hung in the air. Tommy couldn't stop the tears as he blurted: 'You could give me my daughter back . . . alive!'

There was another silence. Austin cleared his throat.

'I'm very sorry, Tommy. I should have known you would say that.'

Tommy got up and excused himself. Still crying, he

stumbled to the restroom, taking a few minutes to regain his composure before returning, red-eyed, to the conference room.

Austin said: 'Is there anything you would like to ask Gabe?'

Tommy, calm again, looked directly at Gabe who was sitting across from him against the far wall, his face expressionless. 'Yes there is.'

'Well, go ahead,' said Austin.

'When Tina gave you the thumbs-up signal to surface, why didn't you just take her directly to the surface?'

Gabe did not look at him. Instead, he looked down and then to his left towards the corner of the room.

'She did not give me a thumbs-up signal to surface. She gave me a thumb signal toward the anchor rope.'

Gabe demonstrated with his left thumb pointing away from his body, still avoiding eye contact.

'Do you have any other questions?' Austin asked.

'No,' replied Tommy, stunned, the words of Ken Snyder still ringing in his ears. Gabe had just contradicted what he had told Tommy, Cindy and Alanda on the phone from Townsville.

'Not any more.'

'By the way,' Austin mentioned, 'Gabe does not have any insurance on Tina.'

'I don't remember asking if he did,' Tommy responded icily.

'We just wanted you to know – if you were wondering about it,' Austin countered. 'Now, aside from bringing Tina back, which obviously we can't do, much as we'd like, is there anything else we can do for you?'

'What about the business with the flowers?' Tommy replied. 'I'm told that none of the flowers and plants . . . that weren't put on the grave, were allowed to be given to my family, regardless of who sent them. Most of them were taken before I even got back there to pay the funeral costs. The rest were just left there to die.'

Again, Austin spoke smoothly as though prepared for all of these missives. 'Tommy, I'm sorry about that. There seems to have been a misunderstanding about the flowers and also about anything said that you took to mean that you, or any of your family, might be removed from the viewing or the funeral. I'll see to it that the misunderstanding surrounding the flowers is corrected.'

He rose to indicate the meeting was over. Gabe remained behind. Tommy got up and headed for the door.

Thanksgiving, always on the last Thursday in November, is a family gathering that, for many Americans, is bigger than Christmas as the festive meal of the year. This Thanksgiving was the first commemorative event the Thomas family had to face in Tina's absence. The table was laid beautifully, but try as they might, the empty place where Tina would have sat resonated.

From his position at the head of the table Tommy suggested: 'Why don't we go to Australia?'

He gestured to the table laden with traditional Thanksgiving turkey and too many dishes to eat.

'I don't really want to spend our first Christmas without Tina here. It's almost more than I can bear to have Thanksgiving without her.'

'Yes, let's,' said Cindy, then glanced with a small frown at Alanda, coming up to her sixth month of pregnancy.

'How do you feel about that?' She looked questioningly at her daughter. 'Do you think they'll let you fly? You'd be seven months by then.'

261

'I think that's a great idea. We can visit all the places we've seen in the photos that Tina loved in Sydney.'

Tommy smiled. 'And what I would really like to do as well is to go to Townsville and see the people who were on the *Spoilsport* and thank them for what they did, especially the guy who brought Tina up . . .'

Everyone was in agreement.

On 18 December, Amanda Phillips was opening some Christmas mail that had arrived. She pulled one of the cards out of the envelope, not recognising the handwriting, and gasped. It was a wedding photo of Tina and Gabe smiling at her from inside a green border. Inside, Gabe had written: 'Who's the sexy-looking guy next to Tina? Oh yeah, that's me.' There was a big smiley face next to it. For Amanda, this was the final straw. 'It's just too weird for me,' she said to her husband Jimmy, who agreed with her. From that moment on, she severed contact with Gabe. All around the United States, others received similar cards. Paula and Ken Snyder, Ginger and Doug Milsap, Melinda and Adam Kayton, and Tom and Shelley Jackson. The cards contained the same message: 'Guess who the good-looking one is?' Melinda's card included the following: 'Get in touch with me in the New Year and we will get together and look at pictures.'

On 21 December, the Thomases flew out of Birmingham. It was a clear day and the temperature had steadily risen from below freezing to a relatively balmy 10°C. Travelling via Chicago and San Francisco to Sydney, they arrived early the day before Christmas Eve, carrying their heavier clothing.

It was a pleasant 21°C in Sydney, where they had a brief stopover. Then, they flew to Townsville.

Although they were prepared for the change to a tropical climate, they were nonetheless startled when they landed in North Queensland. A blast of humid heat hit them as they stepped out into the glare and palm trees surrounding the one-storey terminal in Townsville, the small airport for the region's capital city. They began to sweat, like everyone else, with the humidity up near 80 per cent. Alanda, despite her confidence about travelling, was not feeling well. December in Townsville is heading towards cyclone season and the hottest time of the year. Apart from the general hubbub around Christmas festivities, it is the low season for tourists.

Basing themselves at the Holiday Inn, Tommy, Cindy and Alanda walked around Townsville in a daze, trying to keep awake until nightfall. Jetlagged and emotional, they were nevertheless pleased to be in the place Tina had explored on her last day on land and where her body had been taken to. They spent Christmas Day in the town, walking through the largely deserted mall and then down Flinders Street East.

There was comfort for Tommy in being where his daughter's spirit had left her. Although most people they had spoken to in the days after Tina's death were now on several weeks' Christmas break, Tommy did manage to get hold of some people by phone. He took pictures of Tina to the police station for Senior Constable Glenn Lawrence. He also contacted the Mike Ball office and was delighted when Wade Singleton rang him back despite having just left on a *Spoilsport* expedition. Tommy and Cindy had particularly wanted to meet and thank him personally for trying to save their daughter.

Tommy was impressed when Singleton spoke about his memories of Tina. He smiled when he heard how Tina had joked about holding Wade's hand if he became scared on the night dive.

'Is there any possibility of meeting with you before we leave, Wade?' Tommy asked.

'If you are still here on the twenty-eighth, there's an opportunity for you to see the *Yongala* site pretty much as it was configured on the day, Tommy. We'll be there. The *Jazz II* is coming out and a third boat will be on the same mooring as where the *Adrenalin* was. If you can make some arrangement to come out with the *Jazz II*,' Singleton told him, 'I can probably get over and see you for a little while.'

Tommy discussed this with Cindy and Alanda after he hung up. In their heightened emotional state they felt unable to make the journey. The thought of taking a boat out to the lonely stretch of water where Tina died was more than they could bear. Their flights back to Sydney had been booked for 27 December, the day before the *Spoilsport* would be out at the *Yongala*. There was no way Alanda could go on a day-long open sea voyage. Besides, Cindy was worried about her daughter's health after the flight and the tropical heat.

They decided that Cindy and Alanda would leave as planned on the twenty-seventh and Tommy would go out to the *Yongala* site and then meet them in Sydney.

After visiting the *Jazz II* office and accepting the offer of a ride the next day, Tommy presented himself at the pier at 6.30 a.m. on 28 December, a hot, humid and cloudy Townsville day.

The *Jazz II* crossed Cleveland Bay, stopping briefly at Magnetic Island to pick up passengers, and then crossed the bay again, this time heading farther south. Tommy watched the rugged coastline, land Tina would never have seen, as it was pitch dark when she had left Townsville. She would have been chatting at the bar and receiving her gift of champagne from Wade Singleton by then. In a way, he had been dreading arriving at the site of the SS *Yongala*, but once there, Tommy was glad he'd made the trip. After the engines were cut and the vessel tied on the mooring, he welcomed the silence. The *Spoilsport* was moored there already. Tommy looked across, taking in all of the details of the vessel where Tina had spent her last hours. Once the divers were in the water, Wade Singleton was brought over to the *Jazz II*. Tommy looked at this slightly built man who had tried so hard to save his daughter's life, whose handshake was firm and his heartfelt sorrow for their loss obvious. They chatted for a few minutes.

'Why don't you come and look over *Spoilsport*?' Singleton offered.

This was more than Tommy had hoped for. He sat on the tender as they took off across the water to the bigger vessel. As they drew closer, Tommy tried to imagine Tina on the dive deck pulling on her fins. Tommy stepped onto the platform, then up the stairs to the blue outdoor carpet on the deck, past where the air tanks were kept. Singleton showed him the stairs onto the empty sundeck. Then, he took Tommy back down the stairs into the saloon with its big plasma screen and the turquoise carpets and curtains and wicker chairs. Tommy imagined how excited Tina must have felt that first night, toasted on her honeymoon, chatting to everyone, probably – knowing her – anxious about what the next day would bring, but excited nevertheless. He dragged his eyes away from the lounge setting as Singleton beckoned him back out to the dive deck. From here they walked into a corridor and Singleton opened the door of the first cabin on the right. This had been the honeymoon suite, he said, where Tina had spent her last night.

Tommy glanced inside, taking in colourful fish on the wall in a gold frame and the small portholes looking out to sea; the double and single bed and the en suite gleaming white. Singleton waited quietly in the corridor. After Tommy had finished, his eyes damp with tears, Singleton took him up to the wheelhouse where he was introduced to the ship's master at the helm. Singleton managed all of this so smoothly that Tommy had no time to feel uncomfortable. Singleton and the skipper answered Tommy's questions, discussing the events of the day, as they were still fresh recollections.

Tommy did not feel he should share what he had heard from Ken Snyder. The tour came to a close with an amicable soft drink each on the back deck of the *Spoilsport*. Singleton presented Tommy with a small blue hardback book: Max Gleeson's S.S. *Yongala: Townsville's Titanic*.

Tommy flicked through it, intrigued by the photos of the wreck lying on its side on the sandy ocean floor, black-and-white portraits of Captain William Knight and his crew and colourful underwater shots of coral-encrusted bathtubs and the ship's name on the bow. At the back he found a detailed diagram of the *Yongala*.

'Look Wade, can you please show me on here where you found Tina? It's . . . it's important,' Tommy said. Singleton obliged, explaining exactly where he was when he'd seen Tina lying on the bottom.

As the tender was brought back to the dive deck, Tommy climbed on board to return to the *Jazz II*.

'I want to tell you, Wade,' Tommy said, tears that came so easily now welling again in his eyes, 'how much Cindy and Alanda and I appreciated what you tried to do for Tina. I'm sorry my wife and daughter could not be here today, but they did want me to pass on their heartfelt gratitude for everything.'

Singleton too was teary.

'That's okay. I only wish I could have saved her.'

The two men gripped hands.

The *Jazz II* arrived back in port in Townsville about 4.30 p.m. Later, Tommy dined with the crew. The humidity continued to rise. At 8 p.m., the low grumble of thunder sounded on the horizon. Lightning flickered above the towering monolith of Castle Hill, which was perpetually lit at night, standing guard over the city below.

Seagulls wheeled in the cloudless blue sky, screeching for scraps from the tourists thronging on the wide promenade between the ferry terminals at Circular Quay in the heart of Sydney. The gulls provided a high-pitched contrast to the intermittent low boom of ferry horns signalling departures to beachside Manly and Luna Park, some making a short stop before heading under the Sydney Harbour Bridge and disgorging a busload of tourists at Darling Harbour, the next big inlet to the west.

The Thomases took in the magnificent view of the azure harbour and the iconic bridge while making their way from the Quay along Bennelong Point to the Sydney Opera House. Shops and restaurants shaded by white umbrellas filled the air with the smells of seafood and gourmet pizza.

This was a quintessential Sydney summer day, the temperature a pleasant 26°C. It was still warm for Alanda, especially in the sun. But the Thomases, due to return home the next day, had one goal in mind: to find the spot where Tina had sat on a seawall with the Opera House in the background.

To passersby, the trio looked like any other tourists, except if they had looked closer, they would have seen that Cindy was clutching a photo of Tina.

After a while Cindy began to cry with frustration. 'I've got to find it, I have to,' she wailed as she ran along the wide path beside the wall leading around Farm Cove, searching for the exact spot. Alanda and Tommy walked quickly to keep up with her, caught up in the urgency of her mission.

'It's okay, honey,' Tommy assured her. 'We'll find it.'

And they did shortly afterwards, sitting tired and hot but relieved on the exact spot, with the Opera House and Sydney Harbour Bridge framed in the background. They stayed there for a long time, looking out over the water imagining Tina taking in the view.

The next afternoon, the Thomases flew out of Sydney just as the large crowds began to congregate to choose sites around the harbour foreshores to witness the annual New Year's Eve fireworks against the backdrop of the Harbour Bridge. The Thomas family, settled into their seats, needed no festivities. They had seen what they needed: to see what Tina had seen and be where she had been as the happy bride.

When Tommy and Cindy arrived back at Seattle Slew Drive, it was close to midnight but still New Year's Eve due to the 17-hour time difference with Sydney. A letter was waiting from Unum Provident, the group carrier for Parisian's group life insurance.

Tommy held up the cheque from the mail that had accumulated during the trip to Australia. It was made out to him. The payout figure was US$33,024.41.

CHAPTER 17

Gabe moved into Oak Leaf Circle in Hoover in December as winter set in. Frosts covered the lawns growing down to meet the bitumen on the quiet suburban street of conventional middle-class houses, some devoid of flowerbeds. Tina and Gabe's house was three down from the top of the street on the left.

That December morning, Gabe opened the front door with trepidation. Tina had only stayed in Oak Leaf Circle for one night, but his memories of the place were entangled with thoughts of her and all of the complications that involved. Gabe had been concerned, initially, with the idea of sleeping there alone. One of his brothers had moved in with him for company, saying he'd stay a few days. On the first night, almost as though fulfilling his fears, as he walked down the hallway he saw a figure in front of him. He knew right away who it was. She had visited him at the Holiday Inn. Gabe, however, rubbed his eyes, convinced he must be seeing things. Perhaps it was his brother? Fleeing down the hallway, he pushed open his brother's bedroom door. Even before it opened properly, Gabe could hear him snoring. The image of the figure stayed with him as he slowly crept back to bed. For days afterwards he felt disturbed and he even rang Tina's friend, Amanda Phillips, and told her. She tried to reassure him. It was probably a bad dream, she said.

Early in the new year, at his mother's instigation, Gabe attended a three-month session with the Alabama Grief Support's young widow group. The newly bereaved people sat around sharing their experiences. Gabe had entered a new phase: 'widowhood'. He was provided with advice on how to cope and what to expect. He even wrote political letters to the government complaining about the lack of support for young widowers like himself. Craig Greer offered him counselling. Gabe was referred to the Alabama Psychiatric Services (APS), a casual suggestion from his brother Daniel shortly after Tina's funeral. Gabe was prescribed Ambien, a drug for sleeplessness.

Craig Youngblood kept in touch with Gabe to see how he was coping.

'I'm having a hard time of it,' Gabe told him during one conversation. 'With the costs of paying off the house and everyday things, you know? Also there's no insurance for Tina's life, so there's no money there. My parents paid off the trip costs but I'm really finding it hard to make ends meet.'

Gabe had ninety days from Tina's death to lodge a claim with Travelex Insurance Services for all of the associated costs he stated had been incurred since her death. On 12 November he lodged a claim for the medical expenses he incurred afterwards – but gathering receipts for the rest of his claim took longer than Gabe had anticipated. Finally on 20 January 2004, his claim form, under the joint letterhead of Old Republic and Travelex, was signed – ninety full days since Tina's death. He attached receipts and bills claiming a total of US$10,134.92 for reimbursement of medical and travel expenses. This included Glenda's return flight to Australia. Asked what other life insurance the deceased carried, Gabe had written: 'unknown'.

In mid January, just before the birth of Alanda's baby, Cindy opened a letter from Bob Austin demanding that the family turn over all of Tina's belongings to Gabe. The letter suggested that there had been ample time since the meeting in Austin's office in late November to comply with the agreement. Tommy was away again, but when Cindy rang to tell him, he was angered by its tone. Cindy had already suffered two near breakdowns in the aftermath of Tina's death. Tommy was concerned that this kind of pressure may well send her over the edge. The Australian trip had been a diversion of sorts, but it would never bring Tina back. In many ways, the journey underlined the finality of it all.

Tommy and Cindy decided it was time to engage legal representation of their own. Tommy called Alton Parker Jr., a lawyer at Spain & Gillon, one of the oldest law firms in Alabama. The firm had a general civil law practice that embraced a range of practice groups including estate administration.

It was nearly 3.30 p.m. on Friday, 23 January 2004 when Tommy entered the Zinszer Building, built in 1888 on 2nd Avenue North, Birmingham, one of the few cast-iron-front Italianate Victorian buildings to survive in Alabama.

Sitting opposite Parker, a member of the firm for nearly twenty-five years, Tommy told him his story and sought advice on how to deal with what he believed was the harassment and stress his family had suffered.

The following Wednesday, Tommy and Cindy Thomas became grandparents for the first time. The stress of the past three months, including the long flights to Australia and back, had taken its toll on Alanda. Named William, after his grandfather, the baby was born almost a month early. Alanda's joy at seeing her newborn son was tinged with sorrow at Tina's absence. She remembered how excited Tina had been, her ear to the stethoscope listening to the baby's heartbeat. William Matthew would never know his aunt, who had wanted children and a white picket fence, someone to love and someone who would love her back.

Senior Constable Glenn Lawrence returned from leave in the early part of the new year. He began going back through his notes on the Watson case, completing an internal report he had compiled for the CIB and his supervising inspector, Warren Webber. Returning afresh to the investigation, he became even more convinced about the inconsistencies in the evidence that he detailed in his report. He prepared a PowerPoint presentation to fellow superior officers outlining his concerns. Mostly, they related to Gabe's conflicting statements to police. Among the questions he raised, which none of the available evidence seemed to be able to answer, was why Gabe had not made more effort to assist and rescue Tina; why his rapid-ascent alarm did not activate on his dive computer if he'd been going to the surface as quickly as he'd said; and why Tina's BC had not inflated if she had air in her tank.

Flicking through the PowerPoint slides, Lawrence asked his audience: 'Why did they go alone when they had never dived on this wreck before?

'I also have questions in relation to how Tina, being

smaller and below Gabe when he was towing her, can then reach up around him, above him and with enough force to dislodge his mask and regulator at the same time?'

Lawrence told them how Gabe had said, in one of his two interviews, that he checked his own equipment. But there was no indication of him cross-checking the equipment of his buddy, as is usually done, especially as his wife was a relative novice. Nor could Lawrence find anyone who matched the description Gabe had given of the Asian diver who Gabe claimed to have tapped on the shoulder after leaving Tina to fall to the bottom of the ocean. There were other matters that were inconsistent with available evidence. For instance, in his second record of interview Gabe had said that there had been no offer of a dive instructor to accompany them on the wreck. Wade Singleton's statement, however, said that it had been not only offered, but recommended. Gabe's assertion that there were no warnings about the current had been refuted by many of the other passengers on board.

'Gabe said: "I wasn't going up faster than my bubbles."' Lawrence pointed to the next slide on the PowerPoint presentation. 'That doesn't indicate rocketing to the surface like he told us. Not going up faster than his bubbles indicates a controlled ascent that was not rapid, and it also tallies with his dive computer not alarming.

'I couldn't find any evidence, any suggestion from Gabe at all that he made any attempt to provide Tina with either buoyancy, air or anything apart from kicking her loose.'

Also unlikely, Lawrence stated, was the sequence in which Gabe said he had turned back, cleared his mask before realising that his regulator wasn't in his mouth. Usually it would be the other way round. A diver would need the air from the regulator, and sometimes quite a bit of it, to exhale through his nose to expel water from the mask. There were many

273

inconsistencies too with the Workplace Health and Safety Officer's reports and Gabe's accounts. None of it seemed to add up.

In mid February, Gabe received the letter he had been waiting for, the envelope marked Travelex Insurance Services. He ripped it open.

Dated 10 February 2004, after expressing condolences on the passing of his wife, it acknowledged receipt of Gabe's claim for trip interruption and medical benefits. It asked him to refer to the attached insurance policy under the heading 'General Exclusions and Limitations'. Part 'g' of benefits not payable for sickness, injuries or losses stated 'while participating in skydiving, hang gliding, bungee cords jumping, scuba diving or deep sea diving'. The file indicated the reason for Gabe's trip interruption and medical expenses was not covered under the policy wording and 'all payments are governed by the terms and conditions of the policy in force at the time of the claim'.

Regretfully, the claims examiner concluded, Travelex was unable to be of service.

Gabe read it again. A brochure was enclosed with the letter. Curious, he went through his old paperwork, comparing it with the one he had been given when he booked his trip with Freida Gammill. The brochure enclosed with the Travelex letter denying his claim was dated 2004, while the brochure he had taken from Get Away Travel was dated 2002. There was one major difference: the 2002 brochure did not contain any of the general exclusions and limitations contained in the 2004 brochure.

***

On Monday, 9 February, Tommy Thomas made his routine visit to Tina's grave. Each visit, he would kiss the ground before he left and tell Tina how much he missed her. Parking on the small roadway at the top of the hill in the cemetery, he headed across the lawn. Tina's was the only grave with no gravestone, despite the fact that she had been dead for almost four months. This pained Tommy, but nothing prepared him for the sight that now met his eyes. The yellow roses and white daisies that the family always placed at the head of Tina's gravesite had disappeared. Usually out of town all week on business, it had been Tommy's habit to replace the artificial wreaths each month. Sometimes the family left other mementos and messages: 'Gone yet not forgotten, although we are apart, your spirit lives within me forever in my heart' or Alanda's message: 'Sister, you are the one that I turn to when I need encouragement.' However, apart from the wreaths placed there by the Thomases and, he presumed, the Watsons, Tina's grave always looked bare. Tommy's immediate thought was how much this latest development would upset Cindy. He got back into the car and drove to a florist to replace the missing wreath.

Every fortnight after that, instead of every month, he began replacing the flowers on a Saturday or Sunday. A pattern emerged. By Tuesday or Wednesday of the following week they were gone.

'Daddy, the flowers are gone again,' Alanda told her father regularly by phone, as she visited Tina's grave during the week while he was away.

A month after Tommy and Cindy received Bob Austin's letter, on Saturday, 20 March, Tommy's next-door neighbour, Mike Brashier, borrowed a pick-up truck and, with his son Andrew and Tommy, they loaded Tina's remaining belongings from Seattle Slew Drive onto the back. There was a mattress set, some bedding items and several wedding presents. It also included items that Alanda had removed from Tina's desk at Parisian, an inclusion agreed to through their lawyer, Alton Parker. They delivered everything to Oak Leaf Circle.

The flowers continued to disappear.

Not long after his twenty-seventh birthday in March, Gabe penned a letter to a Senator, angered that he was not entitled to Social Security benefits because he and Tina were married for only 11 days and had no children, and that the information available for widows had not been updated in thirty years.

'Let me tell you how pathetic that is,' he fumed about a one-off government payment of $225.00 paid to bereaved spouses. 'I had to spend over $12,000 to have her body flown back to the states [sic] for burial . . . $225.00 does not even cover the cost for them to dig the hole, its [sic] $700.00 . . .' Why would the government 'hand out money to crack whores who continue to have children just to get more government money on the first of the month' while he faced losing his house if he was unable to pay a mortgage based on two salaries now that there was only one wage coming in?

On 9 June, Alanda walked towards Tina's grave and immediately noticed little orange flags around the site. With a sinking feeling, she asked the funeral home what they represented.

She rang her father straightaway, sobbing, to tell him that the Watsons were having Tina moved the following Monday.

Even when Tommy Thomas was angry he was eloquent,

able to draw on the right vocabulary for the best effect, while at the same time maintaining his dignity. He had tolerated so much, but this was enough. His daughter had never been allowed to rest in peace, ever since being placed in her vault. Battles had raged above ground, but to shift her from her final resting place was, he believed, the height of indignity. Tommy rang the Townsville police and the police in Helena, as well as his lawyer, Alton Parker – anyone he could think of. There was nothing they could do, he was told. As Tina's spouse, under Alabama law Gabe had the legal right to move her, as well as any rights over details of the funeral and burial. Tommy was given no reason for the move, nor did he have any idea about where Tina would be moved to.

On Monday, 14 June, there was a brief reprieve when rain intervened. Several reschedulings followed. Again rain, or other reasons, kept delaying the disinterment of Tina's vault. Tommy was thankful that in July 2004, his efforts in contacting the Queensland police resulted in the Shelby District Attorney halting the move. The mysterious weekly disappearance of the Thomas flowers also stopped around this time.

Gabe engaged Birmingham lawyer Keith T. Belt Jr., then of Bowman and Bate, to assist him in his dispute with Travelex Insurance Services Inc and its underwriter, Old Republic Insurance Company. In a letter dated 15 June 2004, Belt wrote to Carolyn Johnson, the author of the February letter Gabe had received denying him insurance coverage under his policy.

He asked that Ms Johnson accept Gabe's claim for trip interruption, accidental medical expenses, medical evacuation and common carrier accidental death insurance claims, and pointed out that the exclusion she had cited did not appear in the Travel Plus brochure provided to Gabe when he bought the insurance. Nor was it in the confirmation of coverage form provided when Gabe paid his $484 premium. Those two documents, which under Alabama law would serve as the terms and conditions of an insurance policy, did not contain any exclusions for scuba diving, Belt claimed.

'Consequently it is immaterial if you changed your policy or if latter policies had these included as these exclusions were never provided to my client . . . Needless to say,' Belt continued, 'this is an airtight case under Alabama Law and I would ask that you immediately accept this claim and pay the losses.' Failure to do so within 21 days, he warned, would force him to 'file a law suit for bad faith'.

On 25 June, Sergeant Joe Kitching, a prematurely balding red-headed man in charge of the Townsville CIB, wrote the first of a series of emails to Gabe's lawyer, Keith Belt Jr., informing him that Townsville police were still investigating the case and were preparing a report for the Coroner. He stated that further inquiries were expected to be made in the United States. He also informed Belt he was unable to release his client's dive property until the investigation was finalised and a direction given by the Coroner as to whether there would be an inquest into Tina's death.

Gabe personally responded to Kitching: 'I am wondering why this is my 4th attempt in as many weeks trying to contact you and you have not responded.' Gabe declared that he was 'pretty much resigned to the fact' that the police had no intention of finishing the investigation into Tina's death 'in order to protect the dive industry . . . I have no intentions [sic] of going away,' he stated, threatening to speak out against both the dive industry and the Townsville police 'for years to come'. Gabe said he also intended to file complaints against both the police and Kitching, the nominal head of the investigation, as well as with the US Department of State, warning of the dangers to US citizens planning dive trips to Australia. Once he had handed over information collected on his perceived lack of safety in the dive industry, all his comments would, from then on, be on public forums. 'I promise you I will not go away,' he finished off.

Belt wrote again to Kitching on 13 July stating that his client had just received Tina's death certificate and that the only listed cause of death was 'drowning'.

'Consequently, I am very concerned about the diving equipment and whether it may have malfunctioned,' he wrote.

On 16 July 2004, Belt wrote to Kelly Brennan, a lawyer at established Birmingham law firm Balch and Bingham, representing Travelex and its underwriter Old Republic. Following up a telephone conversation between them, Belt informed Ms Brennan that the total amount of the claim 'not including death benefits, is [US]$10,134.92. This amount includes the unused part of the dive trip, airfare, hotel, taxi, emergency phone calls and medical expenses'. In addition to that amount Belt said his client was also claiming the [US]$10,000 accidental death benefit and the [US]$25,000 common carrier accidental death benefit.

Sergeant Gary Campbell was the sergeant-in-charge of the Townsville Break and Enter Squad on the day that Tina died. He had been responsible for dispatching general duties officers to take statements. He was a straightforward cop who did not waste time in idle chat. When he turned his mind to something, he was difficult to shake off. Up until this point, he had been peripherally involved in the investigation into Tina's death, but after the case was forwarded to the CIB, he was appointed to review the investigation on 10 July.

The investigation had been codenamed 'Operation Charlie Oswald'. Campbell began by reading the documentation and then started an occurrence sheet, where he recorded the contacts made with the various witnesses locally, nationally and internationally. Campbell listed the exhibits: Tina's black wetsuit top and bottom, her dive tank and serial number, purple face mask and snorkel and her black and silver Atomic Aquatics fins and size 5 black boots; and the two Oceanic brand dive computers: Gabe's DataTrans Plus model and Tina's less expensive Versa model. He also included the thirty photographs that Gary Stempler had burned onto a CD for police, photos of the post-mortem and the dive entry/exit profile sheets. He and Kevin Gehringer, who was still on the case, took possession of the evidence collected by Glenn Lawrence of the Townsville Water Police. They were to report to the Coroner, David Glasgow, a man who specialised in marine and dive inquests.

Sergeant Joe Kitching corresponded with Gabe's legal representatives. On 21 July, he informed Keith Belt that he would be lodging a submission to Interpol about the US side of the investigations into Tina's death by the end of the week.

Belt had warned Gabe that the police had not concluded

their investigation and would be seeking to undertake further investigations such as interviewing US witnesses. 'Sit tight for a little while until they finish,' Belt advised.

Sergeant Gary Campbell tracked down the now fourteen-year-old Jarrod Fisher and one of the commercial divers who hadn't been interviewed, as well as Tina Graves, who repeated her concern about Gabe Watson telling her that he had pushed his distressed new bride away. Campbell, methodical as always, ordered the meteorological observations on the date of Tina's death at several locations near the *Yongala* shipwreck. He collected a series of images of the wreck from the Museum of Tropical Queensland's website, which identified mooring points, the isolated danger marker, diver access points and the *Yongala* itself as well as their relationship to each other. He also sought help from a scientist at James Cook University, who provided a three-dimensional computer-generated image of the SS *Yongala*, used to study the behaviour of bull sharks, to calculate the leaning angle of the wreck. Campbell collected several addendum statements from witnesses.

He commissioned reports on the quality of air in Tina's Sea Hornet scuba tank in case something in the tank had contributed to her death. Lab tests indicated that the percentage of carbon dioxide found in the tank 'was not significant medically', even if it was slightly over the conservative Australian standard. 'There's certainly nothing . . . that would contribute to her loss of consciousness or distress from the air content,' the report concluded.

Campbell also had the Sea Hornet aluminium scuba cylinder hired from the *Spoilsport* and her regulator and octopus and extra-small-sized BC checked. She had carried over 9 kilograms (about 20 pounds) in weights. According to a police report Tina's personal dive equipment 'was of excellent quality and cleanliness' with no life-threatening faults.

On 1 November Campbell flew to Melbourne and then drove to Sorrento, a seaside town in Victoria, with Gabe's dive computer. Adam White, the Customer Service Manager of Oceanic Australia, told him that if the batteries of the dive computer worn on the wrist were put in back to front, not only would the unit not operate, it would neither display nor record any information, nor would it give off any warnings such as Gabe Watson had described. White pressure-tested the dive computer and found it was 100 per cent accurate. He also found that the dive computer battery had been removed just before Gabe's last four dives. Removing the battery, White told Campbell, meant the dates on subsequent dives reverted back to the original factory setting of 1 January 1996, so an incorrect date would have been recorded for the actual dives. The last dive recorded, Tina's fatal dive, showed that Gabe Watson had been underwater for 7 minutes and had reached a maximum depth of 16.5 metres.

Adam White advised that he was unable to download dive profiles from Tina's more basic dive computer.

CHAPTER 18

It was November 2004 in Townsville and the thermometer was creeping up. The humidity was back after the cooler winter months and the cyclone watch was beginning. Weather, sport and crime never fail to make front-page regional news in the *Townsville Bulletin*. This year had been a good year, in particular, for sport. The Crocs, Townsville's professional basketball team, had four players named in the National Basketball League's All Star Game. The North Queensland Cowboys, Townsville's professional rugby league football team, had their first free-to-air televised game after making Australia's NRL finals series.

Crime reports in this military town often centred on disgraced soldiers dealing in drugs pleading post-traumatic stress disorder or stoushes on the Flinders Street nightclub strip. On 4 November, local journalist Andy Toulson, a senior reporter with the *Townsville Bulletin*, marked the first anniversary of Tina's burial by publishing an interview with Tommy Thomas. It was Toulson who had spoken to Gabe Watson the day he was interviewed by police in Townsville, which led to the newspaper article with the grieving widower. Coincidentally, it was also Toulson who

283

picked up the phone when Tommy, desperately seeking information, rang the newspaper from the United States when he could not find his son-in-law in the days that followed Tina's death. Asked how he was coping, one year on, Tommy told her how Tina's death had 'ripped a great hole' in the family and that the past twelve months had been 'absolute hell'. 'God we miss her so much,' Tommy told Toulson. 'She was such a special, beautiful girl with the most amazing, playful personality.' He still found it hard to talk about her without crying but felt that 'somehow, she is what is pulling both of us through'. He spoke of his pride that Tina, who had 'such ambitions', had been the first on the Thomas side to graduate from college. 'It just isn't right that she is gone.' Tommy thanked the people of Townsville for being 'so incredibly supportive to us throughout this whole horrendous time'. Toulson's long association with the family had begun.

A year after her death, Tina's presence continued to occupy the minds of those in both hemispheres, from Birmingham, Alabama, to the regional city on the edge of the Great Barrier Reef.

Sergeant Gary Campbell's investigations were ongoing. He showed Wade Singleton a document depicting a bird's-eye view of the SS *Yongala* and displaying the moorings of the various vessels so he could better visualise the position of the wreck and the mooring sites. He corresponded by email with Dr Stanley Stutz, who was the last person to see Tina alive, and other key witnesses. In December, he visited Professor David Williams, the forensic pathologist, and Dr David Griffiths, the Chief Medical Officer of the Townsville Hospital's Hyperbaric Medicine Unit, providing them with reports on Tina's equipment as well as statements from witnesses such as Wade Singleton, John Downie and Craig

Stephen, so that these experts might comment further on the post-mortem findings.

Sergeant Brad Flynn sat at his desk in the one-storey Helena Police Department building. It was approaching noon on 22 December 2004. The heavy rain earlier in the morning had eased to a drizzle. Flynn was sending an email to customer service at Travelex Insurance, the latest in a long line of emails to help the Queensland police investigation. Flynn had only recently got to know Tommy Thomas but he knew instinctively that Tommy was an honourable man. Where any man would have been driven to rage, Tommy remained calm, always wanting the best for his daughter. Flynn typed:

Mr Watson is suspected in the death of his wife while on a diving trip to Australia last year. Mr Watson purchased a Travelex policy on his wife and himself for their trip. Mr Watson has been attempting to cash in on the outstanding policies he had on his wife during the past year, but all the others have withheld the payment due to the qustionable [sic] *circumstances involving her death. I have some information on the policy but need to ensure that the claim has not been paid.*

The email was sent to Cassandra Timms, the manager of travel claims with a subsidiary company of Old Republic Insurance. Responsible for the claims unit that denied Gabe Watson's travel insurance claim, she forwarded it, just after noon the next day, to Kelly Brennan at Old Republic's law firm, Balch and Bingham, in downtown Birmingham. The news eventually filtered through to Hoover. Just over a year after his wife's death, Gabe Watson went from a man lodging an insurance claim expecting a payout, to a man under suspicion of foul play.

After serving ten years with the Office of the State Coroner in Townsville, David Glasgow was nearing retirement. Like other Coroners in North Queensland, he divided his time between hearing inquests and sitting in the lower courts as a Magistrate. When Tina Watson's file arrived, it was a death at sea, but one that still warranted further investigation. It would probably be his last case as Coroner.

Glasgow had been a diver himself, more than twenty years earlier, and had presided over some controversial local cases. Specialisations were divided up among the Coroners, and the diving deaths usually landed on Glasgow's desk. In the early days of his involvement, any next step hinged on whether or not the police charged Gabe Watson over his wife's death. If not, a Coronial inquest would be necessary. Glasgow's first task was to talk to the police officers.

'We're carrying out further investigations because we have concerns,' Sergeant Gary Campbell said evenly when they met one morning in Glasgow's office.

'Well, you don't really have to tell me anything about that, because if you've got suspicions you might end up charging someone over that. There's going to be a Workplace, Health and Safety prosecution, because of what happened out at sea – with the boat – I'll just leave the file so you can do the report,' Glasgow said.

Campbell made several visits to the Coroner's office. On one visit, he confided to Glasgow that he believed that a request he had made to visit the United States to complete investigations into the Watson case was being blocked. Glasgow knew the entire case was cost prohibitive with so many overseas witnesses. He offered to write a letter to Campbell's superior officers. Before him, he saw a police officer dedicated to the investigation who clearly had concerns and should be supported. Glasgow sent the Watson file to the Deputy State Coroner, Michael Barnes, seeking his support to make submissions to the Deputy Commissioner of Police for further investigation.

On 17 January 2005, he wrote to Michael Barnes: 'I am in no doubt that there is every reasonable expectation by the deceased's father, and his local senator, that the investigation should be completed with Queensland police travelling to the United States. Unless there is some decision on the matter soon, the father will generate considerable publicity over the perceived lack of action over the death of his daughter.'

This lack of action would by implication, he continued, reflect badly on both the Queensland police and the Office of the Coroner and he was concerned the matter had 'real potential for political embarrassment of a major nature'. More importantly, he added, he did not think enough consideration had been given to it by the state's Commissioner of Police.

For some time, Glasgow heard nothing. Then he contacted Barnes again. The file, he discovered, had been archived, probably accidentally. He told Barnes he wanted it back and that it wasn't closed. The call had the desired effect and the file arrived back in Townsville.

Campbell was once again in Glasgow's office. The officer's tenacity was impressive.

'Don't you ever get angry about it?' Glasgow asked him.

'No,' Campbell said. 'I've learned not to get angry . . .' He paused, sitting forward on his chair, his hand rubbing his forehead. 'It's just that it doesn't sit right, you know, and every time we asked him a question, during the taking of the statement, and the record of interview, we'd end up with different answers . . .'

Campbell described a list he had compiled of the pros and cons of all the conflicting points. Besides, and perhaps most importantly, he added, Gabe Watson was a trained rescue diver.

Glasgow thought back down the years to his own diving days. He listened and took notes, typing them up later himself as budgetary constraints had cut back administrative support.

On 8 February, Gary Campbell followed up on his earlier visit and interviewed Dr Griffiths at the Hyperbaric Medical Unit at the Townsville Hospital. Divers from all around Australia trained in the hyperbaric chamber there. Griffiths noted in his statement that Tina Watson had been treated for a cardiac problem that may, if exacerbated by a physically or emotionally stressful event, provoke anxiety. That anxiety, he hypothesised, may have been brought about by the strong current. He said that Gabe Watson's evidence fitted with the theory of Tina becoming more anxious, developing an abnormal heart rhythm and losing consciousness. When she had stopped convulsing, she would have become limp, Griffiths wrote, and then she would have started to sink 'probably without starting to breathe' even if her regulator was in her mouth. However, he suggested that the opinion of a cardioelectrophysiologist may be helpful in determining whether a serious cardiac event had led to Tina losing consciousness as that was not his area of expertise.

'A severe anxiety attack causing Christina to pull off her husband's mask is unlikely to be a satisfactory explanation of events in the absence of a serious heart disturbance. Panic alone would be likely to cause hyperventilation and not unconsciousness.' Death, he said, would only be likely following panic if the victim lost her scuba regulator or ascended to the surface while breath-holding. In Tina's case neither of those things had happened.

Dr Griffiths tested Gabe Watson's dive computer in the hyperbaric chamber on 14 February. Turned on with the battery correctly inserted, the computer was put in a bucket of salt water and then pressurised in the chamber. Once the pressure reached the equivalent of about a metre in depth, beeps were audible and a 'low air pressure' message flashed on the screen, visible to Griffiths and Campbell who were watching through a viewport. The depth gauge and timer function operated normally. But no beeps were audible when the battery in the computer was reversed and the procedure was repeated in the chamber. The screen remained blank. Once the battery was reversed, the dive computer just didn't work.

Dr Griffiths noted in his report afterwards that the demonstration of no beeping when the computer was pressurised underwater at a depth of between 1 and 5 metres was 'contrary' to what Gabe had told police was the reason for the aborted first dive. He added a qualification: 'However, the computer <u>does</u>' – Griffiths underlined the word 'does' – 'emit beeps when its battery is fitted correctly but it is not correctly connected to a source of compressed air'. Griffith was not given the transmitter that connected to the dive computer because it had been taken home by Gabe Watson.

On 15 March, Detective Sergeant Gary Campbell, Sergeant Joe Kitching, Senior Constable Glenn Lawrence and Senior Constable Paul Campbell received an email from

Gabe Watson. The subject line read: update on investigation (Tina Watson).

After nearly eighteen months Gabe was 'wondering where you were at on the investigation'. He also asked: 'Secondly, why is it you guys objected to me moving Tina from one side of the cemetery to the other?' He wrote that he had not been contacted by anyone from the Queensland police with concerns and 'the first I ever heard of it was when you had the Shelby County district attorney file a court action to stop the move'.

Gabe also wanted to know whether there was any intention to return Tina's dive equipment as well as his computer, log book and all his certification cards. 'I still have the company that financed Tina's equipment asking me what the timetable is for the return . . . as there is not enough money in her estate to cover the debt they would like the equipment back to cover their loss.'

Gary Campbell forwarded the email to the CIB.

Among the industrial and impoverished scars of housing commission estates in downtown Birmingham, Alabama, are many examples of the Art Deco sophistication underlining the architectural foresight of its early citizens. One of those buildings is the Jefferson County Courthouse. Built in 1931, the imposing grey edifice built from reinforced concrete and faced with granite and limestone could pass for the Gotham City Hall in the old *Batman* TV series. Two towering flagpoles bearing large US flags stand on either side of the wide steps that lead to the now modified main entrance tacked on to provide space for a bag scanner and metal detector. *'Equal and exact justice to all men of whatever state or persuasion' Thomas Jefferson* is emblazoned above the entrance. The fluttering flags are the only colours that contrast with the grey steps, railings and walls. The building houses the Jefferson County Probate Court, its Circuit (or trial) Court in which cases are heard before a judge and jury, and the Jefferson County Supreme Court, to which losing sides from the Circuit Court may appeal decisions.

On the fourth floor, outside the marbled foyer in front of the elevator bank, is the Circuit Court registry, which does a roaring trade in filing fees for the civil cases and accompanying motions, responses and replies lodged there every day. Exact money is preferred for all transactions as no change is given.

Civil Case CV005 1837, containing a sixteen-page complaint by David Gabriel Watson against Old Republic Insurance Co, Travelex Insurance Services Inc, and Get Away of Birmingham Inc, lodged on 30 March 2005, was a reasonably standard sort of claim in the court registry. The complaint alleged breach of contract, bad faith, fraud and suppression against the three defendants. Mr Watson wanted damages for economic loss and also claimed he had suffered mental anguish as a result of the denial of the claim. Interest from the date of injury on any amount awarded and the costs the case would amass were also sought.

'Further,' the complaint stated, 'Plaintiff requests that the jury selected to hear this case render a verdict to Plaintiff and against each Defendant, and that it award punitive damages in an amount which will adequately reflect the enormity of the Defendants' wrongful acts and which will effectively prevent other similar wrongful acts.'

This request for punitive damages, not generally available in Australian civil actions, meant Gabe Watson was seeking a sizeable award that was intended to punish any perceived wrongdoing and to act as a deterrent to any companies in the position of the defendants in the future. Effectively he was seeking compensation from three potential pots of money: damages, interest and punitive damages.

On 11 May, Professor Williams, the consultant forensic pathologist, also provided a statement to Sergeant Campbell. Williams had an impressive list of qualifications including a Bachelor of Science from the University of Wales, a Bachelor of Medicine and Bachelor of Surgery from the University of Glasgow as well as a PhD in Forensic Medicine from the same university. He had more than thirty years' experience in forensic medicine and had authored an international textbook on forensic pathology.

Williams confirmed that he had found the cause of Tina's death to be 'drowning', as was noted on her death certificate. He stated categorically, however, that her death had not been caused by arrhythmia from her previous heart condition.

His last comment on the statement read: 'The post-mortem examination did not reveal why she had an apparent problem while diving. It is possible, in my opinion, that she had deprivation of oxygen prior to drowning.'

The 10-kilometre drive to the Southern Heritage Funeral Home and Cemetery had become a ritual for the Thomas family. 'Going to see Tina' was a regular event for all of them, including Alanda's little boy William.

For six months, the flowers the Thomas family had regularly placed on Tina's grave had remained there. Far worse than flowers going missing, though, was the threat that Tina would be exhumed and moved from her resting place. After February 2005, the flowers began to go missing again. When Tommy arrived for his weekly visits, he felt the familiar sense of anxiety, checking to see whether the offerings had been moved. He was never sure whether he would find an empty space at the head of her unmarked stretch of lawn or their bouquet. This bizarre ritual gnawed at any sense of peace. Worst of all, he felt that Tina had no peace. Each weekend, he placed new flowers on the grave. Each Monday, they would disappear. They had vanished by the time he visited the grave.

Sergeant Brad Flynn of the Helena Police Department rang Tommy in late September and Tommy told him about the missing flowers.

'Look Tommy,' Flynn said. 'I wanted to be the first to tell you. Gabe has contacted the funeral home and told them the investigation has been concluded and that he wants Tina moved on October 7.'

Tommy felt as though he'd been punched. To have lost her was bad enough. He wanted a grave with his daughter's name properly marked as befitted anyone who had died. He wanted to be able to engrave the family's thoughts onto a gravestone. It was an ordinary wish, nothing more, a right those who grieved for their lost ones took for granted.

Detective Senior Sergeant Scott Knowles from the Homicide Investigation Unit, State Crime Operations Command, in Brisbane, had been asked by Townsville CIB to review the Watson case. Gary Campbell flew to Brisbane, bringing with him the documentation, including photographs of equipment, reports, statements, data from Oceanic and running sheets. Knowles agreed there were suspicious circumstances that warranted further inquiries locally, nationally and internationally before the brief could reasonably be brought before a court.

On 6 October, the day before Tina's body was due to be moved, the flowers on her grave were removed again, except for one arrangement that Tommy had looped with a bicycle chain to a yellow stake in the ground at the head of the grave.

Tommy was the only family member to attend the re-interment. That morning, on 7 October, Tommy entered through the gates of the funeral home, drove around the roundabout with a line of small deciduous trees, then headed left to where all of the flags that had ever flown over Alabama stood grouped at the top of the hill. It was a sombre, drizzly morning matching his mood. Now, almost two years after first making this journey, Tina was to be raised from the ground. Ever punctual, Tommy arrived early and walked across the wet grass to his daughter's grave. His friend Buddy Womuchil had come with him for moral support. The Helena police were there: Sergeant Brad Flynn and Chief Jones, along with Doug Glascock, who was the director of the funeral home. David Watson and Bob Austin stood separately. Gabe was absent. Tommy's heart was beating fast and he felt faint. He breathed deeply. He was glad that Cindy and Alanda hadn't come. The rain continued to drizzle, pooling around the holes dug by the backhoe. He prayed silently. Standing on the grassy knoll as the machinery cut into the earth around Tina's grave, Tommy was adamant this was unnatural, in spite of the funeral director explaining that re-interments occurred each year for various reasons. The director had explained that people sometimes acquired more plot space or, for their own reasons, wanted their loved ones moved.

Sergeant Flynn, who was privately seething that Gabe had sent his father instead of turning up himself, brought his video camera out. Shielding it from the rain with his hand, he began filming.

Tommy stood with his hands clasped in front of him. The vault was lifted out of the earth from the unmarked grave and then loaded onto the back of a dump truck to be transported to the new site about 90 metres away. Since he last hugged his daughter goodbye at the elevator, Tommy had felt a continuing sense of powerlessness. Eleven days later, when she was so far away, his world had fallen apart. The frantic phone calls; finding out her body had travelled alone back to Alabama and then her burial, all happened in quick succession less than a month after she had stood in white at the altar. Two years later, they seemed no closer to getting answers about what had happened. Today, though, was the ultimate disempowerment as he stood, a spectator once again.

Tina's new place of rest was between two children: a grave with a stone angel and a rabbit marking the short two years of life of a little girl, Mary, and a grey speckled marble headstone with an engraving of a boy holding a baseball bat marking the final resting place of 'Las Vegas Brendan'.

After everyone had left Tina's new gravesite, Tommy stood silently in the drizzling rain. Several tall trees, oak and hickory, grew down the hill towards the road and from here there was a panorama of Oak Mountain, one of Tina's favourite views, still visible through the mists, with forests blanketing the lower hills and leading into the distance. Soon he would see the grass grow slowly over the newly dug earth in the same way he had watched it after Tina was first buried.

The next morning, Tommy returned early to re-stake and chain the flowers from her previous gravesite. A week later, the flowers were gone.

Sergeant Brad Flynn was working on the humdrum inquiries that formed the beat in a county police station when the phone rang. Tommy Thomas's voice was near breaking point.

'The flowers have gone missing again as well as other items that we've put there.'

'Well,' Flynn said. 'I reckon you should be filing police reports for each flower theft with the Pelham Police Department.'

On 15 October Tommy filed the first report.

On 7 November, Sergeant Flynn arrived at Tina's grave, bending to read the card on the bouquet of yellow and white flowers: 'Tina, we love you. Mom and Dad.' Positioning himself behind some trees where he could still observe Tina's gravesite, he sat down to wait, his twenty-odd years in the force providing him with the patience for such a task. After five-and-a-half hours, moving stiffly from one position to another in the chilly November air, he was rewarded. A black SUV came to a stop on the roadway near the grave. Flynn began filming as Gabe Watson, dressed in a horizontally striped blue-and-white polo shirt and tan pants, got out of the car and approached Tina's grave. Gabe paused momentarily, looking down, and returning to the car, came back with a set of red bolt cutters. Through the viewfinder, Flynn could see Gabe bending over the grave and using the bolt cutters to cut at something on the grave. Walking away in the direction of the road, the flowers across one arm, Gabe dumped them beside the roadway. Flynn knew this was the practice adopted at the cemetery: if flowers were to be discarded, staff would come around to collect and dispose of any lying on the roadway. He saw Gabe dump the cable into a nearby rubbish bin before getting back inside the car and driving off. Flynn waited until Gabe had left, then stopped recording and walked across to the grave. The flowers were by the side of the road. He picked them up, noticing the card was missing.

Tired of waiting for answers, in March 2006 Cindy and Tommy planned to cross the Pacific Ocean for a second visit to Australia. Before they arrived, a small spat arose between the two police forces across the globe. Andy Toulson had written another story about the protracted nature of the police investigation. Shortly before the Thomases arrived in Australia, the Queensland Police Minister, Judy Spence, issued a press release stating that her office would follow up with US officers in a bid to 'speed up the investigation'. Helena Police Chief, Lieutenant Doug Jones, was irate. The only delay, as far as he was concerned, was 'the Australian end' refusing to fund Australian officers to travel to the United States to finalise the investigation. He had written to the Queensland Police Commissioner, Bob Atkinson, to tell him so. So far, the US authorities had not been contacted by any senior Australian police. Indeed, Jones added, the US police had even offered to fund the Australian officers' costs for the overseas trip. Tommy Thomas joined the outcry about the lack of support from 'middle management'.

On 22 March, the Thomases met Detective Inspector Mike Condon from the Brisbane Homicide Investigation Unit. The next day, they flew to Townsville, arriving to autumn weather in the north: hot, blustery, still cyclone-prone and unpredictable. Gary Campbell and Kevin

Gehringer met the Thomases at the airport. The following day they took them to the Northern Regional Police Headquarters for a meeting with senior police. Later that day, they were also introduced to the Coroner, David Glasgow.

Glasgow had the face of a congenial grandfather. This, combined with a natural curiosity, made him easier to read than most of the pokerfaced legal fraternity. His voice was deep, unhurried and authoritative. Wearing his heart on his sleeve, he was the sort of man who cared deeply about his responsibilities, but who managed paradoxically to wear them lightly. He had the ability to be empathetic, putting himself in the grieving parents' shoes as he listened to the angst the Thomases had endured through two-and-a-half years not knowing why or how their daughter had died. Cindy broke down often, exhausted and jetlagged. Mostly, in spite of occasional grief-stricken outbursts, she deferred to Tommy. Tommy was courteous and controlled while describing his anger at the length of the investigation. Glasgow was frank. The investigation was being blocked, in his opinion, because of money. The authorities had refined the travel down to the cost of one police officer visiting the United States to carry out further inquiries. Until that occurred, he said, the report could not be finalised.

'So, what can we do?' Tommy asked.

'Either see a politician or see the Commissioner of Police if he'll see you,' Glasgow advised.

'Justice delayed is justice denied,' Andy Toulson quoted Tommy, her copy picked up in other News Limited newspapers. Meanwhile, the Thomases engaged a Townsville barrister, Harvey Walters, to represent them at any Coronial inquest.

***

In the early hours of 27 March 2006, the Thomases chugged out of Ross River Creek on board a Townsville Water Police vessel, heading south. It was almost exactly two-and-a-half years since Tina died and coincidentally the same month as the anniversary of the sinking of the SS *Yongala*. When the Thomases arrived at the wreck site it was still dark. As the sun's rays struggled above a grey horizon, the first light of day struck the uneven waves that slapped against the boat. Tommy and Cindy threw flowers into the lonely stretch of water that had claimed their daughter's life. For Cindy, it was her first visit to the place she had long imagined. She was close to where Tina spent her last few moments, but the dismal sight robbed her of comfort. The petals bobbed on the dark ocean above the wreck that housed all of the other lost souls. On the way back to Townsville, Cindy stayed below, curled up into a ball on a bunk, sobbing. Tommy had been concerned about her reaction, but he knew it was something that she had to do for her self-preservation. He remembered his last journey when Wade Singleton had acted as his guide. This time, in the slow light of dawn, the loneliness of the place seeped into him. He cried into the changing winds, praying that his daughter had gone to a better place.

If the Thomases had been seeking comfort from the series of meetings they had set up with Australian politicians and police, the final interviews before they headed back to the United States fell well short of the mark. The Assistant Commissioner of Police in Townsville, John McDonnell, was an ex Homicide detective, with a firm handshake but a set expression.

'The best decision, as far as I'm concerned, is to let

the American police conduct the interviews in the US,' McDonnell said. 'Look, I understand your need as a father to expedite the investigation, but I'm not going to change my mind. I will make a commitment, though, that within twelve months the findings of the investigation will be before the Coroner to make a decision about where to go from there.'

Two days after the Thomases' visit to their daughter's place of death, the Mayor of Townsville, Tony Mooney, wrote to Gabe Watson, responding to an email Gabe had sent two weeks earlier. He apologised that while the Queensland police were conducting 'a very thorough investigation' into Tina's untimely death, 'I am sorry there are still a number of issues that have not been resolved'. With a copy of Gabe's email attached, Mooney said he had written to the Commissioner of Police in Townsville 'seeking his assistance on this matter'.

CHAPTER 19

Shortly before 10 a.m. on Tuesday, 4 April 2006, two very tall young men walked briskly towards the Alabama Power Company building in the crisp 13°C morning. Morris Lilienthal, a young associate of Keith Belt, was accompanying his client, Gabe Watson. Lilienthal was about to turn twenty-nine, as Gabe had four weeks earlier.

Once through the handsome brass doors marking the entrance to 1710 6th Avenue North, Lilienthal pressed the up button on the bank of elevators. The litigation section of Balch and Bingham was on the tenth floor.

It was just over a year since Gabe Watson had launched his lawsuit. It had reached the stage of a deposition, a pre-trial conversation held in a legal conference room. No such tool operates under the legal system in Australia, where pre-trial evidence is limited to the production of documents. US-style depositions, like those portrayed on *LA Law* and *Boston Legal* where characters sit around a large conference table and lawyers exchange knowing looks, provide an opportunity for follow-up questions. Documents do not.

Gabe's responses would be treated as sworn evidence as though he were giving it before the judge and the jury he had requested for his civil trial. During the deposition he would be asked questions under oath to be recorded in a transcript, giving the defendants – the insurance companies – an opportunity to hear his story and test his answers. It is a useful way to hear from plaintiffs and, sometimes, key witnesses for defendants, before proceedings began in court.

As the elevator surged silently upwards, Lilienthal inquired, 'You okay?' He was conscious that Gabe would be grilled by two lawyers that day, one for Old Republic Insurance and Travelex Insurance Services Inc, and the other for the travel agency, Get Away of Birmingham Inc, through which all Gabe's non-diving travel and accommodation had been booked.

Gabe nodded.

'Don't forget to listen carefully to the questions. Take your time and don't jump in with any old answer,' said Lilienthal, delivering a standard pre-deposition pep talk to a client unfamiliar with the process.

Stepping out onto the marble flooring of the firm's litigation section, the two men were ushered down a hallway to a long room behind the elevators. Gabe Watson followed Lilienthal across the deep tan carpet and took the seat indicated at one end of a long brown granite conference table that could easily have accommodated twenty. Today he was one of just six.

Lilienthal, who sat to his immediate left, exchanged brief greetings with the two other lawyers present.

Julie Pearce, representing Get Away, a partner in Birmingham firm Gaines, Wolter & Kinney, was already seated halfway down on the opposite side of the long table with her client, Freida Gammill. Freida was a likeable, sixty-two-year-old grandmother and veteran of the travel industry. She had organised Glenda Watson's urgent journey to Australia after Tina's death, and annual holidays for Gabe's paternal grandmother Jenny Watson. As a party in the proceedings, Gammill could be present, even though she was the next witness to be called after Gabe.

Travelex and its underwriter, Old Republic, were represented by Eric Langley, one of the newer partners at Balch and Bingham, and a dead ringer for a young James Spader, the actor who portrayed Alan Shore in *Boston Legal*. He sat directly opposite Gabe. Between them, at the head of the table, was Laura Nichols, the official reporter, with her high-tech stenographic machine recording the transcript.

The lawyers agreed to 'the usual stipulations'. Whatever Gabe might say could be used at his pending trial or any other legal proceedings. While the deposition was just like thousands of others carried out every week, this one stood out to both Langley and Pearce. In a run-of-the-mill insurance tussle involving travel it was unusual to be dealing with a claimant who had lost his wife on his honeymoon.

Langley was first up, aware that the transcript would be avidly read in two hemispheres. In the official file was Sergeant Brad Flynn's email of December 2004 describing Gabe as a suspect in his wife's untimely death. Flynn had told Langley about the discrepancies in Gabe's previous versions and the suspicions that gave rise to the protracted, ongoing police investigation. He had also mentioned his surveillance of Tina's grave six months earlier, which had been deliberately kept quiet at the request of the Queensland police. This last point was largely irrelevant to Langley's case, which had a single, simple issue: was scuba diving excluded from the travel insurance policy? Establishing that Tina's death had been scuba-related was clearly important. But even then, the position of his clients remained the same:

there was no insurance recovery possible because scuba diving was excluded from the policy.

Langley looked down at his legal pad as Gabe was sworn in by Laura Nichols. He scanned the list of issues he needed to raise – subjects he might return to several times – and certain questions he wanted to ask in a particular way. Down near the bottom was a separate one-word heading: FLOWERS.

Gabe's deposition began with a series of background questions about where he lived and worked and his tertiary qualifications.

Then the questions began about his relationship with Tina. She was buried in a Watson family plot, Gabe told the hearing. They had been married at the Southside Baptist Church, even though neither of them worshipped there. He no longer attended Shades Crest Baptist Church in Hoover, nor did he worship elsewhere. He did not know where Tina had worshipped 'off and on'. And no, he was not in touch with Tina's parents. Asked why not, he replied: 'They have done some things that made me just decide I am better off not talking to them.'

Gabe's responses suggested his memory for specifics was not good. He said he had to guess, as he did several times throughout the deposition, when he first began diving.

'I am going to say late nineties, but, you know, I don't know.'

Asked why the Townsville police had retained all his diving certificates, his log book and dive computer, he said he had been told nothing would be released until the investigation was complete.

'Is this an investigation relating to the cause of Tina's death?'

After Lilienthal objected to form, Langley amended his question to add, if Gabe knew this.

'You have got me . . . I don't know what the deal is,' Gabe replied.

He said that while the police were not investigating the conduct of Mike Ball Dive Expeditions, he knew that Queensland Workplace Health and Safety was.

Asked if he believed Mike Ball Dive Expeditions had done anything to contribute to his wife's death, Gabe replied: 'Yes, sir . . . in my opinion, I believe that they started out with a too extremely difficult dive, especially for somebody that was a beginner diver . . . It is open water, middle of the changing tide; it is a wreck; from what I was told, it is 100 feet deep, murky water. It wasn't even a dive that *I* would have felt all that comfortable going on.'

When asked why he went on the dive, he replied: 'Because we didn't know any of that stuff until we were in the water.'

'You learned that stuff later?' Langley asked.

'Yes, sir . . . from being in it . . . I believe less than 15 minutes.'

Pearce and her client leaned forward slightly as Gabe was taken to the heart of his claim. Prior to his honeymoon in 2003, Gabe said he had had three or four meetings with Freida Gammill, then a Hoover-based travel agent. During one of these meetings, she had suggested travel insurance because her quote for flights, accommodation, an Opera House booking and dinner, was around US$5000 – that was without the dive component that Gabe had booked himself.

On his next visit, Gabe said Freida had showed him the Travelex brochure. She had recommended it because it included coverage for a terrorist attack. The first Bali bombing had occurred ten months earlier.

'And then I remember asking her, you know, if it would

cover diving since, you know, a large portion of the trip was going to be diving. She thumbed through it and said if it is not explicitly excluded, then it is considered to be included in the coverage.'

Gabe said he had read the brochure, which also had an enrolment form on the back. Page seven of the brochure had a 'restrictions of coverage' section, which listed conditions, exclusions and limitations, 'as set out in the evidence of coverage and confirmation of coverage'. It also referred the reader to the company's website for a list of the limitations and exclusions.

Gabe said he had not looked at the website 'because at the time I was in the process of moving house. Just about everything I owned, other than clothing, was in boxes'. And, 'having hardly even worked during that time', he only had occasional access to one of the two office computers at his father's company premises.

He said he had specifically asked Freida if diving would be covered so that if 'one of us ruptured an ear or something like that', and had to miss a flight it would be covered.

Gabe said he had never applied for travel insurance before that and the only other insurance he had bought through O.M. Hughes Insurance was for the house he had bought with Tina in 2003, and car insurance at the same time. His Blue Cross health insurance was paid for by his father's company, as employers commonly do in America.

When asked about his ear injury on the *Yongala* dive, he told Langley: 'I had, I believe she called it – oh wow, severe barotrauma. I think that is correct.'

Gabe was unsure how many, if any, saltwater dives Tina had done or if she had done any other open-water dives apart from at Alabama Blue Water Adventures after her certification before the trip to Australia. He said he had not dived since his return from Australia. He agreed he did not know what to expect on the *Yongala* wreck dive.

'Had you done any research on the *Yongala* wreck before your trip?'

'No, I don't believe so.'

Having previously been a member of the Divers Alert Network (DAN), he purchased a 30-day DAN policy by ticking a box on the form he signed the first night on *Spoilsport*.

He said there had been a general briefing after boarding 'of how everything was going to go down. I think they showed a video that had . . . all the different stuff to look for, the fish and all that, and that was pretty much it.'

There was no discussion that night, Gabe said, of the dive itself or any hazards. He was not asked whether any briefings were given on the dive itself the following day, when the main, detailed and compulsory *Yongala* briefing had been given by Wade Singleton.

Then, the questioning began about the day Tina died. Langley asked: 'Were y'all wearing weights this day?'

'Yes.'

'Both of you?'

'Yeah, I am pretty sure Tina was.'

'You don't know for a fact if she was or not?'

'No.'

Gabe said he used weights, he guessed 'maybe thirty pounds', because 'you use more in saltwater than in freshwater'.

'But you don't remember if Tina actually used weights or not?' Langley asked again, and got a different answer.

'I know she used weights.'

'But you don't know how much?'

'No. She normally used twenty pounds.'

'How do you know that?'

'Because that is what she said that she had used [back in the United States].'

'So she wasn't going to use any more because she was doing a saltwater dive?'

'No, she wouldn't need to.'

'Why do you say that?'

'Because the heavier you are, the more buoyant you are. And I am a whole lot heavier than her, so in saltwater I float a whole lot easier. She was skin and bones so it didn't matter, you know, saltwater, freshwater.'

Asked about irregularities with his dive computer, Gabe said: 'The first time we got in the water, my computer battery was in backwards so when we dove off the back of the boat, I got down to, like, 3 feet [1 metre], the computer started beeping so we went right back up, went back to the boat, changed the battery around, then went back out.'

The single battery, he said, was 'one of those weird ones like the size of the tip of your pinkie'. He 'just switched the positive and negative [ends of the battery around] because it was in backwards'.

Langley: 'But it was still beeping?'

Gabe: 'Yeah.'

'Even though it was turned around?'

'Yes.'

'Was that normal?'

'Yes.'

'Have you seen that happen before?'

'Yeah, it is set up so that if that happens, it gives you an audible beep and it says gas alarm so that you know you have got a problem.'

Gabe went through the details of how they had descended to the wreck, how Tina had been unable to swim for long,

308

how she'd knocked his mask and, how, after he had fixed it and turned around, she'd already started to sink.

Langley asked if there were other divers around at the time.

'Yeah,' Gabe replied, though he had not previously been so specific, 'there were people coming and going up, down, all over.'

'But was there anyone that was within eyesight of you when all this was happening?'

'Yeah.'

'I take it they didn't realise what was going on, though, as far as you know?'

'No. Because I swam – when I left and did the 45-degree angle, there were some people on the rope. And I remember I swam straight to them. And I remember this guy was there, and I was trying to – obviously I wasn't thinking – I was trying to talk with my regulator in and he just kind of looked at me. When I realised he had no idea what I was talking about, I shot up to the surface.'

'Was the current the reason that you were not able to go down and try to get Tina and bring her back?'

'No, my experience was the reason I couldn't go down and get her.' Gabe made no mention of any problem with his eardrums.

'You are not allowed to go any deeper?' Langley asked.

'No, I am. But I couldn't have done anything, I don't think. I mean, I don't know. But I figured at that point it was a lot smarter decision to go up and try to find somebody that is certified and knows how to help somebody in that situation than to go down and do whatever.'

'. . . in your training and in your rescue certification training, is this the type of thing that y'all had discussed?'

'No.'

Gabe said he had 'no idea' what time or when he learned that Tina could not be revived. He said that 'John', the emergency surgeon from Chicago, another *Spoilsport* passenger, 'might know'. John had later told him about the failed resuscitation attempts. 'They got him [Dr Downie to go to the *Jazz II*] because they [those then on board] didn't know what to do.'

Gabe had not, he told Langley, talked with anyone from Mike Ball Dive Expeditions since his return home. Nor had he filed a lawsuit against Mike Ball and had 'no idea' about whether he intended to initiate legal action. He had learned from the internet that his time to sue ran out in six months, the third anniversary of Tina's death.

'Did you ever see Tina lose consciousness during the incident?' Langley asked.

'I never saw her,' Gabe replied. 'I mean, the last time I saw her, her eyes were open.'

'And she was falling down?'

'Right.'

When the deposition resumed after a lunch break, Langley returned to the issue of Tina failing to inflate her BC.

Langley: 'At that time did you believe that her BC was not working?'

Gabe: 'I don't think I believed one way or the other. I just know she grabbed it and it didn't inflate. I mean, she could have not hit the right button. She could have – I mean, there's – I mean, just –'

'You just don't know?'

'Anyone's guess is as good as someone else's.'

'Did you reach over to try to do it for her?'

'No, I didn't.'

'Was she out of reach at that point?'

'We were probably about 5 feet from each other, something like that.'

'Did you try to, at some point, swim over to her?'

'That was when – when it didn't do anything, that was when we turned to try to swim back, you know, stick your arm out,' referring to grabbing Tina's outstretched left hand and towing her towards the drop line.

'At some point you were able to make contact with her and grab her, correct?'

'Correct.'

'And then somehow your face mask and regulator came off?'

'Correct.'

'Do you know if that was because she was panicking and pulled it off or whether you knocked it off?'

Gabe made no attempt to repeat his previous explanations to police. In his first statement he had said that he or Tina had grabbed his mask and pulled it back, causing it to flood, and in the record of interview he'd stated that her hand had come across his face and hit his mask and he had found himself without his regulator in his mouth. Now he merely answered: 'I have no idea. I really don't.'

Later, Langley returned to Gabe's knowledge of the *Yongala*, asking again whether Gabe had done any research on the *Yongala* wreck dive prior to the trip.

'No,' replied Gabe.

'You hadn't bought any books about it or anything like that –'

'No.'

'– or done any internet research?'

'No, nothing prior to the trip.'

'You told me earlier about barotrauma to your inner ear.'

311

'Correct.'

'Did you have medical treatment in Australia for that?'

'I did.'

'Who treated you?'

'I don't know. Some lady.'

Following Tina's funeral, the travel insurance 'was the only claims form I filled out', Gabe said.

Langley: 'Did you have any, for example, life insurance on Tina?'

Gabe: 'No.'

'Did she have any life insurance through her job?'

'Nothing that was – that I was named beneficiary to. You would have to ask her parents about all the others.'

'Do you know if she had some that were in her parents' names?'

'She might have. I don't know. They told us, talking about Parisian, that they had a burial policy, but, I mean, whether they did or not, I don't know.'

'Did you actually talk to someone from Parisian?'

'Yes, I did.'

'Who?'

'Somebody in Human Resources.'

'And ultimately, though, you didn't get any money from that policy?'

'No.'

'Do you know one way or the other whether Tina's parents did?'

'I don't know. I'm not sure that there was a policy. But if there was, there was somebody other than me.'

'This conversation that you had with someone in Human Resources, was this in person or on the phone?'

'On the phone.'

Gabe had told Amanda Phillips that he was going to

312

Parisian personally to collect Tina's personal possessions and finalise insurance matters, taking Tina's death certificate with him. He had been directed to see Human Resources staff by Tina's manager, Caesar Lamonaca, when he went into Parisian after 12 November, 2003.

'Was this the only conversation that you ever had with anyone at Parisian about her benefits?'

'I believe so.'

With a few objections from Gabe's lawyer, Langley questioned Gabe about his travel insurance claim that was denied by Old Republic in the letter dated 10 February 2004. Gabe said that after receiving a document prior to the wedding called a 'Confirmation of Coverage' he believed he was covered and it was paid for. He denied receiving another document in the same envelope headed 'Evidence of Coverage', which was routinely sent to all policy holders along with the 'Confirmation of Coverage'. Although he now knew that scuba diving was specifically excluded in the 2004 brochure, he said he had seen nothing that indicated it was *not* covered in 2003. Even if Travelex showed him something in the 'Evidence of Coverage' that specifically stated that scuba diving was excluded, it would not change his mind, because he denied that he had received any 'Evidence of Coverage'.

Langley asked Gabe about the Tina Thomas Watson Memorial Fund.

'Is it money contributed to a charitable cause?' he asked.

Gabe answered: 'It is money that is just sitting in an account right now.'

'Is it ultimately going to be given to some charity in her name?'

'I haven't made any kind of determination on it.'

'Is there a board or some group of people that make that decision?'

'No.'

'Just you?'

'Yes.'

When Langley asked Gabe to separate what part of the mental anguish he claimed was the result of something Old Republic or Travelex had done, he replied: 'Out of everything? Well I mean, obviously, the financial part. I still don't have the money to put a tombstone up yet.'

When questioned about the nature of his mental anguish claim, he complained that 'it was too broad of a question . . . I mean this is all a three-part thing . . . Well, I am [then] twenty-six, and I am widowed; my insurance company just denied my claim. And then trying to figure out what do I do, so I mean – there's not one answer to cover all that.'

He said that not being able to sleep was the least of his problems.

Even though more than two years had passed he was 'probably not' any closer to figuring out what to do, he said. 'I mean it is an ongoing thing.'

He'd had a few dates with women but 'nothing that I would call "meet the family because, you know, there's wedding bells down the road"'.

Probably, 'a third' of his mental anguish was the result of the denial of the insurance claim, he conceded, but friction between him and the Thomas family was not part of it. Nor was the police investigation in Townsville. 'I mean there's nothing I can do about it,' Gabe said.

He believed, however, that both Old Republic and Travelex, in denying his claim, should be punished and that punitive damages should be awarded against them. They had been 'manipulative' in attaching to the denial letter the 2004 brochure that contained the specific exclusion against scuba diving, when Tina had died in 2003.

'Has there ever been a headstone on Tina's grave?' Langley asked.

'No.'

'I understand that at one point the gravesite was moved?'

'Yes.'

'Why was that?'

'We had picked out a spot on the other side of the cemetery that we liked better.'

'You said "we" – is that you and Tina?'

'No, we got a family plot.'

'Who made the decision to bury her where she was buried the first time?'

'The fact that it had been ten days since she died and we needed to do something fast. So we just said: "Find us somewhere".'

'Did you have to apply for any kind of court order to get that done [move the body]?'

'No, just filled out documents [from] the internet, something the funeral home has.'

'Did you get any push back from Tina's family on that?'

'No, not from her family.'

'Now, I understand there's been some issue with flowers being removed from her grave. Do you know anything about that?' Langley looked straight at Gabe.

Gabe looked at him impassively and said: 'Flowers being removed from her grave?'

'Yeah,' the lawyer replied, looking down to leaf through his legal pad. 'I had heard somewhere –'

Gabe replied: 'I have not had anything that we put out there removed.'

Langley looked at Gabe across the granite conference table. Gabe clearly knew what he was referring to. His answer was well crafted, allowing him to effectively dodge any admission.

Langley continued his questioning: '. . . that is someone, I don't know if it was her parents or you, had filed some sort of incident report. Do you know anything about that?'

'No, I don't.'

Julie Pearce swapped seats with Langley to begin her questions.

Gabe agreed that in an email of 19 May 2003, Shelley McLaughlin from Mike Ball Dive Expeditions had recommended travel insurance with Travelex or another insurance company and provided him with a telephone number and website address. Gabe had not pursued the information because: 'I had never dealt with it [travel insurance] so I didn't know if it was done through her or somebody else. And there was never any mention of it again by her, so it was just kind of dropped at that point.'

Pearce asked why Gabe had decided it was best not to communicate with his in-laws.

Gabe: 'How long have you got?'

'As long as you need,' she replied.

'Well, first one was just because her mom and her dad and her sister and her aunt and her – whoever else tried to take over the funeral – had hissy fits with every decision we did. Later found out – and I'm just going to give you the abbreviated version, later found out that her mom had returned all the McRae's wedding gifts to McRae's, you know, that they – she actually cancelled one wedding registry, created another, returned the gifts so that it would match what we had. I mean, her mom went around telling people that, you know, I had a million-dollar life insurance policy and, you know, several months back, she was starting a new rumour that I was now in jail for murder, this, that and the other. So, with all that going on, I just decided it is not worth it. So I maintained a relationship with her grandmother and I am satisfied with that.'

Gabe went on to claim that there was a family dispute when Tina moved out into an apartment and that Tina and her mother did not have a good relationship before her death.

The allegedly misleading information on scuba diving coverage he claimed was given to him by Freida Gammill had 'ultimately led to the claim being denied' and contributed to his mental anguish. He said he had no evidence that Freida had intended to mislead him but 'we are going to court to let the jury decide' whether her actions warranted the punitive damages he was claiming.

Gabe's deposition ended at 2.57 p.m.

Freida Gammill's deposition began at 3.10 p.m.

When Gabe contacted her the first time in August 2003, which she thought was 'awfully close' to the honeymoon, Freida said that she had known he was going scuba diving and had been completing that part of his booking himself, as his mother had mentioned it to her.

'The first time he came in the office, I know he told me he had booked the dive trip . . . and that he had to have insurance for that . . . that's what I remember,' Freida said.

Gammill said that before recommending travel insurance, she was aware that the Travelex policy did not cover scuba diving. It would 'never' have been proper to recommend the Travelex insurance policy for someone going on a scuba diving trip, she told Lilienthal. 'I don't know of a travel insurance that covers scuba diving. It has its own little niche.'

She had recommended it merely to cover his flights and hotels in Sydney and Townsville and for the Opera House component, the cost of which was about US$5000.

Gammill said she did not recall Gabe ever asking if scuba diving was excluded. She agreed that the wording on the 'Evidence of Coverage', which he had denied ever receiving, gave a choice of what to refer to for details of exclusion – either the brochure or the website.

Lilienthal: 'So it's your recollection, then, that you specifically informed Mr Watson that this policy didn't cover scuba diving?'

Gammill: 'Yes, that's correct.'

'And when was that?'

'Probably when I offered him the policy.'

'This would have been the timeframe after the initial numbers were completed and you knew what the total cost of the trip was going to be?'

'Exactly, the total cost of the part I was doing.'

'You would disagree if he said that he specifically asked you: "Did this policy specifically cover scuba diving?" and he said that you looked through the brochure and said, "If it's not excluded in this particular brochure, then it's included"? You would disagree with that?'

'I would disagree with that statement, yes.'

Gammill said she recalled that after Gabe's return from Australia in November 2003, he had arrived at her shop to get a telephone number to begin lodging his application to claim against his insurance.

On another occasion – she thought it may have been in January 2004 – Gabe had come in, perhaps to get another brochure or get some copies of his invoices 'to assist him in filing' his claim.

'I talked to him somewhere, because I think he told me he was going to use Bobby Austin [as his lawyer], who I graduated from high school with. That's the reason I had that little bit of remembrance.

'I knew that he had – was getting an attorney, and I'm not sure when that happened, because I think I remember saying something, "Well, you know, the policy that you got from me didn't cover that. You'll have to file on your dive policy" or – I just have a vague remembrance of that.'

She said Gabe had responded: 'It's probably not going to cover it, but I'm going to file anyway' or something to that effect.

Lilienthal: 'He said that?'

Gammill nodded.

'Do you have an independent recollection or are you –'

'It was two-and-a-half years ago. A lot has happened in my life since then. But I just have these little snatches of conversation . . . We had that little bit of conversation sometime . . .'

On 12 April Detective Flynn rang Sergeant Gary Campbell in Australia. Gabe Watson had given sworn evidence in a deposition relating to an insurance claim.

CHAPTER 20

Immediately after Tina Watson's death, online forums had buzzed with theories ranging from detailed scientific explanations about the mixture of oxygen and carbon dioxide in Tina's dive tank, to speculation about how quickly she had surfaced and whether that had contributed to her death. As the third anniversary of Tina's death loomed, online dive forums began to hum again.

'Cindy', who labelled herself as 'Non-diver/Housewife', wrote on 18 April 2006:

The death of Tina Watson, the American on Mike Ball's Spoil Sport [sic], *is still being investigated. No accident, that is certain!!!*

'Shelley, Non-diver/Accounting' wrote:

Actually, Gabe is a certified Rescue Diver.

The media coverage began again. Gabe's lawyer, Bob Austin, told Andy Toulson in an interview published in the *Townsville Bulletin* in early May that his client had nearly drowned trying to save his bride. Gabe, too, he said, was 'hoping, by now, to have some idea about the cause of death, aside from drowning . . . He is not talking to the media, as he is a very private person, and he has had a hard enough time. Nothing they do or say is going to change anything – he is still going to be a widower. He just wants closure.'

In the article Austin alleged that the Watsons had not been properly briefed on the conditions underwater the day Tina died.

The Helena Police Department was undertaking the US investigations into Tina's death. Police Chief Jones had talked to the Justice Department and the FBI and had organised to send his detective, Sergeant Brad Flynn, to Florida, Illinois and Colorado to complete the remaining interviews. Jones was hoping to finish up by late June. Meanwhile, Campbell continued reinterviewing the Australian witnesses. On 19 June, he visited the North Sydney police station where, in the foyer, he met Tina Graves, who with her husband had migrated to Sydney from Colorado. She handed over copies of the emails she had sent Mike Ball Dive Expeditions shortly after the fatal dive. She then provided Campbell with a statement.

In August, the online forums buzzed louder. There was a barrage of emails on Scuba Forum – the same website the online identity 'Jason' had used the day after Tina's death to query the reputation of Mike Ball Dive Expeditions on safety.

One message, posted on 26 April 2006, was penned by 'Kim, Rescue Diver/Diver', who said he had been on *Spoilsport* that day:

Maybe the reason all this is coming up IS because there IS a lot more to it that the investigators are unable to release at this point. There are a lot of questions: why a husband had so much insurance on a brand new wife before he even got back from the honeymoon. It was the 2nd dive I was on the boat so he knew the current – why did he take her back down if not a good idea. She trusted him. He gave 5 different stories as to what happened and they do have evidence or it would not be with the homicide in Brisbane. I guess we will all see. But if you think about it all what else could it be he took her down 2 times and then he LEFT her, watched her going down, could still SEE her. We should all be hoping for wrongs to be righted for this sweet girl that I only got to know for 1 night. SHE SHOULD NOT BE DEAD!!!

'Kendra, Non-Diver (never plan on doing it)/Nursing Student' posted on 1 May 2006:

If Gabe didn't have anything to do with his wife's death, then he should have nothing to hide. If he did do something to cause Tina's death, then hopefully the law will do what it was meant to do and try him. I know what I think, and that's all that matters to me until a proper investigation is finalized, that is all anyone can do: hold their own opinions. I also know that she shouldn't have died and that many people's lives are different know [sic] because she is gone.

. . . I know for a fact that just a few days after Tina's death Gabe commented on how well he had been sleeping. I know that if anything ever happened to my fiance that I would not be sleeping at all . . .

Others were more sympathetic. 'Jenny, Art Director' posted on 25 July 2006:

I find it appalling that you would post such a message. They were on their honeymoon. They loved each other. Tina loved diving. Gabe was forced to make a choice and as far as I know was not a 'rescue' diver at all. He is the one who has to live with the guilt of possibly having made the wrong choice. Not you. We miss her. You did not know her. You did not know of her relationship with her family and how tragic this story really is of a girl who finally felt as though she was released from the grasp of her mother only to be forever caught up in the drama of her own death and horrible accusations of the man that she loved.

Later the same day, 'Jenny' wrote:

The reason for all of these investigations is easily answered: Tina's family. They have been pushing since the beginning; blaming Gabe for taking Tina away since the first day. Trust me when I say there are no facts to support these alligations [sic]. Just some parents who have forced the authorities to go above and beyond.

And even later:

I don't know where you people get your mis-information but there was no insurance on Tina. Period. All the money to get her home and get her buried came out of her husband of 11 days' own pocket. Maybe you should check your sources before you spread your rumors. I heard of what happened the day after it happened and have never heard a different version from Gabe – ever. Try talking to someone who knew Tina AND Gabe for more than a day.

And there were territorial squabbles about who qualified to be counted as a friend of Tina and more personal insults. One post claimed that Glenda Watson had not only laughed at Tina's funeral but that she'd said: 'Oh! This is like a teachers' reunion!'

Then, there were pacifist posts cautioning calm. 'Amanda, Non-Diver/Engineer' posted on 19 August:

While everyone on this board might feel that they are seeking the truth for Tina in their own way, I think everyone has forgotten what happened. Tina has passed, and there is no one that can replace her.

I know that I have spent the last ~3 years living without her. I don't care what took her. While I would hope that if it were some-one who took her from my life and they currently stood on this Earth, that they would be judged quickly but I can't control that. I pray every day that Tina has found out what it's like to have His face before her and that she knows His sanctuary.

I understand that everyone here cared for Tina very much. It's not much hope but He has carried her home and there is no sense to carry on this way. She was a positive person and would have wanted her friends and family to get along. Anger and revenge are feelings that He does not heal. You must do that yourselves.

If you have anything of use to provide that would help any investigation, please provide it to the Queensland Authorities. If you are with the truth, it will be evident.

The Queensland Police Service Diving Squad is housed in the Brisbane Water Police complex, 10 kilometres down-river east of the Brisbane CBD in the suburb of Lytton. Police divers conduct dirty work, including entering vehicles, planes and contaminated waterways. Re-enacting a suspected crime scene is not, however, a run-of-the-mill request. Operation Charlie Oswald had been running for six months when Sergeant Gary Campbell first contacted the officer in charge of the squad, Sergeant Adam Reid, and one of the part-time members, Sergeant Owen Law, a recreational dive master as well as a commercially trained police diver. Campbell had approached Wade Singleton on 8 February 2006 and asked him to comment on the currents on the day Tina died and to identify exactly where he had found her on the ocean floor. Singleton agreed to brief the squad members taking part in the re-enactment. Gabe Watson's initial statement and record of interview were sent to the Diving Squad as part of the preparation for the dive.

Inside the Diving Squad base, large laminated photos of the *Yongala* sat next to Gary Stempler's photo of Tina, her arm outstretched, lying on the seabed. Using Stempler's photo, a diagram had been marked up with approximate positions where Singleton and his orientation group had entered the water and where Gabe and Tina had then swum off. The position on the seabed where Singleton discovered Tina was marked as well.

Campbell also sought further details for the re-enactment of the events of 22 October 2003. In March 2006, he had contacted Dr Richard Brinkman, an oceanographer at the Australian Institute of Marine Science in Townsville. Brinkman was an expert on the main features of tidal flows and currents within the complex circulation on the Great Barrier Reef. Brinkman's mission was to find three envelopes of time in which underwater conditions were comparable to the day Tina died. He began by studying the interaction between the tides and associated north–south flowing currents. These also interact with the far slower but still influential east Australian current, which flows south on the edge of the reef on the Continental Shelf. On top of that, Brinkman had to consider the circulation driven by winds, which can be so strong that they blow the east Australian current into reverse, forcing it to run north on the surface. Compounding all of that, it was difficult to predict what the surface current would be compared to the current at deeper levels. This could vary. As well, Brinkman had to find a meteorologist to predict the weather many months in advance.

For Brinkman, attempting to target similar conditions was the easy part. The tides, he knew, are largely predictable. 'An educated guess', he declared to police, could be made about some of the conditions with the east Australian current. But the weather itself, on the days chosen, would be 'quite challenging', he told Campbell, and would require a judgment call at the time.

Campbell had provided him with the time the fatal dive took place – allowing for the lag after the high tide. The three suggested envelopes of time resembling conditions on 22 October 2003 were in August, September and October 2006. For each envelope, Brinkman recommended specific days and specific times on those days where the currents driven by the tides would be very similar to those on the day Tina died.

Nearly three years after retrieving Tina Watson from the ocean floor, Wade Singleton had left the dive industry and was working as a paramedic with the Queensland Ambulance Service. His new career focused on saving lives, mirroring the sort of compassionate man he was. The death of Tina Watson had marked him. Singleton had already made four statements to Townsville police. As he was ushered into a meeting room on the afternoon of 21 June 2006, he saw Gary Campbell, who smiled a greeting. Nodding back, Singleton was then introduced to

Sergeant Adam Reid, the officer in charge of the squad, and another younger officer, Joshua Kinghorn. Kinghorn was a slightly built young senior constable who had been diving to advanced level recreationally for about eight years and to level 2 of the Australian Diver Accreditation Scheme for commercial divers. His job was to coordinate and formulate the dive plan for a re-enactment of the fatal dive to Campbell's requirements. If conducted properly, the re-enactment should either substantiate or negate elements of Gabe's version to police about what happened when Tina died.

Of critical importance to the overall plan was pinpointing the position on the seabed where Singleton had found Tina. From there, measurements could be taken, and the police divers could then re-enact the embrace witnessed by Stanley Stutz, followed by some test drift dives to re-create the circumstances in which Tina sank.

Singleton listened as the officers discussed with Campbell the tasks that could form part of the operation.

'You can see the debris from the wreck in Gary's photo,' Singleton told the diving squad. He pointed with his finger moving across the laminated blow-up and stabbing at a point beyond where the fallen mast of the vessel jutted out from the side of the *Yongala*.

Kinghorn asked: 'So if we can set up a dive plan to re-enact certain situations indicated by Mr Watson in his statements to police, you feel you could quite comfortably pinpoint where you found the deceased?'

'No problem,' replied Singleton.

Dr Richard Brinkman's September envelope of opportunity, chosen by police as the month for the re-enactment operation, provided a range of days between 19 and 22 September with dive times roughly between 10 a.m. and noon on each successive day.

Monday, 18 September 2006 dawned partly cloudy in Townsville with the temperature steadily rising to 26°C by late morning. A Police Air Wing aircraft from Brisbane landed at Townsville airport in the afternoon disgorging diving squad officers Reid, Law, senior constables Robert James and Scott Cornish and constables Stephen Doyle and Chris O'Brien. They were met by Senior Constable Joshua Kinghorn and his fellow full-time diving squad officer Constable Ricky Murdoch, who had both driven more than 1300 kilometres – a twenty-odd-hour trip – from Brisbane to Townsville for the re-enactment. Later that day, joined by Sergeant Wayne Oldham from the Forensic Services Branch police photographic section, they loaded their gear aboard an Australian Customs Service vessel docked at the Townsville port.

As there were winds of up to 37 kilometres per hour forecast for the following day, it was agreed the operation would be postponed a day.

The weather around Townsville on 20 September, although slightly cooler, was remarkably similar to the skies that had greeted the *Spoilsport* passengers on 22 October 2003 as they rose for breakfast. But instead of the comfort of the large catamaran and its platters of fresh fruit, cooked breakfasts and hot coffee, Wade Singleton was boarding an austere ocean-going patrol boat belonging to Australian Customs to visit the SS *Yongala* dive site with Detective Sergeant Gary Campbell and the police divers as his escorts. The *Dame Roma Mitchell*, a Bay-Class patrol vessel, was solid grey metal with sharp lines, no-nonsense winches and towers protruding from behind the wheelhouse. It offered an operational dive platform for this key part of Operation Charlie Oswald. A locked exhibit box containing Tina's scuba diving equipment sat on the deck.

The eight divers in the team were assigned tasks based on information from Gabe's, Tina's and Singleton's dive computers, so as to make the re-enactment as accurate as possible. On the 2-hour journey to the wreck site, Singleton and Constable Ricky Murdoch, a former Navy clearance diver, again scanned the large photographs of the sea floor, the wreck and its debris, which petered out into sand. This was the spot where Tina was found after her freefall from about 15 metres, near the top of the wreck where Gabe had stated that they separated when he went for help.

Senior Constable Kinghorn briefed the divers on their responsibilities and safety issues. He noted all activity on a running sheet in his laptop computer. Murdoch and Singleton were to undertake the first task, to place markers indicating where Tina had been found. Other divers would place markers at relevant points and take measurements while Kinghorn and Law laid a heritage line – a line of white rope – to demonstrate the path estimated to have been taken by Gabe and Tina from the diver access line at the bow and along the top of the wreck to a point just beyond where he said they separated. The exercises that involved measuring distances and ascent times and re-enacting the embrace would be videotaped and photographed.

Murdoch and Singleton, the veteran of many *Yongala* dives, both knew that any debris would be found close to the wreck and that the rest of the seabed would just be sand. If there was debris in Stempler's photo and Tina was also visible, it made sense that she couldn't have been too far from the wreck.

The *Dame Roma* arrived at the SS *Yongala* wreck site about 9.20 a.m.

'I'll let you leave the surface first and I'll follow you down,' Murdoch told Singleton as they boarded the Custom's inflatable dinghy at 10 a.m. for the short trip to the diver access point.

At 10.05 a.m., only a few metres underwater, Murdoch could see the structure of the *Yongala* below with visibility of about 20 metres. Once on the seabed, Singleton swam along the starboard side of the wreck. He reached a point just before the cargo hold area and then turned and swam, without hesitation, directly out about 10 metres to a place on the sea floor. He turned back to Murdoch. As they had earlier agreed, he placed his hand in the sand indicating where he had found Tina, to within 'a metre or two'. Murdoch placed a marker directly into the seabed at that point and secured it with two augers – corkscrew-shaped tools that he bored into the seabed and then attached to the marker with snap shackles and line. After Singleton placed a second marker under the bow of the *Yongala* and a third at the point where the fallen mast met the sand on the starboard side of the wreck, their task was complete.

Twenty-five minutes later, Singleton and Murdoch surfaced. The completed task was reported to Kinghorn who entered the details onto the running sheet.

Murdoch remarked to Singleton: 'The visibility was pretty good down there, wasn't it?'

'This is the visibility of the actual day,' he replied. 'And the current at this stage was like it was on the day, too,' he added, mindful that they were the first divers down and the current could change unpredictably.

Senior Constable Robert James was tasked to set a grid square around Tina's last position from which a variety of measurements would be taken. Unlike Tina's last day, he found the surface conditions 'relatively rough' with a 1.5-metre swell. When he entered the water just after 11 a.m., the visibility was no more than 15 metres but once on the seabed, he found there was little current operating over the wreck.

Kinghorn and Law had the next underwater task, to indicate the route Gabe and Tina were thought to have taken once they left the drop line. At a depth of 15 metres, around the maximum depth recorded on Gabe's dive computer, one end of the line was tied to the bow and pulled along the mid-deck area of the wreck to a point where it was tied off past the cargo hold area.

Kinghorn was the closest among the divers to Tina in size. He was 167 centimetres tall and weighed 77.5 kilograms compared to Tina, also a small build, a similar height and weighing 63 kilograms. Kinghorn followed the line back to about halfway over the first cargo hold where he had the diver access line at the bow still in view. This was where Gabe had told police the trouble began – he could still see the drop line when he and Tina had turned to swim back. Kinghorn then swam down and across to the point where Tina had sunk.

Law, slightly taller than Gabe at just over 212 centimetres and weighing more than 104 kilograms, noticed that Kinghorn had to use his fins constantly to fight the current to get to Tina's marker position.

Back on the surface, Kinghorn said: 'I found that with the way the currents were it would have been impossible in those conditions for the deceased to end up at the point in which I was finning over to, if she was in a limp state.'

What police now described as the 'bear hug' that had been witnessed by Stanley Stutz was to be simulated the following day.

**

Shortly before 7 a.m. on 21 September, the *Dame Roma Mitchell* departed Townsville port. After arriving at the dive site, Kinghorn moved to the back of the patrol boat and unlocked the exhibit box which, for more than two years, had housed Tina's dive equipment. He put on her BC with its integrated weights system and attached that and her first-stage regulator to a blue diving squad air tank. He conducted a successful check of the equipment. A photograph was taken of him wearing the gear. Using Tina's purple mask, he and Law descended to the 15-metre mark and followed the heritage line they had laid the previous day. Videotaped by Sergeant Reid and photographed by Senior Constable Cornish, Law attempted to re-enact what he believed Stutz had witnessed: he wrapped his large arms around the shoulders of the much smaller Kinghorn, groping with his hands, his mask very close to Kinghorn's head. He found he could indeed comfortably reach the tank valves on the scuba cylinder.

Kinghorn also conducted a series of drifts in which he swam along the heritage line at a depth of 15 metres to the cargo hold area and, when he turned around and had the diver access point in sight, emptied all residual air from his BC, replicating the way Singleton described he had found Tina's BC. Kinghorn then went limp and sank straight down into the cargo hold on the deck of the *Yongala*. On his first freefall, Kinghorn fell 16.6 metres away from Tina's final resting position. On his second attempt he fell a similar 16.7 metres away and straight onto the deck again. Kinghorn then swam to Tina's position, lying as she was first discovered from Stempler's photograph. He was photographed on the sandy bottom. Sergeant Reid was filming all the while. Afterwards, Singleton, who had also dived to the bottom to test the conditions of the day, surfaced to tell Kinghorn: 'The conditions are near identical to the day of the death. If anything the current may have been a little bit stronger today over the top of the wreck.'

On 22 September, the final day of the operational tasks, conditions were again rough with the swell at around 1.5 metres. The sky was cloudy with winds of about 24 kilometres per hour and temperatures hovering around 25°C. Kinghorn and Law conducted another re-enactment followed by drift exercises in open water 10 metres out from the bow of the wreck at a depth of 15 metres. Kinghorn checked the depth gauge on his wrist.

The results, dutifully recorded afterwards on his running sheet, showed he had fallen 7.7 metres from Tina's marker position on the first open-water drift dive and 7.2 metres on the second. Although it was a similar distance for both drifts he noted a stark difference in the directions of the two landing points. A third drift dive, again conducted over the top of the wreck, had him land 16.6 metres from Tina's marker – identical to the previous day and on the same spot.

Singleton, who had dived down for these last exercises, said afterwards: 'The conditions are nearly identical to the day when she died – if anything the same as yesterday. The currents are a little bit stronger but running the same way.'

The exhibit lock box containing Tina's dive gear was to be taken with the divers and their equipment and returned to the Queensland Police Service Diving Squad in Brisbane.

Later, after compiling all his data and reading Gabe's statement and transcript, Kinghorn concluded in his notes: 'There is no possible way, if she separated from the defendant like he stated in a limp position from the mid deck area in approximately 15 metres of water, that the deceased could have ended in the position she did . . . She could only have gotten to that position from the front of the wreck out from the side and in open water.'

Middlemore Hospital in Hospital Road, Oathuhu, opposite the Auckland Golf Club, is one of the largest tertiary teaching hospitals in New Zealand, specialising in plastic surgery, burns, spinal injury rehabilitation, renal dialysis, and neonatal intensive care.

Gabe Watson had arrived there in an ambulance on 1 November 2003, ten days after Tina's death, en route to the United States. On 5 October 2006, six months after Gabe gave his sworn deposition in his lawsuit against the insurance companies and travel agency, the New Zealand police seized his medical notes from the hospital and forwarded them to Queensland police. The Patient Report form, headlined 'Auckland International Airport', detailed that the chief complaint from 'David Watson', from Oak Leaf Circle, Hoover, Alabama, was 'an earache'. Gabe Watson had arrived at the Emergency Medicine section at 7.40 p.m. with 'suspected barotrauma' as noted by the examining doctor, Dr David Scott, who also noted that the patient had taken Sudafed.

He was told he was safe to fly and that his ears looked 'normal'. Tina's body had continued on to Alabama alone.

The records from Dr Kerry Gillespie, the doctor Gabe had visited with his mother when in Townsville, were also seized. Dr Gillespie's notes confirmed that she had considered Gabe well enough to fly home when she saw him for the second time on 30 October.

The date for a trial before a jury was set for Gabe's civil action: 5 February 2007. In early December, Gabe's legal team objected to a notice of intent by defendants Old Republic and Travelex to serve non-party subpoenas on the Alabama Grief Support Foundation and Alabama Psychiatric Services. In the formal objection filed with the court on 8 December 2006, Gabe's lawyers accused the defence of seeking information that was privileged and confidential, irrelevant and immaterial to the issues of the case and purely for the purpose of 'annoyance, embarrassment or oppression'.

In their response to Gabe's objections, filed on the last possible day of the year – Friday, 22 December 2006 – the defendants claimed there was no evidence that counselling was given by a licensed counsellor, psychologist or psychiatrist as required by the law and, if that was the case, Gabe could not claim privilege, because privilege was confined to communications between a licensed person and a patient. In the cut, thrust and parry before the court case began, Old Republic and Travelex offered to withdraw the notice of intent to serve the subpoenas, but only if Gabe withdrew his mental anguish damages claim or would agree to the court inspecting the documents in a closed court, to investigate whether they contained references to the defendants or to the insurance claims. Separately but on the same day, Old Republic and Travelex also filed a motion to stay proceedings until the completion of the criminal investigation into the death of Christina Watson, or adjourn the 5 February trial until a date after the investigation had finished.

The insurance companies argued that if the proceedings were not delayed until the completion of the investigation, expected in the first half of 2007, they would be 'greatly prejudiced' due to certain exclusions contained in the policy at the heart of the case. Any change in date would not prejudice Gabe Watson, it was claimed.

Gabe's lawyers responded by urging the court not to delay the trial. Old Republic and Travelex, it was argued, had known, at least since the case was first filed in March 2005, that a criminal investigation had been under way in Australia, but they had waited until the eve of the trial, nearly two years later, to file the motion.

'The defendants make the statement that the relevance of the ongoing criminal investigation could impact the . . . action, but fail to state how . . . The defendants seem to insinuate by the filing of this motion that the ongoing criminal investigation somehow implicates the defendant. There is absolutely no evidence that the plaintiff is in any way implicated in this ongoing criminal investigation.'

Arguing that it was Alabama law and public policy not to pay insurance claimants pending the outcome of a criminal investigation, Balch and Bingham attached Sergeant Brad Flynn's email of December 2004 as evidence that Gabe was regarded as a suspect since that time. It was all to no avail. By mid 2007, and for the seventh time, Judge Ramsey set the trial date for 5 May 2008.

CHAPTER 21

After his stint at the Townsville Hospital Emergency Department, Dr Stanley Stutz had returned to practice in Providence, Rhode Island, in the United States. As the only witness so far who had seen Gabe and Tina in the critical moments when they left the drop line and disappeared into the depths, Stutz was vital to Sergeant Gary Campbell's investigation. Besides, it could be argued that Stutz's qualification as an emergency doctor put him in the class of expert witness. Now, though, almost four years after Tina's death, Campbell was up against time and memory.

Campbell had already requested Sergeant Brad Flynn to interview Stutz, which he had done, in January 2006, in Boston, Massachusetts. On 18 April 2007, Campbell was to meet Flynn for the first time. Finally en route to the United States, Campbell had spent several days in Brisbane with Detective Senior Sergeant Scott Knowles planning a line of inquiry before they flew direct to Los Angeles to wrap up further inquiries internationally. From Los Angeles, the two police officers had made the long journey across America to Rhode Island on the east coast.

Stutz had gained his open-water dive certificate when

he was twenty. While studying hard through medicine and going on to complete a specialist degree at the Albany Medical Centre in Albany, New York, he had still found time to dive, but it had taken a move across the world, and a further ten years, before he had signed up for his advanced open-water dive certificate.

Campbell had organised for the interview to take place at the Providence Police Department. Once they settled in the interview room, after introductions, Campbell came straight to the point.

'I'd like you to demonstrate with Inspector Knowles the position that you saw Diver 1 and Diver 2 when they were under your observation – standing up, of course,' Campbell said.

Stutz obliged, awkwardly embracing Knowles in the nondescript interview room. Campbell took two photos, then clicked on the display-image settings to show them to Stutz. Peering at the screen, he agreed that they were an accurate representation of the embrace he had seen Divers 1 and 2 in, except, he qualified, the divers had been in a horizontal position.

In his interview with Brad Flynn, Stutz had positively identified Diver 1 as the deceased, Tina Watson. Her expression, he said, when he had first seen her underwater was imprinted in his memory. He had known right away that her disorganised movements were those of someone who was in distress. Besides, he had seen 'fear and distress' on her face and she looked 'awful'. He had the feeling she knew she was in danger. Diver 2, who was much bigger and wider than Tina, had come along shortly after Stutz sighted her, approaching from her left. Diver 2 had moved on top of her. Tina's legs were still 'flapping slowly up and down' as Diver 2 encircled her torso with his arms. Stutz said he could not see Diver 2's hands as they were behind Tina's back, so he could not confirm what he had been doing. The whole embrace, Stutz thought, lasted about 30 seconds, or even as little as 10 seconds. He repeated, from his first statement, how he had seen Diver 2 ascend, and then Tina's movements grow weaker as she sank and disappeared.

The next day, 19 April, Knowles and Campbell flew into Birmingham, Alabama. Sergeant Brad Flynn was now heavily involved in the case. The four police officers discussed the investigation at length before Campbell and Knowles met with Tommy and Cindy to visit Tina's still-unmarked grave. It was now almost three years since Operation Charlie Oswald had begun.

The next day Campbell and Knowles visited Alabama Blue Water Adventures in Pelham. Campbell walked around the wooden duckboard and took fifteen photos of the facility that so far he had only been able to imagine.

Four days after Campbell and Knowles landed in the United States, a warrant to search the premises of David Gabriel Watson of Oak Leaf Circle, Hoover, was sworn in the office of the Federal District Attorney, Herbert Henry. That same day, Campbell took a statement from Jimmy Phillips Jr., who corroborated most of what his wife, Amanda, had so far told police. The following day, Saturday, 21 April 2007, at the Helena police station, Campbell took a lengthy statement from Amanda Phillips, which was finished the following day. Campbell showed her photos of Gabe's dive watch, which she confirmed as being the same one she and Tina had collected from the dive shop days before the wedding.

Amanda also signed a series of emails she had sent Campbell. Later on 21 April, Paula Snyder gave an addendum to her statement of 2003 and provided Campbell with her journal, which contained her entries for the *Spoilsport* expedition. Addendum statements were also provided by her husband, Ken, and Doug and Ginger Milsap.

Gabe Watson's neighbour from a few houses down had only ever said hello once to Gabe as he passed with his black gambolling labrador pup en route to the park. His son had earned extra pocket money mowing Gabe's lawn. Sometimes, he'd noticed cars in the driveway and a speedboat on a trailer. Other than that, Gabe's house, which sat on the dogleg of the street, was like every other house in the neighbourhood, its occupant mostly keeping to himself. So that morning, 23 April, the neighbour was thoroughly unprepared for the scene that unfolded as he opened his front door. He had not witnessed anything like it in all his decades of living there. Always an early riser, the neighbour enjoyed the peacefulness of the dawn, the time when the streetlights were still on from the night before and the sun's rays had yet to illuminate the day. But today, Oak Leaf Circle looked like the set of *CSI*. Armed officers with weapons drawn surrounded the home. There were Helena police cars and white FBI cars with the trademark blue stripe down the side parked every which way on the road. Officers swarmed around the house. The media, too, had clearly been tipped off, as broadcast cameras and a film crew had assembled outside.

Unlike their target inside, the police had risen well before the sun, planning tactics for the raid. Special Agent Greg Gauger was the leading investigator from the Federal Bureau of Investigation. For Brad Flynn, and more especially Gary Campbell, this was an important development after years of work. As they drew up, Campbell spoke into his recorder.

'Time is 6.15 a.m. Today is Monday, 23 April 2007, attending to Oak Leaf Circle, Hoover, to execute search warrant on residence of David Watson, David Gabriel Watson.'

Campbell was concerned Gabe may have received a tip-off, but as they banged at the front door they heard a dog barking incessantly and then the sound of someone's voice trying to quiet the animal.

Two-and-a-half minutes later, one of the officers said: 'He's home.'

'Are you coming to the door?' the same officer asked loudly.

There was a muffled assent from inside the house and a command to the dog: 'Get down.'

Special Agent Gauger executed the search warrant as Gabe Watson blinked into the daylight. He was handcuffed and immediately cautioned that he would not be allowed back in the house if he decided to leave. After the FBI had entered through the front door, the Australian officers were invited in. Campbell had already been told that although they were not allowed to take part in the search of the premises, if they observed anything of interest, they should point it out to the other officers.

As Campbell entered, he recognised the tall well-built man in the corridor immediately.

'Gabe, my name is Gary Campbell. I'm a detective sergeant of the Townsville CIB. This gentleman here is Detective Inspector Scott Knowles from the Brisbane Homicide Squad. Now I warn you, you don't have to answer any further questions or make any further statements because anything you do . . . say, or statement you do make, is recorded and can be later used as evidence in court to either acquit you or convict you of any further offence. Do you understand that? You are also entitled to access a lawyer or a solicitor prior to discussing this matter with us any further. You are also entitled to contact or access a support person if you wish to do so before you discuss this matter with us any further. Do you understand that?'

Gabe mumbled that he did.

Campbell told him they were looking for several items, hence the search warrant.

'If you wish to access your lawyer and bring it to our attention, then reasonable efforts will be made to give you access to a phone . . . okay?'

Gabe told them he wanted his lawyer.

It was almost 7 minutes into the raid.

'Gabe would like to call his lawyer now,' Campbell said to the police nearby. 'Whereabouts is the telephone?' he asked Gabe.

'My cell phone is to the right of the bed on the charger,' Gabe said, adding that he was 'stumped' that Townsville police had come all this way to search his house and asked why they weren't investigating Mike Ball.

'All right, the court case in relation to Mike Ball is in relation to safety breaches under the Workplace Health and Safety Act, all right? . . . We're actually investigating the actual death of Tina and the consequences of that death.'

Gabe made no response.

'Can you check the house is clear so I can give Gabe access to the telephone?' Campbell called.

Gabe was asked about the insurance paperwork he'd compiled for his Old Republic case. It was all boxed up, he replied.

The black labrador, having proved his worth as a guard dog, was panting heavily.

'How old is he?' Campbell asked.

'She's almost turned four.'

'She's in good nick.'

But Gabe was in no mood for small talk. He picked up the phone. From what Gabe said, Campbell guessed he was speaking to his father.

'Call Austin. Tell him he can't come in my house, but to come to my house. I have Australian authorities, Helena authorities and FBI and I'm handcuffed right now. So tell him . . . yeah . . . my . . . He says they talked to the uh . . . the uh . . . uh Old Republic people. But, I'm sure a lot of it is . . . It looks like they're packing up my computer and all that . . . But tell him to get over here because I've got a feeling he's gunna need to look into this more, because my guess is there were conversations with the Thomases that led to this along the way . . .'

Almost half an hour into the raid the phone rang. Gabe answered.

'Yep. Hi. Yep. He says I'm not under arrest. He says I'm free to go, but I'm handcuffed. There's Helena dudes, FBI dudes and there's these little CSI blue lights flashing,' he said.

Campbell waited until Gabe had finished before he spoke.

'It's my understanding, Gabe, that when your lawyer turns up, he can't come inside the premises but I can take the cuffs off you and you can go outside and talk to him if you like. Okay?'

Campbell spoke softly but there was an edge to his politeness.

Gabe answered a muffled question asked by one of the police officers.

'Straight down the hall in that bedroom under the bed,'

he answered. 'It should be a green and black case. Yeah, I think it should be a solid black case . . .'

The search continued. An officer came out carrying dive photographs. Gabe told him they were of Cozumel, Mexico.

'How about your book here?'

'You what? . . . I don't know,' Gabe said.

The labrador was panting solidly now, unsettled by the activity.

Ten minutes later, an FBI officer appeared. Gabe told him his lawyer was Bob Austin.

'Civil attorney, isn't it?' the FBI officer asked. 'Isn't he representing you in the civil deposition? Is that the same guy? No? When he comes, though, he can talk to you outside and we'll take those off. Like I said, you're free to go.'

The FBI agent produced the search warrant and gave Gabe a copy. Asked if anyone else lived in the house, Gabe said he lived alone.

David Watson arrived shortly afterwards with Bob Austin. Campbell outlined his purpose and role and Austin agreed that Campbell could interview his client at a later time.

In just over an hour, the whole thing was over. Oak Leaf Circle was waking up and people were peeking through curtains at the activity outside.

The next day, detectives Campbell and Knowles turned up at Bob Austin's office and made their way past the gathered media. Gabe was already in Austin's office. The lawyer was guarded but Campbell pressed ahead. After all, they'd been allowed this far.

Austin was on the offensive immediately, asking when his client was going to get copies of what had been taken from the raid. He also wanted to know when his client's things would be returned. Campbell told him that would depend on the FBI.

'You'll be headed back – when? Or you don't know?' Austin asked.

'Not sure yet,' Campbell said. 'Basically, we're heading for the FBI Friday and we have to comply with their evidence-handling procedures. Now, that will be Friday morning, at this stage, because while they enabled us to have initial viewing of the material, we weren't given full access to it. So, on Friday I'd like to think we'd have a lot better idea of what we can return and what we can copy, and if there's any other circumstances there to be able to advise you of the status of the exhibits.'

Austin said that his client would have to buy a replacement computer if his wasn't returned to him shortly.

'That's more than a fair concern,' Campbell said soothingly, but he repeated that the FBI had told them to wait until Friday.

Knowles cut in, adding that the FBI was preparing a back-up of the hard drive so there would be no reason to hold on to Gabe's computer.

Gabe had been silent up to this point. Now he ventured: 'It's okay for a week or two, but if it ended up being several months or so, I'd have to figure something out.'

There had been enough banter. Campbell rushed in with the real purpose of the visit.

'As I said over the telephone to you yesterday, what we'd like to do is have Gabe go through with us personally what occurred on the day of the deceased's death. Is that still an option at this stage?'

'Well, you can have the witness statement that was taken and you've got the videotaped statement that was taken,'

Austin said. 'I think it would probably be more productive, if you've got any questions, from having gone through that statement . . . is just to ask him. Have questions about specific things, I think would be more productive than making him relive this whole episode again.'

'Well,' Campbell countered, 'in the process it's still going to take Mr Watson back to that incident . . . I would prefer to hear from the actual person in their own words their account of that incident. Obviously, if Mr Watson doesn't want to, all he has to say is "No".'

'Well, he'd be happy to answer questions . . .'

'But he doesn't wish to recount that . . .'

'Well, where's your starting point?' Austin wanted to know.

'Well, the night before from when Mr Watson got on the boat. I'd like to hear from him about these briefings, how detailed they were . . . what was involved with them, who actually gave them? As I said to you on the phone, we get information from numerous different sources . . .'

Campbell said that he had to investigate everything all sources told him.

'That's a good approach to take. But, now are you going to let him just tell the story? Are you going to record it?' Austin asked.

'Just going to tell the story . . .' Campbell confirmed.

'Are you recording it? Are you going to interrupt him?'

'No I'm not,' Campbell said. 'I will outline his rights to him. He was the only person with the deceased at the time and you did ask me, "Is he a suspect?" and yes, he is. So it's a requirement of our law, just like I believe it is here, to outline a person's rights in any investigation.

'Let me just outline your rights and if you wish to make any comments, that will be fine. I warn you, you don't have to make any further statements or answer any further questions because any statements you do make can be used to convict you of any offence or acquit you of any offence. Do you understand that? Do you understand that you are also entitled to access legal representation? As I understand it correctly, Mr Austin is here. You have had an opportunity to speak to Mr Austin before speaking with us?'

'Yes,' Gabe answered.

'Hold on a second,' Austin cut across the exchange. 'You're going to be taking notes?'

'That's correct.'

'And you're saying that what you write down could be used against him?'

'That's correct.'

'No,' Austin said suddenly.

'No?'

'No . . . we're not going to agree that any of your notes can be used against him, because there's no way of [us] knowing the accuracy of what's said.'

'He's given an opportunity to read through our notes and adopt those notes [or] to say these aren't true and accurate,' Knowles added quickly.

'So you're going to have to read your notes and he's going to have to read your notes . . . It seems a little convoluted . . .' Austin still wanted convincing.

'We're just complying with our legislative requirements,' Campbell said.

'Well, and I'm saying if you had something written down for him to read and sign, I would agree with that, but just your notes of what you're taking down and interpreting what he's saying . . .' Austin said doggedly.

Knowles urged that this was Gabe's opportunity to put his point of view, and it was Gabe's choice as to whether he agreed with them or not.

'We're cooperating with you, but let's do it in the best and fairest way possible for both sides,' Austin said at last.

Campbell began his questions immediately.

'When you boarded the boat, can you say what briefings were ever said to you at that point . . . the actual process of what happened?'

Gabe answered in the same perfunctory tone of his earlier interviews. Yes, there had been a general overview; they had gone upstairs and had been assigned their cabins and had then met at 'the big room up top'. He went through that night's activities. Campbell asked when the first specific dive briefing was, and Gabe replied that it was after breakfast when they were shown out on the back deck where all the dive equipment was kept. He described how Wade Singleton had gone through a 'little chalkboard picture of the dive and did his dive brief'.

Campbell scribbled as Gabe spoke.

'Did he mention currents at all?' Campbell wanted to know.

'He did. He did say that you could go down . . . he was talking about when you were going across to the bottom. He said you could go to the bottom. You could swim and then you could drift with the current . . .'

'Have you got experience in diving?' Campbell asked.

'You guys have got all my stuff,' Gabe countered.

'Did Tina check any of her dive equipment?' Campbell asked.

'What do you mean? She was going through the motions . . . everyone was doing the same thing,' Gabe said.

Gabe provided more details of what was happening on deck until Campbell returned to the issue of safety checks.

'So you tested "the reg" to see if it was working?' Campbell asked.

'Yes, I tested my equipment.'

'Check your computer?'

Gabe hesitated.

'You see there's a button . . . it wouldn't activate until you're in the water.' Gabe went into a long explanation. Then there was discussion about when Tina had bought her gear.

'Did you check Tina's gear?'

'As far as what?' Gabe didn't answer the question.

He went on to outline what happened that day leading up to the aborted dive.

'We went in. They made us drop in. Go straight to the line. We dropped in, went under the boat and the computer was beeping. I don't even know if our tanks were under the water. You know, I mean, it wasn't like we were halfway down to the thing . . .'

He said Tina had barely got her hair wet and she popped up. He'd told her: 'My computer's messed up', so they had got back into the tender.

'And back to the main vessel?' Campbell asked.

'Yes.'

'Did you see anybody when you got back?'

'Almost positive his name was Uzi . . . I asked for a quarter. Told him the battery wasn't working.'

The interview ran for 2 hours. After it was completed, Campbell and Knowles left. As they walked out onto the footpath, Campbell noticed the media presence had grown and that Austin was heading outside to face the cameras.

Before the two Australian detectives returned home, they interviewed Gabe's friends Craig Youngblood and Mike Moore. On 30 April, Mark Hughes, an insurance agent and friend of Craig Youngblood, faxed Campbell the notes he had made on quotes Gabe had sought before leaving for the honeymoon on life and business insurance relating to paying off the mortgage if one spouse died. On 8 September 2003, Hughes had noted: 'Gabe wants to take a look at life insurance after wedding. Touch base in early December [2003]'. And beneath 9 October 2003, two days before the wedding, was a notation: 'Need to call Gabe about life and ask him about his business insurance renewal.'

On 9 May in the Cairns Industrial Magistrates Court, Magistrate Suzette Coates found against Mike Ball Dive Expeditions in its prosecution under Section 28 (3) of the Workplace Health and Safety Act 1995. The Magistrate found that Tina Watson was certified but still fairly inexperienced. 'The dive she was undertaking was difficult for her level of experience. The company had procedures in place to identify inexperienced divers and ensure they were accompanied on "orientation dives" by qualified workers. No orientation dive was conducted and the diver was not supervised in the water by a qualified worker.' The Magistrate noted that Mike Ball Dive Expeditions now had documented procedures in place to identify inexperienced divers and ensure they were accompanied on 'orientation dives' by qualified workers. No conviction was recorded. Mike Ball Dive Expeditions was fined AU$6500. The maximum fine under the act was AU$187,500.

As the inquest approached, the chattering on the Scuba Dive Forum began again, both for and against Gabe.

Sue – Non-diver/Teacher
September 7, 2007 at 17:13:53

Kari, I think I knew Tina about as well as anyone, but had not been in contact for a few years. I was at the funeral and had to ask which "mourner" was her husband. I was looking for a young man with grief on his face, swollen eyes, and that blank stare that is usually the case in an accidental death of a young person. When he was pointed out to me, I saw a man who looked more like he was at his wedding than a funeral, and he swaggered around like he was on cloud nine. I wasn't judging him for her death at the time because as far as we knew it had been a horrible accident. I told my husband at that very moment that there was something strange in his behavior. My family will always love Tina like a daughter. She had faults just like us all, but I think the worst one was her choice of a husband.

CHAPTER 22

Harvey Walters' chambers were inside a small modernised cottage in Wills Street immediately behind the massive four-storey concrete structure of the Townsville Law Courts. The Thomases sat in the small tiled reception area waiting to meet the man they had entrusted with Tina's 'day in court'. A portrait hung in the foyer of the fully robed and wigged Sir George Kneipp, the judge for whom the chambers had been named. The helpful bright-eyed young woman who offered them a drink made them feel at home.

Walters turned out to be a seasoned, sharp operator, sympathetic to a point, professional characteristics he had perfected after so many criminal trials. He had seen it all over the years, representing a lion's share of those accused of crimes in the north, ranging from alleged 'criminals' who kept too many chooks in the backyard, to murderers. As he appraised his new clients, Cindy, he could see, would have difficulties coping with the days ahead. A southern belle with the captivating drawl from the south, she was prone to emotion and was outspoken. He warmed to Tommy right away, deciding he was the 'till death do us part' kind of guy, a dignified old-fashioned type driven to do the right thing by his daughter.

That day, 19 November 2007, the heavy humidity had lifted and early-morning drizzle had set in. For the Thomases, the visit marked their third journey across the world. After four years of public grief, speculation, hostility, controversy, media courting and politicking, they were finally here. In the tropical heat heading towards summer, this man and the building opposite represented their hopes and fears.

From Harvey Walters' chambers, it was a short stroll across the street to the court complex, which straddled an entire block of the Townsville city centre. Built in 1975, with precast concrete panels and concrete slabs projecting well past the building to keep the heat at bay, its architecture would have looked more at home on an administrative building in New Delhi.

The expected phalanx of cameras and microphones greeted the Thomases as they approached the high-arching walkway. Then they walked up the concrete stairs to level B.

Detective Sergeant Gary Campbell's report to the Coroner was delivered only shortly before the inquest. It had caused a buzz inside Gabe Watson's legal team, who could see that the brief overall was damning of their client and suggested that foul play had led to Tina's death. If the evidence persuaded the Coroner, it led one way or another towards a potential murder charge. Gabe could well be the subject of an adverse finding, and because of this he was entitled to be legally represented. Rohan Armstrong of Roberts Nehmer McKee lawyers in Townsville was his solicitor, and Steve Zillman, a thirty-year veteran of the Queensland bar who practised exclusively in the criminal area in Brisbane, had been briefed as his barrister.

As the minutes ticked over towards 10 a.m., Tommy and Cindy perused the bar table and the backs of suited barristers who were all foreign to them except for Harvey Walters.

Counsel assisting the inquest was John Tate, the Crown lawyer who would run the show, examining each witness based on original statements and any addendums made in the years following.

Along the rest of the bar table were the three barristers representing interested parties who had been granted leave by the Coroner to appear. They could cross-examine witnesses to protect their clients' interests. Next to Steve Zillman sat Harvey Walters and, finally, Damien Atkinson, the son of former high-profile Brisbane mayor Sally-Anne Atkinson, representing Mike Ball Dive Expeditions. Atkinson was the only scuba diver among them, having attained his open-water accreditation thirteen years earlier. He had lost a young child the previous year and was acutely aware that Tina's parents were present.

All the legal representatives had to master a variety of issues, outside the usual questions of how the death occured, when and where and who, if anyone, might be responsible. A host of matters were on the table for examination: a basic knowledge of scuba diving; the operation of dive computers and whether the data that could be downloaded could accurately ascertain how long a person was in the water at a certain time; the possible causes of an accidental drowning at depth; heart arrhythmia; the police re-enactment; and the position where Tina came to rest according to a replication of tides and currents similar to the conditions on the day in question. Then there was the significance of Gabe's status as a rescue diver; both Gabe and Tina's dive experience; and other conflicting evidence such as whether any diver, particularly one of Asian appearance, had been approached by Gabe on the descent line. Not to mention the complexities of the employment-related life insurance system that operates in the United States. And there were other issues that had become part of the story such as Tina's disinterment and Gabe's removal of the artificial flowers from her gravesite.

For all the lawyers, the inquest promised to be a memorable one, not least because of the publicity the story generated locally, nationally and internationally, from wire agencies to major US TV networks. It had the hallmarks of a great story: a beautiful bride who had died on her honeymoon, with her husband the suspected villain.

Inside Court Five, the high-ceilinged, cedar-panelled courtroom especially designed to help acoustics, the bar table was already piled high with documentary exhibits. The twelve seats for the jurors were vacant. Paper exhibits were also stacked on legal trolleys, ready to be handed up to the Coroner. Thick legal texts were placed around the bar table. A mass of documents, with some yet to come, formed the core of the exhibits. They included the police and witness statements, expert reports and attachments, medical records, faxes, affidavits from American witnesses, and email exchanges between police and witnesses. There were also Gabe Watson's deposition transcript from 2006, dive training manuals, Christmas cards sent by Gabe to friends in 2003, dive computer training manuals, photographs, tidal information, photocopies of handwritten notes of police and civilian witnesses, passenger diaries, the *Spoilsport* incident report forms of eleven staff and passengers, Gabe and Tina's Mike Ball Dive Expeditions booking forms, documents identifying mooring points, diver access points and measurements at the *Yongala* wreck site, the invoice for the purchase of *Top Dive Sites of Australia* by Glenda Watson, newspaper articles, credit card statements, photocopies of diary entries and police running sheets, hard copy and digital images and drawings.

'Watch your step,' one of the lawyers was warned as he trod warily around a protruding box containing videotapes of interviews with American witnesses.

Bulkier exhibits were stored behind the bar table in boxes and on the courtroom floor. Tina's dive equipment and the three dive computers that told the story of the emergency ascent were there, together with mini digital video cassettes of more American witness interviews; police notebooks; DVDs showing Tina's disinterment and Gabe removing flowers from her grave and audio tapes and dive training videos.

A loud knock on the door heralded the entry of the Coroner, David Glasgow, at 10 a.m. After a decade as a Magistrate sitting in such far-flung settlements as Bamaga, the northern-most town in Australia, Thursday Island and Palm Island, this was his last inquest. Behind him on the wall was the coat of arms. Glasgow sat on the large turquoise chair, his Rumpole-like eyes looking out over the court.

'Today commences my inquiry into the death of Christina Mae Watson,' he said, surveying his court from the bench, 'formerly Christina Mae Thomas, a citizen of the United States of America; [she] was born in Germany on the thirteenth of February 1977, married to David Gabriel Watson on the eleventh of October 2003 and died during a dive on the site of the *Yongala* wreck, some 89 kilometres south-east off the port of Townsville on the twenty-second of October 2003.'

Many witnesses would give evidence from interstate and overseas via telephone and video-link and it was hoped, he said, that the proceedings would conclude in two weeks. The inquest would be conducted under the Coroner's Act of 1958, not the current Act of 2003, which had come into effect six weeks after Tina died. That timing would have a major impact on everything that followed.

As all the lawyers were aware, two major differences separated the old Act from its successor. First, under the old Act a person of interest and against whom adverse findings might be made could claim privilege and decline to give evidence on the grounds that it might tend to incriminate them – directly or even indirectly. No adverse inference could be made against persons exercising their right to silence. But, if the Coroner did make an adverse finding and felt a jury could convict on the evidence before him, he could name and charge the person when he made his findings.

Under the new Act a person could claim privilege against incrimination but if it was found to be in the public interest, that person must nonetheless give that evidence. However, that evidence could not be used against that person in subsequent proceedings. Since 1 December 2003, when the new Act came into force, Coroners have been restricted to finding the facts of a death, without determining blame or publicly naming someone as suspected of criminal activity who might never be charged. The Coroner could merely refer an unnamed person to the Director of Public Prosecutions in criminal matters, for consideration of charges being brought.

Although it was a fairly standard inquest setting for some, it was unusual for Gabe's legal team. Their client was not even in the country let alone the courtroom. He wasn't compelled to be there, living outside the jurisdiction. But, it was felt by the legal team that there was a very real risk of apprehension if he did return. Gary Campbell's report to the Coroner clearly pointed to suspicious circumstances due to continuing inconsistencies in the evidence. If Gabe Watson, the last person to see Tina alive, took up the offer of the court to be flown to Australia and accommodated for the expected fortnight of evidence he could be arrested as soon as he set foot on Australian soil, if police believed there was a strong enough case.

Steve Zillman, who had indicated at a preliminary directions hearing that Gabe would not travel to Australia, said that his client would be prepared to give evidence via telephone or video-link. It was assumed, therefore, that Gabe would be the last witness.

The rules of evidence do not apply at inquests, so hearsay evidence is allowed. With no traditional prosecution or defence, a Coroner presides over a wide-ranging fact-finding exercise led by the counsel assisting in an attempt to hear everything relevant and find the truth of why, how and when a person died in unusual or abnormal circumstances. As in any court-related proceeding, arbitrary time limits may blow out causing inconvenience, added stress and of course, extra expense. Apart from John Tate, who was a salaried Crown law officer, each of the other three barristers was likely charging several thousand dollars a day with added loadings for travel away from their home base. Instructing solicitors charged by the hour. Gabe faced major legal costs in Australia for however long the inquest ran. The legal team involved in his civil case continued to rack up costs with each new motion and reply as the discovery process led up to the February trial.

At the inquest, the first of what would ultimately be sixty-two oral witnesses was Detective Sergeant Gary Campbell.

'Now, Sergeant,' Tate asked after taking him through the start of his leading role in the investigation from about July 2004 to his interview with Gabe following the FBI raid in April 2007, 'am I right in understanding this from your report to the Coroner . . . that there are at least some sixteen different potential words or versions and so it's been very difficult for the police to actually gain an accurate understanding of exactly what happened during the course of the second dive?'

'That's correct.'

'And am I also correct in assuming that you've spent considerable time and energies looking to see how Gabe's versions of events might be corroborated or confirmed by many of these other witnesses?'

Tate took Campbell through twelve points that remained of general concern to police, which included the apparent malfunction of his dive computer, which Campbell stated 'does not seem possible'; going for help rather than using his qualifications and training as a rescue diver to rescue Tina; conflicts between the accounts of Gabe and Stanley Stutz, as well as reports from the two doctors who Gabe consulted about his ears; the lack of confirmation that he approached any other diver underwater; his apparent slow rate of ascent given the emergency; his behaviour at the cemetery; insurance issues; and Gabe's conflicting versions to different people.

Campbell concluded that he had been 'unable to identify a non-suspicious cause of death in relation to the death of Christina Mae Watson née Thomas. And in addition I am unable to exclude suspicious circumstances surrounding [her] death'.

The phone bill for Queensland taxpayers began ascending from the first day with the questioning of the initial international witnesses. Gavin Docking, the master of the *Spoilsport* on the day, on the phone from Fort Lauderdale, Florida, told of tides and current directions, mooring positions and safety procedures on board the *Spoilsport*.

From Alabama, Birmingham cardiologist Professor Andrew Epstein outlined Tina's medical history regarding her heart ailment and firmly ruled out any cause of death being attributable to her former arrhythmia.

'Anxiety could trigger the arrhythmia,' he said. But he had successfully burned off the extra node that was the cause of Tina's problem and the arrhythmia had not returned following the operation. Thus, he explained: 'Anxiety can't trigger an arrhythmia using a pathway that doesn't exist.'

From the start, the two-week deadline on evidence imposed a sense of urgency with a constant juggling act between those waiting in different time zones across the world and those queued outside, some having flown from nearby Cairns where the *Spoilsport* was now based. One Cairns witness, Uzi Barnai, the videographer from the *Spoilsport*, had a wife who was about to give birth. But none of this stopped the lawyers arguing strenuously for their own positions.

Early on the second day, Zillman began dissecting Tommy Thomas's statement in a bid to argue how certain parts of it, and at least ten others largely from Thomas family and friends, were inadmissible as either irrelevant, supposition or hearsay.

'But that is the statement of a distraught father,' the Coroner began, before Zillman successfully argued his point. As Cindy and Tommy listened intently to the often arcane legal references, Atkinson boiled it down simply with a submission of his own when asked what his interest was: '. . . because it involves my client to the extent that there's really three issues . . . canvassed by Detective Campbell yesterday, in terms of causes of death. One was the heart problem and the other was an equipment failure and the third was foul play.'

Coroner: 'I thought the doctor acquitted the heart problem almost immediately?'

Atkinson: 'And I understand that in due course there will be evidence about equipment. And then there's this third issue of foul play. And what Your Honour will be asked to make findings about in due course is the fact that Tina had a buddy and that the buddy, apparently, on the evidence that we've heard from Detective Campbell, didn't make strenuous efforts to save her at the very least. And the evidence that's . . . presently being discussed, is evidence to the effect that even though they were married, their relationship wasn't as strong even at the outset as one might expect.'

It was agreed that contentious parts of witness statements could be argued as witnesses were called. Glasgow looked down from the bench, peering over his reading glasses.

'. . . a great deal of flexibility is given to parties, particularly those that are distressed, and it's quite clear on the material between them, that there is considerable animosity between sections of various families,' he said. He said he did not want to 'unnecessarily restrict' any witness, including Gabe Watson, whose barrister he 'understood fully' saw his client subject to the possibility of an adverse finding or a warrant being issued for his arrest.

Atkinson was first to cross-examine Campbell, who had resumed his lengthy spell in the witness box following the interposing of Docking and Epstein. Atkinson asked whether, apart from her old heart condition, equipment failure was another consideration.

Campbell agreed but stated that even if Tina was over-weighted it would not explain why she died with her regulator still in position, nor why she would stop breathing or self-rescuing (as she had done back in the quarry during her certification). He agreed that there was no reason to doubt the good working of the equipment, which was triple-tested in different conditions, nor the safety procedures on board the *Spoilsport*.

'It's a dance of love,' muttered an amused spectator in the court at the unusual sight of a police officer happily agreeing with everything put to him under cross-examination by a barrister protecting his own client's interests. The opposite was usually the case.

Atkinson led Campbell through a list of twenty issues that the officer concurred were 'hard to explain'. Chief among them was evidence of Tina aspirating, or drowning, yet when Singleton found her, the regulator was still in her mouth and able to be purged, the air valve on her gas cylinder was on and she had plenty of air left.

Gabe's dive computer had recorded the penultimate or aborted dive. Despite his claims that the battery in his dive computer was in backwards and this was why it had beeped, causing him to abort the first dive, tests by an Oceanic technican had shown that with the battery incorrectly inserted, nothing was recorded. Another issue of concern was that if Gabe had descended, like he told police, to reach Tina, according to his own dive computer he didn't go down more than 3 metres – less than two of his own body lengths – because there was no indication of a sudden sharp descent.

Campbell also agreed that Gabe's claim that he was mainly taught to self-rescue and to go for help contrasted with the statement of his own dive instructor, Tom Jackson, who would testify at length about everything Gabe had been taught, including dealing with panicked and unconscious divers and ascending with them to the surface.

Campbell also agreed that three simple steps might have been used by a buddy with Gabe's training to assist Tina: dropping her weights, sharing air from a second regulator and inflating either her or his BC for a controlled ascent to the surface. As well, Gabe took longer to ascend 50 feet (15 metres) than Wade Singleton's 92 seconds to travel almost twice that distance while carrying Tina. And despite speaking to all twenty-five paying passengers on the *Spoilsport*, its twelve crew and the three commercial divers on board, as well as everyone aboard the *Jazz II*, Campbell had not been able to find an Asian diver or anyone else who had been approached by a distressed Gabe on the descent line.

Asked if Gabe had ever admitted embracing his wife underwater, as Stutz appeared to have witnessed, Campbell replied: 'He denies actually reaching her while attempting to catch up with her.'

One of the last things Tina had done was to grab for her husband's mask and regulator, indicating that she may have been lacking air, Campbell said.

Atkinson: 'Did your investigators disclose . . . any explanation for Mr Watson going to the surface rather than going down to offer the regulator [once Tina had grabbed at his mask and primary regulator]?'

Campbell: 'A possibility I did consider was maybe he just straight out panicked, but the rate of ascent would appear to negate that . . . I think it's unlikely that he panicked but . . . I can't say with certainty.'

***

During his cross-examination by Harvey Walters, Campbell went further, saying it was his opinion that it was 'highly unlikely' that Tina had met her death as Gabe said it had occurred, given the numerous versions he had given. Poor recollection, or being distraught or panicked afterwards could have accounted for some of the different versions Gabe gave to people on the day that Tina had died, Campbell agreed. But while Dr Stutz may have had similar difficulties judging distance and time in his three separate official recountings, Stutz was consistent in his statements about the embrace he says he saw Tina being given, and this version of events was, Campbell said, 'totally at odds' with any of Gabe's versions.

'The act of actually swimming down onto the diver, maintaining that embrace and then separating, I would see as inconsistent – totally inconsistent with the panic option,' Campbell said.

Gabe's first account to police of the strength of the current at the *Yongala* – a five out of ten and not as strong as he had experienced at Cozumel years earlier – also 'appears to have evolved further' in his second record of interview where it was 'stronger' than Cozumel, Campbell agreed. By the time of the deposition for Gabe's civil action more than two years later, the severity of the current had 'increased substantially', he said.

Walters asked if Campbell had conducted investigations of Mr Watson's equipment. Campbell replied that Gabe had taken his own dive equipment with him after Tina had died, so police had not been able to examine it.

Cross-examined by Zillman, Campbell agreed that Tina had no estate to speak of, that the house she had bought with Gabe was heavily mortgaged and all that was left was her Jeep. On her death she had about a year's salary owing to a beneficiary, her father, through her employer, Parisian.

***

Uzi Barnai, whose wife was three days past her due date, was interposed during Campbell's continuing cross-examination, the end of which was put off until the last day of the inquest.

Asked to swear on the bible, the former Israeli army officer said flatly, giving a rare moment of humour in his thickly accented English: 'I can swear on it if you like, but it's not my bible.'

Barnai gave a detailed account of his interaction with Gabe regarding the dive computer battery and coin, as well as his sustained efforts with Tina. Of his 40-minute non-stop mouth-to-mouth resuscitation in tandem with Singleton's chest compressions, he said he would do nothing differently.

'There is no – nothing else to do. I was there from the beginning to the end, never paused, never stopped.'

Barnai, like Barton Painter, skipper of the *Jazz II*, was personally thanked by Walters on behalf of Cindy and Tommy, for his efforts to save Tina. After praising the efforts of everyone involved in Tina's attempted resuscitation, Painter remarked that: 'it certainly helps with the closure for me as well'. It was a sentiment that could have been echoed by the two most important witnesses to events underwater – Wade Singleton and Stanley Stutz. Each man was openly distressed during his testimony (Stutz's supplied through video-link much later in the inquest). They were both individually thanked by Walters on behalf of the Thomases, following their lengthy evidence.

The medical evidence, although technical and difficult to follow at times, showed that while Tina's lungs contained no obvious water by the time of autopsy, the vomit and foam and microscopic fluid found in her lungs indicated that she might have ingested water. Professor David Williams, the forensic pathologist who conducted Tina's autopsy 22 hours after her death, well outside the preferred 8 hours, commented that while her lungs did not have the usual over-inflated appearance of someone who had died with lungs full of water, her lungs were heavier than he would have expected.

However, he said when a person drowns, it is very common for them to swallow water that could be regurgitated as what appears to be vomit, but is really water with stomach contents. Foam, seen by several witnesses on Tina's mouth and which Barnai had to wipe away several times as he performed mouth-to-mouth resuscitation, was really water and air that indicated an ingestion of water into the lungs.

'I was unable to find a natural cause of death for the deceased,' Professor Williams told the inquest, suggesting the Coroner should look at non-medical causes for this drowning. If there had been deprivation of oxygen during Tina's dive, he would find it hard to demonstrate during an autopsy.

Harvey Walters then played his trump card. Because he would have no legal right to make submissions on behalf of the family at the end of the inquest, Walters put forward a theory about how Tina died. The theory, he said, would help explain Gabe's multiple versions of Tina's movements underwater with Stutz's witnessed 'bear hug'. It would also explain why her dive equipment, including her regulator, were in excellent order as well as the satisfactory mix of gases in her Mike Ball scuba tank. According to the theory, those elements then fitted together in a fairly logical, if unprovable, sequence. It would also contribute a missing piece of the jigsaw puzzle as to why she had drowned if she had not died from natural causes.

'Doctor,' Walters began, as the news reporters without shorthand began writing furiously, trying to keep up, 'I have a theory, based upon the evidence, that during the dive of Tina with her husband . . . her gas supply . . . from the tank was turned off. And during the process that it was turned off, she struggled, dislodging the mask of the person who was holding her, causing her to be released, wherein she descended to some degree then that person took hold of her, again holding her from the front with the arms around, this person being much larger than she, and as a result of that the breathing apparatus in her mouth was pressed up against that person's chest preventing it from being spat out as is often the case in these scuba diving incidents of persons who are suffering oxygen deprivation. And subsequently the person holding her has seen some other divers who have arrived on another vessel which he did not know about and he has turned the air back on in that position and suddenly left the scene, causing her at this stage to descend to the bottom of the ocean.'

Gary Stempler's underwater shot of Tina Watson's prone body on the bottom of the ocean filled more than a million Australian TV screens as viewers of Channel 9's *A Current Affair* tuned in on the night of Thursday, 22 November 2007. The reporter was dwarfed by the image he stood before as he announced to viewers: 'Tina's parents want to know why Gabe is not in that photo.'

After four days of evidence so far in the inquest, the reporter told his audience, it appeared Tina may have been deprived of oxygen before she drowned.

Cindy Thomas then filled the screen: 'When you think about your child being underwater and not being able to get to the top. Whatever happened that caused that – you dream about it, you think about it every day.'

Tommy Thomas: 'We've just got to know exactly what happened. Not one of sixteen versions but as close as possible to what is the truth.'

The stinger, though, was the 'never before seen' surveillance footage, an exhibit at the inquest, of Gabe cutting the bicycle chain from the stake holding Tommy's artificial flower arrangement at the head of Tina's grave two years earlier.

'How do you explain that?' asked Cindy.

Until he took a radical career detour into carpentry, Adam White was the most knowledgeable man in Australia on Oceanic dive computers. Based at Sorrento outside Melbourne, he'd been the US company's customer service manager for fifteen years when Sergeant Gary Campbell had approached him in late 2004 to ask what information could be extracted from Gabe and Tina's dive computers. Tina's basic Versa model was not able to be downloaded. The most useful information gained from scrolling through its screens was her maximum depth of 27.1 metres on the day of her death, and that she had spent a total of 10 minutes underwater before she surfaced, not breathing, with Wade Singleton. The inquest was told that Oceanic could provide no more data than was viewable on the screens.

Gabe's DataTrans Plus model that he'd bought in 1998 was one of the Oceanic's early wireless, air-integrated models. It was comprised of two parts – the transmitter section on the top of the octopus on the first-stage regulator near the dive tank that relayed air cylinder pressure, and the dive watch worn on the wrist. Both were battery operated. White had told Campbell that if the battery in the dive computer was not inserted properly, it would not operate. He also said that by removing the battery, the dates on the subsequent dives would revert to the factory settings. He found that the battery had been removed prior to the last four dives being recorded on the dive computer and that these dives were recorded as having various dates in 1996.

During the inquest, White confirmed to John Tate that the air cylinder pressure was relevant because the computer needed to receive that pressure, otherwise, as a safety feature, it would sound alarms to indicate the dive computer was not receiving, or the air cylinder was not turned on. Gabe's dive computer had been set to accept a radio signal and was activated. When White obtained it from police, he was not provided with the transmitter.

White agreed, as also shown by other independent tests, that if the battery was inserted incorrectly into the data module on the diver's wrist, it was essentially 'dead', with no display at all. But the transmitter section took a slightly different battery. White agreed that an occasion could arise where the battery was inserted upside down in the transmitter section but the separate data module on the diver's wrist could operate to the limited extent that it still recorded depth and time in the water.

'So,' said Zillman, 'you can conceive of a situation where a diver, having the computer system . . . in two components – that is the transmitter and data module – inserting the battery into the module correctly but inserting the battery into the transmitter incorrectly?'

'Yes,' replied the former technician.

Zillman: 'That person gets into the water, descends to a depth of . . . 6 feet or whatever, there's not going to be any proper signal coming from the transmitter?'

White: 'No.'

'An alarm will beep?'

'Yes.'

'And flash. But the dive will be conceivably recorded?'

'Yes.'

'Until rectified, until something's done about it?'

'Yep.'

'So the only way to rectify that is to turn about the battery in the transmitter?'

'If . . . that was the cause of it, yes.'

White agreed that the only way for a diver to access the battery in either the data module or the transmitter was with a coin – such as an American quarter, or an Australian five-cent piece.

As part of his role-playing of Tina in the 2006 re-enactment of the fatal dive, Senior Constable Joshua Kinghorn had tested another of Gabe's claims to police: his explanation of why he had to let go of Tina when his mask and regulator were knocked, and how he had then cleared his mask, and then realising his regulator was not in his mouth, found his octopus from which he took his next breath. Many divers, Kinghorn stated, might find it impossible to clear their mask using only the air left in their lungs and then to locate and insert another regulator and take a breath, particularly following the type of exertion Gabe claimed to have expended towing Tina against the current. Kinghorn said he had tried to simulate this explanation while using his fins in a swimming pool and just could not do it.

However, at a time after giving his statement in January that year, he told the inquest he had since managed to do as Gabe described, but only when he was in a relaxed state on the bottom of the pool.

The court was also treated to the scene of two male divers in an embrace on day seven of the inquest. The police video of the re-enactment had shown Sergeant Owen Law putting his arms around the shoulders of the much smaller Kinghorn to see if Law could reach the valve on Kinghorn's gas cylinder. He could. However, he had not tried to do it from under the armpits, as described by Stanley Stutz. Sergeant Law demonstrated again for the court: wearing clothes and a diver's mask, and with Kinghorn decked out in Tina's dive equipment, they embraced standing up, so they could be more easily seen.

'So, coming up underneath,' said Law to the Coroner, putting his arms under Kinghorn's. 'Okay. That's easier . . . bearing in mind I don't have the shoulders to go around . . . from here I've got easy access . . . I've still got good purchase . . . to grab the tank valve . . .'

The subject of the dive computers came up again on day nine during the evidence of Workplace Health and Safety inspector Christopher Coxon, the principal advisor for diving with Workplace Health and Safety Queensland. He explained that for the computer to perform its functions for the diver, it gathers 'a wealth of data', recording every second in real time. This is far more information than is represented in the data that can be downloaded from the module worn on the wrist in either table, graph or in summary form. Dive computers, he said, were 'very concerned about the time spent underwater, the depths reached and the rate of ascent . . . Those are the three variables that affect a diver's health underwater in terms of decompression illness, embolism.'

A dive computer was not designed to give a truly accurate picture of what happened between snapshots, he explained. Gabe's DataTrans Plus merely took a snapshot of information via distance, that is every 3 metres or 10 feet, to assess the variables. Wade Singleton's dive computer, in contrast, calculated the same information in a different way, by taking snapshots in time – every 20 seconds. Dive computers don't begin recording until the diver reaches 1 metre, or roughly 3 feet, underwater. They deactivate upon reaching the same depth of 1 metre below the surface, during an ascent.

Gabe's computer had a separate function to record the maximum depth on his last dive – 16.5 metres or 54 feet, but in its continuous snapshots of descent, it never recorded anything over 15.2 metres or 50 feet. Thus a built-in error rate of about 3 feet, or 1 metre, on either side of any depth recorded had to be taken into account. Gabe had been underwater for 7 minutes, according to the computer – that meant somewhere between 7.01 minutes and 7.59 minutes, but it was impossible to say any more than that.

The last dive Gabe had completed, according to the dive computer, was clearly the fatal dive. With the last dive logged appearing first in the list, the fatal dive, however, was dated 1 January 1996 – not 22 October 2003. The penultimate dive, which listed a maximum depth of 1.5 metres, was dated even more strangely – 9 January 1996. The presence of these dates, and the two following, which were also 1 January 1996, indicated that the battery had failed or been removed at least twice.

Coxon couldn't explain the anomaly with the 9 January 1996 date. Unlike Adam White, he was not confident enough to say this was indeed Gabe's aborted dive, even though Gabe had dived on 22 October 2003 to both 16.5 metres and 1.5 metres, the shorter depth occurring, as he told police, on the dive he aborted as a response to the beeping alarm.

What Coxon could say from documents shown to him was this: Gabe's log book recorded fifty-six dives, the form he filled out for Mike Ball when he embarked on the *Spoilsport* stated he had dived fifty-five times and the computer printout of his dive computer showed fifty-four downloadable dives. None of the figures was consistent, Coxon agreed, and the three dives recorded on the computer between May 2002 and 22 October 2003 came nowhere near the twelve dives in the past twelve months that Gabe had officially stated he had completed.

After at least ten revised witness lists in the first week alone, it was clear that the evidence was going to take far more time than the allotted two weeks for the Coronial inquest. Coroner Glasgow made an early call. Schedules were reorganised and another two weeks were set down in the traditional legal holiday period in January. The inquest had to finish by 1 February 2008 before the regular sittings of the court commenced. Cindy and Tommy left behind the tropical humidity of Christmas in Townsville and flew back to Birmingham to spend Christmas with Alanda, who had since remarried, and their grandchildren, including the latest arrival, Michael.

CHAPTER 23

On the night of 22 January, *A Current Affair* ran another segment containing more 'never before seen' footage showing the police dive re-enactment with Sergeant Owen Law and Senior Constable Joshua Kinghorn demonstrating, with the slow arm movements of humans underwater, how Gabe could have reached around and turned off Tina's oxygen. The report was set against a backdrop of honeymoon video grabs – Tina at Darling Harbour, walking into the Sydney Aquarium, on a ferry to Taronga Zoo, kissing goodbye to the camera for a 'before' shot while packing and Gabe explaining he was taking the video 'in case we get eaten by a shark'.

Tommy and Cindy, fortified from their seven weeks back home, were also interviewed.

Cindy: 'We just want to know the truth, what happened to our child.'

Tommy: 'This was our daughter . . . We asked to know exactly what happened in the beginning and we thought we got those answers and we didn't . . .'

In the last two weeks of January 2008, it was cool relief from the relentless summer heat inside the air-conditioned walls of Coroner Glasgow's courtroom. Tommy and Cindy, swapping their winter coats for short sleeves in another abrupt seismic shift from their usual world, listened grimly. Some days, especially when events were discussed in such detail about what had happened underwater, Cindy had stayed inside the hotel room, unable to face the evidence – as a growing scenario of foul play seemed to unfold.

One after another through the majority of the US-based witnesses, the inconsistencies or gaps in Gabe's underwater accounts were poked and prodded. Most of the divers on the *Spoilsport* were far more seasoned divers than Gabe. Some provided personal damning opinions on the decision Gabe had made that effectively left his wife to her fate while he went to the surface for help. Paula Snyder said she thought he had clearly panicked. The Snyders and Doug Milsap gave their evidence via telephone from Florida late at night their time, on the thirteenth day of the inquest. But Australian police witnesses, and professional divers including Wade Singleton – all with far more diving experience – placed great emphasis on Gabe's status as a rescue diver. All believed he should have had the skills to bring his panicking wife to the surface alive.

Sergeant Glenn Lawrence, since promoted and having left the Water Police for the Townsville Crime Prevention Unit, was questioned on Gabe's record of interview. He gave evidence about his investigation and Gabe's contrasting statements, including saying that he was 'rocketing' to the top and risking the bends in one account and in another account admitting that he had not ascended faster than his bubbles.

'. . . if he . . . wasn't going up faster than his bubbles,' stated Lawrence, 'that definitely is not an emergency or a rapid ascent. It's a controlled ascent. That brought me back to the question I had in relation to his dive computer not alarming on his indicated rapid ascent whereas . . . on both Wade and Tina's – both [their computers] alarmed' indicating a 'too fast' ascent.

John and Tina Graves gave evidence by phone link from Sydney to the inquest and repeated what they had already told police, including Gabe apparently playing cards in the saloon within hours of Tina's death. They conceded during Zillman's cross-examination that Gabe may have been sitting with card players, rather than actually playing. Lou Johnstone, whose diary had been included in the documents before the inquest, was further questioned on her recollection of the conversation with Gabe in his cabin after Tina had been declared dead.

The emotional impact of Dr Stanley Stutz sobbing while recounting how Tina sank before his eyes had affected everyone in the courtroom. Tommy was glad Cindy was absent that day.

As Stutz told John Tate, in his evidence-in-chief: 'So, what I saw was her looking up at us – or me. She was off to my left. He [a male diver who was bigger] was also somewhat to my left but came across really in front of me almost . . . came across to her and then sort of came on top of her – swam on top of her [indicated two divers facing one another horizontally] . . . and then just met up with her, was on top of her and looked to me like he was trying to bring her to the surface.'

Stutz said he couldn't see if the male was flush upon the woman or there had been a gap, but after being together in that embrace position 'for a period of time' they had 'split apart' and he didn't know why.

Stutz was asked by Tate what happened to the lady.

'She sank. I mean, she sank . . . And she just couldn't

swim. I don't know why she – she couldn't swim; there was something wrong and she couldn't swim . . . But I can tell you that there was something wrong before he got to her.'

He said Tina's position was horizontal throughout the period he saw her, at first moving her arms and legs and 'then in general' her arms were out, almost in a crucifixion shape.

Zillman cross-examined Stutz on his recollection of the timing of events four years on. There was conflict between Stutz and other witnesses on the time of the dive. He thought it may have occurred around noon, while everyone else testified that it was earlier.

'After I lost eye contact with her, and she went into the depths, I looked around,' Stutz recounted. 'It looked to me like nobody else had seen . . . And at some period of time after that, I saw another diver come in from above, and make a beeline straight to the bottom.' It was his impression at the time that this third diver was the diver who rescued Tina from the seabed.

Stutz said: 'I didn't see his face or anything when he went down. And then I saw him come up with her. It struck me as the same diver . . . because . . . they were related in terms of, you know, I saw a diver go straight down the bottom and [in the time it took] for me to go [to] my dive instructor and then I saw a man who looked the same size with a body coming up. That's how I told myself they were they same person.'

Stutz was adamant the diver taking Tina up had initially come from above him when he was at 5 metres depth on the drop line, not from below him. But the inquest had already heard from Wade Singleton, Gary Stempler, Dawn Asano and Claudia Petersen that Tina was spotted on the ocean floor while they were around 20 metres below the surface when Wade saw her and took her up.

Re-examined by John Tate about his memory of the events, Stutz told the inquest: 'I've gone through this evidence multiple times since it happened. I mean, first of all . . . an event like that is obviously shocking and . . . you remember those kinds of things. Secondly . . . I'd never seen anything – I mean outside work – like that in my life . . . So yeah, I mean, it was pretty fresh because it's been in my mind the whole time, you know. I mean, I've been seeking closure to this, too.'

Much of the evidence about tensions in the relationship between Tina and Gabe was successfully kept out of the inquest evidence following objections by Zillman and by agreement with the other barristers. This included events such as the weekend Tina had visited Amanda Phillips' cousin, Xander, in Atlanta, during the protracted lead-up to the proposal, and observations about Gabe and his behaviour towards Tina by her family and friends. Certain sections of some of the statements of her friends and family were ultimately not admitted into evidence by the Coroner. Some who had made statements were not called as witnesses.

Two of Gabe's friends were called to give evidence via telephone link from Birmingham. Michael Moore recounted how Gabe had acted quickly and decisively in response to what could have been a dangerous situation when he dropped half his diving weight during their long-ago trip to Cozumel. He also told the court that Gabe suffered from sinus trouble and was 'a moderate swimmer' as well as diver 'at best' despite his height and body size.

When he had arrived to give his personal condolences to Gabe at Gabe's parents' house on the night he returned from Australia, Gabe had showed him the honeymoon video of Tina and himself and some photographs of the wedding and trip to Australia.

One specific picture stuck out.

'It was a picture of Tina and she was leaning up against the sign that . . . either said "caution undertow" or "danger undertow", and the reason I remember this so vividly is that – is the fact that Gabe showed us that picture and he said, "Look at this picture." He said, "This is a picture we took a couple of days before this dive." And he said, "Isn't this just ironic that here . . . she is leaning against the sign after what happened?" '

Moore said this led to Gabe talking about what happened with Tina, a few hours into the conversation. He said Gabe told him that Tina had knocked his regulator and his mask off and was having some type of difficulty before she drifted away when he let go to replace them.

As she drifted down, Gabe had said he tried to swim back to her but 'he said that his eardrums had busted or ruptured or some type of pain in his ears, and that he . . . could not equalise [the] pressure in his head to get to her' so he immediately went to the surface for help. Moore said when he had asked Gabe what the problem was with Tina's equipment, he had replied that he didn't know.

'He said, "I just – to be honest, I didn't take the situation as serious as I should have". He said, "I thought maybe her vest was coming off or something wasn't right and so, when I let go of her to put this equipment back on myself I just didn't think it was, you know, going to be an outcome like it was. I thought it was just something, she would stay there beside me, I'd get my mask back on and we could fix whatever it was and continue with the dive".'

Moore told the inquest how about seven months afterwards, at a lunch with Gabe and high school friend Craig

Youngblood, Gabe told them how he had trouble sleeping at night, wishing he'd done things differently. He'd had some trouble with Tina's parents. He also found it difficult to get the picture of the ocean out of his mind.

Craig Youngblood also told the inquest that Gabe had told him from Townsville that he had 'hurt his ear' during the dive. And Tom Jackson, questioned on the topic by Zillman, insisted that Gabe had told him he had 'ruptured his ear drum' when he tried to kick back and help Tina who had been pushed down and away from him by the strong current.

Tom Jackson, Gabe and Tina's dive instructor, had already attended the Helena police station three times to complete his lengthy statement and produce various dive instruction manuals. At the inquest Jackson was questioned at length about the various dive certification levels and what each entailed as far as dealing with panicking and unconscious divers and how to rescue them. He disagreed with Gabe's statement to police that much of his rescue training had dwelt on self-rescue, and was 'surprised' to hear that Gabe told police he had gone for help because he didn't know what he could do. This flew in the face of everything he had taught Gabe. 'None of [it] makes sense,' he said. It was true, he conceded to Zillman, that someone's knowledge, gained through certification, could fade if not used. Unlike with open and advanced levels where it was possible to take refresher courses, there was none available to recreational divers who had completed their rescue certificate but had not taken it further. Rescue skills were repeated and refined only for those who went on to train for the dive master certificate.

***

As the inquest neared the end, the issue of life insurance was aired through the testimony of several witnesses close to Tina. Tommy Thomas recounted his conversation with Tina two weeks before the wedding, during which Tina told him that Gabe had asked her to increase her work group life insurance benefit to the maximum and to change Gabe to be the sole beneficiary but that she had not done this. Tommy remained the beneficiary. Sonja Jordan, a Parisian work colleague, recalled a conversation about mortgage insurance about a month before the wedding and Tina saying she and Gabe already had that type of insurance and had just taken out 'huge' life insurance policies. There was no other evidence called that corroborated this statement.

Amanda Phillips told of her conversation with Gabe on 12 November 2003 during which he told her that he was going to Parisian the next day with Tina's death certificate to finalise any paperwork, including insurance, and to clean out Tina's desk. According to Amanda, Gabe had told her of a conversation he had with Tina in September that year about life insurance. He told Amanda Tina had received information about the rates and payments per month for different life insurance payouts. In her police statement Amanda had related: 'At that time he and Tina had laughed that for ten dollars more Tina could have had a million dollar policy. Gabe said that it was a good thing that they didn't get that policy because he would be sitting in an Australian jail now on involuntary manslaughter charges. That was kind of laughed off,' she added.

Caesar Lamonaca, the store manager at Parisian, remembered Gabe arriving at the store in November 2003. He had directed Gabe 'to Human Resources to inquire about an insurance policy'.

Sergeant Gary Campbell re-entered the witness box on

the last day of the inquest. He was cross-examined by Zillman and tidied up some loose ends, confirming that Dr
John Downie was unavailable due to his schedule to give
oral evidence of his attempts to resuscitate Tina. Although
initially cooperative when first approached in October and
November the previous year, the two Korean divers on the
Jazz II declined to submit themselves to further questioning. Email exchanges to Campbell via a police interpreter
with the Asian Specialist Unit were tendered as exhibits.
They indicated that no-one had approached them on the
diver descent line. Han Gyu Kim, the male Korean diver,
was unwilling to be questioned further about the diver he
had seen reaching over the top of Tina's dive tank.

Zillman questioned Campbell about Gabe's contact with
insurance agent Mark Hughes a month before the wedding.
Documents faxed to Campbell from Hughes in April 2007
showed that Gabe's initial inquiries to Hughes had been
about life insurance for either himself or Tina so that the
mortgage might be paid off if there was a death. Gabe was to
be contacted again by Hughes after the wedding with a view
to follow-up. Hughes sourced a quote through Zurich Life
Connections for Gabe to be insured for a sum of US$250,000
and an identical sum for Tina on a separate page. Zillman
questioned him about a computer printout.

'So,' said Zillman, 'what the document shows us, rather
than Gabe being anxious to take up insurance on Tina's life
prior to the wedding, he was declining to do so?'

Campbell replied: 'With that organisation, on the face of
it, yes.'

In the end, Gabe Watson did not testify at the inquest. The
Coroner had earlier offered that the court would pay for

his airfare and accommodation. But Zillman informed him that Gabe intended to claim privilege, and as such his testimony would merely be about him defending that privilege, so it was decided not to go to the expense of hearing it. Although in legal terms a witness's right to silence was not something that any court could draw an adverse inference from, it fuelled speculation that Gabe would be the subject of an adverse finding by the Coroner.

On the eighteenth day of sittings, the Coroner had told Zillman that although he had not yet come to a conclusion on the evidence, 'it is quite clear to me that your client is at risk of the possibility that he could face a criminal charge as a result of it, subject to a thorough review of the proceedings and submissions that are made'. Harvey Walters, he ruled, was not entitled legally to make submissions on behalf of Tommy and Cindy Thomas, and he stated that he did not intend to make adverse findings against Mike Ball Dive Expeditions.

'A prosecution has been dealt with in the Magistrates Court, Cairns and your client's been fined,' he told Atkinson. 'If they intended to prosecute anybody . . . such as Wade Singleton, the time limit has well and truly passed. The evidence given by – as I recall it, the officers from the Department and . . . Workplace Health and Safety [was] that your client is well regarded within the industry and has taken steps to ensure that their policy and practice is complied with. That it breached it, was evident from the conviction.' Glasgow praised the police for their efforts.

While Glasgow waited for Tate and Zillman's written submissions, and before he intended to make his findings public in late April, the blogosphere began to hum again.

On the Tina Watson Diver Death forum on the topix. com website, comments had been posted from Birmingham by those who had seen the surveillance tape on *A Current Affair* of Gabe removing flowers from Tina's grave with bolt cutters the previous November.

After a five-month lull, out of the blue 'Jason' from Birmingham, Alabama – the same penname used by the online participant who had sought information about Mike Ball's track record the day after Tina died – posted a comment on 11 April 2008.

I am a friend of Gabe's and he says the flowers the Thomas[es] left violated cemetery policy. As a matter of fact, he says that just about everything they have left violates their policy. The rules and regulations for the cemetery are about 12 pages long. But regardless of why he removed them, as her next of kin and property owner he can remove what he wants and leave what he wants. He says the Thomas[es] have never asked his permission to leave anything out there. Also, he got a hold of Tina's psych records. I have a feeling after the end of the inquest he is going to make them public . . .

This was followed, on 20 and 21 April 2008, by a vigorous exchange between 'Jason' and others in Birmingham, elsewhere in America, and in Brisbane, Australia.

In answer to 'John Wayne' from Brisbane, 'Jason' said:

. . . Just curious there Duke, what is your basis for saying he murdered his wife? WE learned at the inquest he didn't have any insurance on her, so what was his motive? Boredom? Just for the hell of it? If you are convinced he killed her, tell us why and how please?

'Ralph' from the United States suggested on 21 April 2008 that Gabe might be escaping the real questions by not appearing at the inquest.

'Clarice Jones', also from the United States said:

Question: Would someone planning on murdering their wife be dumb enough to actually purchase a large amount of insurance on their wife before doing it? I know their [sic] are a lot of stupid criminals, but jeez???

'Jason' replied immediately:

Actually the police gave him no assurances they would actually compensate him for two months of missed work by attending the hearings. Since he did not have life insurance on Tina, like her parents did, he didn't have 30K sitting around to take time and travel to Australia. The dive computer thing is interesting, you do realize there are two pieces to his dive computer and the police only tested one piece? How do they know he wasn't talking about the other piece? Answer, they never asked him.

How do you know the people who say he gave varied statements to are remembering it correctly? How do you know he didn't give them the cliff notes version so they would stop asking him? So I guess he decided to lease her a car 30 days before killing her in his name, buy a house, pay for a $10k honeymoon as well as expatriation of the wife he was going to kill? So seriously, someone please answer me this? Again, what was his motive? No motive = please for the love of God fill me in on why he would have done it.

And for Clarance [sic]: If he didnt [sic] have life insurance what would his motive have been then? Also you do realize the one and only eye witness to the whole thing, Dr. Shultz, or stultz [sic] or Something like that testified he was trying to save his wife, not do her harm right? How can you take a statement of someone saying he saw Gabe trying to save his wife and turn it into something else?

After several more replies on a similar theme, 'Jason' added:

Who cares what you would want on your loved ones [sic] grave, he is [the] property owner and can do as he wishes. Again, how one controls ones [sic] grave do [sic] not make them a murderer. Something from before the fact should be presented. Anyone? Anyone? Might be waiting for a while on that one huh?

After more mockery, 'Jason' added a few posts later:

Still waiting on someone to post a possible motive. And to Clarance's [sic] commnent [sic] on why would he be dumb and purchase insurance if he was planning on killing her? Why would he spend $10k to go to australia [sic] to do it in front of 25 others when just a month before he was diving with her in an abandoned quarry where they were the only two out there? Since you seem to think he did it for fun, why didnt [sic] he do it then? So again, I will sit back and wait for someone to enlighten us on a motive. Please bring your facts with you.

In the midst of these posts, there were accusations that 'Jason', with all of his apparent inside knowledge, was not a 'friend of Gabe's' but Gabe himself.

On 23 April, 'Kendra' from Lubbock, Texas, asked why Gabe's parents arrived at the Thomases' house before Tina had been buried to take her car and wedding presents and why he moved her plot, took the flowers and refused to get Tina a headstone.

. . . It wouldn't surprise me if you were Gabe! Make sure you tell him I said hello! And ask him how he's been sleeping lately!

Three weeks later, on 13 May, after more speculation on the forum, 'Jason' intervened again saying he had been away.

. . . So again, no motives presented. You guys talk about me bringing up pointless stuff, ummm, how many times have you guys brought up him removing flowers from the cemetery? Like every post just about. Motives are not made after the fact, but before the fact. And someone said he was just mean. Ok, so you going with malice as motive. Now present your supporting facts for malice. ie: they were in a fight or he has a history of abuse. I will be anxiously awaiting another nonsensical post about something he did after the fact. Oh yea, [sic] and someone said he researched extradition and knew it would take a long time to get to him? Where was the evidence of him doing this? Sorry, but theories and guesses are not evidence. Support your arguement [sic] with something that is fact based. You know, something that you have evidence of. In case you arent [sic] sure, webster.com has a definition of motive and evidence if you need to freshen up on the difference between fact and theory. Sorry Duke, still laughing at you calling me an idiot for calling you Duke. What a tool. You guys make me smile. Keep it up. haha, and you freaks think I am Gabe. Like he cares whats [sic] posted on a message board. He thinks its funny people quote Andy Toulson.

'Lauren' from Fort Worth, Texas, joined in:

Jason, you have got to let go of the idea that a psycho needs any kind of motive whatsoever to kill someone. If you are truly a friend of Gabe's why would you . . . take part in making him look like more of a moron than he already is?

'Jason' fired back:

So lauren, what is your 'reasonable' explanation? Prove he is a psycho then. If he is a psycho, surely you have evidence to support this? Cause you wouldnt [sic] want to libel yourself would you? Again, use stuff from Pre-Death. Cause I am sure you are smart enough to figure out on your own that anything after her death would not be allowed as this is seen as acting under a post traumatic situation and therefore, inadmissable [sic]. So psycho acts pre Tina's death. I will be waiting on your response of nothing material or factual.

Still on 13 May, 'Meghan' wrote:

jason, i think you should just stick with kicking puppies cause it seems like the only thing you are good at. you obviously don't know what you are talking about. All you do is twist around other people's comments and make yourself look foolish. Half of what you say doesn't even make sense. You may want to get some new material too, and it may just be me but 'evidence & motive' are getting old. Ever heard of an opinion?

At blog post 57 of what went on to be 121 on that forum, 'Jason' fired the blowtorch one last time:

Meghan, omfg, you cut [sic] little downie. It only took 3 pages and you actually just made my point for me that I have been trying to get across to you joobs. Sad thing is, Meghan is reading her previous post and has stopped reading this one. She probably has a crossed eyed look right now cause she is too stupid to understand how she just made my point. Its [sic] ok Meghan, arguementation [sic] does not seem to be your strong point. Stick with making babies and cooking meth. Well, my job is done on this meesage [sic] board. Never thought one of you guys would actually make my point for me though.

Oh ya and Franklin, again I wouldn't believe everything the Townsville Bulletin reports. My friend, that is a front because of a settlement. Thats [sic] how insurance companies save face when the [sic] settle.

Lauren you need to go buy a law book . . . It only matters what is admissable [sic]. And i told you, what he did during the times they were planning a funeral and after burial would never see the light of day in a court room. So if you werent [sic] calling Gabe a psycho, why do you think he killed her? Now you don't [sic] not have malice, or greed to support your reasoning. By the way, you have to prove one of those to prove murder. Just an FYI for ya. You just argued yourself out of the arguement [sic].GG.

Its [sic] official, the ruling is in. I WIN!!!! Peace I am Outta HERE. Later Nubs. Enjoy your 'opinion' filled arguements [sic]. Still laughing at the one. OMFG

Oh yea, Duke, your [sic] still a d-bag ;-P

In an interview with Leisa Scott in the *Courier Mail's Q Magazine*, published in April 2008, Tommy and Cindy once again thanked the Queensland police for their perseverance.

'They have cared so much about a 26-year-old girl on her honeymoon who didn't come home. They never gave up,' said Cindy. 'They could have just said, "Hey, accidents happen," but they cared about this girl they never knew.'

Said Tommy: 'For over four years, we knew where and when [Tina's death] happened and we've been trying to find out what happened, how it happened and why did it happen. I think we're a lot closer to the "what" and the "how", but I'm not sure we'll ever know why. And even if we did,

I have come to the realisation I still wouldn't be able to get my head around it.'

Despite the fact that the date of the Coronial finding was set at 24 April, John Tate was late with his submissions. Zillman, who was to receive them first, thus had no time to prepare his own in time, and Coroner Glasgow had to resign as a Magistrate to take up his new position as Family Responsibilities Commissioner on 25 April.

The next date when everyone was free was 19 June 2008, for oral submissions followed by the handing down of the Coronial finding the next day. In the meantime the law had to be checked about the unprecedented situation Glasgow found himself in: would the Act governing Magistrates and Coroners need an amendment for him to be temporarily reinstated as a Magistrate with all the powers that flowed from that in order for him to hand down his findings? Legal advice indicated that his role as Coroner did not rely upon him being a Magistrate. To bring down his findings he was appointed a Coroner for the day.

In May 2008, just over two years since he filed it, Gabe Watson had dropped his travel insurance-related civil action. His application for an adjournment had been refused and the Supreme Court of Alabama refused to hear his appeal against that decision. So he requested that the action be dismissed. His lawyers had stated that he risked incriminating himself in proceedings in Australia. On 2 May 2008, Judge Ed Ramsey dismissed the case with prejudice, which meant it could not be revived at a later date.

Bob Austin confirmed the dismissal to the media. The

case had been dropped, he said, because the Australian legal team believed it was not in Gabe's best interest to pursue the damages claim. Mr Austin added that his client would not be voluntarily returning to Australia. Gabe's Australian legal team had not been briefed on his civil action in Alabama and was focusing on completing written submissions for the Coroner.

In mid May, just as Coroner Glasgow received both sets of legal submissions, an American film crew arrived in Townsville to film scenes in the town and at the *Yongala* wreck site for a planned 90-minute special on the highly acclaimed NBC current affairs program *Dateline*.

'The program will look at whether what happened was an accident or something else . . . a dream vacation or something gone bad,' producer Tom Keenan told the *Townsville Bulletin* as he and cameraman Craig White shot footage of the Townsville Water Police headquarters and the concrete monolith, the courthouse.

When the documentary first screened, on 19 May 2008, Paula Snyder and Ginger Milsap provided the opening voiceovers, describing their *Yongala* dive.

'I remember Tina being very loving and complimentary toward Gabe,' said Ginger.

Paula Snyder added: 'She was just an absolute little princess. And he was tall and strapping and, you know, here they are on their honeymoon.'

Cindy Thomas appeared on the screen briefly: 'I worried, and she would say, "Mom, he's a certified rescue diver. You do not have to worry."'

Craig Cleckler returned to Blue Water and showed the spot beyond the duckboard containing the 1-metre and

3-metre platforms where Tina had surfaced after her panic on the 6-metre platform.

Amanda Phillips cried as she remembered Tina.

'You would see a smile. She would have a huge smile on her face. She'd draw up some kind of joke, punchline. She'd fill a room with her body . . . loved making everyone laugh.'

Tina, she said, was a natural drawcard. 'It seemed like she could pick and choose who she wanted to date.

'My happiest memory? She's laughing at me for being silly . . . for being here crying for her right now. She'd try to come up with some joke to make me laugh. She'd like everybody to be happy.'

Tommy and Cindy smiled in shared reminiscences at 'Tina's eclectic taste in music', her one-time passion for the singer formerly known as Prince and escapades she got up to with friends, especially Amanda.

But it was Ken Snyder and Doug Milsap's on-camera comments that gripped the audience as they relayed their versions of what happened.

Tommy Thomas said: 'He [Gabe] said he was holding her and calling to her while they were trying to resuscitate her.'

Ken Snyder: 'He never went over to her. That would have been a normal male response. He would have jumped over the side of the boat and swam to his wife – just would have went to her. I mean, if you deserted her once, you wouldn't desert her again. I mean it was just unbelievable.'

Tommy Thomas: 'He didn't go over until after he knew she was dead.'

Doug Milsap: 'None of this makes sense and it all indicates that he's not telling the truth about something.'

Sergeant Brad Flynn also provided commentary to the program describing how the Australian police felt. 'They could not say, "We look at this as being just an accident."'

When the reporter, Dennis Murphy, asked was it possible that the real story was 'about a moderately competent diver who just panicked?' Flynn replied: 'Sure, but if that happened, why don't you tell us? Why don't you get that off your chest, you know . . . We seem to believe that to have a murder, you have to have a motive of sex or money. None of that really comes into play here. But that doesn't rule anything out. I have to follow the evidence regardless of where that leads me.'

John Tate, counsel assisting the inquest, also made the headlines, telling the Coroner when the inquest reconvened for final submissions on 19 June 2008: 'The account given by Mr David Gabriel Watson does not stand against the evidence nor the inquiries made subsequently by police. There are too many unanswered questions.'

Tommy, Cindy and Alanda Thomas watched the proceedings from a large screen in Texas. It was Zillman's turn. Like any good counsel, he attacked the weak links in the case: the lack of motive for Gabe to kill his new wife; how the autopsy did not shed any light on how she drowned; how her scuba diving equipment was found to be working perfectly; how his client had been denied the presumption of innocence by police and particularly the media; and how the emails from two Korean divers presented as evidence at the inquest before they declined to testify – emails that claimed they had not been approached by another diver – would not be admissible in a criminal proceeding.

'The police have, at some point, determined that Gabe was guilty of murder and have endeavoured to construct a case to that end rather than to simply gather evidence,' Zillman told the crowded courtroom.

He argued that the evidence relied upon by Tate was largely circumstantial, but to support such a serious allegation it must be 'such as to exclude any reasonable hypothesis consistent with innocence'. He pointed to inconsistencies in the evidence, particularly of Dr Stutz. As well, he looked at the conclusions and assumptions that both the police and witnesses had made in relation to evidence from dive computer readings, estimates of Gabe's ascent rate after leaving Tina, his previous and recent dive experience, his actions as a trained rescue diver and the evidence of the current above the *Yongala* that day, saying that they were mistaken interpretations of the evidence.

There was, he said, no 'logical and identifiable' motive. 'Other than in extreme cases, it is not the way of the world that a husband would kill a bride of eleven days,' Zillman argued, looking briefly around the court and glancing at the large screen from which the Thomas family sat immobile.

There was no evidence, Zillman said, that it was a crime of passion or an act by a mentally deranged husband. And he discounted as hearsay Tommy Thomas's testimony of Gabe wanting Tina to increase her life insurance policy with Parisian. In addition, Gabe had himself deferred discussion of a substantial insurance policy amounting to US$250,000 until after his honeymoon.

What the public had been prejudiced by, he told the Coroner, was the surveillance footage – of Gabe using bolt cutters to remove plastic flowers from Tina's grave – which, he stated, was irrelevant to the purpose of the inquest.

At least four possible, innocent explanations for Tina's drowning, including an arrhythmia, obstruction by vomiting, laryngospasm, and anxiety or panic, he said, could not be detected during a post-mortem examination.

Tate, however, in his reply, described those possibilities

as 'at best remote, and bordering on the fanciful'. By noon they had finished. Another night of waiting lay ahead for the families and friends of Gabe and Tina Watson.

The test for David Glasgow, when considering committing someone for trial for murder or manslaughter under the old Coroners Act 1958, was whether 'the evidence from the inquest was sufficient to put a person . . . [on] trial . . .' In other words, could a jury conviction be reasonably anticipated? It wasn't a question, Glasgow knew, of whether a jury *would* convict Gabe Watson. It was a question of whether they *could*. Glasgow had wrestled with this question for months. He had begun his new role as Family Responsibilities Commissioner and was now spending time in Far North Queensland in Indigenous communities. But, as he worked on his findings, while mowing the lawn on his suburban block near the river, Glasgow tried putting himself in Gabe Watson's shoes, seeing it from his perspective. Was he the coward who abandoned his wife, someone who had made a bad decision, or was there some other, more malevolent force at play? Whichever way he looked at it, it came down to a basis of logic: he could find no alternative explanation than murder on the evidence before him for why Tina Watson had drowned. He went through Zillman's succinct submissions and still came back to one factor: dry drowning. What's the explanation for that? How did Tina asphyxiate if air was in her tank when she was found? A jury, he believed, would have to query why this was the case. No plausible explanation, he believed, had been given in all of the evidence, including 150-odd exhibits and the subsequent submissions he had both heard and read. On Zillman's submissions it was murder or nothing: an open finding. But open findings led nowhere. They meant no closure for anyone and a wasted investigation. Stutz's evidence was the clincher for him, and what had Stutz seen if it wasn't evidence of foul play?

By the end of the inquest, he had read all the authorities on circumstantial evidence. One case in particular had resonated. It used the phrase 'the golden thread'. A case had to fit together and make logical sense. But there could not be a break in the thread. If there was, there was no case. Glasgow satisfied himself that, in this inquest, the thread had not been broken.

Winter in tropical North Queensland is high tourist season, where the temperature is usually around 28°C. Stinger season is over and, for six months the region appeals to visitors from all over Australia. While the southern states pull on winter woollies, summer clothes with a light cardigan can still be the order of the day, as it was on the morning of 20 June 2008.

After the loud knock preceding any judicial officer into court, Acting Coroner Glasgow walked towards the bench in a different court from where the inquest had been heard. It was to be his last appearance in such a role. A large media contingent filled the public gallery. Sitting at the depleted bar table were John Tate and Rohan Armstrong, the latter appearing in the absence of Zillman who had been excused due to another commitment. None of the lawyers present was holding his breath for an open finding.

The large TV screen showed the Thomas family and supporters in the United States holding hands in prayer at a large round table. At the Coroner's suggestion, court staff swung the camera – usually trained on him – around

396

the courtroom so the Thomas family could see who was present, before he began to outline the Act under which he would make his findings, the purpose of the inquest, and the submissions leading to his decision.

The court became quiet as those present, and the family on the big screen, waited for his finding. Suddenly, loud music broke the silence, belting out the first few bars to a 1970s rock 'n' roll song. Mobile phones in some courts are banned, even confiscated and the subject of severe reprimands. Hands flew to coat pockets and handbags. Forced to carry around his first-ever, newly acquired mobile phone thanks to his new appointment, the Coroner felt around in his own pockets and seized on the quivering instrument.

'It's mine,' he admitted sheepishly, after pressing frantically on any button he could find to stop the tune. The court audience laughed, particularly the media contingent. For Glasgow, the solemnity of the occasion lightened a little.

'I do apologise,' the nevertheless embarrassed Coroner said, before reading aloud from his twelve pages of findings.

Tina Watson, he found, had drowned about 11.27 a.m. on 22 October 2003 during a scuba dive on the historic shipwreck *Yongala*.

'There are only two persons who know or knew what in fact actually occurred. One is Tina, who cannot tell us, and the other Gabe. It appears certain that at some point in time investigators considered some of Gabe's explanations lacked credibility and it further appears to me that investigators gave Gabe the opportunity to clarify matters which may have caused concern.'

Touching on the 'significant delay in completing investigations which caused significant concerns to family of the deceased and other persons interested in the outcome', the Coroner alluded to the competing factors of staff availability and 'ability and willingness of officers in charge to expend funds' to carry through recommendations by investigators and/or the Coroner.

'Such delay also contributed to the fact that as time progressed memories of events for some witnesses became less clear and, of necessity, investigators were required to revisit witnesses to obtain further statements to clarify information obtained by previous interviewers.'

The Coroner was satisfied that the four possible explanations submitted by Zillman for accidental drowning had been excluded by the evidence. Significantly, he believed that Tommy Thomas's evidence that Gabe had asked Tina to increase her company insurance to the maximum and make him the beneficiary, would be admissible in a criminal proceeding 'and may be such to provide a possible motive'. Dr Stutz was 'a significant observer of the events under the sea' and the Coroner had 'listened carefully' to his evidence and later reviewed it. 'I found him to have provided an honest and reliable account of his recollections,' he said.

Glasgow challenged Zillman's specific submissions of inconsistent evidence, saying 'there is evidence of sufficient reliability on each of these identified matters which, when viewed in the context of all of the evidence, satisfy me, that a properly instructed jury could make a finding of guilt against David Gabriel Watson on a charge of murder'.

It was a surreal moment for the bar table. The accused was not in court, so Glasgow effectively had to charge Rohan Armstrong, in the absence of his client, with murder.

'David Gabriel Watson, I formally charge you,' he intoned, 'that on the 22nd day of October 2003 at the site of the historical shipwreck *Yongala* 48 nautical miles southeast from the port of Townsville in the state of Queensland David Gabriel Watson murdered Christina Mae Watson.'

Armstrong stood mute and the barristers looked on, having never seen one of their profession standing at the bar table to be charged with murder. The Thomas family and supporters, the tension gone from their faces, gazed at each other as the Coroner told Gabe, through Armstrong, that he was not obliged to enter a plea, would have the opportunity to give evidence and call witnesses and was warned that anything he said would be taken down and might be given in evidence at his trial.

Asked if David Gabriel Watson wished to say anything, Armstrong replied: 'No, Your Honour.'

With no actual person to charge or commit for trial in person, the Coroner directed that a warrant for the commitment for trial be issued for Gabe's arrest pending his committal for trial to the next criminal sittings of the Supreme Court of Queensland to be held in Townsville.

Tommy Thomas spoke from inside the TV screen, the measure of closure the decision had given him evident on his face.

'Thank you, Your Honour.'

Another legal chapter in the case had begun: the potentially long road to extradition.

To the Thomases, Gabe's earliest comments to them that he would have to be dragged back to Australia 'kicking and screaming' had a different meaning as the legal fraternity discussed outcomes. No final decision could be made, however, until Gabe Watson stepped off a plane onto Australian soil and presented himself for trial.

When the Coroner's finding was handed down, Gabe, so newspapers claimed, was 'enjoying' a pizza with his parents, David and Glenda Watson, at his home in Hoover.

The Watson family continued with their policy of ignoring the media and stayed behind closed doors when the pack arrived outside. Bob Austin, instead, addressed them, issuing a statement that he was 'shocked' by the decision of the Australian court and that he would be discussing how to fight the allegations with his client's legal team.

CHAPTER 24

'She was a beautiful girl both inside and out – just a treasure to us – fun-loving, always joking and cuttin' up. She made life fun for all of us.'

Tommy's soulful eyes and mellow southern accent addressed each viewer of the NBC *Today* show as though speaking to them in person. He was what's known in the trade as 'natural talent'. By now, he had a good measure of what the media wanted and delivered his opinions in considered bites. The Coroner's finding the previous Friday provided another opportunity to air the story. This time the headline on *Today's* exclusive on msnbc.com ran: 'Did Husband Kill Wife on Honeymoon?'

The studio was bright, as befitted a chat show, with a vibrant purple backdrop and matching mauve flowers in vases on the coffee table. Tommy was dressed in a charcoal grey suit and tie. Alanda, who sat next to him on the beige couch, wore a mint-green top with a small bow. Her long brown hair was loose behind her trademark fringe.

Long-time NBC *Today* show host Matt Lauer began by saying that Gabe had been asked to do an interview but had declined. Now the dust had settled after the finding, neither

Tommy nor Alanda looked jubilant. Having lived through the momentary elation of the Coroner's decision they had slipped back into their lives, knowing it was not over and that justice was not going to bring Tina back.

Alanda spoke in her mellifluous voice of the fairytale wedding her sister had always wanted. Tina, the princess bride. Matt Lauer shifted gear, stating that he had heard that they both had misgivings about Tina's choice of husband before the wedding.

'What made you uneasy?' Lauer asked.

Alanda hesitated.

'Give me an example,' he probed.

Alanda looked down as she described how Gabe had once thrown a pizza at her sister in a restaurant. When asked whether Tina had told her about any issues in her relationship with Gabe, Alanda said that Tina was not the sort of person who wanted to burden people with her problems.

The interviewer moved on to events on board the *Spoilsport* and the day Tina had died. Tommy said that at first he had thought her death was an accident.

Did he agree with Gabe's version that Tina had panicked?

'The fact of the matter is that the version about her panicking . . . does not really stand up to the fact that she had shown a real keen sense of self-rescue and, had she panicked, unless something prevented her, in 40 feet of water she would have made it to the surface.'

Asked about the motive, Tommy said there had been a number of factors discussed in the court case: financial, jealousy and obsession, but that they would have to wait for the courts to sort it out.

***

After the Coronial finding was handed down, the Townsville Regional Crime Coordinator, Detective Inspector Warren Webber, had the task of telling the media outside the court what would happen next. Webber told the waiting media contingent that a warrant would be issued for Gabe Watson's arrest. The Queensland Director of Public Prosecutions would then approach the Federal Attorney-General, who would liaise with American authorities to begin extradition proceedings, which would take 'some period of time', he warned. Watson was to stand trial at the Supreme Court in Townsville on a date to be set.

Megan Palethorpe, a young journalist from the ABC in Townsville, had prepared her questions:

'You must be happy to see that the Coroner has exercised his power to formally charge him today?' she asked.

Webber avoided any implications behind that question: 'I get no pleasure to see that a young woman who was apparently travelling to Australia and having a great time was apparently being murdered on her honeymoon, by her husband . . .'

Elsewhere across the globe the media ran with the breaking news.

The Thomases were interviewed in Nashville, Tennessee. They stood in a line, with a darkening sky behind them, joined by other members of the family, to answer questions. It was already night-time, given the 14-hour time difference. Cindy said: 'You never think your daughter will leave for her honeymoon and her husband will kill her.'

Alanda added: 'It's just one more step closer for justice for Tina.'

'Words,' Cindy added, 'cannot explain for our entire family . . . it's been devastating.'

Tommy told the waiting media: 'It's an unbelievable

relief . . . that is really the first word I can think of. It has been a very long four years and eight months. It was just so emotional and intense when we heard the Coroner say those words . . . "charged with murder" . . . Cindy has just been pulled from one end of the spectrum to the other, from being as torn up as she could be, to now just being so relieved. The Coroner's decision really validates what we have been working towards . . . getting justice for Tina for the past four-and-a-half years. People have thought we were crazy in still pushing so hard after all this time to get answers and keeping our hopes alive that we would see justice for our little girl. It is such a hard situation for people to wrap their heads around. The whole process has been so drawn out because of the sheer enormity of the investigation and the police having to interview more than sixty witnesses from all around the world . . . We were stunned when we heard Mr Glasgow issue the warrant for Gabe's arrest immediately. This is absolutely the most positive move we have yet seen in the whole, long process . . . We know that there is still a long battle ahead of us but what is important, for us and our family now is to just keep it going for Tina and see it through. Tina is going to get her day of justice in court and today was our first real indication of that.'

Tommy thanked the Queensland police again.

'[The investigation] can only be described as one of the most challenging investigations on a truly global scale,' he said. 'It is much more than just commendable, it is remarkable on a scale of effort alone.' Australia, he added, had become 'such an important part of our lives'.

Greta Van Susteren, in her Fox News program *On the Record*, talked with Sergeant Brad Flynn. In her combative style, she grilled him on everything from Gabe Watson's motive to why Flynn refused to reveal information that had already been aired at the inquest. Flynn spoke of the multiple discrepancies in Gabe's interviews. The program replayed the coverage of Gabe with bolt cutters removing the Thomas family's flowers. Later, Greta interviewed Tommy, live from Virginia, going over again how he had felt when he heard the news of Tina's death.

Bloggers speculated about Gabe Watson's motives, now he was charged with Tina's murder:

Nancy Grace [an American cable show host and former prosecutor famously tough on defendants and suspects] *featured a psychologist who explained this* [Tina and Gabe's relationship] *as a typical abusive spousal relationship. A weak-willed spouse with low self-esteem allows herself to be controlled by an abusive husband. She is to blame for everything. If Gabe were actually sorry that Tina slipped out of his grasp, he would have blamed himself in uncontrollable sorrow in his videotaped testimony for allowing this to happen. Instead he blames everybody and everything except himself – the non-existing* [sic] *current, Tina's panic, the Thomases, the dive insurance, brutal police interrogators and even the blogosphere. Drowning Tina when she looked him in the eye was his ultimate sociopathic means of control. Unfortunately for him, prisons also have violent control freaks.*

On the US ABC TV news site, following a segment aired on the Coronial finding, 'Alrocks', who claimed to be a friend of both Gabe and Tina, said she had spent time with them when they were dating and engaged.

. . . both appeared to be so in love & happy . . . Gabe seemed to be a truly crushed soul at her funeral and for some time after . . . I

*had heard through the grapevine that Tina's parents were try-
ing to get her death investigated, but according to Gabe so was
he. Since then, some of the evidence has come out that makes me
question Gabe's innocence . . . Personally if he's guilty, I'll forever
question my judgment of character, be haunted that I have will-
ingly been in the presence of a murder [sic] & and be sickened that
my friend's life was cut short by the hands of a man that she loved,
laughed w/, & trusted.*

In early July 2008, the site that 'Jason' had frequented a
couple of months before began to hum with different
rumours – Gabe Watson was dating again.

'Lisa' from Birmingham, Alabama asked:

*I'm curious. Who is this 'new friend' of his? Is this the girl that is
living with him? Do you know how long they have been together
and living together? Do you know what her name is?*

Others followed suit. 'Amy', also from Birmingham, asked:

*Is this the same girl he was dating in the following months after
Tina died?*

Then, in mid July, 'Lisa' from Alabama was back on the
scuba dive forum site asking for the name of the woman
Gabe was allegedly dating. She suggested it might be 'Kimberley'. There was further discussion that 'Kimberley' and
Gabe Watson might have been going out since 2004.

Others joined in Gabe's defence while still others sar-
castically called themselves 'Free Gabe'. Then after more
posts about Gabe's relationship with Kimberley, one blog-
ger, 'Jennifer', as though announcing secret celebrity gossip,

made the surprise announcement that Gabe was to get married on 22 August.

'He's already married' posted back 'Jenny', one of the regular contributors and a fan of Gabe. On 20 August, 'Gabe's Best Friend' enquired if they had already left for the honeymoon? And 'Amy' asked if Jenny was one of the bridesmaids.

The wedding between Gabe Watson and Kim Lewis, a science teacher, took place on 15 August 2008, a date kept from the media. Eight people attended. Kim Lewis had been introduced to Gabe by one of his former girlfriends and had reportedly sold her house in Hoover in 2007 before moving into Oak Leaf Circle. She was two years younger than Gabe and had also gone to Hoover High.

Gabe's new bride had shoulder-length fair hair; like Tina, she parted it to the left. She had a similar body shape to Tina. The media seized on the connection. On 22 October Brisbane's *Courier Mail* ran the headline: 'Suspected dive killer Gabe Watson marries lookalike bride'. The new bride kept well out of the limelight, but the media ran with rumours that she holidayed in Italy prior to the wedding with her future mother-in-law. The date of 22 August, listed on an online wedding gift registry, was said to be deliberately false so as to deflect media attention. Nothing was posted about the location of their honeymoon.

Having initially declined to comment on the wedding, now Tommy spoke out in Brisbane's *Courier Mail* saying: 'Who is this girl? Has she been living in a cave?' Later in the article, he said: 'She is probably a nice girl, but it boggles my mind. These two go and get married two months after he is ordered to face murder charges. It totally blew me away.'

Commenting on the drawn-out legal process, in the same

newspaper article, Tommy said: 'I'm thinking maybe they are a little gun-shy and are trying to get this brief watertight but they won't tell me anything.'

On 13 October, the *Shelby County Reporter*, a weekly newspaper in Alabama with a circulation of 8000, ran a story headlined: 'Arrest in Watson case imminent'. The journalist quoted Sergeant Brad Flynn saying: 'We're sitting on "go" and as soon as they get the paperwork together we'll do whatever we need to do.' Flynn said that Queensland authorities would be forwarding the papers through Interpol, the world's largest international police organisation, to the US Department of Justice. From the Justice Department, the papers would go to the US Attorney's Office in Birmingham. Helena police, with the assistance of US Marshals, would then issue an arrest warrant for Gabe Watson and extradite him to Australia. The report stated that Watson had been under surveillance since returning to the United States, but Flynn would not disclose further details.

A few days later, on 18 October, Andy Toulson wrote a story in the *Townsville Bulletin* focusing on the lead-up to the fifth anniversary of Tina's death. She quoted State Opposition spokesman, Mike Horan, saying the government needed to act on the extradition process.

Tommy Thomas was also quoted saying he was concerned nothing would be done before the cut-off date of 20 December and that the paperwork had not yet even left for Brisbane: 'With December being what it is and many government personnel shutting down for most of the month, my concern is that we have only about six weeks truly left to get this done. We always understood that the legal process would be time-consuming, and we have absolute faith in the Queensland legal system and the police efforts. But we are worried that time is fast running out for the indictment to be made, and the arrest warrant to reach the US authorities.'

The DPP responded, citing the complexity of the case. '. . . prosecutors were "more than aware of the six-month time restraint" on handing down an indictment,' a spokesman said. 'And we're "working around the clock" on the matter. The department was "looking at using the full time frame allowed to process the very complex paperwork".' The spokesperson stressed that the matter was 'a priority' for DPP Tony Moynihan.

While the blogosphere eagerly awaited news, another development in mid October briefly took the focus away from Gabe Watson and on to another case bearing striking similarities to the Watson case. It involved a husband standing trial on charges of drowning his wife while scuba diving. Like the Watson case, police had taken years before charging David Swain, a former dive shop owner of Jamestown, Rhode Island, with the murder of his wife, Shelley Tyre, on a romantic getaway to the Caribbean. At first police wrote off the 1999 death of Tyre as a tragic accident, but, after relentless pursuit by Tyre's parents, authorities in the British Virgin Islands had charged Swain with murder despite the circumstantial nature of the case.

'Pete the Diver', who announced the case on one forum, wrote on 20 October:

. . . if they were premeditated then Gabe and Swain would have made sure that the bodies and equipment were never found. Of course murderers do not usually act logically. The strangest part

of the Watson murder is Gabe drowning Tina in the first minute of the first Ocean dive. He couldn't have waited several minutes, or several days? Also, if committing a scuba diving murder for a large insurance payoff, then why take out a policy that excludes diving? My feeling is that Gabe did not originally know how he was going to murder Tina, and he acted impetuously at the first opportunity, i.e. the first ocean dive, and this is why he bungled the insurance. He also didn't have time to perfect an alibi or even a cogent story, because he acted impulsively at the first opportunity to kill Tina. For whatever reason, he became enraged and had to act at that moment. He thought up his story to the cops on the fly and that is why the story changes and is full of holes. Also, the cemetery shenanigans are a result of impulsive anger, [sic] But all this is theory, and we'll see what happens with the extradition and ensuing trial. My bold prediction – Gabe doesn't go peacefully, either fleeing . . . If he does make it to trial, watch him plead guilty to a lesser charge or reduced sentence.

A month later, on 15 November, Toulson reported that the Thomas flowers on Tina's grave were going missing again. Alanda had found some flowers she had placed on her sister's grave thrown down a hill nearby. Unlike her parents' flowers, they had not been chained to the site. Tommy again filed a report with Helena police. A few days later, an exclusive was aired on ABC 33/40 with the reporter, Yonu Wodejo, standing in the night air in the Southern Heritage Cemetery in Pelham reporting on the thefts of the flowers and keepsakes placed on the grave by the Thomas family. Wodejo cut to footage of Alanda that day visiting the grave with her little boy.

'It's painful. It's upsetting. It's just incredible,' Alanda said, explaining that sometimes the flower thefts would stop for six or seven months and then start up again. Sergeant Flynn was also interviewed by Wodejo, noting that it was three years almost to the week since he had filmed Gabe Watson removing the flowers from Tina's grave with bolt cutters. 'Why,' he asked, referring to that earlier theft, 'would anyone be driving around with 3-foot [1-metre] bolt cutters in the back of the car? . . . I don't think we are dealing with logic here,' he said.

On 28 November, the *Courier Mail* ran a story stating that Queensland prosecutors were ready to move on 'accused honeymoon killer Gabe Watson, with a murder indictment likely to be filed within days'. Headed by barrister Ross Martin, SC, a legal team had completed the paperwork in a five-month investigation to extradite the American to face trial for murder, the newspaper stated. Queensland's DPP was reportedly ready to present a brief of evidence for a murder indictment in the Supreme Court. After that, the lengthy extradition process would begin. Bob Austin had indicated Watson would oppose the extradition, describing the DPP case as 'weak as well-water' and lacking motive. Australian National University Professor of International Law, Don Rothwell, was quoted as saying that the extradition process would be 'fairly straightforward'.

'Provided US authorities don't have any doubts about the evidence, it would be extremely unusual for the US to question the arrest warrant,' he said.

The story appeared the same day that the DPP presented an indictment in the Supreme Court in Townsville charging Gabe with murder. Justice Kieran Cullinane ordered Gabe to appear for mention before the same court on 3 February 2009, the first day of criminal sittings for the year, or he would face arrest for extradition to Australia. Justice

Cullinane began the long process of clearing his cases to accommodate what promised to be a lengthy trial. The indictment was to be forwarded to the Commonwealth Attorney-General's Department in Canberra, and then sent to the US Attorney-General's Department in Washington, DC, where an application would be made seeking approval for a US warrant for Watson's arrest. But the indictment was never to leave Brisbane. Toulson reported in the *Townsville Bulletin* that Gabe was under surveillance to prevent him becoming 'a flight risk'. A red flag was put on his passport.

On 3 December, Tommy made another national media appearance, speaking from San Diego in California to Meredith Vieira on the NBC *Today* show. He confirmed that if Gabe refused to fly back to Australia, he would have to be extradited.

'It's good . . . Tina will finally get her day in court and the justice she deserves,' Tommy said.

In late January there was a meeting between the investigating police and the DPP to discuss changing the charge from murder to manslaughter. That same month, Steve Zillman and Rohan Armstrong flew to the United States and finally met their client for a conference. The lawyers explained matters that anyone in his position would need to ponder: what powers existed to have him extradited, under which circumstances extradition could be achieved, which legal tests applied under which an extradition order was able to be challenged, if a challenge was mounted what that then entailed, and any other options open to him. If Gabe consented to be extradited that meant other procedures came into play.

CHAPTER 25

On 3 February 2009, the media filled the dark cedar benches inside the courtroom in the Townsville Courts of Law building. Would Gabe Watson appear in court? Even the media with the best court contacts had no idea. Justice Kieran Cullinane walked in and sat behind the bench. His associate and the legal teams sat at the bar table. It was clear as everyone waited, feet shuffling on the blue and purple carpet, that Gabe was not going to appear. The previous November, Justice Cullinane had warned that if he did not appear, he would face arrest and extradition to Australia. Rohan Armstrong, at the bar table, stood to tell the judge that Gabe Watson was still in the United States and that the defence needed more time to take further instructions from him. When the DPP, too, requested more time, Justice Cullinane adjourned the case to a date to be fixed.

On Tuesday, 12 May 2009, having had several months to make his preparations for what might be an extended period away from the United States, Gabe did what Bob Austin was to describe as a 'back-flip' on his long-stated aim to fight extradition. He left his family and friends in Birmingham, Alabama, crossed the country and then the Pacific Ocean from Los Angeles and arrived, alone, to greet the sunrise at Brisbane International Airport. His voluntary arrival was not disclosed to the media. Gabe was arrested when he stepped off the plane at 5.15 a.m. by Detective Sergeant Gary Campbell and his partner, Senior Constable Kevin Gehringer. He was escorted under security to the Brisbane watchhouse, where he was processed, photographed and fingerprinted, and then placed in a holding cell. He remained there during the brief mention of his matter in the Supreme Court before Justice John Byrne at 11.30 a.m. The judge ordered that Gabe be formally remanded in custody until his next court appearance on 29 May – sixteen days away.

Gabe knew he was in a 'no-win situation', Austin told reporters in Birmingham. 'He has gone to Australia to say, "I am here to answer the charges and I am not guilty of those charges." He wants to get it over with,' said Austin.

The Queensland DPP, Tony Moynihan, said afterwards he was pleased Mr Watson had decided to return to Australia to face trial.

'This has avoided the need for a complex and lengthy extradition process,' Mr Moynihan said in a prepared statement. 'Given that this matter is now before the court, it would not be appropriate to comment further.'

The Thomases were surprised by the abrupt change in events. Tommy revealed to Toulson in the next day's edition of the *Townsville Bulletin* that the lead prosecutor in the murder case, Assistant Director of the Queensland Department of Public Prosecutions, Brendan Campbell, had rung him early that morning with what he described as 'good news'.

'We were totally taken by surprise at what has happened . . . This is the biggest step that has been taken so far in the five-and-a-half years since our daughter died, and hopefully, it will expedite Gabe facing trial over Tina's death. We are very grateful that Tina will finally have her day in court.' The family, he said, would be there 'ringside' for the trial.

By Thursday, 14 May, both Brendan Campbell and Detective Sergeant Gary Campbell, together with a Queensland DPP communications officer, were on a flight to the United States. They arrived in Birmingham the same night and spent part of the weekend of 16–17 May 2009 meeting with Tommy, Cindy and Alanda Thomas. The prosecutor explained the events of earlier in the week and what would follow.

'Tommy,' said Brendan Campbell, addressing the head of the family, 'we want you to know that Gabe's surrender to the Australian authorities was an unconditional voluntary surrender.'

Cindy, Alanda and Tommy stared at the two men as he spoke. It was quite unbelievable. After all this time, the no-show at the inquest, the refusal to testify, it seemed bizarre to them.

'There were no deals made to negotiate his return,' Campbell stressed. 'And I might add that it is not DPP policy to pursue such negotiations.'

'So,' said Tommy, not quite believing what he was hearing, 'all of a sudden, out of the blue, with no real warning, he decides to fly to Australia and surrender – it's surreal,' he said, repeating the sentiments he had expressed to a Brisbane newspaper reporter earlier in the week.

The family was briefed on the Australian court system and the legal process as Tommy was likely to be a witness. Brendan Campbell also canvassed the family's view on a plea of manslaughter, assuring them it would still mean a substantial sentence.

'There is a real difference between our system in the US

and the Australian process,' Tommy told the *Birmingham News* on 18 May.

On 28 May, *Good Morning America* ran a segment entitled: 'Honeymoon Drowning Mystery'. Tommy, this time in tears, was filmed bending over Tina's grave. During his interview, he told the journalist of his frustration at seeking justice for his daughter: 'I just tell her that I love her and I just keep telling her I'm going to keep going until I can help her rest and be at peace.'

The news that there would be a hearing on 6 June was as abrupt as the news of Gabe's voluntary return to Australia. Tommy and Alanda barely had time to put in leave requests and book flights to Australia. They had a week to pack. Cindy was ill and could not travel, so Amanda Phillips made a rushed decision to leave her two young children in Louisiana with their father, take leave from her civil engineering practice and step into Cindy's shoes to represent her best friend. After months of nothing, suddenly Gabe Watson was to appear in court.

Shortly before, one of the key legal identities close to the inquest was told by a source: 'The thing will be over fairly soon.' When it was queried whether this meant a deal had been done, the answer came back, 'You might be surprised.'

The Queensland Supreme Court is in the heart of the city of Brisbane, on the corner of George and Adelaide streets, across the river from the Gallery of Modern Art. It's a modern, boxy white structure that replaced the former Supreme Court building partially destroyed by fire in the late 1960s. The statue of Themis, the Goddess of Justice, highlights the building's purpose. Standing in a small garden under an alcove, she holds scales in her left hand and a sword in her right. From George Street, a spacious façade forms the entrance to The Law Courts through an open quadrangle, surrounded by palm and jacaranda trees and stonewalled gardens and sculptures.

On Friday, 5 June 2009, as Cindy Thomas lay in an intensive care unit in Birmingham mystifying doctors with unexplained haemorrhaging, the cameras crowded around the quadrangle waiting to shoot footage of the rest of her family. Even more sought-after, though, than the statuesque figure of Amanda Phillips, was a fresh face for the camera on the Thomas side – Kim Lewis Watson. No-one had any footage of her.

By 10.15 a.m. Gabe Watson was sitting in court dressed in a dark jacket, blue shirt and yellow tie, his arm loosely draped across the bench seat in the dock, his new wife behind him. When called to enter a plea to a charge of murdering his first wife, Christina Mae Watson, he had stood in the dock and calmly announced he would plead 'not guilty to murder [but] guilty to manslaughter'.

It was one of those imperceptible silences that sometimes descends in courtrooms; the moment when the unbelievable has been voiced, and no-one wants to breathe in case the next moment is missed. The prosecutor, Brendan Campbell, got to his feet and stated that he had accepted the plea. Justice Peter Lyons perfunctorily told the court that he would sentence Watson immediately after hearing submissions. Those media players filing for radio and online news departed the courtroom hurriedly to report the news flash. Back in the courtroom, the prosecution asked for a five-year jail term with parole after eighteen months. Steve Zillman countered, saying it was too long. He asked instead for four years with non-parole period of twelve months. Zillman pointed out that since Gabe had made admissions at the time to investigating police officers which became the foundation of the Crown case, they had all the 'necessary detail that might have caused his arrest' for the offence to which he had just pleaded guilty.

'You have to take into account my client's decision to voluntarily return to Australia,' he addressed Justice Lyons, adding that a lesser sentence should also be considered given that the case had attracted intense publicity.

'Thousands upon thousands of words have been written concerning this matter, at least on the internet. He has been for a long period of time publicly accused of a crime or crimes for which he is not guilty. He has had to endure that situation for a period of up to six years.

'It was not until such time after his return that the DPP indicated that they would accept a plea of manslaughter in discharge of the indictment,' Zillman continued. 'And the last matter is, of course, he is not a citizen of this country and all of his family and friends reside in the US, and so any time in prison that he is required to serve will be harder for him than it would be for an Australian citizen.'

The facts, he told the judge and the world at large, were clear: 'He panicked. He ought . . . to have remained, but he did not. He panicked. He was in difficulty. She was panicking and he then panicked.'

Gabe had finally admitted he'd done the wrong thing.

Campbell told the court that under Section 290 of the Criminal Code, Gabe Watson 'was to be held criminally responsible for Tina's death as he failed to perform his duty . . . to act as her buddy . . . and the accused had taken on that responsibility'.

'It must of course,' Campbell said, 'also be taken into the mix for Your Honour's consideration that . . . his previous accounts . . . had involved falsehoods and attempts to wrongly shift blame.'

'Your Honour, this is a case where the sentence must reflect the very serious obligation that a person undertakes as a buddy,' the prosecutor said. 'It is a case that calls for a deterrent sentence, in this context reinforcing that persons must take their responsibilities, as a buddy, very seriously.'

When Lyons came back, more than 4 hours later, to deliver his sentence, he directed Gabe to stand up. The judge began:

'You stand convicted on your plea of guilty of the offence of manslaughter causing the death of your wife . . . The deceased experienced difficulties during the dive. You made some attempts to assist her but these were unsuccessful. In the course of this, your face mask and regulator were dislodged. However, you were able to replace your face mask and to get an alternative oxygen supply from what is referred to as a safe second.

'When this happened, you could see that the deceased was sinking but you formed the view that there was nothing you could do and you swam away with a view to getting assistance. There are circumstances, beyond those I have just described, which are relevant to determining your sentence.

'You were clearly a far more experienced diver than the deceased was. The deceased had what is called an open-water certification, which I understand to be a basic diving qualification and which she had attained some months previously. The dive at the *Yongala* was a significant challenge for a diver of the level of experience and competence of the deceased. On the other hand, you were a diver with substantial experience, although it is pointed out that much of your experience was not in open waters where significant

currents could be encountered. You had a number of qualifications, including a rescue diver certificate which you had
obtained some four-and-a-half years before these events.
The dive was carried out using the buddy system. As your
wife's buddy for the dive, you took responsibility for providing her with assistance if she encountered difficulty.

'The Crown alleges against you that you failed to carry
out your duty to her in a number of significant ways. I accept
that you failed to do so in the following respects: you failed to
ensure that when the deceased had encountered difficulties
she had a supply of oxygen available to her and, in particular, you failed to share your oxygen supply with her; having
released the deceased to recover your face mask and oxygen
supply, you did not then take hold of her again or stay with
her, or follow her as she sank; you did not attempt at any
time to inflate her buoyancy control device [compensator] or
remove the weights which divers often carry to assist them to
descend.

'It follows from these matters, that you failed to make
any reasonable attempt to take the deceased to the surface. I
therefore accept that you are guilty of a very serious departure from the standard of care which was incumbent upon
you with the result that your conduct is deserving of criminal punishment.

'An offence such as manslaughter which involves the
loss of a human life is obviously a very serious matter. The
deceased was twenty-six. You were recently married. She
had every reason to look forward to a long and happy life.

'Her death is also a great tragedy for her family. I have
read the victim impact statements. They demonstrate
that she and her family were very close and that she was
very close to her friend [Amanda]. They demonstrate how
deeply her loss is felt by all of them. Her family, obviously

and naturally, take a very serious view of your conduct and that, not surprisingly, appears in their statements. However, there is much in those statements from which I do not gain assistance in determining your sentence . . .

'You have voluntarily returned from the United States and have surrendered yourself into custody in Australia. In my view, it is quite significant that at the time of your return you did not know that the Crown would not persist in charging you with murder, which carries a mandatory sentence of life imprisonment. You no doubt expected that you would be sentenced to a term of imprisonment for a substantial period in what for you is a foreign country.

'You have, in fact, acknowledged that you are guilty of manslaughter. You do not seek to pretend that your actions were other than what they were. In doing so, you have spared the deceased's family the agony of a trial.

'While in the context of the loss of the deceased's life it may not be of great significance, it must also be recognised that you have saved the community the expense of conducting a trial. I regard your conduct as a recognition by you of your wrongdoing and an expression of remorse. I am conscious that you have no criminal history. There is, naturally, no suggestion of a risk of reoffending.'

The judge referred to a number of references regarding Gabe's character from people who knew him well. Dr David Fancher, a church elder from Alabama, had described Gabe as a man who remained calm in situations that could have angered him. He also described how he always wanted to help others. Once, he said in his reference, Gabe had driven 600 kilometres to help Fancher's daughter, a near-stranger, move into a new house. Craig Youngblood, Gabe's old friend, described Gabe as one of the most even-tempered people he knew. One of his strongest attributes, said Youngblood, was making Tina happy. He had never seen Gabe lose his temper or act in a spiteful way.

Justice Lyons said that the statements, which flew in the face of victim impact statements given by Tina's family and friends, confirmed that Gabe Watson was 'of good character'.

'They also reveal that you are a person who is known to help others and that you loved your wife and were devastated by her loss.

'I have referred to the delay in the prosecution of the case against you. It is a plainly considerable delay. When there is delay in the prosecution of a criminal charge, a major consideration, which often works in reduction of the sentence, is that rehabilitation may have occurred in the period since the offence. That is not a relevant consideration in this case. However, you have carried the burden of these events for a substantial period. That is a matter to which I am prepared to give weight.

'I consider that that burden has been increased by the very extensive publicity which these events have occasioned. That is demonstrated, to some extent, by the obvious presence of a significant number of representatives of the media in the court today. I also accept that in that period you have been subject to accusations of matters of which you are not guilty . . .

'There have been, in some of your statements, some inconsistencies and some attempts to put blame on other people. There does not seem to be any persistence in your attempt to put blame on anyone else and I accept that the responsibility for this loss is yours alone. The inconsistencies and those attempts, to me, while they do not speak particularly well of you, should be looked at in the circumstances in which they occurred. That is, they occurred shortly after the dive and at a time when you, no doubt, were deeply upset by the events which have occurred . . .

'The precise time is unclear, but it can only have been of the order of 2 minutes from the time that the deceased first started to encounter difficulties until you surfaced, and the time within which you made your initial decision to leave her was obviously significantly less.

'I suspect that once you had made that decision and decided to go to seek other assistance, there would have been difficulty in reversing your decision and turning back again to try to assist her. I accept, nevertheless, that there is a very serious departure in your case from the requirements of the duty of care which you had undertaken in the course of this dive.

'The seriousness of the matter, notwithstanding the factors which I take into account in mitigation, means that it is necessary to impose a penalty which provides for a substantial period of imprisonment.

'I therefore propose to impose a head sentence of four-and-a-half years.

'Because of the mitigating factors which I have identified and because I accept that for you in Australia time in prison will be harder than it will be for people who serve a sentence of imprisonment in their own country, I intend to fix a suspension date a little earlier than might otherwise have been the case.

'Accordingly, I order that you be imprisoned for a period of four-and-a-half years. I declare that the period of twenty-three days from the 13th of May 2009 until the 5th of June 2009 be deemed time already served under the sentence.

'I order that the term of imprisonment be suspended after a period of twelve months' imprisonment which will take into account that twenty-three day period.

'I am required to inform you that you must not commit another offence punishable by imprisonment within a period of four-and-a-half years to avoid being dealt with for the suspended term of imprisonment.

'For the avoidance of any doubt, I order that a conviction be recorded.' He adjourned the court and everyone stood.

On one side of the courtroom, the Thomases and Amanda Phillips looked at each other in despair.

Outside, Tommy addressed the waiting media in the quadrangle. Cameras flashed as he spoke.

'I believe that probably the entire Australian nation, as well as our own country back home, shares in the shock with us of what we have seen. Because, it's total injustice. It's ludicrous what we have seen. And today, he's allowed to take the easy way out. He pleads guilty to manslaughter and then laughingly, it looks like he was the victim as the sentence is being read.'

Tommy said the outcome of the case was 'an embarrassment I think to everyone involved. It's an embarrassment to all Australians, it's an embarrassment to police here, the police in our country and to everyone who has been involved in this investigation,' he said.

'I'm sure that it's an embarrassment to all the people who were out there on that day, who did everything they could to try to save our daughter.'

Reporters asked a few questions, allowing him to state his mind, which he did volubly: 'It's a slap to the Australian people and the justice system. It's a slap in the face to the police on both sides, both in the US and Australia that spent time investigating this case . . . and the four-and-a-half years here is a joke.'

Alanda had not seen Gabe Watson since Tina's funeral. She told the media she was in 'complete shock, complete shock, so complete injustice to Tina, I can't even begin to describe how hard it was to sit there and hear him say . . . how little my sister's life was valued to them. It was very painful.'

Even Amanda, often preaching calm, was outraged: 'I never thought it would be this minimal. Michael Vick [an American football quarterback who spent twenty-one months in jail not long before for his part in an illegal inter-state dog fighting ring] will have spent more time in jail for dogs than Gabe will have spent time for Tina. And she was a person.'

The three figures linked arms and walked stoically across the quadrangle. There were no tears.

Meanwhile, the pack was on to the next task. An AAP photographer, followed by TV cameramen, raced away and ran down the stairs to get a shot of Gabe Watson's new bride clutching a bottle of water while shielded by friends. Wearing a brown figure-hugging dress and black stilettos, she kept her head down as she hurried away into the Brisbane traffic.

The shock news reverberated across the world. The investigating police, who had spent so many years preparing the case, would not comment. But, now promoted, Lieutenant Brad Flynn of the Helena Police Department did not hold back: 'I am very shaken. You dedicate yourself, like, five-and-[a]-half years of your life to the case and you want to see resolution, you want to see some closure, [we] didn't get that today . . .'

He told Andy Toulson: 'It turned out to be one big pity

party for Gabe. The whole tone of the court hearing was patronising in the extreme towards the pain, loss, suffering and desire for justice by Tina's family. They said it was going to be hard for Watson to be away from his friends and family in an Australian prison – but the Thomas family are never going to see their daughter again. I am disgusted by what has happened – I have not put five-and-a-half years of my life into this investigation to see this happen. I am not in the business of doing deals – I am in the business of gathering evidence and presenting that evidence in court before a jury. Despite what they say, they made a deal weeks ago. We had our legs chopped out from under us today, and there was nothing we could do about it.'

Wade Singleton had also attended the sentencing. In his first public comments outside the inquest, he told the media that he, too, was deeply disappointed. 'Well, to put it simply,' he told the media, 'to leave someone down there, [is] signing a death warrant, you are leaving them to die . . . as long as they are underwater and they're not breathing there is no chance of survival . . .'

Harvey Walters was in Ingham, about an hour's drive north of Townsville, when he heard the news. He immediately bought a *Townsville Bulletin* and sat down in a coffee shop to digest it. Tommy Thomas, he read, had 'extremely serious doubts' that there hadn't been some sort of deal between the DPP and Gabe's defence lawyers. Why else would he come back to Australia on his own after five-and-a-half years if a deal wasn't in place, unless he knew he wasn't going to have to face trial for murder?

Tommy had fired both barrels in the interview with Andy Toulson: 'I think it was a straight business decision . . . a trial potentially lasting several months, involving sixty-five witnesses testifying in person could cost millions. We think this is the primary basis of their decision, but to us, they took the easy way out. The DPP did not work for the victim here, or the victim's family. They just did not listen to us and they seem to be accountable to no-one.'

His words almost shouted from the newsprint: 'Do I think Gabe killed Tina? Hell yes, he killed her. He should have gone to prison for murdering our little girl. And what is our daughter's life worth? Just eleven months in prison for a man who admitted causing her death. We've got more questions today than we had when we started. But this will not be the end of it.'

In the hubbub that followed the news, it was Tommy Thomas's statement during his impromptu press conference that stuck, foreshadowing what was to lie ahead. Outside the Queensland Supreme Court in Brisbane in front of the bevy of TV cameras, radio mikes and note-booked reporters, he said, his voice barely containing his anger: 'This is not justice and this is not over.'

AFTERMATH

June 2010

Almost seven years after Tina Watson sank to her death near the wreck of the SS *Yongala*, the case is nowhere near over, nor is there any clearer picture about what exactly happened that day. In early 2009, a memorial website was set up for Tina by her sister, Alanda, containing more than seventy photos, a timeline, a memory book and a journal. Comments were added from friends and relatives, and Tina's birthday and other special dates were commemorated in both the memory book and online journal. Other entries were from strangers touched by Tina's story or acquaintances from years ago. Alanda also set up an online legacy page for Tina, and since then a 'Justice for Tina Watson' Facebook group page appeared, attracting at least 160 followers. Later in 2009 a Facebook fan page was set up by the Watson family to support Gabe while he was in jail. More than 140 fans signed up.

In a show of support for Gabe, blue ribbons, the colour of the sea, appeared on houses in Oak Leaf Circle where Gabe's wife, Kim Lewis, still lives. The same ribbons appeared on bouquets placed on Tina's grave and on the balustrade outside Gabe's parents' house in Hoover, his brother's condo and at the homes of other supporters, including his friend Craig Youngblood.

Like the polarised positions adopted by Australians over whether a dingo took baby Azaria Chamberlain from her parents' tent at Uluru in 1980 or whether her mother, Lindy, murdered her, a similar schism developed over whether Gabe Watson killed his wife through criminal negligence or whether he intended to murder her.

The debate generated after the sentence was handed down pitted neighbour against neighbour in Gabe's street, and divided friends of both Tina and Gabe, lawyers and politicians on both sides of the world.

Amy Walker, one of Gabe's neighbours, told the CBS42 television news in Birmingham that she couldn't believe a neighbour 'right next door' may have killed his wife.

The neighbour on the other side of Gabe Watson's house told the authors while she stood at her door between two blue ribbons of support: '. . . Gabe was always a good neighbour.'

If the Office of the Director of Public Prosecutions (ODPP) in Queensland had hoped that the legal saga might end with Gabe Watson's jailing, it had underestimated Tommy Thomas. Outside the Supreme Court after the sentencing, Tommy had told the media that the words of the judge to Gabe congratulating him for saving Queensland the expense of a criminal trial were 'a very harsh slap in the face for us'. Even more accusatory were Tommy's comments about the existence of a secret plea deal between Gabe Watson's lawyers and the ODPP. After all, it had indicted Gabe Watson for murder in December 2008. Six months earlier a confidential review endorsed by its outgoing head, Leanne Clare, had found it so 'under-funded, under-resourced and inexperienced' that 'senior staff fear miscarriages of justice could occur', according to a report in *The Australian*. The review recommended forty-nine prosecutors be appointed immediately and $5.9 million provided for the following three years. The report stated that the limited funding for the ODPP for criminal matters 'gives the impression that funding for criminal matters favours the accused rather than the victim'.

Whether Gabe Watson had thought it likely that the charge against him might be downgraded to manslaughter when he arrived in Australia is unknown. Steve Zillman had told the sentencing court that Gabe had voluntarily returned to Australia on 13 May 2009, knowing he would face a murder charge. Brendan Campbell, speaking for the DPP, did not object to this statement. Indeed, this fact significantly influenced the sentencing judge's decision on the length of Gabe's custodial sentence as well as the appeal judges' decision when they were asked to review the sentence.

As far as the Thomases were concerned, at the time of Brendan Campbell's visit to the United States on 16 May 2009, little more than two weeks before Gabe was sentenced, they still believed that the available evidence was to be put before a jury on a charge of murder. The Thomases had clearly voiced their concerns at this meeting when the issue of manslaughter had been raised by Brendan Campbell, even though he had said any such change would still mean a substantial sentence. They were also told that it was not DPP practice to negotiate plea deals. Alanda Thomas would later reveal they were encouraged not to alert the media.

On 3 June 2009, two days before the sentencing, Tommy Thomas met with Brendan Campbell at the ODPP. Tommy later told the ABC radio *AM* show that he became 'upset' as he realised a deal had been made.

Investigations for this book revealed that a meeting initiated by the ODPP took place in late January between the prosecution and investigating officers where the issue of the charge being changed from murder to manslaughter was discussed. A Freedom of Information application was lodged by the authors requesting emails from 1 November 2008 to 31 May 2009, between Brendan Campbell and Tony Moynihan, SC, about the Watson case. At the time the book went to press, the Department of Justice and Attorney-General said that the 'vast majority of documents qualified as legal professional privilege'. Questions were also put to the ODPP by the authors, which included: whether Gabe Watson knew the charge of murder would be changed to manslaughter before he left for the US, or whether he knew it was likely; at what point after the ODPP presented the indictment for murder to the Supreme Court of Queensland in December 2008 was it decided to change the charge to manslaughter; and whether financial considerations and expediency were major factors in the decision to accept any plea deal. The response to our questions was the same as the statement made by Queensland DPP, Tony Moynihan, SC, four days after the sentence.

'The decision to accept Mr Watson's plea of guilty to manslaughter was made after a careful and thorough examination of the admissible evidence, and was not taken lightly. Given the complex circumstantial nature of the case, Mr Watson's admission that he breached his duty to render assistance to his wife ultimately meant there was no reasonable prospect of proving, beyond a reasonable doubt, that he was guilty of murder.'

This appears to convey that the DPP was unable to proceed with a murder charge once Gabe Watson admitted he was negligent in causing his wife's death.

***

Within two weeks of Gabe Watson's sentencing, the Queensland Attorney-General, Cameron Dick, announced he would appeal on the grounds that it was 'manifestly inadequate'. In a one-day hearing on 17 July 2009, the state's Solicitor-General, Walter Sofronoff, QC, suggested to the three-member Court of Appeal that the sentencing remarks of Justice Peter Lyons read more like a civil negligence judgment and that the judge had failed to grasp the gravity of Gabe Watson's criminal negligence. A more appropriate head sentence, he urged, was seven years imprisonment with actual jail time of two-and-a-half years before it was suspended. The original sentence, Sofronoff submitted, 'does not adequately reflect the community's justified revulsion at conduct admitted to be criminally culpable and by which the respondent killed a young woman'. Suspension of further jail time was favoured over parole because it freed the prisoner to leave the country or be deported, rather than be tied to onerous parole reporting in Australia for the rest of the head sentence. Gabe's barrister, Martin Burns, SC, submitted that his client's split-second decision to go for help on the surface rather than stay and aid his wife, was wrong in hindsight. Mitigating factors such as the intense media scrutiny with the innuendo of murder hanging over him for five years had been correctly considered before Gabe's sentencing, he said.

On 18 September 2009, the Queensland Court of Appeal varied Gabe Watson's original sentence. While the original head sentence survived, Watson's jail term was to be 'suspended after 18 months'. Each judge delivered his own opinion.

'It is not an exaggeration to describe the circumstances as unique,' Justice Richard Chesterman declared.

There were no 'truly comparable cases' with which to

compare sentences as most case law on criminally irre-
sponsible manslaughter involved actions rather than Gabe
Watson's inaction, or 'conscious abandonment to obvious
danger' of his wife.

'It is obviously right to designate the respondent's omission to assist his wife as serious, indeed grave,' the judge
stated. 'It is not just that the omission caused her death. It
must have been obvious to him that when he himself swam
to the surface he was leaving his wife to die. He was her
only means of survival and he turned away. He was capable
of affecting her rescue, either by inflating his own buoyancy device or hers. He knew she was inexperienced and
depended upon him for her safety. He knew she had declined
an orientation dive because of her trust in his competence
and capacity to protect her.'

Although Justice Chesterman was sceptical that Gabe
truly panicked, because that excuse was only given for the
first time at his sentencing, 'it is, I think, likely that the
respondent left his wife because when confronted with a
novel, difficult and dangerous situation, he lacked the qualities of character, and the skills to deal with it'.

Justice Chesterman corrected two of prosecutor Brendan
Campbell's submissions to the sentencing judge, Justice
Lyons: that Tina Watson drowned and that Gabe had not
ensured she had oxygen to breathe.

'When the dive master from *Spoil Sport* [sic] found the
deceased on the seabed her regulator was in her mouth. It
was attached to her air tank by a hose and was in good working order. It must follow that throughout the dive, until she
died, Mrs Watson had her own supply of oxygen and did
not need the respondent to supply it, and he did not omit to
do so. It follows also from the fact that the deceased maintained the regulator in her mouth that she did not drown.

The cause of death was asphyxiation. For some reason, wholly unexplained in the materials provided, the deceased ceased to breathe.'

While Gabe's different accounts varied in 'detail and content and there are some inconsistencies between them', Justice Chesterman didn't attach the same significance to the inconsistencies as Brendan Campbell had during his sentencing submissions, 'given the circumstances' in which Gabe gave them 'and the respondent's evidence and understandable distress at his wife's death'.

Justice Chesterman singled out four of Gabe's various accounts. The first account was to Wade Singleton – how Gabe was unable to 'tow' Tina after she tried to grab his regulator and mask, and he had let go and she sank quickly as he surfaced for help. To Paula Snyder, Gabe's account was that Tina was 'too heavily weighted', the judge said. Tina had knocked his mask off, tried to grab his regulator, panicked, and had sunk to the bottom, the judge related, after she had tried to inflate her buoyancy device. Gabe had decided 'in a split second' not to dive after her but to surface for help. To Craig Stephen, the Mike Ball company operations manager, Gabe had described swimming back to the descent line but that Tina had stopped swimming, and after he had turned around she had knocked his mask off and the regulator out of his mouth. Once he had cleared the mask and found his second regulator he had looked down and seen his wife sinking, motionless. He swam after her 'but desisted because of pressure in his ears', the judge related, and decided to surface and seek help.

Finally, Justice Chesterman cited Gabe's initial statement to police when he relayed the circumstances leading him to tow Tina, the dislodging of his mask and regulator and, on replacing them, how he saw that Tina was out of reach,

5 or 10 feet below him, sinking. When he swam down, he 'realised there was nothing he could do'.

The judge said, 'it may be thought that the account given to the police is likely to be the most accurate', in a formal interview situation with hours in which to have recovered some composure and collect his thoughts.

'It is apparent from the respondent's dive computer that he did not descend more than 10 feet in the effort to reach his wife who had sunk . . . He did not attempt to rescue her.'

Of the seven mitigating factors taken into account by the sentencing judge, Justice Chesterman found that three – Gabe's voluntary return from the United States to face a charge of murder, the apparent 'unnecessary' delay in charging and bringing him to trial which 'seems to have been caused by the attempt to prosecute the respondent with murder' and the wide publicity and being 'wrongly accused in the public eye of murder' causing Gabe 'considerable anxiety' – were of 'particular importance'.

'Recognising the difficulty, weighing and balancing the need to denounce the respondent's criminal conduct with the unique circumstances of the offence and the factors in mitigation', the judge felt that suspension after eighteen months, rather than the usual period of half the sentence, was 'justified by the strength of the case in mitigation'. The original twelve months in custody was, he said, 'insufficient denunciation of the respondent's abandonment of his wife' which 'deserves stronger censure'.

In contrast, Justice John Muir would have dismissed the appeal and left the sentence intact. He said the 'evidence was unclear as to why' Gabe Watson made his 'flawed decision' to surface rather than rescue his wife. Both the sentence and appeal hearings had been told that Gabe had panicked.

'The respondent himself did not advance that explanation in any of his accounts of the incident but his counsel submitted that it was not surprising that he would not wish to advance an explanation which cast him in a poor light. If [Gabe] did not panic, it seems plain that, in the absence of a sinister explanation for his conduct (and no intention to harm or abandon the deceased is alleged) [he] was unable to cope with the situation in which he found himself . . . In the result [Gabe] failed, catastrophically, to fulfil his duty and to heed what would surely be a basic human instinct: to go immediately, directly and with determination to his wife's rescue.'

Justice Muir pointed out that on the evidence before the court Gabe had no intention of harming his wife, and he had helped her initially.

'Stupidity is revealed rather than wickedness. Malice is nowhere to be found,' the judge wrote. 'His reprehensible decision to swim for assistance was made in a hostile environment when he was under stress. That he acted as he did in an attempt to obtain help is relevant, even though any assistance from others would almost certainly have come too late to benefit the deceased.'

The judge sided with Justice Lyons, who in sentencing Gabe had taken into account 'powerful factors in mitigation: including Gabe's lack of criminal history; his genuine remorse; his voluntary return from America to face trial in a foreign country, obviating the need for expensive and lengthy extradition proceedings; and the fact that for a lengthy period of time, [he] endured the opprobrium of facing the charge of murdering his wife'.

'Minds may well differ as to whether the suspension [after twelve months] was overly generous,' Justice Muir stated, but did not find it warranted any variation.

The Chief Justice of the Supreme Court of Queensland, Paul de Jersey, who headed the appeal panel, would have allowed the appeal and made the jail term different again from Justice Chesterman – half the original head sentence, thus making Gabe serve two years and three months in jail. He found that Gabe Watson's lack of action, described as 'a case of panic', was diminished in significance by the absence of any such claim before his plea.

Gabe Watson's 'breach of duty [as Tina's dive buddy] was fundamental', the Chief Justice pointed out. And as the Attorney-General had made clear in written submissions, it was not merely momentary, '. . . it is almost inexplicable that he made the decision to leave her'. Justice de Jersey felt Justice Lyons was 'unduly influenced by circumstances personal to [Gabe Watson] and unfortunately distracted from a sufficient acknowledgement of the gravity of the crime'. If Gabe had pleaded not guilty and been convicted of manslaughter after a trial, six to seven years in jail would have been appropriate, he thought.

However, he stated: 'It must be emphasised that the respondent did not plead guilty to any intentional inflicting of harm. Some of the reported public reaction to this sentencing may have overlooked that.'

It should also be remembered, the Chief Justice said, that Gabe Watson had pleaded guilty not just to causing Tina's death negligently, 'but criminally negligently: a breach of duty of such substantial proportion as to attract sanction in the criminal court'. In those circumstances a twelve-month term in jail 'was plainly unacceptable'. With the rest of the court divided, he said that to 'secure an operative order of the court' he was prepared to join with Justice Chesterman in an order for suspension after eighteen months.

Gabe Watson is eligible for parole on 13 November

2010. Speaking from Alabama, after the addition to Gabe's sentence, Tommy Thomas told a local television station that the decision was 'disgusting but not unexpected'.

'With the Department of Public Prosecutions allowing [Gabe] to plead guilty to manslaughter instead of facing a trial for murder before a jury as he had been charged and indicted, we knew that the appeal would only be based on the sentencing and the remarks that occurred in court on June the 5th and nothing else . . . none of the other evidence was considered. So we expected it.'

Just hours after the appeal decision, Alabama Attorney General, Troy King, announced that he would pursue a capital murder charge against Gabe Watson based on any alleged evidence of pre-meditation on US soil of planning to murder his wife. King instructed investigators and prosecutors to immediately begin compiling evidence for presentation to an Alabama grand jury. Alabama is one of the states in the USA where capital murder can result in either life imprisonment or execution. Lethal injection is the primary method of execution unless the condemned person elects to be electrocuted. At the time of writing, there were 205 inmates on death row – ninety-seven black males, one hundred white males, two black females and two white females – with the most recent execution carried out on 11 June 2009.

In late October, 2009, David Swain, the dive shop owner from Rhode Island, was convicted of murdering his wife a decade earlier while they were scuba diving. On 19 November, Tommy Thomas went public to the *Brisbane Times* about similarities between the diving death of his daughter and this case, dubbed 'a near perfect crime'.

Forty-three-year-old David Swain and his wife, Shelley

Tyre, forty-six, a school headmistress, had been on holiday, sailing with friends in the British Virgin Islands. The couple had entered the water together and then parted to explore different parts of the wrecks of two boats. Not long after, Swain had surfaced alone. More than 30 minutes later, Shelley Tyre's body was found. She was lying on the sandy bottom in 24 metres of water, face up, with no mask and her regulator out of her mouth. One of the friends, Christian Thwaites, spotted one of Shelley's fins and then found her body. He surfaced with her and began trying to resuscitate her in the water. After Swain had met them in a dinghy and dragged Tyre on board, Swain had performed additional CPR for several minutes, to no avail. The next day a local diver found Tyre's other fin, embedded blade-down in 30 centimetres of sand with its heel strap still fastened tightly, as well as her mask with its strap hanging loose from its anchoring pin, and her snorkel, the mouthpiece detached. Like Tina Watson, Shelley Tyre was healthy when she died, and her equipment was in good working order. The regulators worked, air pressure in her tank was operational with plenty of air left and her buoyancy jacket was able to inflate and deflate. Again, like the Watson case, her husband was the only diver in the immediate vicinity at the time of her death. Unlike Tina Watson, though, the petite Tyre was an experienced diver, having logged 354 dives.

For a decade Swain was not charged over the death. But Swain was pursued by Tyre's parents, just as the Thomases pursued Gabe Watson, seeking justice for their daughter. Six years later Shelley's parents successfully sued Swain in a wrongful-death suit against their only daughter in the Providence Superior Court at Rhode Island. In 2006, after Swain chose not to attend most of the hearing and not to defend himself, the civil jury found him responsible for his wife's death on the lesser burden of proof than the criminal standard of beyond reasonable doubt. It awarded Tyre's parents US$3.5 million. However, Swain, who had already filed for bankruptcy, did not pay. Authorities in the British Virgin Islands then charged him with murder a year later, largely based on the circumstantial evidence put forward at the civil trial.

Swain's lawyers had accused Tyre's parents of never having liked their son-in-law. The lawyers said that the Tyres had 'channelled their understandable grief into the office of a plaintiff's lawyer who has tried at every step to transform Mr Swain into a killer which he is not'.

Prosecutors had accused Swain of killing his wife so he could pursue an affair with a chiropractor, Mary Basler, who had been one of his dive students. Swain also inherited US$630,000 in life insurance and other assets on Tyre's death that he would not have been entitled to had they divorced, under the terms of their pre-nuptial agreement.

Swain continued his pursuit of what would be a year-long romance with Basler soon after his wife's death. Several letters to her were tendered at the trial, one of which was dated five months before Tyre died and described Basler as Swain's 'soulmate'. Crown witnesses also testified about the signs of violent struggle on Tyre's damaged mask, her snorkel with its missing mouthpiece and the unusually embedded fin. Expert evidence was put forward, in the absence of eyewitnesses, suggesting Swain had wrestled his wife from behind, torn off her mask and shut off her air supply while diving on the wrecks.

An expert in hyperbaric medicine told the trial Shelley Tyre had probably stopped breathing about 8 minutes into the dive, judging from the air left in her tank, and drowned. Her damaged equipment, spread over a wide distance, indicated violent activity that did not equate to panic in such a benign dive spot with little current. As with Tina Watson, there was no equipment or environmental causes to indicate why Shelley Tyre had stopped breathing. In the trial, the doctor said the only other person with her was her husband who must have killed her. An American pathologist, giving expert testimony, described the death as a 'homicidal drowning' having ruled out accident, suicide and death from natural causes, all of which were also discounted in the case of Tina Watson. The defence also described the prosecution case as weak, lacking in physical evidence and eyewitnesses, built on speculative theories and with a poor autopsy report that could not discount medical reasons including a heart attack or stroke during an accidental drowning. Swain's two children from his first marriage denied he could have killed his wife. The nine-member jury did not agree and unanimously convicted him on 27 October 2009, shortly before he turned 54, after a three-week trial in the Eastern Caribbean Supreme Court.

When she sentenced him, on 10 November 2009, to at least twenty-five years jail, the trial judge, Justice Indra Hariprashad-Charles, singled out Swain's actions after his wife was found at the bottom of the sea.

'Mr Swain also displayed strange behaviour after his wife's death.' This had included, she said, refusing to perform extended CPR on his wife on the surface, stating after about 3 minutes that she was dead, preventing Thwaites from sending a mayday call when back on board their holiday vessel, and twice asking the man who had found and isolated Shelley Tyre's equipment the following day to give the items away.

Police investigating the Watson case were familiar with

the Swain inquiry. Tommy Thomas told the *Brisbane Times* that it was impossible not to connect the crimes of Swain and his son-in-law.

'When we first learned of this story, we couldn't help but wonder if this is where the idea originated for [Gabe] to do what he did to Tina,' he said.

'My understanding is that the [Swain] story had been publicised to some degree in diving news and the media . . . as a diver [Gabe] would have quite possibly known of this story and learned from it that underwater crimes are amongst the most difficult, if not the most difficult, to prove, especially where murder is involved. What happened to Tina happened four years after the death of [Shelley Tyre], and it appeared that Swain would not be charged, much less arrested and tried at the time.'

In January 2010, a war of words erupted publicly over the Queensland authorities' refusal to send the original brief of evidence and exhibits to the Alabama authorities. This was to form the bulk of the evidence to be put before a grand jury, the panel of twenty-three that decides in private whether or not there is enough evidence to indict an individual or corporation on criminal charges.

Alabama's Assistant Attorney General, Don Valeska, was already on the record saying, 'As far as this department is concerned, the crime started in America and was then committed in Australia. We would definitely arrest him [Gabe Watson] when he gets back but whether two countries can charge someone over the same [crime] remains to be seen. A judge here may turn around and say that he can't be put in jeopardy for the same crime twice.'

In the United States, it is a constitutional right not to

be placed in jeopardy twice. But there is a 'separate sovereigns' exception to double jeopardy stemming from a 1978 Supreme Court case on tribal law which means that states are sovereigns as well as the US federal government. Double jeopardy attaches only to prosecutions of the same criminal act by the same sovereign.

Tommy Thomas joined the fray on 14 January, publicly accusing the Queensland DPP of withholding vital evidence from US authorities to save itself international embarrassment and cover up an under-the-table manslaughter deal.

'I know they made a deal with Gabe . . . the DPP admitted it to my face,' Mr Thomas said. 'What I think is happening is that they made notes regarding the deal on the evidence that has created a paper trail they don't want revealed.

'But I don't care they are trying to cover their tracks . . . just send the evidence we need to the Alabama Attorney General so we can finally go to trial and see justice.'

Meanwhile it was reported widely that deportation was the most likely option for Gabe Watson after the Queensland and federal governments indicated that they could not support any moves by the US to extradite him, should he be indicted by a grand jury, if it meant he would face the death penalty on conviction.

Under Australian law, the government is not permitted to surrender anyone to another country if there is a possibility of facing the death penalty. Under Section 25 of the Commonwealth Extradition Act, the Federal Attorney-General is not permitted to issue a surrender warrant to the extradition country if the offence is punishable by a death penalty unless the death penalty is not imposed after a trial or even if it was imposed, that it would not be carried out. Foreigners imprisoned for more than twelve months are generally deemed by the Federal Department of Immigration and Multicultural Affairs to have a 'substantial criminal record', which would be the case for Gabe Watson. Mostly, in these cases, such people are deported promptly, although each case is assessed individually. Gabe Watson could still apply for special consideration to remain in Australia. Another alternative, if the threatened murder charge eventuated, according to Bob Austin, could be that Gabe does not return to Alabama.

At the end of January 2010, Cameron Dick announced he had sought his own legal advice from the federal government to ensure any cooperation did not breach Commonwealth laws or international agreements. In the meantime, Alabama authorities were sent, 'as a first step', the Coroner's inquest transcript, excerpts from court proceedings and other publicly available information – which US prosecutors already had. By mid February 2010 the Queensland government had made it clear it would not send anything else without an undertaking from Alabama that it would not pursue the death penalty. Attorney General Troy King refused, labelling the Australian actions as 'blackmail' and 'an outrage'. The stalemate continued for months.

Throughout all the brouhaha that had followed his sentence and appeal, Gabe Watson served his time at the privately run medium to high security Borallon Correctional Centre near Ipswich, west of Brisbane. Local media report links pasted on his 'Support Gabe Watson' Facebook fan page told of him playing the part of the nobleman, Lennox, in an in-house production of Shakespeare's *Macbeth* in April 2010. His heavily tattooed cellmate, 'John', was reported in the *Brisbane Times* as participating in an 'adopt a puppy program' and walking a black labrador who would eventually provide companionship to a person with disabilities.

Days after Tina would have turned thirty-three, on 15 February 2010, David Watson, sitting in a high-backed green chair in the family home, spoke out for the first time on CBS42 television in a news segment broadcast. Breaking the long-standing family policy of making no public comment on Gabe's case, his father stated that the family feared their Attorney General's stated intentions of pursing a capital murder charge.

'It is utter nonsense that he would do something like this,' said David Watson. 'We are scared to death. That keeps me awake at night . . . And now Troy King, without knowing anything about the case, wants to put my son to death,' he said. 'It is time to speak out.'

David Watson used the interview to shoot down a number of allegations levelled against his son, including reports that Gabe had a significant life insurance policy on Tina that had led to speculation about a financial motive for her death.

'At the inquest the police agreed or acknowledged there was no insurance of any kind. He did not have not [sic] one dime of insurance on her,' Dave Watson said. As had been shown at the inquest, further action on some quotes obtained for mortgage-related life insurance had been deferred until after the honeymoon. And Gabe had not been the beneficiary of Tina's modest Parisian life insurance policy, the program stated.

The family had also questioned reports that a witness had seen Gabe hold Tina in a bear hug and that he took his time ascending for help. The 'bear hug' incident, they claimed, was a rescuer taking Tina to the surface. Inquest testimony showed that Gabe had burst out of the water calling for help and when his son attempted to go back down to save his wife, he was restrained, David Watson said.

'The testimony is that when he came to the surface . . . he burst out of the water to his sternum and [the tender driver] had to actually hold him to restrain him to keep him from going back.'

Mr Watson said his family believed that 'Tina encountered some medical event' that led to her death.

Three months later, just before this book went to press, both David and Glenda Watson were interviewed for a lengthy article in the *Birmingham News*. Having spent hundreds of thousands of dollars defending their son, they said that the threatened legal action of Troy King had prompted their new stance, against their own legal advice.

The Watsons were photographed for the article standing next to the blue ribbons tied to a post on their front porch. They accused the Thomas family and Troy King of conspiring together. There was no motive, no evidence, no logic for murder, they said.

'We feel like we've been tied to the railroad tracks and run over and over,' said Glenda Watson. 'In and of itself, any one thing is horrendous but it just doesn't stop. Tina would be just horrified if she could see the things that have gone on.'

The Watsons believe Gabe has paid very highly for his decision to leave Tina.

'He was not found guilty of murder. Any blame has been paid for,' his mother said. 'His whole life has been in upheaval. His name has been slandered. His whole personality has been on public display, and it has not been accurate.'

In the same article, Craig Greer, the pastor who married Gabe and Tina, described the Thomas family's actions since their daughter died as 'vindictive grief. Somebody has to pay for what happened.'

Added Bob Austin, who had advised Gabe legally, without payment, since he returned from his honeymoon: 'Gabe spent almost $5000 on the funeral. He would get less than he spent if he ends up with the estate. It was an insolvent estate.'

'To think somebody would kill somebody for $30,000 when they had just taken on $12,000 of their debt and spent $10,000 on a honeymoon trip, the logic just escapes me,' Austin said.

The Watsons said they were not surprised at the Coronial decision.

'Remember now, for the three or four years prior, through the newspapers, the blogs, the Thomases, [Gabe] had been called every vile, vulgar, vicious name you can imagine,' David Watson said. 'At this point, he had already come to the conclusion that the entire world was against him.'

'He insisted on going [to Australia] by himself,' said his father. '[Gabe] said, "I don't want anybody crying, everything will be fine". He left America with an outstanding murder indictment. He left here fully expecting to stand trial for murder.'

David Watson said: 'I think we were aware the Thomases and Troy King were conspiring, but I'm not sure I appreciated the significance at that time. I was still under the impression [Gabe] would come home and we would begin to put our lives back together. It's scary.' But they had followed early legal advice to remain silent and allow the legal system to work.

'I'd be reluctant to go against our attorneys, but in my heart I think, had we been just as vocal and just as outspoken, had we made *The Jerry Springer Show* and all that years ago, would it have changed anything?' David Watson asked. 'We really felt like we were giving Tina a measure of respect by not engaging in this.'

Close friends like Craig Youngblood and Jeremy Bearden described Gabe in the article as laid back and slow to anger.

'Never in a million years would anybody who knows Gabe think he did this,' Youngblood said. 'There's never been a doubt in my mind that this was anything other than an accident,' Bearden said. 'Gabe had a boat, a lake house. He was not in need of money. He had investments. He was making better than the average Joe, and he never cared about money.'

Glenda and Kim Watson visited Gabe in jail in November 2009 and found him coping well.

'I was really afraid of what I would see,' Glenda Watson recalled. 'I was afraid of seeing a dead-panned stare. But I looked in his eyes and the twinkle was still there.'

In Townsville, in the same month, the investigating detectives, Gary Campbell and Kevin Gehringer, also broke their silence after the most complex, protracted and demanding case of their careers. They told the *Townsville Bulletin* they had no doubt their original investigation conclusions were right and there remained sufficient evidence for Gabe Watson to stand trial for murder. The facts had never been properly tested before a jury, they said.

At the Southern Heritage funeral site, Tina's gravestone faces away from the foot markers dug into the grass in September 2009 commemorating the deaths of Gabe's paternal grandparents U. G. 'Watt' Watson and Geneva 'Jenny' Watson. Tina's plain gravestone has etchings of a koala and a panda bear on either side of the simple inscription of her name and the dates of her birth and death. The Watsons had purchased the plot at the Southern Heritage Cemetery in 2004, and Gabe's grandfather was then moved there. Tina's disinterred remains were also moved there in 2005.

Whether Tina will remain buried in the Watsons' plot was unknown at the time of writing. In December 2009, Tommy filed a petition with the Jefferson County Court to re-inter her remains to a place where her grave can be visited in peace by her family. Tommy asked the court to support his petition to move Tina, citing that Gabe Watson had admitted guilt in the death of Tina and that allowing him to control the burial place of his deceased victim allowed him to profit from his wrongdoing, which is not permitted under Alabama law. This was despite the fact that, generally, Alabama courts had held that a surviving spouse had the right to decide the burial arrangements of the deceased. With no case law as a precedent on this point, Tommy pointed to the rule not being absolute and allowing for special circumstances which he asked a Probate Court judge to take into consideration.

'Her family is unable to pay their respects to her final resting place, a resting place among her killer's family . . . Christina remains victimised to this day,' the petition stated.

Gabe's new lawyer handling his estate, Joseph A. Fawal, has applied to have the requested order to exhume Tina's body heard along with other matters, including a petition for final settlement of Tina's estate, after Gabe's release from prison.

The Thomases, meanwhile, steadfastly continue their fight for 'justice for Tina'. As the seventh anniversary of her death approached, another battle was playing out. Tina's estate, which included just over $3000 in assets including her bank account, wedding band set, clothing and bed, dresser and two night stands, remained in dispute between Gabe Watson and Tommy Thomas. Tommy had replaced Gabe as executor of Tina's estate after his successful application once Gabe had been charged with murder. On 17 November 2008, in granting the letters of administration to Tommy, Judge Alan King noted that Gabe's attorney disputed that the Coronial findings constituted a formal charge of murder and noted that extradition had not been ordered. Gabe was nonetheless ordered to remit all the assets of Tina's estate within fifteen days, an order that was immediately challenged and remains contested. Belongings sought back from Gabe include gifts she bought her family while in Australia, all her school and university paraphernalia including yearbooks, class photos, diplomas, ID cards and video recordings, her driver's licence, school band gear, her entire *Gone with the Wind* collection and AOPI collection including dolls and pandas, the personalised licence plates AOQTPI, Tina's wedding dress, veil, pearl necklace and earrings, postcards, letters, photos, cards, trinkets, frames, books, CDs, notebooks, folders, clothes and china passed from her maternal grandmother to Cindy and on to Tina.

As Gabe Watson's release from prison approached, the case remained a divisive issue in newspaper comments, in cyberspace, between Attorneys-General, and especially between the families and some of Tina's and Gabe's friends.

Troy King's office has described the political stalemate as a 'Catch 22' situation. Whether or not capital murder was the appropriate charge to pursue could not be decided until they received the evidence from Queensland. Without the evidence, however, particularly the physical exhibits including the dive computers and Tina's equipment, an informed decision could not be made.

On 1 June 2010 Troy King lost the Republican Party's primary vote to be its candidate in elections in November, ruling out another four-year term for him as Alabama Attorney General. Instead, standing against the Democrat candidate for that office in November would be the new Republican nominee, Birmingham lawyer and former Washington lobbyist Luther Strange. Gabe Watson's Facebook support page had urged Gabe's fans and friends to vote for Strange over King. Tommy Thomas, however, remains confident that no new Attorney General 'would do otherwise than continue to seek justice for a victim of a crime who was a citizen of our great state'.

Don Valeska, Assistant Attorney General and head of the violent crimes division of the Attorney General's department, and an employee of the state who has served under eight Attorneys General, told us that generally 'cases go forward no matter who the Attorney General is'. He remained confident at the time of writing that with the full brief and exhibits from Australia, together with other evidence that had not been admitted at the inquest, Gabe Watson could stand trial in Alabama. If so, he confirmed he would be the lead prosecutor at what was likely to be a lengthy trial.

'I would say we have evidence that has not come out yet,' he told the authors. 'It's not a smoking gun or some huge elephant in the bathtub. We expect to have a few other things that come forward depending on what the defence raises . . . We think Tina is worth more than a year or eighteen months in jail.'

Examples of evidence not before the inquest included what prosecutors believe was an alleged visit by Gabe to Parisian before he was married, and Gabe's travel insurance claim for up to $75,000 with the additional claim for punitive damages which could have resulted in an award 'in the millions' had he won, Valeska said.

'The fact that he sued and he dropped it,' Valeska explained. 'That's the kind of stuff we consider new evidence.'

Meanwhile, in spite of legal proceedings drawing to a close in Australia, there remains a lack of closure. The Watson family thinks the Queensland Court of Appeal got it right: Gabe has paid a price for a bad decision he thought best at the time.

But for the Thomas family, devastated by the loss of their daughter, nothing short of a criminal trial, with all of the evidence put before a jury, will mark an end to the ongoing saga. Just as this book went to press, Troy King backed down and took the death penalty off the table. In a widely quoted letter to Cameron Dick he laid out his plans to continue 'with determining whether sufficient evidence exists to bring and prosecute charges against Gabe Watson in our state'. The maximum penalty he would seek would be life in jail without parole. He would not renege and later re-seek the death penalty, he wrote in the letter. 'Under United States Supreme Court law, an offer made by a prosecutor is binding.'

If legal action does continue in Alabama, it will be, like so many aspects of this case, according to a spokesman for Troy King, pushing through 'unchartered territory'.

Index